Economic Growth and International Trade

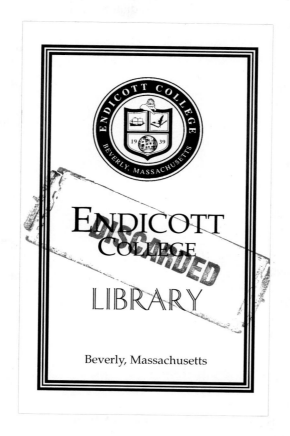

Review of International Economics

Economic Growth and International Trade

E. Kwan Choi and Bjarne S. Jensen

Iowa State University and Copenhagen Business School

BLACKWELL *Publishers*

ISBN: 0631218114

First published 1999

Reprinted

Blackwell Publishers Ltd
108 Cowley Road
Oxford OX4 1JF, UK

Blackwell Publishers Inc
350 Main Street
Malden, Massachusetts 02148, USA

British Library Cataloguing in Publication Data has been applied for

Library of Congress Cataloging in Publication Data has been applied for

Typeset by Best-set Typesetter Ltd., Hong Kong
Printed and bound in Great Britain
By MPG Books, Bodmin, Cornwall

This book is printed on acid-free paper

Contents

Contents

Introduction

E. Kwan Choi and Bjarne S. Jensen

This volume is devoted to new research combining the theory of economic *growth* with the theory of international *trade* and international *factor mobility*. As growth theory, it addresses fundamental issues associated with models of deterministic and stochastic dynamics of trading economies. As theory on trade and factor mobility, it deals with the evolution of gains from trade and the dynamic welfare effects of regulation, strategic trade policy and skilled worker migration. This introduction can only offer a brief account of the work collected here from an international selection of contributors.

The mechanisms of endogenous growth and divergence in population growth rates across countries are juxtaposed by Deardorff, and the relative performance of countries under various growth scenarios is critically analyzed. The prospects for international inequalities in per capita income, world trade (export/import) shares, and domestic ownership of capital are illustrated. He also extends the results obtained to other standard models of trade with monopolistic competition.

Allowing for uncertainties in the process of factor accumulation, a stochastic neoclassical two-sector growth model of a small trading economy is presented and fully examined by Jensen and Wang. After obtaining the crucial boundary inaccessibility conditions for the diffusion process, they derive a steady-state probability distribution of the capital-labor ratio. They obtain the sample paths of the geometric Wiener process as the uncertainty analogue of deterministic endogenous growth paths.

Kemp and Shimomura show that free international trade may be both deterministically chaotic and gainful (in the sense of Pareto) for a participating country. They prove their theorem on the existence of a chaotic solution with trade gains by using an OLG dynamic general equilibrium model, by showing the existence of period-3 solutions, and by applying the Li-York theorem.

From the perspective of economic theory, Wan and Weisman examine the crucial role (in bringing about economic efficiency) played by well-informed intermediaries in a dynamic world of imperfectly informed agents. For trade relations between China and the rest of the world, Hong Kong's success, in the past two decades and in the future, as a channel of information and middleman in trade is seen as important for the unprecedented growth in quantity and value of Chinese manufacturing exports.

The potential for emerging economies to catch up is investigated by van de Klundert and Smulders in an open two-sector model with one exposed sector producing a tradable good and the other sheltered sector producing a non-tradable good. The exposed sector of the backward economy has a knowledge gap that gives investment in R&D a relatively high rate of return and that drives the process of convergence. They analyze two regimes: balanced trade and perfect capital mobility. The latter is shown to speed up convergence at the expense of accumulating foreign debt.

Regulation of the sheltered sector entails welfare gains, which are largest under capital mobility.

Stark and Chau emphasize that, while the possibility of migration expands the set of employment opportunities, it also gives a new incentive structure for endogenous human capital (skill) formation at home. Combined with assumptions about the information environment (monitoring capability of employers), their model displays the dynamics of human capital formation and the corresponding intertemporal pattern of migration and return migration. They demonstrate that skilled worker migration ("brain drain") and welfare gains of the home country need not be mutually exclusive.

Under whatever cultural backgrounds children are brought up, they are strongly influenced by their parents. Nishimura and Shimomura assume that the consumption pattern of each parent generation has an externality effect on the preferences of the next child generation. They show that, with such child-parent externality in a simple overlapping generations model, a small open (in contrast to autarkic) economy can exhibit chaotic equilibrium dynamics.

Learning-by-doing is one of the important sources of economic growth. Many Japanese and East Asian firms are believed to have obtained their dominant market positions through learning processes, possibly with the help of their governments to ensure significant local market share. Long, Benchekroun and Tian analyze several models of international market share rivalry and the appropriate optimal strategic trade policies of the home government. To conduct effective trade policy, they show that a government must know how sophisticated firms are behaving in their dynamic games. It illustrates the complexity of intervention in a world of imperfect information.

In contrast to the celebrated Balassa-Samuelson hypothesis, many fast-growing Asian countries (Japan excepted) have experienced little trend real exchange rate appreciation. Devereux explores a mechanism for long-run real exchange rate determination that is an alternative to the Balassa-Samuelson model, but which includes it as a special case. The model is designed to address two main issues: the tendency for long-run exchange rates to be dominated by differentials in traded goods prices, and the tendency for many faster-growing Asian economies to see real exchange depreciation against Japan and the US. The model stresses the importance of endogenous productivity growth in the distribution services sector.

Wong and Yip examine one of the pressing issues facing developed and developing countries: how the growth of an economy may be affected by international trade, industrialization, and the timing of free trade. An economy, which is experiencing asymmetric growth of its two sectors due to differential rates of learning by doing, may not grow under free trade, depending on its autarkic growth rate relative to that of its trading partner and on when free trade is allowed. In some cases, the growth of an economy could be deterred by free trade, but in other cases its growth is perfectly anchored to that of its trading partner. One important feature of the model covered in the present paper is that the relative prices in the economy and the world are constantly changing even along a balanced growth path. This feature introduces a new dimension to the theory of economic growth and international trade: the timing of free trade. The importance and consequences of this dimension may have vital policy implications.

The macroeconomic importance of residential capital has been highlighted recently. Usually, nondurable consumption is the only argument in the utility function. Leung extends the EKLR model by incorporating residential capital as both an investment good and a durable consumption good. He focuses on the comparison of growth and welfare effects of different tax policies: income tax, property tax, and tariffs. The choice of optimal policy depends on the amount of initial wealth.

The contributions to this volume were presented at the conference "*Dynamics, Economic Growth and International Trade, II*", held in Hong Kong, July 1997. The conference was sponsored by the Copenhagen Business School, the Danish Society for the Advancement of Business Education (FUHU), the Central Bank of Denmark, the Otto Moensted Foundation, and the Chinese University of Hong Kong.

We are grateful for their support and financial contributions.

1
Diverging Populations and Endogenous Growth in a Model of Meaningless Trade

Alan V. Deardorff*

Abstract

The endogenous growth literature raises the possibility that countries may grow without bound in terms of per capita income, and that they may do so at different rates. This possibility also exists in neoclassical growth models with diverging populations—populations that grow at different rates. In both cases, however, this means that international inequality of per capita incomes will not only exist but also get worse over time. This paper examines that possibility within a very simple one-sector model that allows for both diverging populations and endogenous growth.

1. Introduction

The "New Growth Theory," characterized by growth rates that depend even in the long run on savings and other parameters of behavior and thus "endogenous growth," has caused a revival in a literature that had lain dormant for over two decades.[1] In the international context, endogenous growth has been applied primarily to searching for a better understanding of how international trade and investment may influence national growth. However, endogenous growth also has a much more straightforward implication that I seek to explore in this paper. If countries can grow indefinitely at different rates, then their per capita incomes will grow further and further apart, implying increasing international inequality and perhaps an increase in envy, resentment, and conflict among nations. That is a concern that I noted earlier in Deardorff (1994), where I observed that even without the usual mechanisms for endogenous growth such as endogenous learning-by-doing and technological progress, the presence of differences in population growth rates across countries can give rise to the same phenomenon. In this paper I combine that paper's assumption of diverse population growth rates—what I call diverging populations—with a very simple model of endogenous growth. My purpose is to examine the circumstances under which international inequality will emerge and even increase over time.[2]

The growth model examined here will be of the "AK" variety.[3] That is, endogenous growth will be made possible by assuming a technology that includes a lower bound on the marginal product of capital in producing new capital. In such a model, if enough output is saved and invested, it may be possible for the capital stock to grow indefinitely relative to the labor force. I incorporate this assumption into the simplest possible model of a world economy, one in which there is only one homogeneous good. Such a model would not normally be thought to include trade, but I will allow for trade anyway, and also on occasion international direct investment, both of which will be assumed to arise randomly when free markets make international transactions a matter of indifference. Since this trade does not actually accomplish anything that could not

---

* Deardorff: University of Michigan, Ann Arbor, MI 48109, USA. Tel: (734) 764-6817; Fax: (734) 76309181; E-mail: alandear@umich.edu. I have benefited from discussions on this topic with Pat Deardorff, Bob Stern, and participants at the Hong Kong conference.

be done without trade, I call this a model of "meaningless" trade. However, I show later in the paper that it behaves similarly to other more standard models of trade. Indeed, it is equivalent to a version of Krugman's (1979) model of trade with monopolistic competition that is the cornerstone of much of the New Trade Theory.

In section 2, I analyze this meaningless trade model, leading to a table of results (Table 2) that I work through in the text. Since the model includes a number of objectionable assumptions, I examine some of these in section 3, where I try to convince the reader that the model is not as silly as it may at first sound. Section 4 concludes.

2. The Growth Model with Meaningless Trade

The simple version of the AK model that I will use is as follows: Country i produces a homogeneous product, Y^i, using inputs of capital, K^i, and labor, L^i, in a production function that has a lower bound, b, on the marginal product of capital. For simplicity I go further than that, letting the production function be linear:

$$Y^i = aL^i + bK^i. \tag{1}$$

The labor force grows with population at a constant rate, n^i:

$$\dot{L}^i = \frac{dL^i}{dt} = n^i L, \tag{2}$$

while the capital stock grows with investment, I^i:

$$\dot{K}^i = \frac{dK^i}{dt} = I^i. \tag{3}$$

Growth of Individual Countries

In principle I will sometimes allow for international investment, but right now there is no reason for it, since the return to capital is its marginal product, b, and equal across countries. Therefore I assume for now that the source for domestic investment is domestic savings, which I take to be a constant fraction of national income, Y^i:

$$I^i = s^i Y^i. \tag{4}$$

Suppose initially that there is no trade or other interaction between the countries. Then this is an example of the familiar AK model of a closed economy that was introduced by Solow (1956).[4] Equations (1)–(4) combine to yield a single differential equation in the capital–labor ratio, $k^i = K^i/L^i$:

$$\dot{k}^i = \frac{dk^i}{dt} = s^i a + (s^i b - n^i)k^i. \tag{5}$$

The solution to this equation is

$$k^i(t) = (k_0^i - k^{i*})e^{(s^i b - n^i)t} + k^{i*}, \tag{6}$$

where k_0^i is the country's initial capital–labor ratio and k^{i*} is given by

$$k^{i*} = \frac{-s^i a}{s^i b - n^i}, \tag{7}$$

which turns out to be the steady-state capital–labor ratio in the case where growth converges to a steady state.

Specifically, let $G(x) = d(\ln x)/dt$ be the growth rate of any variable, x. Then the relevant properties of this solution can be summarized as in equations (8) below. Performance of a country over time depends critically on whether the exponential in equation (6) is positive or negative. Since the exponent is positive for high saving and low population growth, both of which show a certain restraint on the part of the people in the country, I refer to the countries in that case as "abstemious." The opposite case, of low saving (thus high consumption) and high population growth suggests a greater eagerness for current enjoyment, and I call these countries "hedonistic."

Hedonistic countries: If $s^i b < n^i$ then

$$k^i \to k^{i*} = \left(\frac{s^i a}{n^i - s^i b} \right) > 0,$$

(8a)

$$y^i \to a + bk^{i*} = a + \left(\frac{s^i ab}{n^i - s^i b} \right),$$

(8b)

$$Y^i \to \infty,$$

(8c)

$$G(k^i), G(y^i) \to 0,$$

(8d)

$$G(Y^i) \to n^i.$$

(8e)

That is, if the savings rate is low enough compared with the population growth rate, then the capital–labor ratio converges to a constant, as does the per capita income of the country, and the growth rates of both converge to zero. Variables that are not in per capita terms, however, including national income, Y^i, grow without bound, with growth rates converging to the rate of population growth, n^i.

Abstemious countries: If $s^i b > n^i$ then

$$k^i, y^i, Y^i \to \infty,$$

(8f)

$$G(k^i), G(y^i) \to s^i b - n^i,$$

(8g)

$$G(Y^i) \to s^i b.$$

(8h)

That is, if the savings rate is high enough (only possible if $b > n^i$), then even the per capita variables grow without bound. Their growth rates converge to $s^i b - n^i$, while that of total income converges to $s^i b$.

The distinction between exogenous and endogenous growth can be seen in these solutions. In an exogenous growth model, either sustained per capita growth is impossible, as in the low-saving case here, or it occurs only due to exogenous technological progress, which is omitted here. In an endogenous growth model, sustained per capita growth *is* possible, and the rate of growth of per capita variables depends endogenously on behavior in the model, as in (8g) it depends on s^i and n^i.

Trade Patterns

So far I have allowed for no economic interaction between these countries, such as international trade or capital movements. But if I now allow for either of these, there is no positive reason for these interactions to occur. The model has only one good, so there is no incentive to exchange consumer goods. And while there could nonetheless be trade over time if one country were to invest capital in another at one time and receive returns on that investment by importing the consumer good later on, there is no incentive for this form of trade either, since the return to capital is fixed by assumption at b in all countries.

This will not stop me, however, from extracting information about trade and capital flows from this simple model. For while there is no positive incentive to trade here, there is no reason not to, either. In Deardorff (1998), I found it useful to depart from an old convention in trade theory, which is to assume that when buyers and sellers are indifferent among sellers and buyers with whom to trade, they always resolve that indeterminacy in favor of domestic exchange. I assumed instead that agents resolve such indeterminacies randomly across all agents among whom they are indifferent, so that international trade may become as likely as domestic exchange, if not more so. I recognize that this is an extreme assumption and one that many will object to. But it is not logically more extreme than the assumption of zero transport costs and other trade barriers on which it is based, and in any case I think it bears looking at as a limiting case. As I will note in section 3, the implications are similar to some other approaches to international economic modeling that have been popular of late, and they are identical to one of them in particular. However, under my assumptions here this trade does nobody any good (or harm) and I therefore refer to this as a "meaningless" trade model.

I will consider two cases: with and without international capital flows. Consider first, then, the case of a prohibitive barrier to international capital movement but free international trade.

Without international capital flows, demanders (consumers and investors) in each country are collectively constrained to spend only their own income, but with free trade they will be indifferent among all countries' products and therefore will spend that income on the products of all countries in proportion to their outputs. It is helpful to think of producers in each country, all of which produce the same homogeneous product, as putting their outputs into a common world pool, from which demanders in each country then draw. The result is a good deal of international trade, with demanders importing a fraction of their income equal to one minus their country's share of world output, since this share is their own producers' share of the pool. Their country's producers likewise export that same fraction of their output, and trade is balanced. At each moment in time, very much as in the simple frictionless gravity equation of Deardorff (1998), exports from country i to country j are

$$T^{ij} = \frac{Y^i Y^j}{Y^w}, \tag{9}$$

where $Y^w = \Sigma Y^i$ is world output.

A country's total international trade (exports plus imports) in this case is

$$T^i = \sum_{j \neq i} T^{ij} + \sum_{j \neq i} T^{ji} = 2\frac{(Y^w - Y^i)Y^i}{Y^w}. \tag{10}$$

Not surprisingly, this model has the property that the share of a country's GDP that it trades, $T^i/Y^i = 2[1 - (Y^i/Y^w)]$, depends negatively on its size relative to the world.

Now suppose alternatively that international capital flows are permitted. With equal returns to capital across countries, the normal assumption would be that capital stays home, but this too is arbitrary. If returns really are equal, then potential investors should be indifferent as to where they install their capital, and the location of capital will be indeterminate. As an alternative to keeping capital at home, I will resolve this indeterminacy by assuming that capital is allocated randomly in proportion to population, so that foreign direct investment (FDI) keeps the ratio of installed capital to labor the same in every country. This too can be justified with a minor modification of the model, as I will argue in section 3. Owners of capital in any country will then own it all over the world, with a portfolio that matches in its country composition the distribution of population across countries. They will be paid the competitive return to their foreign capital, b, which they will collect as imports of the produced good. Those imports also measure the value of the exports of capital services.

What, then, will be the trade flows at a point in time with mobile capital? We must first distinguish GNP and GDP, both of which were presented until now by Y^i. Let K^i be the capital owned by residents of a country, and K_i be the capital installed in that country.[5] Then, since all capital earns the return b, GNP of country i is

$$Y^i = aL^i + bK^i, \tag{11}$$

and world output is

$$Y^w (= Y_w) = aL^w + bK^w. \tag{12}$$

Since installed capital is in the same ratio, $k^w = K^w/L^w$, in every country, however, GDP is

$$\begin{aligned} Y_i &= aL^i + bK_i \\ &= aL^i + bk^w L^i \\ &= \frac{L^i}{L^w} Y^w. \end{aligned} \tag{13}$$

In this model, a country's share of world income, Y^i/Y^w, can easily exceed or fall short of its share of world production, Y_i/Y^w, through ownership of capital abroad or through foreign ownership of domestic capital.

To specify international trade in this context of mobile capital, we need to clarify even further how various indeterminacies will be resolved. An owner of capital that is installed abroad who wants to invest the earnings in another foreign country could be assumed to collect its foreign earnings by importing goods, and then to export those same goods for investment somewhere else. But that would amount to no more than re-exports which, if we allow them, could proliferate unduly in the model. Instead I will assume again that all producers place their outputs into a single world pool, and that those who earn any income buy from that same pool at random for both their consumption and investment needs. They then deliver the products either for consumption to their home countries or for investment to the countries where they want to install capital; that is, to all countries in proportion to population. Thus any investment gives rise to trade flows exported from countries in proportion to production and imported into countries in proportion to population. A given trade flow between two countries may be initiated, therefore, by an investor who is not located in either of those countries.

Note that again there is no facility for borrowing or lending, and therefore no possibility of countries spending more or less than their incomes. However, there can be trade imbalances, as usually measured, since net capital flows will be matched by exports of the good (used for investment) in the same direction without any offsetting imports in the same period. The imports come later as income on that capital.

To derive trade flows, we need to consider consumption and investment separately. Let the GNP of country j be divided into consumption and investment: $Y^j = C^j + I^j$. Consumption goods will be purchased from all countries in proportion to their production, as above, giving rise to exports from i to j equal to $(Y^i/Y^w)C^j$. Investment goods will be sourced in the same fashion, but they will be invested in, and therefore exported (from the source country) to, all countries in proportion to their populations. Thus the investment of country h (equal to its savings rate times its income, $I^h = s^hY^h$) gives rise to exports from country i to country j of $(Y^i/Y^w)I^h(L^j/L^w)$. Total exports from i to j are therefore

$$T^{ij} = \frac{Y^i}{Y^w}\left(C^j + \frac{L^j}{L^w}\sum_h I^h\right). \tag{14}$$

Define the world savings rate as the GNP-weighted average of the national savings rates,

$$s^w = \sum_h \frac{Y^h}{Y^w}s^h, \tag{15}$$

and note that investment in proportion to population implies that

$$\frac{L^j}{L^w} = \frac{K^j}{K^w} = \frac{Y^j}{Y^w}. \tag{16}$$

Equation (14) can then be rewritten as

$$\begin{aligned} T^{ij} &= \frac{Y^i}{Y^w}[(1-s^j)Y^j + s^wY_j] \\ &= \frac{Y^iY^j}{Y^w}\left(1 - s^j + s^w\frac{Y_j}{Y^j}\right). \end{aligned} \tag{17}$$

To understand the determinants of trade in this equation, realize first that a country's own savings has a negative effect on its imports, since whereas consumption requires mostly imports in a small country, savings and the consequent investment mostly goes into other countries and therefore requires imports into them, not into the country doing the investing. Likewise, imports depend positively on how much is produced in a country, GDP = Y_j, compared with its residents' income, Y^j, since production is proportional to the labor force and new investment, which in turn uses imports.

Equation (17) says that trade will be given by the simple frictionless gravity equation if *both* of the following are true: the savings rate of the importing country equals that of the world, *and* the importing country has GNP equal to GDP; i.e., it has no net capital flows.[6] Trade between two countries will exceed the simple gravity prediction if the importing country saves less than the world, since it will then be a big consumer and therefore importer; and/or if the importing country is a net host to foreign capital, since its imports for investment purposes will be greater than predicted from its own income and savings.

Growth Effects

Now consider what happens to output and trade over time as the countries follow the growth paths stated earlier in equations (8). There are several cases to consider, depending on the characteristics of the countries involved. These are summarized in Table 2, using the identification of certain benchmark countries that appears in Table 1. Specifically, I denote by $\bar{\imath}$ and $\tilde{\imath}$ the countries with the highest population growth and savings rates, respectively, $\bar{n}$ and $\bar{s}$ being the corresponding rates. Also, looking at per capita income, among hedonistic countries (which do converge to a steady state in per capita terms), I denote by $\hat{i}$ the country with the highest steady-state per capita income, while among abstemious countries I denote by $\hat{\hat{i}}$ the country that tends toward the highest growth rate in per capita income. Countries that save more of their incomes than the world average savings rate defined in (15) are denoted with a forward arrow, while those that save less than the world average are denoted by a backward arrow. Throughout Table 2, rather than squeeze any of these indicators on to country super-scripts, i, an indicator placed directly over any variable denotes that country, as indicated in the footnote to Table 2.

Table 2 then records the ultimate behavior of various shares and other variables that may be informative for the issues raised in the introduction. Specifically, it reports shares of world population, income, and production for countries, indicating whether these are (or asymptotically approach) a constant or the extreme values of zero and one. In the latter case, it indicates which of the benchmark countries, if any, come to dominate the world in the sense of having a share of one.

Next the table reports the behavior of trade shares—exports and imports—not as fractions of world trade but as fractions of a country's own production or income. Again, these shares may become constant at intermediate values between zero and one, or they may converge to zero or one themselves, indicating that trade will appear to become either more or less important over time for the country. The table also includes the ratio of a country's owned capital to the capital installed there, thus indicating its net capital position and therefore its reliance either on capital abroad for income or on foreign-owned capital for production. Of course, in this meaningless trade (and investment) model, neither trade nor foreign direct investment play any substantive role and could be replaced by domestic sourcing and investment without cost. However, these ratios are likely, I believe, to approximate their values in various more complex models where trade and FDI do play real roles, as I will argue in section 3. More important, perhaps, they indicate the sources of international friction that may arise when international disparities in income are accompanied by extreme reliance on trade and/or FDI.

Finally, Table 2 reports what happens to perhaps the most important variable in this model, per capita income. Only that of the most "successful" country is reported, and there only to say whether it approaches a constant or instead grows without bound. More important, however, is the indicator of which country it is that occupies this role, which varies across the cases considered. The final row of Table 2 then reports what happens to a measure of relative poverty, taken to be the ratio of per capita income in a given country to that of the country with the highest per capita income. Again, in this model, the actual performance of every country is independent of both the behavior of other countries and of the permissible interactions among them. Nonetheless, it is relative performance that often gives rise to concern by the public, and I would expect these conclusions to extend to many more complex models that allow for such interdependencies.

The columns of Table 2 correspond to the cases considered. The first four, in columns (3)–(6), concern a world of only hedonistic countries, which therefore all converge to steady states, their per capita variables approaching constants. The last four columns allow for abstemious countries, and therefore endogenous growth. To explore the role of diverging populations, both sets of cases are divided into ones in which all countries share the same population growth rate and ones where they do not. Finally, each of the resulting four cases are in turn divided into ones without international capital

Table 1. Benchmark Countries and Parameters

	Country Indicator	Corresponding Parameter
Highest Population Growth Rate	$\bar{i} = \arg\max_i n^i$	$\bar{n} = \max_i n^i$
Highest Savings Rate	$\tilde{i} = \arg\max_i s^i$	$\tilde{s} = \max_i s^i$
Highest Steady State Per Capita Income and Capital–Labor Ratio	$\hat{i} = \arg\max_i \left(\dfrac{s^i a}{n^i - s^i b} \right) = k^{i*}$	$\hat{k}^*, \hat{y}^*$
Highest Asymptotic Per Capita Growth Rate	$\hat{\hat{i}} = \arg\max_i (s^i b - n^i) = G(y^i)$	$\hat{\hat{g}} = G(y^i)$
Countries with Higher and Lower Savings Rates than the World Average	$\bar{i}$: $s^i > s^w$, $\underline{i}$: $s^i < s^w$	

Table 2 (facing page). Relative Performance of Countries Under Various Growth Scenarios

(1)	(2)	All Countries Hedonistic: $s^i b < n^i$, $\forall i$				Some Countries Abstemious: $s^i b > n^i$, for some i			
		Equal Population Growth Rates, $n^i = n$, $\forall i$		Unequal Population Growth Rates, $n^i \neq n$, $\forall i$		Equal Population Growth Rates, $n^i = n$, $\forall i$		Unequal Population Growth, $n^i \neq n$, $\forall i$	
		NoFDI	FDI	NoFDI	FDI	NoFDI	FDI	NoFDI	FDI
(1)	(2)	(3)	(4)	(5)	(6)	(7)	(8)	(9)	(10)
Shares* of World Population	$\lambda^i = \dfrac{L^i}{L^w}$	$\lambda^i = \dfrac{L_0^i}{L_0^w} = \text{const}$		$\bar\lambda \to 1$, $\lambda^i \to 0$, $i \neq \bar i$		$\lambda^i = \dfrac{L_0^i}{L_0^w} = \text{const}$		$\bar\lambda \to 1$, $\lambda^i \to 0$, $i \neq \bar i$	
Shares of World Income	$\omega^i = \dfrac{Y^i}{Y^w}$	$\omega^i \to \text{const}$		$\bar\omega \to 1$, $\omega^i \to 0$, $i \neq \bar i$		$\tilde\omega \to 1$, $\omega^i \to 0$, $i \neq \tilde i$		$\tilde\omega \to 1$ if $\tilde s b > \bar n$; $\bar\omega \to 1$ if $\tilde s b < \bar n$	
Shares of World Production	$\gamma^i = \dfrac{Y_i}{Y^w}$	$\gamma^i = \omega^i$	$\gamma^i = \lambda^i$	$\gamma^i = \omega^i$	$\bar\gamma \to 1$, $\gamma^i \to 0$, $i \neq \bar i$	$\gamma^i = \omega^i$	$\gamma^i = \lambda^i$	$\gamma^i = \omega^i$	$\bar\gamma \to 1$, $\gamma^i \to 0$, $i \neq \bar i$
Export Shares of Production	$\chi^i = \dfrac{X^i}{Y_i}$	$\chi^i = 1 - \omega^i$	$\tilde\chi^i \approx 1 - \omega^i$	$\tilde\chi \to 0$, $\chi^i \to 1$, $i \neq \bar i$		$\tilde\chi \to 0$, $\chi^i \to 1$, $i \neq \tilde i$		$\tilde\chi \to 0$, $\chi^{i \neq \tilde i} \to 1$ if $\tilde s b > \bar n$; $\bar\chi \to 0$, $\chi^{i \neq \tilde i} \to 1$ if $\tilde s b < \bar n$	
Import Shares of Income	$\mu^i = \dfrac{M^i}{Y^i}$	$\mu^i = 1 - \gamma^i$	$\tilde\mu^i \approx 1 - \gamma^i$	$\tilde\mu \to 0$, $\mu^i \to 1$, $i \neq \bar i$		$\tilde\mu \to 0$, $\mu^i \to 1$, $i \neq \tilde i$		$\tilde\mu \to 0$, $\mu^{i \neq \tilde i} \to 1$ if $\tilde s b > \bar n$; $\bar\mu \to 0$, $\mu^{i \neq \tilde i} \to 1$ if $\tilde s b < \bar n$	
Owned Shares of Dom. Capital	$\kappa^i = \dfrac{K^i}{K_i}$	1	$\tilde\kappa > 1$; $\tilde\kappa < 1$	1	$\bar\kappa \to 1$; $\bar\kappa > 1, \bar\kappa < 1$	1	$\tilde\kappa > 1$; $\tilde\kappa < 1$	1	$\bar\kappa \to \infty, \bar\kappa \to 0$; $\bar\kappa \to 1, \bar\kappa > 1, \bar\kappa < 1$
Highest Per Capita Income	$y^{max} = \max_i y^i$	$\tilde y = \text{const}$		$\hat y = \text{const}$		$\tilde y \to \infty$		$\hat{\tilde y} \to \infty$	
Relative Poverty	$\rho^i = \dfrac{y^i}{y^{max}}$	$\rho^i = \dfrac{y^i}{\tilde y} = \text{const}$		$\rho^i = \dfrac{y^i}{\hat y} = \text{const}$		$\rho^i = \dfrac{y^i}{\tilde y} \to 0$		$\rho^i = \dfrac{y^i}{\hat{\tilde y}} \to 0$	

$*\ \bar x \equiv x^{\bar i}$, for $\bar\cdot = \tilde\cdot, \tilde{\tilde\cdot}, \hat\cdot, \hat{\hat\cdot}$

mobility or (No FDI), and ones in which savers invest randomly in all countries in proportion to population, as described above.

My discussion of these results will focus on what they mean, rather than on much
detail of their derivation, since many of them are obvious once you understand their
meaning and the model. Despite my best efforts, the notation remains cumbersome,
so that just expressing the results in words may be the larger part of my contribution.

Growth effects on population   Population shares are the most straightforward, of
course, since population growth is exogenous. Without diverging populations, with all
population growth rates equal, population shares are simply constant at their initial
levels. With diverging populations, however, the country with the largest population
growth rate[7] comes to dominate the world population, in the sense that its share of
world population goes to one regardless of how small it may have started.

It is for this reason, I think, that other contributors to the literature on economic
growth have tended to ignore the case of diverging populations, dismissing it as converging to a single closed economy. As we will see, and as I noted already in Deardorff
(1994), this sweeps under the rug a lot of interesting dirt. For one thing, the countries
whose shares of population go to zero nonetheless continue to exist, and their performance matters, not least to them. More importantly, just because a country's share of
population goes to zero does not mean that its share of other relevant economic variables also dwindles to insignificance. Such a country may well come to own a significant and perhaps even dominant share of, say, world capital. That is the possibility
explored in Deardorff (1994) with diverging populations and exogenous growth, and
endogenous growth provides additional mechanisms for it to happen.

Growth effects on income and production   To see this, consider what happens to shares
of world income and production. Ignoring FDI for the moment, these two shares—
denoted ω^i and γ^i in Table 2—are equal. With hedonistic countries per capita incomes
become constant in the steady state, and with equal rates of population growth this
means that total incomes also remain constant relative to one another. With unequal
population growth rates but all countries still hedonistic and hence in steady states,
the fastest growing population has the fastest growing income, and its share of
world income and production therefore also goes to one, perhaps justifying dismissing it as being essentially a closed economy. But if any countries restrain either consumption or population growth sufficiently to be classed as abstemious, then their
incomes will grow faster than their populations in the long run and it is possible
for their incomes to even grow faster than the fastest growing population. If that
happens, especially if the fastest growing population is also hedonistic, as is plausible,
then the abstemious country acquires a share of income that eventually approaches
100%.

Which country is it that comes to dominate the world economy in this way? With
equal population growth rates the answer is simple. From equation (8h), the growth
rate of output is highest for the country that saves the largest fraction of its income, $\tilde{\imath}$,
and its growth rate must also be larger than the common n or no country would be
abstemious. Therefore it is this highest saving country, $\tilde{\imath}$, that asymptotically accumulates a share of world income, $\tilde{\omega}$, equal to one.

If population growth rates are not equal, then there are two growth rates of GNP
that compete for being the highest. One is the growth rate of the highest saving country,
$\tilde{s}b$ from equation (8h). The other is the growth rate of the fastest growing population,
$\bar{n}$. If the former exceeds the latter, then the high-saving country, $\tilde{\imath}$, will again dominate

the world economy. But if $\bar{n} > \bar{s}b$, then even though the high-saving country is growing without bound in its own per capita terms, it is dwindling to insignificance compared with both population and income in $\bar{\imath}$.

Note that in this case the high-population-growth country, $\bar{\imath}$, is itself hedonistic, since if it were abstemious its own rate of growth would exceed $\bar{n}$. Thus we have here a world economy that is not growing in per capita terms, even though there are abstemious countries within it who are enjoying ever-increasing per capita incomes.

Suppose now that capital is mobile. This matters only for the location of capital and therefore production, both of which will now be proportional to population. Shares of world income behave as already described. Shares of world production, however, do not. Instead, these are equal to shares of world population, becoming constant when countries share equal population growth rates and otherwise approaching one in the country with the fastest growing population.

Growth effects on trade   Consider now the share of its output that each country exports, and the shares of its income that it imports. With only a single homogeneous good produced anywhere and both buyers and sellers indifferent among those with whom they might transact, the assumption here is that transactions are determined randomly in proportion to amounts of production and income. That is, all buyers buy from all countries in proportion to their shares in world output, while all sellers sell to all countries in proportion to world demand.

With immobile capital, the resulting trade patterns are straightforward. A country's producers sell to its own market only a fraction of their output equal to their country's share in world income, ω^i. Therefore they export the rest, which is the fraction $(1 - \omega^i)$ of production. Buyers, spending their entire incomes on either consumption or investment, similarly buy from domestic producers only their share of world production, γ^i, and import the rest, the fraction $(1 - \gamma^i)$. These results are reported only in column (3) of Table 2, but they are valid in all of the columns without FDI, where they have been used instead together with the above results on income and production shares to report where the trade shares go to zero and one. For example, in column (5), since with unequal population growth and hedonistic countries both income and production shares go to one in the country with highest population growth, this country's trade also falls to zero since it has nobody of any size to trade with. All other countries, on the other hand, sell essentially all their output to the high-population-growth country, and they import equally from it, because of its dominant share of both income and production.

With mobile capital the situation is somewhat different, as already noted above in equation (17). Each country still purchases goods equal in value to its income for the purposes of both consumption and investment, and it buys them at random from other countries in proportion to where they were produced. However, whereas it imports goods for consumption into its own country, most of what it buys for investment is delivered elsewhere, following its own FDI, into other countries in proportion to their populations and therefore in proportion to their shares of capital and output. On the other hand, while a country's own income may now lead to less imports than before, the country will also be importing goods on behalf of its foreign owners of domestic capital. How all these forces balance out is unclear and complex, as equation (17) indicates. But (17) also shows that as long as savings rates do not differ greatly across countries and countries' GNP and GDP are not too far apart, then trade flows will be approximately what they were with immobile capital. Therefore, in column (4) of Table 2, I have shown the trade shares as being approximately the same with FDI as without, and I have not tried to distinguish the cases of FDI and No FDI in the remainder of the table.

Growth effects on investment   Even more important than trade for the public's perception of the world economy may be the role of foreign direct investment. There are several ways one could measure this, and I have chosen to look at the ratio of capital owned by a country to capital installed in it. Since the former includes capital installed abroad, this does not tell us how much of domestic capital is foreign owned, which I will note separately from the table in the discussion here. Rather, this ratio tells, in the only sense meaningful in this real model, whether a country is a net creditor or a net debtor in world markets. That is, does it own more or less capital than it employs?

Without FDI, of course, this ratio is one. With FDI and also with equal population growth rates, but regardless of whether capital is growing faster than population or not, capital installed in each country will grow at the same rate (since it is invested in proportion to population), while capital owned will grow faster or slower depending on savings. Thus, high-saving countries will accumulate more capital than they can accommodate domestically and will become net creditors, while low-saving countries will become net debtors. This is shown in columns (4) and (8) of Table 2 in terms of the countries that were identified in Table 1 as saving above and below the world average.

With unequal population growth rates, I am pretty sure that the same thing happens, but with one exception. Now the country with the fastest growing population, $\bar{\imath}$, attracts ultimately 100% of investment. Thus it becomes the location for virtually all of world capital. If its share of world income is also one—as it is in column (6) and in column (10) if $\bar{n} > \tilde{s}b$—then its owned and installed capital approach equality. If on the other hand an abstemious high-saving country saves enough to dominate world income, then *it* will own virtually all world capital, which will be installed in $\bar{\imath}$. In that case, $\tilde{\imath}$ owns infinitely more capital than is located within it, while $\bar{\imath}$ owns hardly any. In both cases, all other countries will behave as in column (4).

Growth effects on per capita income   Consider finally per capita income. With only hedonistic countries, all converge to steady states in which per capita income is constant, even though, with diverging populations, total incomes grow at different rates. From equation (8b) we see that if population growth rates are equal, then steady-state per capita income varies only with the savings rate, and is highest for the country that saves the most, $\tilde{\imath}$. With diverging populations, on the other hand, a country can offset a somewhat low savings rate with a low population growth rate, and the highest per capita income may be found in a different country, one I have called $\hat{\imath}$ in Table 1. The per capita income of other countries relative to that maximum—what I have called relative poverty ρ^i—also converges to a constant. How far short of the maximum individual countries fall depends on the variation across countries in savings rates and population growth rates, but it is in any case bounded above zero.

The situation is quite different if any countries are abstemious. Per capita incomes of such countries grow without bound at growth rates that converge to positive constants. Whatever may be the relative ranking of countries by per capita income initially, all that matters in the long run is who grows fastest. That country's per capita income will eventually surpass all others, and it will grow to be infinitely large relative to them. With equal population growth rates, finding that country is easy. From equation (8g) it is again the country with the highest savings rate, $\tilde{\imath}$. With diverging populations, however, slow population growth can again boost a country's growth rate, and the maximum is achieved by the country I have identified as $\hat{\imath}$. Thus the same parameters, savings and population growth, matter and in more or less the same ways for per capita incomes in abstemious countries as in hedonistic ones. But the implications are now far more dramatic, since the abstemious countries achieve long-run growth and therefore approach infinite per capita incomes.

More importantly, perhaps, if residents of these countries begin to compare per capita incomes across borders, what they will find will be much more startling and perhaps more troubling when they compare to hedonistic countries. All but the residents of country $\hat{\imath}$ will find themselves falling ever further behind it in terms of per capita income. And while other abstemious countries will have the consolation that their own per capita incomes are nonetheless rising over time, hedonistic countries won't even have that to console them.

Prospects for Inequality, Envy, and Resentment

I asked at the outset what endogenous growth models might tell us about the prospects of future inequality of incomes across countries. Clearly the model here presents a discouraging picture. Like exogenous growth models, this model says that countries that differ in their saving behavior and population growth rates will also differ in the long run in their per capita incomes. That, no doubt, is as it should be. But the endogenous growth model goes on to say that if countries save enough relative to their rates of population growth for endogenous growth to be possible, then these same differences will lead to increasing divergence in per capita incomes across nations. The possibility of endogenous growth itself is certainly a hopeful implication of the new endogenous growth theory. But the accompanying possibility—which is almost inevitable in the very simple model explored here—is less encouraging. For it means that growth could be accompanied by increasing envy across national borders and perhaps international frictions as a result.

By allowing the model to include both international trade and direct investment, albeit in a very simplified and not very meaningful form, the model also suggests the form that these frictions might take. Note that as we move to the right in Table 2, there is a tendency for the trade shares to become more extreme, and also eventually for the same to happen to some of the owned shares of capital. That is, as savings and population growth parameters become more diverse and abstemious, not only does international per capita income inequality increase; some countries also find themselves depending ever more heavily on trade and, if permitted, on international investment. For example, in columns (3) and (4), export and import shares converge to constants between zero and one. In all other columns, however, the trade shares of all but one country go to one, because all but the largest countries find themselves relying almost exclusively on a single other country to market their products and to source their consumption and investment needs. In some cases though not all, this other country is also one whose per capita income is growing infinitely large relative to their own.

With international investment, this reliance on a foreign, richer, country may be even more pronounced. Consider the case of country $\bar{\imath}$, whose population grows faster than any other country. If the highest saving country, $\tilde{\imath}$, grows even faster ($\tilde{s}b > \bar{n}$), then the owned share of capital in $\tilde{\imath}$ goes to infinity while that in $\bar{\imath}$ goes to zero. What this means is that, in the most populated country, the share of capital owned by foreigners approaches 100%. The high-saving country may not be the richest in the world ($\hat{\imath}$ may be some other country with a lower population growth rate), but it is surely richer than $\bar{\imath}$. Thus the huge population of the poorer country finds itself becoming ever poorer relative to the high-saving country, and because of the latter's ownership of most of its capital, it may feel exploited by it. This is surely a recipe for resentment and worse.

This is a baleful picture I have painted, and one that draws heavily on some very extreme and nonstandard assumptions. Obvious candidates for questioning are my assumptions that population growth and savings parameters are constant and that international trade and investment occur randomly and as a matter of indifference. In the next section I examine each of these assumptions to see whether they are too severe to permit my analysis any credibility.

3. Evaluation of Assumptions

Clearly the assumptions just mentioned are either uncharacteristic of the real world, or unusual in the growth literature, or both. The question is whether they seem likely to have driven the results in ways that more plausible or familiar assumptions would not. I can give no sure answer to that question without actually building and solving the models that these assumptions were in part selected to avoid. But a brief discussion of each can suggest, I think, that the message of the simple model is robust.

Constant Savings Rate

Early growth models like Solow's (1956) that assumed constant savings propensities were soon replaced by models with one form or another of optimal savings behavior. However, tractable versions of these models have replaced the simple constant savings rate with even more implausible assumptions about individual's preferences and biology, such as infinite lives with constant time preference, or two-period lives with ineffectual retirement. And they have not really altered the key feature of the constant savings rate that drives results in this model: that individuals with different attitudes toward the future will save different fractions of their incomes, even in otherwise similar economic circumstances. If differences in culture across countries continue to lead people to save differently, then the aspects of economic performance explored here, which depend on such differences in savings, seem likely to continue to play the sorts of role ascribed to them here. The only way out of this that I can see is for increasing economic interaction through trade and investment to so homogenize world cultures that such differences across countries disappear.

Constant Population Growth Rate

The assumption of a constant population growth rate is more standard in the literature on economic growth than the constant savings rate, but it is probably less justifiable for the purpose of this paper. Evidence abounds that birth rates and death rates, on which population growth depends, vary with income, and in particular that population growth rates are likely to fall as real per capita income rises sufficiently beyond subsistence. This obviously would matter a great deal for the results in this paper. However, a moment's thought suggests that allowing for this would only make matters worse. Countries could now differ in their population growth rates *because* of their differences in income, and those differences in population growth would then exacerbate the differences in per capita income. One does not need this paper to raise concern about the long-run implications of such a mechanism, but it certainly does not assuage concern.

In addition, just as cultural differences across countries might be expected to maintain differences in long-run savings rates under any plausible theory for determining them endogenously, so too will cultural differences cause population growth rates to differ.

The Meaningless Model of Trade

The model of international trade that I have used in this paper is really no model at all. By having all countries produce the same homogeneous good and trade it randomly, I have avoided all of the usual reasons for trade, such as comparative advantage, increasing returns to scale, product differentiation, and so forth. Along with many of these familiar theories of trade go both sources of gain from trade, and possible costs of trade (such as factor dislocation) that my approach also excludes. If these benefits and costs could ever be big enough to swamp the effects of growth that I have looked at, then my results would deserve little confidence.

However, long experience with traditional models of international trade suggests that the static welfare effects of trade are comparatively small, and therefore unlikely to outweigh the effects of growth. More recent models of the New Trade Theory, with their increasing returns to scale, offer the chance for larger welfare effects, but to some extent my choice of the AK model to represent endogenous growth was precisely to capture some of these effects. In any case, it is not obvious to me how allowing more explicitly for increasing returns could undermine the implication of this paper about increasing inequality.

Still, to comfort those who may find my meaningless trade model unsettling, let me note that other more conventional models do exist that ought to behave just like it. The simplest is a variant of Krugman's (1979) model of monopolistic competition.

A monopolistically competitive trade model   Suppose, then, that countries do not after all produce a single homogeneous good, but rather that they produce a potentially unlimited number of differentiated products, each by a single firm, f. Products enter a Dixit–Stiglitz (1977) aggregating function with constant elasticity of substitution:

$$A = \left(\sum_{f=1}^{F^w} (d_f)^{\frac{\sigma-1}{\sigma}} \right)^{\frac{\sigma}{\sigma-1}}, \tag{18}$$

where F^w is the number of firms in the world, d_f is the quantity an agent demands of the differentiated product of firm f, and σ is the elasticity of substitution among varieties. I assume this function to be the same in all countries, the aggregate being equally usable for consumption and investment. Production by a firm requires use of an input that is the same linear composite of labor and capital specified in equation (1) for the one-sector model. The amount of this composite needed by a firm is given by a cost function that includes both a fixed-cost and a constant marginal cost component: $c = \alpha + \beta x_f$, where x_f is the output of the firm and $\alpha, \beta > 0$ are constants. With this formulation, as is well known, demand for each firm's product will have constant elasticity, causing each to price its product with a constant markup over marginal cost. Free entry drives profits to zero, leading each firm to produce the same output and employ the same inputs (except in this case that they may have different mixes of capital and labor, which are perfect substitutes). Output of the (single) industry expands and contracts, not by varying the size of firms, but by entry and exit of identical firms.

This model behaves exactly like the one-sector model of section 2. However, now instead of buyers being indifferent among sellers of a homogeneous product, they actually prefer equal amounts of each firm's output in order to maximize their Dixit–Stiglitz aggregator in the face of equal prices. This in turn requires that they buy from each country in proportion to its number of firms, and thus its output, which is exactly the result that the random trade mechanism of section 2 led to through the law of large numbers. Therefore one can regard the meaningless trade model of section 2 as equivalent to a Krugman-style one-sector model of monopolistic competition.

There is one difference, however, that should be noted. The model now will have a form of increasing returns to scale. This arises not through the technology of the firm, whose increasing-returns component has been deactivated by the constant elasticity assumption of demand that leads all firm outputs to be the same. Rather, increasing returns arises here from product variety, since an expansion of output through entry of additional firms increases the value of the Dixit–Stiglitz aggregator more than in proportion to F^w. This does not invalidate anything said about the one-sector model, except that y is no longer a correct measure of real income, which instead rises more than in proportion to y. This would mean, for example, that even hedonistic countries with constant y in the steady state would enjoy increasing real incomes over time owing to increased product variety, both from their own producers if their population grows at all, and from the world. And since this variety benefits them just as much if it is produced abroad as at home, this would provide a spillover across countries that was not present in the one-sector meaningless trade model.

Rather than pursue these implications here, however, I merely note that they can just as easily be removed. Suppose that the aggregator of the differentiated products takes the following form instead of equation (18):

$$A = \left(F^w\right)^{\frac{-1}{\sigma-1}} \left(\sum_{f=1}^{F^w} (d_f)^{\frac{\sigma-1}{\sigma}} \right)^{\frac{\sigma}{\sigma-1}}. \tag{18'}$$

As shown in Brown et al. (1996), this form of the aggregator neutralizes any benefits of increased variety.

Other trade models   There is at least one other way that the meaningless trade model of section 2 can be reinterpreted to conform more closely with meaningful trade models with which we are familiar. That is to assume that each country produces a different homogeneous product. This could simply follow from an Armington Assumption, that demanders in their own minds somehow differentiate products by country of origin. Or it could follow from a general version of the Heckscher–Ohlin (H–O) model if factor supplies differ sufficiently for each country to be completely specialized in a different product.[8] In either case, although each country will produce only one good, all will demand the products of all countries and therefore will also export their own products to all others as well.

The H–O approach could become tricky as factor endowments then change in the growth model. But note that in the cases of greatest concern, with abstemious countries growing at different rates, their capital–labor ratios will in fact become increasingly different.

Another issue that arises with using either the Armington Assumption or complete specialization in H–O to reconcile with the one-sector model, however, is *relative prices*. As a fast-growing country pours more and more of its product on to the world market, its price will fall. Indeed, to look at just one simple case, if aggregators for both consumption and investment are identical Cobb–Douglas functions, then each country's share of world output at world prices will be constant, equal to the exponents of the Cobb–Douglas function. This constancy is achieved by the price of any country's product falling in proportion to any increase in its output. Therefore much of what may have been interesting about Table 2 would be invalidated. However, as this case may suggest, it seems likely that such a model would conform increasingly closely to the one-sector model of section 2 if aggregators had constant elasticity of substitution (CES) and if that elasticity were taken to be very large. Indeed, I suspect that the one-sector homogeneous product model of section 2 is just the limiting case of such a CES Armington or specialized H–O model as the elasticity goes to infinity.

The Model of International Investment

I assumed in section 2 that if international direct investment were permitted, capital would be allocated at random in proportion to population. That may have seemed especially arbitrary. However, it too can be justified as a limiting case of a more familiar model.

Suppose that the linear production function of equation (1) is replaced with a CES function of labor and capital with elasticity of substitution σ^{LK}. This function will have a return to capital that is not constant, but that instead depends negatively on the capital–labor ratio, k. With freely mobile capital, investment will flow to any country with a lower k than others, since its return to capital will be higher, and therefore in equilibrium all capital–labor ratios will be the same. This is of course a different model than considered above, but as σ^{LK} is taken to be larger and larger, it will approximate the linear technology of equation (1).

4. Conclusion

The conclusion that I draw from this analysis is not, as you might think, that the world is in trouble. I do believe the model when it tells me that, for certain parameters of behavior, a plausible future would include ever-increasing international income inequality accompanied by increased trade and investment that might be blamed for that inequality. But the model does not tell us what the parameters of actual behavior really are, and on that account I remain agnostic. I have not examined actual technology, savings, and population growth parameters to see where they may lie in the context of this model, and I would not trust such a simple model to quantify real world behavior in any case.[9]

Instead, I take some reassurance from the fact that recent literature attempting to find evidence of endogenous growth in the real world has not been notably successful. In particular, several recent papers, most notably Jones (1995a,b), have sought empirical evidence that incomes of countries have diverged over recent decades, as they should have if endogenous growth models were correct, and they have found that the time series evidence does not support the predictions of endogenous growth models. On the basis of that, I conclude very tentatively that both the hope and, as I have argued, the specter of endogenous growth may be downgraded among our priorities for further analysis.

References

Barro, Robert and Xavier Sala-I-Martin, *Economic Growth*, New York: McGraw-Hill (1995).
Brown, Drusilla K., Alan V. Deardorff, and Robert M. Stern, "Modelling Multilateral Trade Liberalization in Services," *Asia-Pacific Economic Review* 2 (April 1996):21–34.

Deardorff, Alan V., "Trade and Capital Mobility in a World of Diverging Populations," in D. Gale Johnson and Ronald D. Lee (eds.), *Population Growth and Economic Development: Issues and Evidence*, Madison, WI: University of Wisconsin Press (1987):561–88.

———, "Growth and International Investment with Diverging Populations," *Oxford Economic Papers* 46 (1994):477–91.

———, "Rich and Poor Countries in Neoclassical Trade and Growth," Research Seminar in International Economics discussion paper 402, University of Michigan (1997).

———, "Determinants of Bilateral Trade: Does Gravity Work in a Neoclassical World?" in Jeffrey Frankel (ed.), *Regionalization of the World Economy*, Chicago: University of Chicago Press (1998).

Dixit, Avinash K. and Joseph E. Stiglitz, "Monopolistic Competition and Optimum Product Diversity," *American Economic Review* 67 (1997):297–308.

Fisher, Eric O'N., "Growth, Trade, and International Transfers," *Journal of International Economics* 39 (1995):143–58.

Galor, Oded, "Convergence? Inferences from Theoretical Models," *Economic Journal* 106 (1996):1056–69.

Jones, Charles I., "R&D-Based Models of Economic Growth," *Journal of Political Economy* 103 (1995a):759–84.

———, "Time Series Tests of Endogenous Growth Models," *Quarterly Journal of Economics* 110 (1995b):495–525.

Krugman, Paul R., "Increasing Returns, Monopolistic Competition, and International Trade," *Journal of International Economics* 9 (1979):469–79.

Long, Ngo Van and Kar-yiu Wong, "Endogenous Growth and International Trade: A Survey," in Bjarne S. Jensen and Kar-yiu Wong (eds.), *Dynamics, Economic Growth and International Trade*, Ann Arbor, MI: University of Michigan Press (1996).

Lucas, Robert E., Jr., "On the Mechanics of Economic Development," *Journal of Monetary Economics* 22 (1988):3–42.

Romer, Paul M., "Increasing Returns and Long-Run Growth," *Journal of Political Economy* 94 (1986):1002–37.

Solow, Robert, "A Contribution to the Theory of Economic Growth," *Quarterly Journal of Economics* 70 (1956):65–94.

Notes

1. See Romer (1986) and Lucas (1988) for the seminal contributions, and Barro and Sala-i-Martin (1995) for a comprehensive treatment of the new growth theory.

2. In quite a different approach to a similar problem of international inequality, I have examined a neoclassical growth model in Deardorff (1997), showing that large enough differences in factor endowments can lead both to the failure of factor price equalization and to multiple steady states. The latter, as in Galor (1996), imply the existence of poverty traps, where per capita incomes differ permanently and substantially, not because of differences in behavior but because of differences only in initial conditions.

3. See Long and Wong (1996) for a survey of models of endogenous growth and international trade, where the AK model is carefully explained.

4. Solow's model, of course, allowed a more general production function than (1), $Y = F(K, L) = Lf(K/L)$ with constant returns to scale. It became the AK model if $\lim_{k \to \infty} f'(k) > n$.

5. K_i is "on the ground," if you like, and thus the subscript.

6. Interestingly, no extra conditions are required for the exporting country.

7. I will assume for this and other identifications of countries with the highest levels or rates of variables that they are unique. In many cases, like this one, if more than one country were to tie for the maximum, we could redefine countries to combine them.

8. Fisher (1995) has examined an AK growth model with two countries that focuses more on situations of incomplete specialization.

9. Actually, I did on one occasion, in Deardorff (1987), attempt just such a quantification. Using a version of the model in Deardorff (1994), modified to better capture certain features of the data, I simulated long-term growth using savings, population growth, and other parameters from the developed and developing worlds. What I found was not suggestive of endogenous growth.

2
Basic Stochastic Dynamic Systems of Growth and Trade

Bjarne S. Jensen and Chunyan Wang*

Abstract

Uncertainties are intrinsic features of dynamic economic systems, and this paper considers the dynamic implications of factor endowment (labor, capital) uncertainties for a small growing trading economy. The stochastic growth models presented extend the open neoclassical two-sector growth model (Deardorff) to a stochastic environment in continuous time, and extend the diffusion dynamics of one-sector growth models (Merton; Bourguignon) to a trading two-sector economy. It is demonstrated that the basic propositions of deterministic steady-state growth and endogenous growth theory, under some specifications and certain parametric restrictions, are preserved within a stochastic framework.

1. Introduction

Stochastic elements will evidently appear in any economic growth process generated by factor endowment accumulation and technological change. It is not possible to know exactly how the labor force will grow. Neither will the actual evolution of capital stock be governed by a purely deterministic process. What happens then in *dynamic trade* models to the *steady-state* or *endogenous* (persistent) *growth* paths, when the traditional assumption of *certainty* is *relaxed*?

In the present paper, we raise this question for neoclassical *two-sector growth* models of a *small* country that is *trading* in both commodities. Within the framework of Ito-Wiener *diffusion* processes for the factor endowment (capital/labor) ratio, particular attention is given to the long-run *probabilities* of *diversification* or complete *specialization*. As to the *existence* of a steady-state distribution, our central problem and objective are to obtain genera *boundary inaccessibility* conditions. Another major goal is to derive the *steady-state* probability *distribution* of the capital–labor ratio in *closed form* for a trading economy. Parameters of stochastic trade models generating *persistent* (endogenous) *growth* per capita are analyzed. The *geometric* Wiener process appears to be the uncertainty analogue of deterministic endogenous growth paths. For our purposes and as benchmarks, sector production functions of the CD and CES form are used.

In the literature on the pure theory of international trade, the implications of *uncertainty* for factor *allocation*, *production*, and *trade* patterns have long ago been studied by Kemp and Liviatan (1973), Batra (1974), Ruffin (1974a,b), Turnovsky (1974), Kemp (1976), Baron and Forsythe (1979), Kemp et al. (1981), Young (1984), and Pomery (1984). Instead of firms maximizing profit or expected profit and hence being indifferent towards risk, the main focus of these authors is upon *risk* averse *producers* max-

---
* Jensen, Wang: Copenhagen Business School, Nansensgade 19, DK-1366 Copenhagen K, Denmark. Tel: (+45) 3815 2583; Fax: (+45) 3815 2576; E-mail: bsj.eco@cbs.dk; E-mail: cw.int@cbs.dk.
We would like to thank Martin Jacobsen (University of Copenhagen) and Preben Kjeld Alsholm (Technical University of Denmark) for their very detailed comments and suggestions. Useful comments were received from Martin Richter and Niels Henrik Børjesson (Copenhagen Business School). This work was financially supported by the Danish Social Science Research Council, grant 9500740.

imizing their *expected utility* from profits in a stochastic environment of random *prices,* *resource* uncertainty (randomness in factor endowments), or *technological* uncertainty (random parameters) in sector production functions. Recognition of these uncertainties and risk aversion tended to *invalidate* the fundamental theorems of *deterministic trade* theory. The latter, however, would carry over to a stochastic environment, if *uncertainty* can be *accommodated* by introducing *contingency* markets of the Arrow–Debreu type (Kemp, 1976; Kemp and Liviatan, 1973) or allowing for trading risk in a *perfect* capital (security) market. For a systematic integration of the theory of international financial markets into international commodity trade theory, see Helpman and Razin (1978) and Grinols (1987).

So far, the analyses of various types of uncertainty and their implications have been conducted within essentially *static trade models* with *constant* expected aggregate *factor endowments.* Although the propositions about uncertainty in static or comparative static analyses (alternative capital stocks) are instructive, the process of capital *accumulation* with *uncertainty* is best represented by *stochastic* versions of economic *growth* models.

The *dynamic* implications of *resource* (labor, capital) *uncertainties* are particularly relevant, since a *small* growing trading country, as is usually assumed, faces *known,* constant world *prices* of traded goods.

Our basic *stochastic growth model* represents an extension of the open neoclassical two-sector growth model originated by Deardorff (1971, 1974), cf. Jensen and Wang (1997), to a stochastic environment in *continuous time.* Our diffusion dynamics extend the continuous-time stochastic one-sector growth model outlined by Merton (1975) and Bourguignon (1974) to a trading two-sector economy.

The structure of the paper is as follows. First, we generalize the deterministic growth models to various stochastic dynamic systems and present the diffusion processes for the state variables: labor and capital. Next, by Ito's Lemma, we derive diffusion processes for the capital–labor ratios. Moreover, the crucial boundary issues of the diffusion processes are examined, and actual *sufficient conditions* for *inaccessible* boundaries are obtained. From the Kolmogorov forward equation for a stationary probability density function, the *steady-state probability* distribution of the *capital–labor ratio* is derived in *closed form* for the trading economy.

2. Structure of Two-Sector Trade Models

General Equilibrium and a Two-Sector Trading Economy

Consider an economy consisting of a *capital* good industry (sector) and a *consumer* good industry (sector), labelled 1 and 2, respectively. The sector *technologies* are described by productions exhibiting *constant returns* to scale:

$$Y_i = F_i(L_i, K_i) = L_i f_i(k_i) \equiv L_i y_i, \quad i = 1, 2 \tag{1}$$

where the *intensive function* f_i is a strictly concave monotonic increasing function on the nonnegative real line; i.e., $f_i(k_i)$, $k_i \equiv K_i/L_i$, $i = 1, 2$, have the properties

$$\forall k_i > 0: \quad f_i'(k_i) = df_i(k_i)/dk_i > 0, \quad f_i''(k_i) = d^2 f_i(k_i)/dk_i^2 < 0. \tag{2}$$

Full employment of labor and capital gives

$$L_1/L + L_2/L \equiv l_1 + l_2 = 1, \quad K/L \equiv k \equiv l_1 k_1 + l_2 k_2 \tag{3}$$

$$l_1 = (k - k_2)/(k_1 - k_2), \quad l_2 = (k_1 - k)/(k_1 - k_2), \quad Y_i = L_i y_i = L y_i l_i. \tag{4}$$

The factor endowments belonging to the *diversification cone* $C_k \subset \mathbb{R}_+^2$ are

$$C_k = \{(L, K) \in \mathbb{R}_+^2 | k_1 < K/L < k_2 \vee k_2 < K/L < k_1\}. \tag{5}$$

The open two-sector economy is assumed to operate under *perfect competition* (zero profit condition); absolute (money) *factor* prices (w, r) are the same in both sectors; and *output* prices (P_1, P_2) represent unit cost. Hence, we have the competitive *general equilibrium* relations, $P_i Y_i = rK_i + wL_i$, $i = 1, 2$, and

$$\omega \equiv w/r = f_i(k_i)/f_i'(k_i) - k_i, \quad r/P_i = f_i'(k_i), \quad p \equiv P_1/P_2 = f_2'(k_2)/f_1'(k_1). \tag{6}$$

A small, *open*, competitive two-sector economy can only remain *diversified* with common positive ω if the *range* of the *terms of trade*, $p \equiv P_1/P_2$, is confined to the zero-profit price interval with the limits (cf. Rybczynski lines in Wong, 1995)

$$k_1 > k_2 : \tilde{y}_2/\tilde{y}_1 < p < (\tilde{y}_2/\tilde{y}_1)(\tilde{k}_1/\tilde{k}_2); \quad k_2 > k_1 : (\tilde{y}_2/\tilde{y}_1)(\tilde{k}_1/\tilde{k}_2) < p < \tilde{y}_2/\tilde{y}_1. \tag{7}$$

With p as a fixed number, we use the symbols $\tilde{y}_i = f_i(\tilde{k}_i(\tilde{\omega}[p]))$, $i = 1, 2$, in (7) for factor endowments $k \in C_k$.

Gross domestic product Y is the monetary value of outputs from both sectors and represents aggregated gross factor incomes (cf. (4), (6))

$$Y \equiv P_1 Y_1 + P_2 Y_2 = L(P_1 y_1 l_1 + P_2 y_2 l_2) = rK + wL = L(rk + w) \equiv Ly. \tag{8}$$

Let Q_i, $i = 1, 2$, denote the quantitative size of the *domestic demand* (absorption level) for good 1 (gross investment) and good 2 (consumption), and Q_i is equal to domestic production, Y_i, minus net exports, $X_i \lessgtr 0$; i.e.:

$$Q_i = Y_i - X_i. \tag{9}$$

The *trade balance* is assumed to satisfy the constraint

$$P_1 X_1 + P_2 X_2 = 0 \quad \therefore \quad Y = P_1 Q_1 + P_2 Q_2; \tag{10}$$

i.e., trade equilibrium prevails with no foreign borrowing/lending allowed.

Deterministic Dynamics for a Small Two-Sector Trading Economy

For the general deterministic dynamic neoclassical model of a small trading economy, a rigorous analysis can be performed by specification of the factor accumulation process. The domestic labor force grows exponentially at an exogenous rate, $n > 0$, and the domestic stock of capital goods increases by gross savings $S = sY$, $s > 0$, with the deduction of depreciation $\delta P_1 K$. Hence we have (8), $L \geq 0$, $K \geq 0$:

$$\dot{L} \equiv dL/dt = Ln, \tag{11}$$

$$\dot{K} \equiv dK/dt = Ls(y/P_1) - \delta K = L(s[y_1 l_1 + (y_2/p)l_2] - \delta k) \equiv Lg(k). \tag{12}$$

Thus, with the *factor endowments* L and K as *state variables*, the complete description of the growth process in the small trading economy is given by the *dynamic system* (11)–(12). This system applies to growth processes with "fixed" sector technologies operating within the *diversification* cone (nonspecialization), as well as to *flexible* sector technologies operating outside the diversification cone.

From (11)–(12), we get for $k \in [0, \infty[$:

$$\dot{k} = h(k) \equiv g(k) - nk = s(y/P_1) - (n + \delta)k = s[y_1 l_1 + (y_2/p)l_2] - (n + \delta)k. \tag{13}$$

The director function $h(k)$ is a C^1-function on $[0, \infty[$, and $h(k)$ is a concave function cf. (2) and has—like the per capita real GDP-function y/P_1—a *linear segment* (flat) within the diversification cone (5); cf. Jensen and Wang (1997).

3. Stochastic Dynamic Systems for Trading Economies

Introduction of Stochastic Elements

Introducing *random* elements (uncertainty) of the growth rate of labor n, the saving rate s, and the capital depreciation rate δ into (11)–(12), we have

$$\dot{L} = L(n + \varepsilon_1),\tag{14}$$

$$\dot{K} = L(s + \varepsilon_3)(y/P_1) - (\delta + \varepsilon_2)K,\tag{15}$$

where the *random variables* ε_i, $i = 1, 2, 3$, are formally represented as

$$\varepsilon_i = \Phi_i(L, K)\,dw_i/dt, \quad \text{or} \quad \varepsilon_i = \beta_i dw_i/dt, \quad \beta_i \geq 0, \quad i = 1, 2, 3.\tag{16}$$

Here $w_i(t)$ are standard Wiener processes (Karlin and Taylor, 1981, p. 342; Øksendal, 1992, p. 14), and $\Phi_i(L, K)$ is either a *nonnegative* function of $L(t)$ and $K(t)$ or, more simply, a constant $\beta_i \geq 0$. At first, we assume that the random variables ε_i of the growth rate of labor, the saving rate, and the capital depreciation rate δ do not depend on the *state* variables L and K. However, we will in section 4 consider the general case of saving uncertainty.

Thus (14)–(16) become the *stochastic differential* equations:

$$dL = L(n + \beta_1 dw_1/dt)dt = L(ndt + \beta_1 dw_1),\tag{17}$$

$$\begin{aligned}dK &= L(s + \beta_3 dw_3/dt)(y/P_1)dt - (\delta + \beta_2 dw_2/dt)Kdt \\ &= L(\{s(y/P_1) - \delta k\}dt - \beta_2 kdw_2 + \beta_3(y/P_1)dw_3).\end{aligned}\tag{18}$$

They express formally that the *infinitesimal changes* $dL(t)$ and $dK(t)$ of the *state* variables L and K between instants t and $t + dt$ are now *random* variables, *conditional* on the values of the random variables $L(t)$ and $K(t)$ at *time t*.

In differential symbols (17)–(18) have the common form

$$d\mathbf{X} = \mathbf{a}(\mathbf{X}, t)dt + \mathbf{b}(\mathbf{X}, t)d\mathbf{w}\tag{19}$$

where $\mathbf{a}(\mathbf{X}, t), \mathbf{b}(\mathbf{X}, t)$ are respectively the *drift* and *diffusion* coefficients.

By comparing (11)–(12) with (17)–(18), it has accordingly been assumed that:

(1) The stochastic process $w_i(t)$ is a standard Wiener process, and hence $dw_i(t)$ is a normal distribution with mean zero and variance proportional to dt.
(2) The *expectations* of (17)–(18) are assumed to be equal to the deterministic relations (11)–(12), which can be seen as a true representation of the dynamics of the expected values, $E[L(t)]$ and $E[K(t)]$. The values of the stochastic state variable $\mathbf{X}(t)$, (19), are determined completely when the Wiener process (path) $\mathbf{w}(t)$ is known up to time t (Karlin and Taylor, 1981, p. 346), and $E[\int \mathbf{b}(\mathbf{X}, t)d\mathbf{w}(t)] = \mathbf{0}$.
(3) The *conditional* variance of $dL(t)$ and $dK(t)$ must necessarily be assumed to be of infinitesimal order dt to avoid any *degeneracy* of the stochastic differential equation (17)–(18) into either the *deterministic* relationships (11)–(12) or into being dominated by the *pure* stochastic terms depending on $dw_i(t)$.

(4) The *drift* and *diffusion* coefficients in (17)–(18) are *autonomous* (i.e., independent of time *t*); hence the *governing functions* ("probabilistic laws") of the economic phenomena are time-invariant.

The *stochastic dynamic system* (17)–(18), defined on the whole *nonnegative orthant* for *L* and *K*, consists of *three subsystems*, allowing for, respectively, specialization in good 1, nonspecialization (diversification), and specialization in good 2. *Explicitly*, (17)–(18) become, with $\tilde{k}_2 > \tilde{k}_1$, cf. (8), (7), (1), (4):

$$0 < k \le \tilde{k}_1 \quad dL = L(ndt + \beta_1 dw_1),$$
$$dK = L(\{sf_1(k) - \delta k\}dt - \beta_2 kdw_2 + \beta_3 f_1(k)dw_3), \tag{20}$$

$$\tilde{k}_1 < k < \tilde{k}_2 \quad dL = L(ndt + \beta_1 dw_1),$$
$$dK = L(\{s[\tilde{y}_1 l_1 + (\tilde{y}_2/p)l_2] - \delta k\}dt - \beta_2 kdw_2$$
$$+ \beta_3[\tilde{y}_1 l_1 + (\tilde{y}_2/p)l_2]dw_3), \tag{21}$$

$$k \ge \tilde{k}_2 \quad dL = L(ndt + \beta_1 dw_1),$$
$$dK = L(\{s(f_2(k)/p) - \delta k\}dt - \beta_2 kdw_2 + \beta_3(f_2(k)/p)dw_3). \tag{22}$$

The case with capital intensity (7) will give a system similar to (20)–(22). The *drift* and *diffusion* coefficients of the stochastic dynamic system (20)–(22) are *homogenous functions* (in the Euler sense) of *degree one* in the state variables *L* and *K*. The homogeneity property allows us to describe two-dimensional systems completely by the dynamics of the capital–labor ratio; cf. Jensen (1994).

Stochastic Dynamics of the Capital–Labor Ratio

LEMMA 1. *For the two-sector trading economy (17)–(18)—with uncertainties in labor growth rate, savings rate, and the capital depreciation rate—the stochastic dynamics for the capital–labor ratio is a diffusion process given by*

$$dk = \{(s - \rho_{13}\beta_1\beta_3)(y/P_1) - [n + \delta - (\beta_1^2 \rho_{12}\beta_1\beta_2)]k\}dt$$
$$- \beta_1 kdw_1 - \beta_2 kdw_2 + \beta_3(y/P_1)dw_3, \qquad k \in [0, \infty[\tag{23}$$

where ρ_{ij} is the time-invariant correlation coefficient between the incremental Wiener processes dw_i and dw_j.
Explicitly, (23) becomes for the three subintervals of k, cf. (20)–(22):

$$0 < k \le \tilde{k}_1 \quad dk = \{(s - \rho_{13}\beta_1\beta_3)f_1(k) - \Theta k\}dt + b_1(k)dw, \tag{24}$$

$$\tilde{k}_1 < k < \tilde{k}_2 \quad dk = \{(s - \rho_{13}\beta_1\beta_3)\tilde{\theta}_2 + [(s - \rho_{13}\beta_1\beta_3)\tilde{\theta}_1 - \Theta]k\}dt + b_2(k)dw, \tag{25}$$

$$k \ge \tilde{k}_2 \quad dk = \{(s - \rho_{13}\beta_1\beta_3)(f_2(k)/p) - \Theta k\}dt + b_3(k)dw, \tag{26}$$

with

$$\Theta \equiv n + \delta - (\beta_1^2 + \rho_{12}\beta_1\beta_2), \tag{27}$$

$$\beta^2 \equiv \beta_1^2 + \beta_2^2 + 2\rho_{12}\beta_1\beta_2, \tag{28}$$

$$\rho \equiv 2(\rho_{13}\beta_1 + \rho_{23}\beta_2), \tag{29}$$

$$b_1^2(k) \equiv \beta^2 k^2 + \beta_3^2 f_1^2(k) - \rho\beta_3 f_1(k)k,$$

$$b_2^2(k) \equiv \beta^2 k^2 + \beta_3^2 [\tilde{\theta}_2 + \tilde{\theta}_1 k]^2 - \rho\beta_3 [\tilde{\theta}_2 + \tilde{\theta}_1 k]k, \tag{30}$$

$$b_3^2(k) \equiv \beta^2 k^2 + \beta_3^2 [f_2(k)/p]^2 - \rho\beta_3 [f_2(k)/p]k,$$

$$\tilde{\theta}_1 \equiv [\tilde{y}_1 - (\tilde{y}_2/p)]/(\tilde{k}_1 - \tilde{k}_2) > 0, \quad \tilde{\theta}_2 \equiv [(\tilde{y}_2/p)\tilde{k}_1 - \tilde{y}_1\tilde{k}_2]/(\tilde{k}_1 - \tilde{k}_2) > 0, \tag{31}$$

and $\tilde{\theta}_1$ is the slope of the linear segment of the GDP-function y/P_1, while $\tilde{\theta}_2$ is the corresponding intercept; cf. (4), (7)–(8), (13).

PROOF. Ito's Lemma: Let $\mathbf{X}(t) \in \mathbb{R}^n$ be a general diffusion process defined as in (19). Let $F(\mathbf{X}, t)$ be an arbitrary C^2-map from $\mathbb{R}^n \to \mathbb{R}$; then

$$dF(\mathbf{X}, t) = F_t dt + F_\mathbf{x}^T d\mathbf{X} + \frac{1}{2} d\mathbf{X}^T F_{\mathbf{xx}} d\mathbf{X}; \tag{32}$$

i.e., $F(\mathbf{X}, t)$, determined by the diffusion process $\mathbf{X}(t)$, is again a diffusion process; F_t and F_x represent the partial derivatives with respect to t and $\mathbf{x}$ of the function $F(\mathbf{x}, t)$, $F_{\mathbf{xx}}$ represents the Hessian matrix of $F(\mathbf{x}, t)$, and the multiplication rules are: $(dw_i)^2 = dt$; $dw_i \cdot dw_j = \rho_{ij} dt$; $(dt)^2 = 0$; $dt \cdot dw_i = 0$.

The expression (23) is obtained after straightforward calculations from (17)–(18) by applying Ito's Lemma (32) to the capital–labor ratio, $k = K/L$; i.e.:

$$dk = 0dt - (K/L^2)dL + (1/L)dK + (K/L^3)dL^2 - (1/L^2)dLdK + 0dK^2. \tag{33}$$

The expressions (24)–(26) are obtained from (23), using (1), (4), (8), together with $l_1 = 1$, $l_2 = 0$ for (24); with $l_1 = (k - \tilde{k}_2)/(\tilde{k}_1 - \tilde{k}_2)$, $l_2 = (\tilde{k}_1 - k)/(\tilde{k}_1 - \tilde{k}_2)$, and (7) for (25); and finally, $l_1 = 0$, $l_2 = 1$ for (26). See Karlin and Taylor (1981, p. 364), Malliaris and Brock (1982, p. 142), Klump (1995).

The expressions (30) of the squared diffusion coefficients are simply obtained by using the multiplication rules in combining the three diffusion terms of (23). □

COROLLARY 1. *If only the labor growth rate and the capital depreciation rate are uncertain ($\beta_3 = 0$), the diffusion process of $k(t)$ is described by, cf. (23):*

$$dk = \{s(y/P_1) - \Theta k\}dt - \beta_1 k dw_1 - \beta_2 k dw_2, \tag{34}$$

or explicitly

$$dk = \begin{cases} \{sf_1(k) - \Theta k\}dt - \beta k dw & = a_1(k)dt + b(k)dw, & 0 < k \le \tilde{k}_1 \\ \{s\tilde{\theta}_2 + [s\tilde{\theta}_1 - \Theta]k\}dt - \beta k dw = a_2(k)dt + b(k)dw, & \tilde{k}_1 < k < \tilde{k}_2 \\ \{s(f_2(k)/p) - \Theta k\}dt - \beta k dw = a_3(k)dt + b(k)dw, & k \ge \tilde{k}_2 \end{cases} \tag{35}$$

where the diffusion coefficient of the combined incremental Wiener process $dw(t)$ in (35) is, cf. (28)–(30),

$$b_i^2(k) = b^2(k) \equiv \beta^2 k^2 = (\beta_1^2 + \beta_2^2 + 2\rho_{12}\beta_1\beta_2)k^2. \tag{36}$$

Note that ρ_{23} does not enter the drift coefficient in (23). Furthermore, note that our introduction of uncertainties (17)–(18) implies that the *deterministic* growth *parameters* s, n, δ only appear in the drift coefficients, cf. (24)–(26), but not in the diffusion coefficients (30). From (23), it is clear that *uncertainty* in the *saving* rate s will always introduce *nonlinear* terms in the *diffusion* coefficient of the capital–labor ratio, creating as is well-known, difficulties in solving (23)–(31). Therefore, with respect to closed-form probability distributions, we will later primarily investigate the situations in Corollary 1.

4. Boundary Conditions, Steady-State, and Convergence

From Lemma 1, with the derived diffusion processes of the capital–labor ratios on the state space $[0, \infty]$, we may now analyze the process evolution of the small competitive trading economy, with emphasis on long-run behavior (asymptotic properties). However, the drift and diffusion coefficients *govern* the process evolution only at *interior* points of the state space. To fully define a diffusion process, the behaviour of any *boundary* points requires *separate* specification. For our purposes of studying the long-run evolution of nontrivial states, careful examination is needed of the *conditions* that will make the *boundaries*, $k = 0$ or $k = \infty$, *inaccessible* for any *finite* time ($t < \infty$). If $a_i(0) = 0$ and $b_i(0) = 0$—as is often seen cf. (24)–(26) and (35)—then $k(t) = 0$ is an *absorbing* boundary; i.e., the sample paths $k(t)$ remain at the zero position once it is attained. Even if $a_i(0) \neq 0$, or $b_i(0) \neq 0$, and hence $k = 0$ is not an absorbing state, we may not admit negative state values of $k(t)$; i.e., a *viable* (working) *economic* diffusion model must require that the *inaccessibility* of the boundary state $k = 0$ is ensured by imposing sufficient *parameter restrictions* on the actual drift and diffusion coefficients.

As the incremental Wiener processes $dw_i(t) \in\,]-\infty, \infty[$ may occasionally take on very large negative values, the drift and diffusion coefficients must indeed be carefully chosen to prevent the random variable $k(t)$ from never hitting the lower boundary $k = 0$. The sort of "boxing match" between $a_i(k)$ and $b_i(k)$ must in the neighborhood of $k = 0$ be won by the drift coefficient $a_i(k)$, which evidently in this neighborhood must be positive and larger than $b_i(k)$. However, the exact inaccessibility *criteria* follows only from rigorous analysis related to the *divergence* of specific improper integrals of the drift and diffusion coefficients; see Appendix A. Primarily the divergence of the so-called *scale function* $S(k)$ at $k = 0$ and $k = \infty$ is used to establish the *sufficient* parametric *conditions* for inaccessibility of the respective boundaries for various diffusion processes below.

Remark 1. It is well-known (Karlin and Taylor, 1981, p. 359), that the solution (Ito-integral) to the stochastic differential equation (17) is the geometric Wiener process with the *continuous sample paths* (stochastic trajectories, realizations)

$$L(t) = L_0 \exp\left\{\left(n - \frac{1}{2}\beta_1^2\right)t + \beta_1 w_1(t)\right\}; \quad 2n \gtrless \beta_1^2 : \lim_{t\to\infty} L(t) = \begin{cases} \infty \\ 0 \end{cases}. \tag{37}$$

Furthermore, the *boundaries* zero or infinity are *inaccessible*, as the sample paths (37) *cannot* attain any of the two boundaries in *finite* time. It will be instructive to prove the latter statement as a prelude to the general procedure of proving inaccessibility below. From (17) and Appendix A, the *scale density* $s(L)$ and the *scale function* $S(L)$ become, cf. (A.2):

$$s(L) = \exp\left\{-2\int_{L_0}^{L} nL/(\beta_1^2 L^2)dL\right\} = (L/L_0)^{-2n/\beta_1^2}, \tag{38}$$

$$S(L) = \int_{L_0}^{L} s(L)dL = L_0/(1 - 2n/\beta_1^2)\left[(L/L_0)^{1-2n/\beta_1^2} - 1\right]. \tag{39}$$

As $S(0) = -\infty$ for $2n \geq \beta_1^2$, the latter is a *sufficient* parameter condition for the *inaccessibility* of the boundary $k = 0$. But despite the finite $S(0) = -L_0/(1 - 2n/\beta_1^2)$ for $2n < \beta_1^2$, the boundary $k = 0$ may still not be attainable.

The *speed density* $\mathfrak{m}(L)$ is, cf. (A.3):

$$\mathfrak{m}(L) = 2L^{2n/\beta_1^2}/(\beta_1^2 L^2) = \left(L_0^{2n/\beta_1^2}/\beta_1^2\right)L^{2n/\beta_1^2 - 2}, \tag{40}$$

and we must now with (39)–(40) and (A.6) evaluate

$$\Sigma(0) = \int_0^{L_0}[S(L) - S(0)]\mathfrak{m}(L)dL = \frac{L_0^{4n/\beta_1^2}}{\beta_1^2(1 - 2n/\beta_1^2)}\int_0^{L_0}L^{-1}dL = +\infty. \tag{41}$$

Thus $\Sigma(0) = +\infty$ says that it takes *infinite* time to reach zero boundary from any interior state; i.e., $L = 0$ is after all also *inaccessible* for $2n < \beta_1^2$, as it *cannot* be attained in *finite* time. The same analysis can be applied to boundary $L = \infty$, which is neither attainable in finite time. From this examination of the *labor diffusion* process (17)—which have no steady-state distribution—it is also clear that boundary problems for the capital–labor ratio diffusion below are essentially due to boundary problems associated with the capital stock diffusion process. $\qquad\triangledown$

Labor Growth and Capital Depreciation Rates are Uncertain

CD case. The general intensive form of the CD (Cobb–Douglas) function is

$$f_i(k) = \gamma_i k^{a_i}, \quad \gamma_i > 0, \quad 0 < a_i < 1, \quad i = 1, 2 \tag{42}$$

with the following limits of $f_i(k)$ and $f_i'(k)$, ("Inada conditions"):

$$\lim_{k \to 0} f_i(k) = 0, \quad \lim_{k \to \infty} f_i(k) = \infty, \quad \lim_{k \to 0} f_i'(k) = \infty, \quad \lim_{k \to \infty} f_i'(k) = 0. \tag{43}$$

From (35)–(36) and the CD functions (42), we have

$$dk = \begin{cases} \{s\gamma_1 k^{a_1} - \Theta k\}dt - \beta k dw & = a_1(k)dt + b(k)dw, \quad 0 < k \le \tilde{k}_1 \\ \{s\tilde{\theta}_2 + [s\tilde{\theta}_1 - \Theta]k\}dt - \beta k dw & = a_2(k)dt + b(k)dw, \quad \tilde{k}_1 < k < \tilde{k}_2 \\ \{s(\gamma_2/p)k^{a_2} - \Theta k\}dt - \beta k dw & = a_3(k)dt + b(k)dw, \quad k \le \tilde{k}_2. \end{cases} \tag{44}$$

THEOREM 1. *The sufficient conditions for the diffusion process (44) of a small competitive trading economy—with CD technologies and uncertainties in both labor growth and capital depreciation—to have inaccessible boundaries are*

$$\text{k = 0: always inaccessible,} \tag{45}$$

$$k = \infty: \ 2\Theta + \beta^2 \ge 0 \ \Leftrightarrow \ 2(n + \delta) \ge \beta_1^2 - \beta_2^2. \tag{46}$$

The parametric condition (46) also ensures the existence and the long-run convergence of the stochastic capital–labor ratio $k(t)$ to a time-invariant (steady-state) probability distribution $P(k)$.

PROOF. Applying (A.2) of Appendix A:

$$s_i(k) \equiv \exp\left\{-2\int_{k_0}^k \frac{a_i(u)}{b_i^2(u)}du\right\}, \quad i = 1, 2, 3 \tag{47}$$

to the system (44), we have

$$s_1(k) = \exp\left\{-2\int_{k_0}^k \frac{s\gamma_1 k^{a_1} - \Theta k}{\beta^2 k^2}dk\right\}, \quad 0 < k \le \tilde{k}_1 \tag{48}$$

$$s_3(k) = \exp\left\{-2\int_{k_0}^k \frac{s(\gamma_2/p)k^{a_2} - \Theta k}{\beta^2 k^2}dk\right\}, \quad k \ge \tilde{k}_2. \tag{49}$$

From (48)–(49), we get by simple integration

$$s_1(k) = (k/k_0)^{2(\Theta/\beta^2)} \exp\left\{\frac{2s\gamma_1}{(1-a_1)\beta^2}\left(k^{-(1-a_1)} - k_0^{-(1-a_1)}\right)\right\}, \tag{50}$$

$$s_3(k) = (k/k_0)^{2(\Theta/\beta^2)} \exp\left\{\frac{2s(\gamma_2/p)}{(1-a_2)\beta^2}\left(k^{-(1-a_2)} - k_0^{-(1-a_2)}\right)\right\}. \tag{51}$$

From (50), we have

$$S_1(0) = \int_{k_0}^{0} s_1(k)dk \equiv m_0^1 \int_{k_0}^{0} k^{2(\Theta/\beta^2)} \exp\left\{\frac{2s\gamma_1}{(1-a_1)\beta^2}k^{-(1-a_1)}\right\}dk. \tag{52}$$

Since $1 - a_1 > 0$ and $2s\gamma_1/[(1-a_1)\beta^2] > 0$, cf. (42), the exponential term in (52) will dominate and explode for $k \to 0$, and hence $S_1(0)$ diverges; i.e., $S_1(0) = -\infty$. Thus, the *lower boundary $k = 0$ is always inaccessible, irrespective* of the size of the drift and diffusion parameters.

From (51), we have

$$S_3(\infty) = \int_{k_0}^{\infty} s_3(k)dk \equiv m_0^3 \int_{k_0}^{\infty} k^{2(\Theta/\beta^2)} \exp\left\{\frac{2s(\gamma_2/p)}{(1-a_2)\beta^2}k^{-(1-a_2)}\right\}dk. \tag{53}$$

Since $1 - a_2 > 0$, cf. (42), the divergence of $S_3(\infty)$ here only depends on the polynomial term in (53) with the exponent $2(\Theta/\beta^2)$. Hence divergence of $S_3(\infty)$ requires that $2(\Theta/\beta^2) \geq -1$, or equivalently $2(n + \delta) \geq \beta_1^2 - \beta_2^2$, cf. (27)–(28). Hence, the *upper* boundary $k = \infty$ is *inaccessible* by imposing the parameter restriction stated in (46).

The *existence* of $P(k)$ and the *convergence* of $P(k, t)$ towards $P(k)$ follow from (A.2)–(A.3), (44), and (A.7):

$$|\mathcal{M}_1(0)| = \int_0^{\tilde{k}_1} m_1(k)dk = \int_0^{\tilde{k}_1} \frac{1}{\beta^2 k^2 s_1(k)}dk < \infty,$$

$$\mathcal{M}_3(\infty) = \int_{\tilde{k}_2}^{\infty} m_3(k)dk = \int_{\tilde{k}_2}^{\infty} \frac{1}{\beta^2 k^2 s_3(k)}dk < \infty. \tag{54}$$

The *finiteness* (convergence) of the *two* improper integrals in (54) is easily verified with a procedure similar to that above to require the *same* parameter conditions as obtained from (52)–(53), of which only (53) imposed effective restrictions as stated in (46). □

Remark 2. Besides the proofs, we may offer some intuition for the results obtained. The general inaccessibility of the *lower* boundary (45) is essentially due to the CD property, $f_i'(k) \to \infty$ as $k \to 0$, (43), which enables the *nonlinear part* of the *drift* coefficient $a_1(k)$ in (44), in the neighbourhood of $k = 0$ to *dominate* the linear drift (Θk) and diffusion (βk) elements. The sufficient inaccessibility condition of the *upper* boundary (46) prevents "explosion" (reaching $k = \infty$ in finite time) of the diffusion process (44). By (46), we see that large values of labor growth (n), large depreciation rate (δ), and large uncertainty (high volatility) in depreciation (β_2) will naturally curb high values of $k(t)$, whereas a very high volatility in labor growth (β_1) spells trouble by giving chances for generating very high values of the ratio $k(t)$. Note that if $\beta_2 = 0$ and $\delta = 0$ (Merton, 1975), then the sufficient condition (46) coincides with the condition for $L(t) \to \infty$, (37). Evidently, large values of n and δ help in preventing $k(t)$ from attaining infinity.

The *divergence* conditions of $S_1(0)$ and $S_3(\infty)$, (45)–(46), are the same as the *convergence* conditions of $\mathcal{M}_1(0)$ and $\mathcal{M}_3(\infty)$, since the scale density functions $s_1(k)$ and $s_3(k)$ entered the respective improper integrals reciprocally.   ▽

CES case. The general intensive form of CES technology, $\gamma_i > 0, 0 < a_i < 1$, is

$$f_i(k) = \gamma_i[(1-a_i) + a_i k^{\rho_i}]^{1/\rho_i}, \quad 0 < \sigma_i < \infty, \quad \rho_i \equiv (\sigma_i - 1)/\sigma_i, \quad -\infty < \rho_i < 1. \quad (55)$$

By evaluating (55), the limits or *dominating* ($\sim$) terms of $f_i(k)$ and $f_i'(k)$ become

$$\sigma_i < 1: \begin{cases} \text{small } k: f_i(k) \sim \gamma_i a_i^{1/\rho_i} k, & \lim_{k \to \infty} f_i(k) = \gamma_i(1-a_i)^{1/\rho_i} \\ \lim_{k \to 0} f_i'(k) = \gamma_i a_i^{1/\rho_i}, & \lim_{k \to \infty} f_i'(k) = 0 \end{cases} \quad (56)$$

$$\sigma_i > 1: \begin{cases} \lim_{k \to 0} f_i(k) = \gamma_i(1-a_i)^{1/\rho_i}, & \text{large } k: f_i(k) \sim \gamma_i a_i^{1/\rho_i} k \\ \lim_{k \to 0} f_i'(k) = \infty, & \lim_{k \to \infty} f_i'(k) = \gamma_i a_i^{1/\rho_i}. \end{cases} \quad (57)$$

From (35)–(36) and the CES functions (55), we get the diffusion process

$$dk = \begin{cases} \left\{ s\gamma_1[(1-a_1) + a_1 k^{\rho_1}]^{1/\rho_1} - \Theta k \right\} dt - \beta k\, dw, & 0 < k \le \tilde{k}_1 \\ \left\{ s\tilde{\theta}_2 + [s\tilde{\theta}_1 - \Theta]k \right\} dt - \beta k\, dw, & \tilde{k}_1 < k < \tilde{k}_2 \\ \left\{ s(\gamma_2/p)[(1-a_2) + a_2 k^{\rho_2}]^{1/\rho_2} - \Theta k \right\} dt - \beta k\, dw, & k \ge \tilde{k}_2. \end{cases} \quad (58)$$

THEOREM 2. *The sufficient conditions for the diffusion process* (58)—*with CES technologies and uncertainties in both labor growth and capital depreciation—to have inaccessible boundaries are*

$$\sigma_i < 1: \begin{cases} k = 0: & 2(n + \delta - s\gamma_1 a_1^{1/\rho_1}) \le \beta_1^2 - \beta_2^2, \\ k = \infty: & 2(n + \delta) \ge \beta_1^2 - \beta_2^2, \end{cases} \quad (59)$$

$$\sigma_i > 1: \begin{cases} k = 0: & \text{always inaccessible}, \\ k = \infty: & 2(n + \delta - s(\gamma_2/p)a_2^{1/\rho_2}) \ge \beta_1^2 - \beta_2^2. \end{cases} \quad (60)$$

PROOF. From (58), we have the expressions, cf. (47):

$$s_1(k) = \exp\left\{ -2\int_{k_0}^{k} \frac{s\gamma_1[(1-a_1) + a_1 k^{\rho_1}]^{1/\rho_1} - \Theta k}{\beta^2 k^2} dk \right\}, \quad (61)$$

$$s_3(k) = \exp\left\{ -2\int_{k_0}^{k} \frac{s(\gamma_2/p)[(1-a_2) + a_2 k^{\rho_2}]^{1/\rho_2} - \Theta k}{\beta^2 k^2} dk \right\}. \quad (62)$$

For $\sigma_i < 1$: From (61) and (56), we have, cf. (A.5):

$$S_1(0) = \lim_{k \to 0} \int_{k_0}^{k} s_1(k)\,dk = \int_{k_0}^{0} (k/k_0)^{-2\left[s\gamma_1 a_1^{1/\rho_1} - \Theta\right]/\beta^2} dk. \quad (63)$$

Hence it follows from (63) that the divergence of $S_1(0)$ to $-\infty$ requires that the exponent must be less than or equal to -1, or equivalently $2_s\gamma_1 a_1^{1/\rho_1} \ge 2\Theta + \beta^2$, which gives the lower boundary condition in (59).

From (62) and (56), we have, cf. (A.5):

$$S_3(\infty) = \lim_{k \to \infty} \int_{k_0}^{k} s_3(k)\,dk$$

$$= \int_{k_0}^{\infty} (k/k_0)^{\frac{2\Theta}{\beta^2}} \exp\left\{ \frac{2s(\gamma_2/p)(1-a_2)^{1/\rho_2}}{\beta^2}(k^{-1} - k_0^{-1}) \right\} dk. \quad (64)$$

The polynomial term in (64) decides the divergence of $S_3(\infty)$; it diverges to $+\infty$ if the exponent $2\Theta/\beta^2 \ge -1$, which gives the inaccessibility condition in (59).

For $\sigma_i > 1$: From (61) and (57), we have, cf. (A.5):

$$S_1(0) = \lim_{k \to 0} \int_{k_0}^{k} s_1(k)dk = \int_{k_0}^{0} (k/k_0)^{\frac{2\Theta}{\beta^2}} \exp\left\{ \frac{2s\gamma_1(1-a_1)^{1/\rho_1}}{\beta^2}(k^{-1} - k_0^{-1}) \right\} dk. \tag{65}$$

The exponential term in (65) will always explode for $k \to 0$. Hence $S_1(0)$ is diverging, and accordingly, $k = 0$ is *inaccessible*, *irrespective* of parameters restrictions.

From (62) and (57), we have, cf. (A.5):

$$S_3(\infty) = \lim_{k \to \infty} \int_{k_0}^{k} s_3(k)dk = \int_{k_0}^{\infty} (k/k_0)^{-2\left[s(\gamma_2/p)a_2^{1/\rho_2} - \Theta\right]/\beta^2} dk. \tag{66}$$

$S_3(\infty)$ is divergent, if and only if the *exponent* of the polynomial in (66) is larger than or equal to -1, which gives the parametric *inaccessibility* restriction as stated in (60). □

Remark 3. A comparison of the sufficient inaccessibility conditions in Theorems 1–2 reveals that the *crucial* strength (size) of *drift* coefficients near the boundaries depends on the savings *parameter s* and the *derivative properties* of the CD and CES functions, (43), (56)–(57). With $\sigma_i < 1$, (59) says that the lower boundary is inaccessible, when s and the derivative $f_i'(0)$, (56), dominate both the linear drift 2Θ and linear diffusion (β^2) elements. The condition (59) for $k = \infty$ is the *same* as (46), cf. the upper limit of $f_i'(k_i)$, (43), (56). With $\sigma_i > 1$, the logic of (60) for $k = 0$ is the same as in (45), cf. the dominating infinity derivative of $f_i'(0)$ in both (43) and (57). Naturally, to avoid explosion of the capital–labor ratio, the saving rate and the upper bound of the derivative, (57), must not be too high, as expressed by (60) for $k = \infty$.

Remark 4. Any *one-dimensional* regular *diffusion* process is *completely* characterized by its *scale* function $S(x)$ and its *speed* measure $\mathcal{M}(x)$, cf. (A.2)–(A.3). It holds with either reflecting or absorbing boundaries. If a regular diffusion on an open interval $]r_1, r_2[$ satisfies the inaccessible boundary conditions, cf. (A.4)–(A.6), and if the diffusion solves a stochastic differential equation, then this solution is unique even if the drift and diffusion coefficients do not satisfy the standard conditions of Lipschitz continuity and the linear growth conditions (see Ito and McKean, 1965).

An unbounded slope of CD and CES functions with $\sigma_i > 1$ at $k = 0$ prevents Lipschitz continuity, but the solutions to (44) and (58) are still unique when inaccessibility of $k = 0$ is ensured by Theorems 1–2. Hence, with inaccessibility we need not be restricted to only the class of bounded slope (see the critique by Chang and Malliaris, 1987).

The Saving Rate is Uncertain

It was seen in (23) that the *uncertainty* in *saving* behaviour will always introduce *nonlinear* terms in the *diffusion* coefficient. Inaccessible boundaries here raise conditions that clash with common deterministic dynamic regularity properties.

CD case. From (24)–(31) with $\beta_1 = \beta_2 = 0$ and the CD functions (42), we have the diffusion process

$$dk = \begin{cases} \{s\gamma_1 k^{a_1} - (n+\delta)k\}dt + \beta_3\gamma_1 k^{a_1} dw_3, & 0 < k \le \tilde{k}_1 \\ \{s\tilde{\theta}_2 + [s\tilde{\theta}_1 - (n+\delta)]k\}dt + \beta_3[\tilde{\theta}_2 + \tilde{\theta}_1 k]dw_3, & \tilde{k}_1 < k < \tilde{k}_2 \\ \{s(\gamma_2/p)k^{a_2} - (n+\delta)k\}dt + \beta_3(\gamma_2/p)k^{a_2} dw_3, & k \ge \tilde{k}_2. \end{cases} \tag{67}$$

CES case. From (24)–(31) with $\beta_1 = \beta_2 = 0$ and the CES functions (55), we have the diffusion process

$$dk = \begin{cases} \left\{ s\gamma_1[(1-a_1)+a_1 k^{\rho_1}]^{1/\rho_1} - (n+\delta)k \right\} dt \\ \quad + \beta_3 \gamma_1[(1-a_1)+a_1 k^{\rho_1}]^{1/\rho_1} dw_3, & 0 < k \le \tilde{k}_1 \\ \left\{ s\tilde{\theta}_2 + [s\tilde{\theta}_1 - (n+\delta)]k \right\} dt + \beta_3[\tilde{\theta}_2 + \tilde{\theta}_1 k]dw_3, & \tilde{k}_1 < k < \tilde{k}_2 \\ \left\{ s(\gamma_2/p)[(1-a_2)+a_2 k^{\rho_2}]^{1/\rho_2} - (n+\delta)k \right\} dt \\ \quad + \beta_3(\gamma_2/p)[(1-a_2)+a_2 k^{\rho_2}]^{1/\rho_2} dw_3, & k \ge \tilde{k}_2. \end{cases} \tag{68}$$

THEOREM 3. *The diffusion process (67) or (68)—with CD or CES functions and uncertainty only in saving rate—will have boundary properties and sufficient inaccessibility conditions as follows:*

$$\sigma_i = 1: \begin{cases} k = 0: \textit{inaccessible, if } a_1 > \dfrac{1}{2}; \textit{ possibly accessible, if } a_1 < \dfrac{1}{2}, \\ k = \infty: \textit{always inaccessible,} \end{cases} \tag{69}$$

$$\sigma_i < 1: \begin{cases} k = 0: \ 2[s\gamma_1 \alpha_1^{1/\rho_1} - (n+\delta)] \ge [\beta_3 \gamma_1 \alpha_1^{1/\rho_1}]^2, \\ k = \infty: \textit{always inaccessible,} \end{cases} \tag{70}$$

$$\sigma_i > 1: \begin{cases} k = 0: \textit{possibly accessible,} \\ k = \infty: \ 2[s(\gamma_2/p)a_2^{1/\rho_2} - (n+\delta)] \le [\beta_3(\gamma_2/p)a_2^{1/\rho_2}]^2. \end{cases} \tag{71}$$

PROOF. See Appendix B.   □

With uncertainty in the saving rate, the *drift* and *diffusion* coefficients in (67)–(68) now have *similar nonlinear elements*, that, if dominating, will prevent us from satisfying a sufficient inaccessibility condition, as the scale function $S_1(k)$ at $k = 0$ is now finite, cf. (B.3) and (B.9), whenever $\sigma_i \ge 1$. It is the infinite derivatives ("Inada property") at $k = 0$, (43), (57), that instead of supporting inaccessibility as before, cf. (45) and (60), now create problems by also appearing in the diffusion coefficients (67)–(68). This derivative problem is not changed by using (24)–(26), which include all the types of uncertainty. We may note that with $a_1 < \frac{1}{2}$, (69), the zero boundary will in fact absorb certain sample paths of (67) in finite time. Thus, uncertainty about the saving rate was recognized by Bourguignon (1974, p. 151) as a serious *obstacle* to the economic *viability* of diffusion processes (67)–(68). The factor accumulation process is likely to be much more severely affected (large volatility) by *uncertainties* about the *saving* rate than by uncertainties in labor growth and depreciation rates. The *lack* of any parametric *restrictions* preventing the accessibility of the absorbing boundary $k = 0$ (implosion, "economic collapse"), cf. (69) and (71), represents a *critical* stochastic dynamic model complication for the system (67)–(68) and a mathematical issue to be adequately resolved below.

General Parameter Uncertainties and Inaccessible Boundary Conditions

To dampen the impact of the Wiener process dw_3 near $k = 0$ in (15)–(16), the random element ε_3 in the saving parameter must be *state-dependent*, and to preserve (20)–(22) as a *homogenous* stochastic *dynamic* system, the function $\Phi_3(L, K)$, (16), must be homogenous of degree zero; i.e., $\Phi_3(L, K) = \phi_3(k)$.

From economic reasons, the *shape* of $\phi_3(k)$ on the *domain* $k \in [0, \infty[$ should be chosen as a monotonically *increasing* curve, but this curve should also—to avoid creating excessive saving parameter volatility—be *bounded* above by a *horizontal* asymptote. With these two stipulations upon relevant selections of $\phi_3(k)$, one choice might be the logistic (S-shaped) curve described by well-known exponential expressions. Among the exponentials, however, a relevant and convenient choice of $\phi_3(k)$, with proper domain and range for our purposes, would be

$$\phi_3(k) = \beta_3 \tanh(\lambda_3 k), \quad k \in [0, \infty[, \quad \phi_3(0) = 0, \quad \phi_3(\infty) = \beta_3. \tag{72}$$

Thus, letting the uncertainty of the saving rate depend on the capital–labor ratio by (72), the stochastic differential equation of capital, (18), becomes, cf. (15)–(16):

$$
\begin{aligned}
dK &= L(s + \beta_3 \tanh(\lambda_3 k) \, dw_3/dt)(y/P_1)dt - (\delta + \beta_2 dw_2/dt)Kdt \\
&= L(\{s(y/P_1) - \delta k\}dt - \beta_2 k dw_2 + \beta_3 \tanh(\lambda_3 k)(y/P_1)dw_3).
\end{aligned}
\tag{73}
$$

With (73) and (17), we obtain as before, using (33) and Lemma 1, the stochastic differential equation for capital–labor ratio

$$
\begin{aligned}
dk &= \{[s - \rho_{13}\beta_1\beta_3 \tanh(\lambda_3 k)](y/P_1) - [n + \delta - (\beta_1^2 + \rho_{12}\beta_1\beta_2)]k\}dt \\
&\quad - \beta_1 k dw_1 - \beta_2 k dw_2 + \beta_3 \tanh(\lambda_3 k)(y/P_1)dw_3.
\end{aligned}
\tag{74}
$$

The formulas (24)–(31) of Lemma 1 still apply after replacing β_3 with $\beta_3 \tanh(\lambda_3 k)$ everywhere.

THEOREM 4. *The sufficient conditions for the general diffusion process (74)—with CES technologies and uncertainties in labor growth, capital depreciation, and saving rates— to have inaccessible lower and upper boundary are*

$$k = 0; \ \sigma_i < 1: \ 2(n + \delta - s\gamma_1 a_1^{1/\rho_1}) \le \beta_1^2 - \beta_2^2, \tag{75}$$

$$k = 0; \ \sigma_i \ge 1: \textit{ always inaccessible}, \tag{76}$$

$$k = \infty; \ \sigma_i \le 1: \ 2(n + \delta) \ge \beta_1^2 - \beta_2^2, \tag{77}$$

$$k = \infty; \ \sigma_i > 1: \ 2(n + \delta - s(\gamma_2/p)a_2^{1/\rho_2}) \ge \beta_1^2 - \beta_2^2 - \Delta, \tag{78}$$

$$\textit{where } \Delta \equiv [\beta_3(\gamma_2/p)a_2^{1/\rho_2}]^2 - 2\rho_{23}\beta_2\beta_3(\gamma_2/p)a_2^{1/\rho_2}.$$

PROOF. See Appendix C.   □

The sufficient inaccessibility conditions (75)–(76) and (77)–(78) reflect, respectively, the requirements $S_1(0) = -\infty$ and $S_3(\infty) = \infty$. Note that (75)–(76) are the same as (59)–(60) and (45); i.e., Theorems 1–2 are confirmed as special cases of Theorem 4 with $\beta_3 = 0$. Furthermore, special cases of (78)—either $\beta_1 = \beta_2 = 0$ or $\beta_3 = 0$—give (71) of Theorem 3 and (60) of Theorem 2. But most important, the *assumption* (72) has *removed* the uncertainty of saving rate $\phi_3(k)$ in (73) entirely from the *lower* boundary problems, cf. (69) and (71), because with (72), we now have that (76) holds, irrespective of the size of *any drift* and *diffusion* parameters.

Stochastic Dynamics and Asymptotic Nonstationary Distributions

Relaxing the sufficient inaccessibility condition $S_3(\infty) = \infty$ does not imply explosion, cf. (A.6) and Remark 1. But to avoid any risk of implosion, we want to keep the condition $S_1(0) = -\infty$. Moreover, together with a finite $S_3(\infty)$, we have the following well-known implications (with probability one):

$$[S_1(0) = -\infty \wedge S_3(\infty) < \infty] \implies \lim_{t \to \infty} k(t) = \infty \implies \lim_{t \to \infty} \mathsf{E}[k(t)] = \infty. \tag{79}$$

A finite $S_3(\infty)$ is simply equivalent to reversing the inequality in (77)–(78), cf. Appendix C. For $\sigma_i \le 1$, the reverse of (77) is $2(n + \delta) \le \beta_1^2 - \beta_2^2$. The latter implies that $k(t) \to \infty$ as $t \to \infty$, but it is a pathological case as the reversal of (77) also implies that $L(t) \to 0$ (although never reached in finite time), cf. (37). In short, no relevant stochastic endogenous growth is possible with $\sigma_i \le 1$. Hence as in the deterministic case, stochastic endogenous economic growth requires that the marginal product of capital is bounded below; i.e., $\sigma_i > 0$, cf. (57).

By reversing (78), the sufficient condition of growth becomes, cf. (79), (76):

$$\sigma_i > 1: \ S_3(\infty) < \infty \iff s(\gamma_2/p)a_2^{1/\rho_2} \ge n + \delta + \frac{1}{2}(-\beta_1^2 + \beta_2^2 + \Delta), \tag{80}$$

which is the *stochastic analogue* to the *deterministic* condition—with only $n + \delta$ on the RHS—of endogenous (persistent) growth (see Jensen and Wang, 1997, p. 93; Jensen and Larsen, 1987).

We see from (80) that it is generally more *difficult* (a higher average saving rate is required) to *achieve* persistent economic growth in the face of uncertainty—as $n - \frac{1}{2}\beta_1^2 > 0$ is now taken for granted in (80), cf. (37), and Δ is always positive when $\rho_{23} = 0$, cf. (78). Uncertainties in the accumulation of capital, (73), ($\beta_2 \ne 0$, $\beta_3 \ne 0$) make the stochastic analogue (80) harder to satisfy.

The *rapidity* of stochastic growth is not directly seen by (80). However, with $S_3(\infty) < \infty$, the stochastic differential equation (74) is asymptotically, cf. (C.11):

$$dk \sim \bar{a}_3 k dt + \bar{b}_3 k dw_3 \equiv \left\{ (s - \rho_{13}\beta_1\beta_3)(\gamma_2/p)a_2^{1/\rho_2} - \Theta \right\} k dt$$

$$+ \left[\beta^2 + \beta_3^2(\gamma_2/p)^2 a_2^{2/\rho_2} - \rho\beta_3(\gamma_2/p)a_2^{1/\rho_2} \right]^{1/2} k dw_3, \tag{81}$$

which is the *geometric* Wiener *process* with the sample paths and expectation

$$k(t) \sim k_0 \exp\left\{ \left(\bar{a}_3 - \frac{1}{2}\bar{b}_3^2 \right)t + \bar{b}_3 w_3(t) \right\}, \quad 2\bar{a}_3 > \bar{b}_3^2 \tag{82}$$

$$\mathsf{E}[k(t)] \sim k_0 \exp(\bar{a}_3 t) \tag{83}$$

It is easily verified that the exponential growth condition $\bar{a}_3 - \frac{1}{2}\bar{b}_3^2 > 0$ in (82) is equivalent to (80). Thus, the stochastic condition (80) is indeed the analogue of deterministic exponential growth. The small trading economy that eventually grows as (80)–(83) is finally specialized in the capital-intensive good.

5. The CD Case with Closed-Form Steady-State Distribution

Having obtained the conditions for the *existence* and convergence to a *steady-state* (time-invariant) *distribution*, cf. (46), we also want to obtain as a *benchmark*—with CD sector technologies of the small trading economy—a *closed-form* expression for the *time-invariant probability density* function $p(k)$ and the *distribution function* $P(k)$ of the diffusion process (44).

It turns out that the benchmark *distribution* function $P(k)$ for the trading economy can be expressed by *gamma* $\Gamma(\alpha)$ and *incomplete gamma* functions $\Gamma(\alpha, x_0)$, which are generally defined, respectively, by the improper integrals

$$\Gamma(\alpha) \equiv \int_0^\infty x^{\alpha-1} e^{-x} dx, \quad \Gamma(\alpha, x_0) \equiv \int_{x_0}^\infty x^{\alpha-1} e^{-x} dx, \quad \alpha > 0. \tag{84}$$

THEOREM 5. *The time-invariant (steady-state) distribution $P(k)$ for the stochastic process (44), cf. Theorem 1, will have a density function $p(k)$, if and only if*

$$2(\Theta - s\tilde{\theta}_1) + \beta^2 > 0 \quad \Leftrightarrow \quad 2(n + \delta - s\tilde{\theta}_1) > \beta_1^2 - \beta_2^2. \tag{85}$$

With (85), the time-invariant probability density function $p(k)$ is in closed form

$$p(k) = \begin{cases} p_1(k) = \dfrac{m_1}{m} k^{-2[1+\Theta/\beta^2]} \exp\{-c_1 k^{-(1-a_1)}\}, & 0 < k \le \tilde{k}_1 \\[2mm] p_2(k) = \dfrac{m_2}{m} k^{-2[1+(\Theta-s\tilde{\theta}_1)/\beta^2]} \exp\{-c_2 k^{-1}\}, & \tilde{k}_1 < k < \tilde{k}_2 \\[2mm] p_3(k) = \dfrac{m_3}{m} k^{-2[1+\Theta/\beta^2]} \exp\{-c_3 k^{-(1-a_2)}\}, & k \ge \tilde{k}_2, \end{cases} \tag{86}$$

where the constants c_1, c_2, c_3, m_1, m_2, m_3 are given by

$$c_1 = 2s\gamma_1 / [(1-a_1)\beta^2], \quad c_2 = 2s\tilde{\theta}_2 / \beta^2, \quad c_3 = 2s(\gamma_2/p)/[(1-a_2)\beta^2]$$

$$m_1 = \tilde{k}_1^{\frac{2\Theta}{\beta^2}} e^{x_1}/\beta^2, \quad m_2 = \tilde{k}_1^{\frac{2[\Theta-s\tilde{\theta}_1]}{\beta^2}} e^{x_2}/\beta^2, \quad m_3 = \tilde{k}_1^{\frac{2[\Theta-s\tilde{\theta}_1]}{\beta^2}} \tilde{k}_2^{\frac{2s\tilde{\theta}_1}{\beta^2}} e^{x_2-x_3+x_4}/\beta^2$$

$$x_1 = c_1 \tilde{k}_1^{-(1-a_1)}, \quad x_2 = c_2 \tilde{k}_1^{-1}, \quad x_3 = c_2 \tilde{k}_2^{-1}, \quad x_4 = c_3 \tilde{k}_2^{-(1-a_2)},$$

and with m involving gamma and incomplete gamma functions

$$m = C_1 \Gamma(\alpha_1, x_1) + C_2 [\Gamma(\alpha_2, x_3) - \Gamma(\alpha_2, x_2)] + C_3 [\Gamma(\alpha_3) - \Gamma(\alpha_3, x_4)],$$

$$\alpha_1 = \frac{1+2\Theta/\beta^2}{1-a_1}, \quad \alpha_2 = 1 + 2(\Theta - s\tilde{\theta}_1)/\beta^2, \quad \alpha_3 = \frac{1+2\Theta/\beta^2}{1-a_2},$$

$$C_1 = [m_1/(1-a_1)]c_1^{-\alpha_1}, \quad C_2 = m_2 c_2^{-\alpha_2}, \quad C_3 = [m_3/(1-a_2)]c_3^{-\alpha_3}.$$

With the stationary density function $p(k)$, (86), the stationary distribution $P(k) = \int_0^k p(k)dk$ can be expressed by incomplete gamma functions as

$$P(k) = \begin{cases} P_1(k) = \dfrac{C_1}{m} \Gamma(\alpha_1, c_1 k^{-(1-a_1)}), & 0 < k \le \tilde{k}_1 \\[2mm] P_2(k) = P(\tilde{k}_1) + \dfrac{C_2}{m} [\Gamma(\alpha_2, c_2 k^{-1}) - \Gamma(\alpha_2, x_2)], & \tilde{k}_1 < k < \tilde{k}_2 \\[2mm] P_3(k) = P(\tilde{k}_2) + \dfrac{C_3}{m} [\Gamma(\alpha_3, c_3 k^{-(1-a_2)}) - \Gamma(\alpha_3, x_4)], & k \ge \tilde{k}_2, \end{cases} \tag{87}$$

and the probability measures of the three factor endowment regions are

$$P(k \le \tilde{k}_1) = P(\tilde{k}_1) = \frac{C_1}{m} \Gamma(\alpha_1, x_1), \tag{88}$$

$$P(\tilde{k}_1 \le k \le \tilde{k}_2) = P(\tilde{k}_2) - P(\tilde{k}_1) = \frac{C_2}{m} [\Gamma(\alpha_2, x_3) - \Gamma(\alpha_2, x_2)], \tag{89}$$

$$P(k > \tilde{k}_2) = 1 - P(\tilde{k}_2) = \frac{C_3}{m}[\Gamma(\alpha_3) - \Gamma(\alpha_3, x_4)]. \tag{90}$$

The distribution $P(k)$, (87), will have finite first- and second-order moments $E(k)$ and $E(k^2)$, if and only if, respectively

$$\Theta - s\tilde{\theta}_1 > 0 \quad \Leftrightarrow \quad n + \delta - s\tilde{\theta}_1 > \beta_1^2 + \rho_{12}\beta_1\beta_2, \tag{91}$$

$$2(\Theta - s\tilde{\theta}_1) - \beta^2 > 0 \quad \Leftrightarrow \quad 2(n + \delta - s\tilde{\theta}_1) > 3\beta_1^2 + 4\rho_{12}\beta_1\beta_2 + \beta_2^2. \tag{92}$$

With (91)–(92), the steady-state distribution $P(k)$ will have first- and second-order moments given by

$$E(k) = \mu_1/m, \quad E(k^2) = \mu_2/m, \quad \sigma^2 = E(k^2) - [E(k)]^2, \tag{93}$$

where the constants μ_1 and μ_2 are given by the following expressions involving complete and incomplete gamma functions:

$$\mu_1 = C_1^*\Gamma(\alpha_1^*, x_1) + C_2^*[\Gamma(\alpha_2^*, x_3) - \Gamma(\alpha_2^*, x_2)] + C_3^*[\Gamma(\alpha_3^*) - \Gamma(\alpha_3^*, x_4)],$$

$$\alpha_1^* = \alpha_1 - (1 - a_1)^{-1}, \quad \alpha_2^* = \alpha_2 - 1, \quad \alpha_3^* = \alpha_3 - (1 - a_2)^{-1},$$

$$C_1^* = [m_1/(1 - a_1)]c_1^{-\alpha_1^*}, \quad C_2^* = m_2 c_2^{-\alpha_2^*}, \quad C_3^* = [m_3/(1 - a_2)]c_3^{-\alpha_3^*},$$

$$\mu_2 = C_1^{**}\Gamma(\alpha_1^{**}, x_1) + C_2^{**}[\Gamma(\alpha_2^{**}, x_3) - \Gamma(\alpha_2^{**}, x_2)] + C_3^{**}[\Gamma(\alpha_3^{**}) - \Gamma(\alpha_3^{**}, x_4)],$$

$$\alpha_1^{**} = \alpha_1 - 2(1 - a_1)^{-1}, \quad \alpha_2^{**} = \alpha_2 - 2, \quad \alpha_3^{**} = \alpha_3 - 2(1 - a_2)^{-1},$$

$$C_1^{**} = [m_1/(1 - a_1)]c_1^{-\alpha_1^{**}}, \quad C_2^{**} = m_2 c_2^{-\alpha_2^{**}}, \quad C_3^{**} = [m_3/(1 - a_2)]c_3^{-\alpha_3^{**}}.$$

PROOF. For the stochastic system (44), the speed densities are, cf. (A.2)–(A.3):

$$m_1(k) = \frac{1}{\beta^2 k^2}\exp\left\{-2\int_k^{\tilde{k}_1}\frac{s\gamma_1 k^{a_1} - \Theta k}{\beta^2 k^2}dk\right\}, \quad 0 < k \le \tilde{k}_1$$

$$m_2(k) = \frac{1}{\beta^2 k^2}\exp\left\{2\int_{\tilde{k}_1}^k\frac{s\tilde{\theta}_2 + [s\tilde{\theta}_1 - \Theta]k}{\beta^2 k^2}dk\right\}, \quad \tilde{k}_1 < k < \tilde{k}_2$$

$$m_3(k) = \frac{1}{\beta^2 k^2}\exp\left\{2\int_{\tilde{k}_1}^{\tilde{k}_2}\frac{s\tilde{\theta}_2 + [s\tilde{\theta}_1 - \Theta]k}{\beta^2 k^2}dk + 2\int_{\tilde{k}_2}^k\frac{s(\gamma_2/p)k^{a_2} - \Theta k}{\beta^2 k^2}dk\right\}, \quad k \ge \tilde{k}_2. \tag{94}$$

After simple integration, we obtain

$$m_1(k) = m_1 k^{-2[1+\Theta/\beta^2]}\exp\left\{-\frac{2s\gamma_1}{(1 - a_1)\beta^2}k^{-(1-a_1)}\right\}, \quad 0 < k \le \tilde{k}_1$$

$$m_2(k) = m_2 k^{-2[1+\Theta/\beta^2 - s\tilde{\theta}_1/\beta^2]}\exp\left\{-\frac{2s\tilde{\theta}_2}{\beta^2}k^{-1}\right\}, \quad \tilde{k}_1 < k < \tilde{k}_2$$

$$m_3(k) = m_3 k^{-2[1+\Theta/\beta^2]}\exp\left\{-\frac{2s(\gamma_2/p)}{(1 - a_2)\beta^2}k^{-(1-a_2)}\right\}, \quad k \ge \tilde{k}_2, \tag{95}$$

where the constants m_1, m_2, m_3 are given in Theorem 5.
By (95), we have, cf. (A.8):

$$m = \int_0^{\tilde{k}_1} m_1(k)dk + \int_{\tilde{k}_1}^{\tilde{k}_2} m_2(k)dk + \int_{\tilde{k}_2}^\infty m_3(k)dk, \tag{96}$$

which gives—after changes of variables and limits of integrations together with rather lengthy calculations—the expression for m as stated in Theorem 5. Thus by (95)–(96), the invariant density function $p(k)$, (86), is established.

Since the *parameter* α in the gamma and incomplete gamma functions has to be *positive*, it is seen from $\Gamma(\alpha_2, x_3)$ that

$$\alpha_2 > 0 \quad \Leftrightarrow \quad 1 + 2(\Theta - s\tilde{\theta}_1)/\beta^2 > 0, \tag{97}$$

which gives the restriction for the existence of the density stated in (85) or rewritten using (27)–(28).

The first- and second-order moments are obtained from the density function as

$$\mathsf{E}(k) \equiv \int_0^\infty k p(k)dk = \int_0^{\tilde{k}_1} k p_1(k)dk + \int_{\tilde{k}_1}^{\tilde{k}_2} k p_2(k)dk + \int_{\tilde{k}_2}^\infty k p_3(k)dk = \mu_1/m,$$

$$\mathsf{E}(k^2) \equiv \int_0^\infty k^2 p(k)dk = \int_0^{\tilde{k}_1} k^2 p_1(k)dk + \int_{\tilde{k}_1}^{\tilde{k}_2} k^2 p_2(k)dk + \int_{\tilde{k}_2}^\infty k^2 p_3(k)dk = \mu_2/m.$$

After several substitutions of variables and lengthy rearrangements, we get the expression for the parameters μ_1 and μ_2 as stated in Theorem 5.

Finally, from the incomplete gamma functions, $\Gamma(\alpha_2^*, x_2)$, $\Gamma(\alpha_2^{**}, x_2)$ we see that

$$\alpha_2^* > 0 \quad \Leftrightarrow \quad \Theta - s\tilde{\theta}_1 > 0, \quad \alpha_2^{**} > 0 \quad \Leftrightarrow \quad 2(\Theta - s\tilde{\theta}_1) > \beta^2, \tag{98}$$

which gives the moment existence restrictions (91)–(92), and Theorem 5 is established. □

We may note that a steady-state distribution such as (87) with moments (93) does not imply that the expected growth rates of labor and capital are the same. *Stochastic steady-state* growth and *balanced* growth are no longer equivalent concepts (Stigum, 1972).

Applications

Let us in the midst of abstract deductions give some illustrative examples of applying the formulas in this paper, and especially Theorem 5. From (6) and (42), we have

$$p = \frac{\gamma_2 a_2 k_2^{a_2-1}}{\gamma_1 a_1 k_1^{a_1-1}}, \quad k_i = \frac{a_i}{1-a_i}\omega, \quad \omega = \left[\frac{\gamma_1}{\gamma_2}\frac{a_1}{a_2}\frac{\left(\dfrac{1-a_1}{a_1}\right)^{1-a_1}}{\left(\dfrac{1-a_2}{a_2}\right)^{1-a_2}}p\right]^{\frac{1}{a_2-a_1}}. \tag{99}$$

Example 1 $p = 1$, $s = 0.2$, $n = 0.02$, $\delta = 0.05$, $\beta_1 = 0.01$, $\beta_2 = 0.03$, $\rho_{12} = 0$, $\gamma_1 = \gamma_2 = 1$, $a_1 = 0.2$, $a_2 = 0.25$.

First we must find the three subintervals of k as given by the *endpoints* $\tilde{k}_1$, $\tilde{k}_2$ of *diversification* cone, cf. (5), (7), and (99). Next, the price and parameter values of Example 1 give together with (42) and (31)

$$\omega = 3.5, \quad \tilde{k}_1 = 0.9, \quad \tilde{k}_2 = 1.2, \quad \tilde{y}_1 = 0.97, \quad \tilde{y}_2 = 1.04, \quad \tilde{\theta}_1 = 0.23, \quad \tilde{\theta}_2 = 0.78, \tag{100}$$

and $\Theta = 0.0699$, $\beta^2 = 0.001$, cf. (27)–(28). The expressions (93) and (88)–(90) give

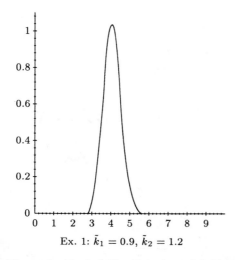

Ex. 1: $\tilde{k}_1 = 0.9$, $\tilde{k}_2 = 1.2$

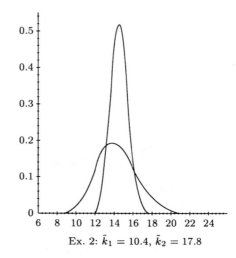

Ex. 2: $\tilde{k}_1 = 10.4$, $\tilde{k}_2 = 17.8$

Figure 1. Probability Density p(k), Equations (86)

$$E(k) = 4.057, \quad \sigma = 0.398, \quad P(\tilde{k}_1) = 0.854 \cdot 10^{-85}, \quad P(\tilde{k}_2) = 0.686 \cdot 10^{-52}, \qquad (101)$$

and the *probability density* $p(k)$, (86), is shown in Figure 1.

On infinite time horizon, any diffusion process will in principle have a nonzero probability of observations anywhere in the state space, here $k \in [0, \infty[$. However, in Example 1, the *region* of *specialization* in the consumer good (all capital goods are imported) contains practically the *entire probability* distribution. The *expected* value $E(k) = 4.057$, (101), is very close to the specialized certainty (deterministic) steady-state value of the capital–labor ratio,

$$\kappa = [s(\gamma_2 / p)/(n + \delta)]^{1/(1-a_2)} = 4.054, \qquad (102)$$

obtained from $f(\kappa)/\kappa = (n + \delta)p/s$, cf. (13), (42) and $p, s, n, \delta, \gamma_2, a_2$ in Example 1.

In our second example, we want a *larger* diversification cone, which requires that the *sector technologies* (parameters a_i) differ more. Higher prices of the capital good also contribute to preserving some domestic production of Y_1.

Example 2 $p = 1.3$, $s = 0.25$, $n = 0.01$, $\delta = 0.02$, $\beta_1 = 0.01$, $\beta_2 = 0.03$, $\rho_{12} = 0$, $\gamma_1 = \gamma_2 = 1$, $a_1 = 0.2$, $a_2 = 0.3$.

From Example 2 and (99), (42), (31), we get

$$\omega = 41.6, \quad \tilde{k}_1 = 10.4, \quad \tilde{k}_2 = 17.8, \quad \tilde{y}_1 = 1.6, \quad \tilde{y}_2 = 2.4, \quad \tilde{\theta}_1 = 0.03, \quad \tilde{\theta}_2 = 1.28, \qquad (103)$$

and $\Theta = 0.0299$, $\beta^2 = 0.001$, cf. (27)–(28). The expressions (93) and (88)–(90) give

$$E(k) = 14.38, \quad \sigma = 2.18, \quad P(\tilde{k}_1) = 0.014, \quad P(\tilde{k}_2) = 0.932, \qquad (104)$$

and the *probability density*, $p(k)$, (86), is shown in Figure 1.

The probability measure of diversification region is nearly 0.92. The *expected* value $E(k) = 14.38$, (104), is very close to the diversified certainty steady-state value of the capital–labor ratio (Jensen and Wang, 1997, eq. (33))

$$\kappa = \tilde{\theta}_2 / [(n + \delta)/s - \tilde{\theta}_1] = 14.31 \qquad (105)$$

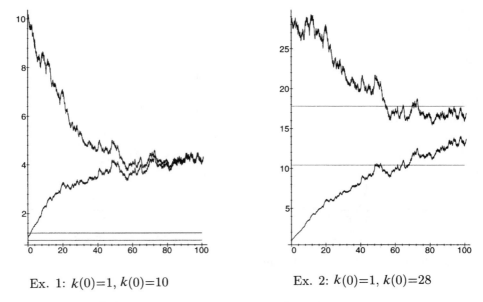

Ex. 1: $k(0)=1$, $k(0)=10$ Ex. 2: $k(0)=1$, $k(0)=28$

Figure 2. Sample Paths for k(t), *Equations (44)*

obtained from (42) and $s, n, \delta, \tilde{\theta}_1, \tilde{\theta}_2$ in Example 2.

In Figure 1, the density function with the same parameter values as Example 2 is also shown for smaller uncertainty parameters $\beta_1 = 0.005$, $\beta_2 = 0.01$. The latter does not change the values of (103) and (105), whereas the moments and the probabilities are now

$$\text{E}(k) = 14.33, \quad \sigma = 1.57, \quad P(\tilde{k}_1) = 0.102 \cdot 10^{-9}, \quad P(\tilde{k}_2) = 0.99997; \tag{106}$$

i.e., the trading economy will always—despite omnipresent uncertainties about the growing factor supplies of labor and capital—have the stochastic factor endowment ratio $k(t)$ between $\tilde{k}_1$ and $\tilde{k}_2$, and hence have *domestic production* of *both* goods. Probability statements (measures) about the *stochastic trade pattern* between $\tilde{k}_1$ and $\tilde{k}_2$ can be calculated from (9)–(10), (35), (87). As may be checked, the parametric values in Examples 1–2 satisfy the restrictions (85), (91)–(92).

The Ito rules of stochastic calculus suggest that the first-order moments are upward-biased estimates of the certainty (deterministic) values (Merton, 1975, p. 382). However, $\text{E}(k)$ and κ in (101)–(102) and (104)–(106) agree remarkably well.

For the parameters of Examples 1–2, Figure 2 shows two simulated sample paths for $k(t)$, (44), using initial values below and above $\text{E}(k)$. The horizontal lines indicate the diversification interval. In the simulations, the same Wiener diffusion (realization) $w(t)$ is employed for all initial values. Hence the two sample paths will converge in the long run. With the parameters of Examples 1–2 and the particular initial values chosen, it takes about 60–80 units of time for the diffusion processes of $k(t)$, (44), to attain their steady-state distributions in Figure 1.

6. Final Comments

In macroscopic and microscopic sciences, no rigid deterministic schemes (rigorously exact laws) are apparent in nature. We are compelled to appeal to stochastic models and probabilities. However, analytical stochastic dynamics of diffusion processes offer exact propositions as in deterministic dynamics. In economics, the study of deterministic models is often a prerequisite for extending dynamic analysis to the realm of uncertainty and probability calculations. If we find the economic universe capricious, the fault lies with our original model—not with the universe. For the basic stochastic models of a small trading economy, we may conclude that uncertainties in labor growth, depreciation, and saving rates still leave fundamental results of deterministic growth models intact, provided that the crucial issue of inaccessible boundary conditions is resolved. The closed-form steady-state probability distribution in the CD case should be useful in comparative probability calculations. The formulas allow us to determine the probability of finding the state variables over the long run in any given region (specialized/diversified) of the state space. The parametric case of stochastic endogenous (persistent) growth establishes asymptotically the natural "uncertainty correspondence" between the sample paths of the geometric Wiener process and the exponential solutions of deterministic endogenous growth models.

Appendix

A. Boundary Conditions and Steady-State Distribution

Let the transition probability of the process (19)—in case of a *one-dimensional* stochastic process $X(t)$—be

$$P(x, t; x_0, t_0) = \Pr[X(t) \leq x | X(t_0) = x_0], \tag{A1}$$

where $X(t)$ is the state of the process at instant t. The transition probability distribution $P(x, t; x_0, t_0)$ is assumed to have a probability density function $p(x, t; x_0, t_0)$, defined everywhere.

Boundary conditions   In terms of notation in (19), we define in the one-dimensional case the following indefinite integrals (functions):

$$J(x) = \int_{x_0}^{x} \frac{a(u)}{b^2(u)} du; \quad s(x) = \exp\{-2J(x)\}, \quad S(x) = \int_{x_0}^{x} s(u) du, \tag{A2}$$

$$m(x) = \frac{\exp\{2J(x)\}}{b^2(x)} = \frac{1}{b^2(x)s(x)}, \quad M(x) = \int_{x_0}^{x} m(u) du. \tag{A3}$$

The functions $s(x)$, $S(x)$, $m(x)$, and $M(x)$ are called, respectively, the *scale density* function, the *scale* function, the *speed density* function, and the *speed measure* of the stochastic processes $X(t)$; cf. Karlin and Taylor (1981, pp. 194–6, 229). Let the diffusion process $X(t)$ have two boundaries $r_1 < r_2$.

Inaccessible boundaries   *Sufficient* conditions: The two boundaries r_1 and r_2 are inaccessible, if

$$\forall x_0 \in [r_1, r_2], \quad S(r_1) = -\infty; \quad S(r_2) = +\infty; \quad \text{equivalently,}$$
$$s(x) \text{ is not integrable on the closed interval } [r_i, x_0] \tag{A4}$$

or else

$$S(r_i) = \lim_{x \to r_i} S(x) = \lim_{x \to r_i} \int_{x_0}^{x} s(x) dx = \mp\infty; \quad i = 1, 2. \tag{A5}$$

The *necessary* and *sufficient* condition is

$$\Sigma(r_i) \equiv \int_{x_0}^{r_i} [S(r_i) - S(x)] m(x) dx = +\infty; \quad i = 1, 2. \tag{A6}$$

Existence of steady-state distribution   A *time-invariant* distribution function $P(x)$ exists, if and only if

$$S(r_i) = \mp\infty \text{ and } \mathcal{M}(x) \text{ is finite at } r_i; \text{ i.e., } |\mathcal{M}(r_i)| < \infty; \quad i = 1, 2. \tag{A7}$$

The existence of steady-state distribution $P(x)$—implying inaccessible boundaries—also implies the *convergence* of the nonstationary distribution functions $P(x, t)$ towards $P(x)$ as $t \to \infty$.

Existence of steady-state density function   A *time-invariant* probability density function $p(x)$ exists, if and only if the *speed* density $m(x)$ satisfies

$$\int_{r_1}^{r_2} m(x) dx < \infty, \quad p(x) = mm(x), \quad \int_{r_1}^{r_2} p(x) dx = 1, \tag{A8}$$

where m is the normalizing constant.

The conditions and formulas above can be applied directly when we have the *same* stochastic differential equation (drift and diffusion coefficients) for the *whole interval* of x. For more details, see Karlin and Taylor (1981) and Mandl (1968).

B. Proof of Theorem 3

CD case   Applying (A2) to the system (67) gives, cf. (47):

$$s_1(k) = \exp\left\{ \frac{(n+\delta)(k^{2(1-a_1)} + k_0^{2(1-a_1)}) - 2s\gamma_1(k^{1-a_1} - k_0^{1-a_1})}{\beta_3^2 \gamma_1^2 (1 - a_1)} \right\}, \tag{B1}$$

$$s_3(k) = \exp\left\{ \frac{(n+\delta)(k^{2(1-a_2)} + k_0^{2(1-a_2)}) - 2s(\gamma_2/p)(k^{1-a_2} - k_0^{1-a_2})}{\beta_3^2 (\gamma_2/p)^2 (1 - a_2)} \right\}. \tag{B2}$$

From (A2) and (B1), we have

$$S_1(0) = \int_{k_0}^{0} s_1(k) dk \equiv m_0^1 \int_{k_0}^{0} \exp\left\{ \frac{(n+\delta)k^{2(1-a_1)} - 2s\gamma_1 k^{1-a_1}}{\beta_3^2 \gamma_1^2 (1 - a_1)} \right\} dk. \tag{B3}$$

Since $1 - a_1 > 0$, $S_1(0)$ will *converge*, and accordingly $k = 0$ may possible be accessible.

To decide whether $k = 0$ is in fact inaccessible, we need further to calculate $\Sigma(0)$. In this CD case, we have for the lower boundary $k = 0$, cf. (A6):

$$\Sigma(0) = \int_{k_0}^{0} [S_1(0) - S_1(k)] m(k) dk. \tag{B4}$$

The limit of the integrand $S_1(k)m(k)$ in (B4) is, cf. (A2)–(A3), (B3), (67):

$$\lim_{k \to 0} S_1(k) m(k)$$

$$= \lim_{k \to 0} \frac{m_0^1 \int_{k_0}^{k} \exp\left\{ [\beta_3^2 \gamma_1^2 (1 - a_1)]^{-1} [(n+\delta)k^{2(1-a_1)} - 2s\gamma_1 k^{1-a_1}] \right\} dk}{\beta_3^2 \gamma_1^2 k^{2a_1} \exp\left\{ [\beta_3^2 \gamma_1^2 (1 - a_1)]^{-1} [(n+\delta)k^{2(1-a_1)} - 2s\gamma_1 k^{1-a_1}] \right\}}. \tag{B5}$$

Since $[\beta_3^2\gamma_1^2(1-a_1)]^{-1} > 0$, the limit (B5) *converges* iff $2(1-a_1) > 1$; i.e., $a_1 < \frac{1}{2}$. Hence with $a_1 > \frac{1}{2}$, $\Sigma(0)$, (B4), will be *divergent*, and thus the lower boundary is inaccessible.

From (A2) and (B2), we have

$$S_3(\infty) = \int_{k_0}^{\infty} s_3(k)dk \equiv m_0^3 \int_{k_0}^{\infty} \exp\left\{\frac{(n+\delta)k^{2(1-a_2)} - 2s(\gamma_2/p)k^{1-a_2}}{\beta_3^2(\gamma_2/p)^2(1-a_2)}\right\}dk. \tag{B6}$$

Since $1 - a_2 > 0$, and $k^{2(1-a_2)}$ is the dominating term, $S_3(\infty)$ will always diverge; i.e., $k = \infty$ is *inaccessible*.

CES case   Applying (A2) to the system (68) gives, cf. (47):

$$s_1(k) = \exp\left\{-2\int_{k_0}^{k} \frac{s\gamma_1[(1-a_1)+a_1k^{\rho_1}]^{1/\rho_1} - (n+\delta)k}{\beta_3^2\gamma_1^2[(1-a_1)+a_1k^{\rho_1}]^{2/\rho_1}}dk\right\}, \tag{B7}$$

$$s_3(k) = \exp\left\{-2\int_{k_0}^{k} \frac{s(\gamma_2/p)[(1-a_2)+a_2k^{\rho_2}]^{1/\rho_2} - (n+\delta)k}{\beta_3^2(\gamma_2/p)^2[(1-a_2)+a_2k^{\rho_2}]^{2/\rho_2}}dk\right\} \tag{B8}$$

For $\sigma_i < 1$: From (B7), we have for small k, cf. (56):

$$S_1(0) = \lim_{k\to 0}\int_{k_0}^{k} s_1(k)dk = \int_{k_0}^{0} \exp\left\{-2\int_{k_0}^{k} \frac{s\gamma_1 a_1^{1/\rho_1} - (n+\delta)}{\beta_3^2\gamma_1^2 a_1^{2/\rho_1}}k^{-1}dk\right\}dk$$

$$= \int_{k_0}^{0} (k/k_0)^{-2\left[s\gamma_1 a_1^{1/\rho_1} - (n+\delta)\right]/\beta_3^2\gamma_1^2 a_1^{2/\rho_1}}dk \tag{B9}$$

$S_1(0)$ diverges if the exponent of k/k_0 is less than or equal to -1, which immediately gives the condition (70).

From (B8), we have for large k, cf. (56):

$$S_3(\infty) = \lim_{k\to\infty}\int_{k_0}^{k} s_3(k)dk$$

$$= \int_{k_0}^{\infty} \exp\left\{-2\int_{k_0}^{k} \frac{s(\gamma_2/p)(1-a_2)^{1/\rho_2} - (n+\delta)k}{\beta_3^2(\gamma_2/p)^2(1-a_2)^{2/\rho_2}}dk\right\}dk$$

$$= \int_{k_0}^{\infty} \exp\left\{\frac{(n+\delta)(k^2-k_0^2) - 2s(\gamma_2/p)(1-a_2)^{1/\rho_2}(k-k_0)}{\beta_3^2(\gamma_2/p)^2(1-a_2)^{2/\rho_2}}\right\}dk$$

$$\equiv m_0^3 \int_{k_0}^{\infty} \exp\left\{\frac{n+\delta}{\beta_3^2(\gamma_2/p)^2(1-a_2)^{2/\rho_2}}k^2 - \frac{2s}{\beta_3^2(\gamma_2/p)(1-a_2)^{1/\rho_2}}k\right\}dk. \tag{B10}$$

As $1 - a_2 > 0$, the constant denominators in (B10) are positive, and since the k^2 term is the dominating term in the exponential expression, $S_3(\infty)$ will always be divergent; hence the upper boundary is always *inaccessible*.

For $\sigma_i > 1$: From (B7), we have for small k, cf. (57):

$$S_1(0) = \lim_{k\to 0}\int_{k_0}^{k} s_1(k)dk$$

$$= \int_{k_0}^{0} \exp\left\{-2\int_{k_0}^{k} \frac{s\gamma_1(1-a_1)^{1/\rho_1} - (n+\delta)k}{\beta_3^2\gamma_1^2(1-a_1)^{2/\rho_1}}dk\right\}dk$$

$$\equiv m_1^0 \int_{k_0}^{0} \exp\left\{\frac{n+\delta}{\beta_3^2\gamma_1^2(1-a_1)^{2/\rho_1}}k^2 - \frac{2s}{\beta_3^2\gamma_1(1-a_1)^{1/\rho_1}}k\right\}dk. \tag{B11}$$

Since $1 - a_1 > 0$, $S_1(0)$ will always converge, and hence $k = 0$ may possibly be accessible. Whether in fact $k = 0$ is attainable in finite time requires similar evaluations as shown above, cf. (B4)–(B5), (41).

From (B8), we have for large k, cf. (57):

$$S_3(\infty) = \lim_{k\to\infty} \int_{k_0}^{k} s_3(k)dk$$

$$= \int_{k_0}^{\infty} \exp\left\{-2\int_{k_0}^{k} \frac{s(\gamma_2/p)a_2^{1/\rho_2} - (n+\delta)}{\beta_3^2(\gamma_2/p)^2 a_2^{2/\rho_2}} k^{-1}dk\right\}$$

$$= \int_{k_0}^{\infty} (k/k_0)^{-2\left[s(\gamma_2/p)a_2^{1/\rho_2}-(n+\delta)\right]/\beta_3^2(\gamma_2/p)^2 a_2^{2/\rho_2}} dk. \tag{B12}$$

$S_3(\infty)$ diverges if the exponent of k/k_0 is larger than or equal to -1, which is equivalent to the condition in (71).

C. Proof of Theorem 4

The hyperbolic function $\phi_3(k) = \beta_3 \tanh(\lambda_3 k)$, (72), is given by

$$\phi_3(k) = \beta_3 \tanh(\lambda_3 k) = \beta_3(e^{\lambda_3 k} - e^{-\lambda_3 k})/(e^{\lambda_3 k} + e^{-\lambda_3 k}), \quad k \geq 0. \tag{C1}$$

It is well-known and easily verified from (C1) that for

$$\text{small } k: \phi_3(k) \sim \beta_3\lambda_3 k, \quad \Leftrightarrow \quad \phi_3(k)/\beta_3\lambda_3 k \to 1 \text{ as } k \to 0, \tag{C2}$$

$$\text{large } k: \phi_3(k) \sim \beta_3, \quad \Leftrightarrow \quad \phi_3(k)/\beta_3 \to 1 \text{ as } k \to \infty. \tag{C3}$$

Lower boundary $\sigma_i = 1$: With the CD production function (42), the scale density function $s_1(k)$ now becomes, cf. (47), (28)–(30), (72), (74):

$$s_1(k) = \exp\left\{-2\int_{k_0}^{k} \frac{[s - \rho_{13}\beta_1\phi_3(k)]\gamma_1 k^{a_1} - \Theta k}{\beta^2 k^2 + \phi_3^2(k)\gamma_1^2 k^{2a_1} - \rho\phi_3(k)\gamma_1 k^{(1+a_1)}} dk\right\}. \tag{C4}$$

Since $a_1 < 1$, the *dominating* term in the numerator and denominator of (C4) becomes for small k, cf. (C2):

$$s_1(k) \sim \exp\left\{-2\int_{k_0}^{k} \frac{s\gamma_1 k^{a_1}}{\beta^2 k^2} dk\right\} = \exp\left\{\frac{2s\gamma_1}{(1-a_1)\beta^2}(k^{-(1-a_1)} - k_0^{-(1-a_1)})\right\}. \tag{C5}$$

Since $1 - a_1 > 0$, it is seen from (C5), that $S_1(0) = \int_{k_0}^{0} s_1(k)dk$ is diverging at $k = 0$ cf. (52), and hence the lower boundary is *inaccessible*.

For $\sigma_i < 1$: With the CES function (55), the scale function with the dominating terms becomes, cf. (74), (56), (C2), (C5):

$$S_1(0) = \lim_{k\to 0}\int_{k_0}^{k} s_1(k)dk = \int_{k_0}^{0} (k/k_0)^{2\left[\Theta - s\gamma_1 a_1^{1/\rho_1}\right]/\beta^2} dk. \tag{C6}$$

Hence it follows from (C6), that the divergence of $S_1(0)$ requires that the exponent $2[\Theta - s\gamma_1 a_1^{1/\rho_1}]/\beta^2 \leq -1$, which is the lower boundary condition in (75), cf. (63).

For $\sigma_i > 1$: With the CES function (55), the scale function with the dominating terms becomes, cf. (74), (57):

$$S_1(0) = \lim_{k \to 0} \int_{k_0}^{k} s_1(k)\,dk = \lim_{k \to 0} \int_{k_0}^{0} \exp\left\{\frac{2s\gamma_1(1-a_1)^{1/\rho_1}}{\bar{b}_1^2}(k^{-1} - k_0^{-1})\right\}dk. \tag{C7}$$

where $\bar{b}_1^2 \equiv \beta^2 + \beta_3^2\lambda_3^2\gamma_1^2(1-a_1)^{2/\rho_1} - \rho\beta_3\lambda_3\gamma_1(1-a_1)^{1/\rho_1} > 0$, cf. (30). Since the parameter $2s\gamma_1(1-a_1)^{1/\rho_1}/\bar{b}_1^2$ in the exponential term is always positive, it follows from (C7) that $S_1(0)$ is always diverging, and hence $k = 0$ is inaccessible, irrespective of parameter restrictions, cf. (65).

Upper boundary   With the CD function (42), the scale density $s_3(k)$ becomes, cf. (47), (28)–(30), (72), (74):

$$s_3(k) = \exp\left\{-2\int_{k_0}^{k} \frac{[s - \rho_{13}\beta_1\phi_3(k)](\gamma_2/p)k^{a_2} - \Theta k}{\beta^2 k^2 + \phi_3^2(k)(\gamma_2/p)^2 k^{2a_2} - \rho\phi_3(k)(\gamma_2/p)k^{(1+a_2)}}\,dk\right\}. \tag{C8}$$

Since $a_2 < 1$, the *dominating* term in the numerator and denominator of (C8) becomes for large k, cf. (C3):

$$s_3(k) \sim \exp\left\{-2\int_{k_0}^{k} \frac{-\Theta k}{\beta^2 k^2}\,dk\right\} = (k/k_0)^{2\Theta/\beta^2}. \tag{C9}$$

The divergence of $S_3(\infty)$ from (C9) is analogous to the result in (53), (46); hence we have (77) for $\sigma = 1$.

For $\sigma < 1$: With the CES function (55), the scale density $s_3(k)$ becomes, keeping the dominant terms for large k, cf. (C8), (C3):

$$s_3(k) \sim \exp\left\{-2\int_{k_0}^{k} \frac{-\Theta k}{\beta^2 k^2}\,dk\right\} = (k/k_0)^{2\Theta/\beta^2}, \tag{C10}$$

which is the same as (C9), and the divergence of $S_3(\infty)$ is analogous to (64), (59).

For $\sigma > 1$: From (C8), (55), (57), (C3), we have for large k:

$$s_3(k) \sim \exp\left\{-2\int_{k_0}^{k} \frac{(s - \rho_{13}\beta_1\beta_3)(\gamma_2/p)a_2^{1/\rho_2}k - \Theta k}{\beta^2 k^2 + \beta_3^2(\gamma_2/p)^2 a_2^{2/\rho_2} k^2 - \rho\beta_3(\gamma_2/p)a_2^{1/\rho_2} k^2}\,dk\right\}$$
$$= \exp\left\{-2\int_{k_0}^{k}(\bar{a}_3/\bar{b}_3^2)k^{-1}\,dk\right\} = (k/k_0)^{\bar{a}_3/\bar{b}_3^2}. \tag{C11}$$

$\bar{a}_3 \equiv (s - \rho_{13}\beta_1\beta_3)(\gamma_2/p)a_2^{1/\rho_2} - \Theta$, $\bar{b}_3^2 \equiv \beta^2 + \beta_3^2(\gamma_2/p)^2 a_2^{2/\rho_2} - \rho\beta_3(\gamma_2/p)a_2^{1/\rho_2} > 0$, cf. (30). $S_3(\infty)$ from (C11) *diverges*, cf. the analogue (B12) and (71), if the exponent $\bar{a}_3/\bar{b}_3^2 \geq -1$. Rewriting the latter, using (27)–(28), gives condition (78), where $\Delta \equiv \bar{b}_3^2 - \beta^2 + 2\rho_{13}\beta_1\beta_3(\gamma_2/p)a_2^{1/\rho_2} = [\beta_3(\gamma_2/p)a_2^{1/\rho_2}]^2 - 2\rho_{23}\beta_2\beta_3(\gamma_2/p)a_2^{1/\rho_2}$, cf. (29).

References

Baron, David P. and Robert Forsythe, "Models of the Firm and International Trade under Uncertainty," *American Economic Review* 69 (1979):565–74.

Batra, Raveendra N., "Resource Allocation in a General Equilibrium Model of Production under Uncertainty," *Journal of Economic Theory* 8 (1974):50–63.

Bourguignon, Francois, "A Particular Class of Continuous-Time Stochastic Growth Models," *Journal of Economic Theory* 9 (1974):141–58.

Chang, Fwu R. and A. G. Malliaris, "Asymptotic Growth under Uncertainty—Existence and Uniqueness," *Review of Economic Studies* 54 (1987):169–74.

Deardorff, Alan V., *Growth and Trade in a Two-Sector World*, unpublished PhD dissertation, Cornell University (1971).

———, "A Geometry of Growth and Trade," *Canadian Journal of Economics* 7 (1974):295–306.

Grinols, Earl L., *Uncertainty and the Theory of International Trade*, Chur, Switzerland: Harwood Academic Publishers (1987).

Helpman, Elhanan and Assaf Razin, *A Theory of International Trade under Uncertainty*, NY: Academic Press (1978).

Ito, Kiyosi and Henry P. McKean, Jr., *Diffusion Processes and Their Sample Paths*, Berlin: Springer-Verlag (1965).

Jensen, Bjarne S., *The Dynamic Systems of Basic Economic Growth Models*, Dordrecht: Kluwer Academic Publishers (1994).

Jensen, Bjarne S. and Mogens Esrom Larsen, "Growth and Long-Run Stability," *Acta Applicandae Mathematicae* 9 (1987):219–37.

Jensen, Bjarne S. and Chunyan Wang, "General Equilibrium Dynamics of Basic Trade Models for Growing Economies," in Bjarne S. Jensen and Kar-yiu Wong (eds.), *Dynamics, Economic Growth, and International Trade*, Ann Arbor: University of Michigan Press (1997).

Karlin, Samuel and Howard M. Taylor, *A Second Course in Stochastic Processes*, NY: Academic Press (1981).

Kemp, Murray C., *Three Topics in the Theory of International Trade—Distribution, Welfare and Uncertainty*, NY: North-Holland/Elsevier (1976).

Kemp, Murray C. and Nissan Liviatan, "Production and Trade Patterns under Uncertainty," *Economic Record* 49 (1973):215–27.

Kemp, Murray C., Ngo Van Long, and Koji Okuguchi, "On the Possibility of Deriving Conclusions of Stolper–Samuelson Type When Commodity Prices Are Random," *Economic Studies Quarterly* 32 (1981):111–16.

Klump, Rainer, "On the Institutional Determinants of Economic Development—Lessons from a Stochastic Neoclassical Growth Model," *Jahrbuch für Wirtschaftswissenschaft* 46 (1995):138–51.

Malliaris, A. G. and William A. Brock, *Stochastic Methods in Economics and Finance*, Amsterdam: North-Holland/Elsevier (1982).

Mandl, Petr, "Analytical Treatment of One-Dimensional Markov Processes," (Die Grundlehren der mathematischen Wissenschaften in Einzeldarstellungen, Band 151), Berlin: Springer-Verlag (1968).

Merton, Robert C., "An Asymptotic Theory of Growth under Uncertainty," *Review of Economic Studies* 42 (1975):375–93.

Øksendal, Bernt, *Stochastic Differential Equations—An Introduction with Applications*, 3rd edn., Berlin: Springer-Verlag (1992).

Pomery, John, "Uncertainty in Trade Models," in Ronald W. Jones and Peter B. Kenen (eds.), *Handbook in International Economics*, Vol. I, NY: North-Holland/Elsevier (1984).

Ruffin, Roy J., "International Trade under Uncertainty," *Journal of International Economics* 4 (1974a):243–59.

———, "Comparative Advantage under Uncertainty," *Journal of International Economics* 4 (1974b):261–73.

Stigum, Bernt P., "Balanced Growth under Uncertainty," *Journal of Economic Theory* 5 (1972):42–68.

Turnovsky, Stephen J., "Technological and Price Uncertainty in a Ricardian Model of International Trade," *Review of Economic Studies* 41 (1974):201–17.

Wong, Kar-yiu, *International Trade in Goods and Factor Mobility*, Cambridge: MIT Press (1995).

Young, Leslie, "Uncertainty and the Theory of International Trade in Long-Run Equilibrium," *Journal of Economic Theory* 32 (1984):67–92.

3
Trade Gains in Chaotic Equilibria

*Murray C. Kemp and Koji Shimomura**

Abstract

It is shown by means of an overlapping-generations (OLG) example that free international trade may be both deterministically chaotic and gainful in the sense of Pareto to a participating country.

1. Introduction

The global welfare economics of international trade contains a handful of propositions, the best-known of which state that:

(i) for any country, free trade is potentially better than no trade;
(ii) given any trading world, however cluttered with import and export taxes, it is always possible for a subset of countries to form a customs union without harming any individual, whatever his country of residence.

These propositions were originally established for finite economies of the Arrow–Debreu–McKenzie kind; see Kemp and Wan (1972, 1976, 1986). However, it is now known that they remain valid for doubly-infinite economies of the overlapping-generations (OLG) type; see Kemp and Wolik (1995), also Kemp and Wong (1995).

The economies studied by Kemp and Wolik are very general. In particular, they allow for the possibility that there are no steady states and for the possibility that capital is over-accumulated. What remains unclear is whether Pareto-improving free trade and Pareto-improving customs unions are compatible with chaotic world equilibria.[1]

We here focus on the oldest and best known of the two propositions, that free trade is potentially beneficial. Now it would not be surprising if it were found that a free-trade equilibrium can be chaotic, for OLG models of Kemp–Wolik type can be highly nonlinear. However, it might well be surprising if it were found that a *compensated* and therefore *gainful* free-trade equilibrium can be chaotic for, in a context of compensation, each trading country behaves like a single price-taking individual endowed with a consistent map of nonintersecting Scitovsky social indifference surfaces. Nevertheless, in the present note we construct an OLG example in which free trade is Pareto-improving and the world equilibrium chaotic. The example is simple; but it is not incompatible with the general model of Kemp and Wolik.

2. A Closed Economy

There are three consumable commodities, labelled 0, 1 and 2. They cannot be produced but are available as given and constant natural endowments in each period of time. Commodities 0 and 2 are perishable; that is, they last for just one period. Commodity 1 is more or less durable, wasting at the constant proportional rate of δ per unit of time, $\delta \in (0, 1)$.

*Kemp: University of New South Wales, Sydney, Australia 2052. Fax: +61-2-9313-6337; E-mail: a.dinel@unsw.edu.au. Shimomura: Kobe University, 2-1 Rokko, Nada, Kobe, Japan 657-0013. Tel: +81-78-881-1212; Fax: +81-78-861-6434; E-mail: simomura@rieb.kobe-u.ac.jp. We acknowledge with gratitude the helpful comments of Nikolaus Wolik, Kar-yiu Wong and a referee.

The population consists of overlapping generations, each of which survives for two periods. The number of births per period and the total population are constant. Moreover, each individual, whatever his date of birth, has the same preferences and the same endowments. Specifically, each young individual is endowed with y_i units of commodity $i, i = 0, 1, 2$. He consumes commodities 1 and 2 only, financing the purchase of those commodities by selling his endowment of commodity 0. Old individuals, on the other hand, receive the null endowment. They consume only commodity 0, financing their purchases of that commodity by selling what is left of their youthful holdings of the durable commodity 1. By normalization, each of the young and old populations is equal to one.

In each period there are spot markets in which the three commodities can be exchanged.

The following additional notation will be employed:

$q(t)$: the price of commodity 0 in terms of commodity 1 during period t
$p(t)$: the price of commodity 2 in terms of commodity 1 during period t
$y(p(t)) \equiv y_1 + p(t)y_2$: that part of the income of the young generation of period t contributed by the endowments of commodities 1 and 2
$x_i(t)$: the demand for commodity i by the young of period $t, i = 1, 2$
$x_0(t)$: the demand for commodity 0 by the old of period t.

The two-period utility function of generation t takes the time separable form

$$u(x_1(t), x_2(t)) + \beta v(x_0(t+1)),\tag{1}$$

where u is an increasing and strictly quasi-concave function of x_1 and x_2, v is an increasing function of x_0, and β is a positive constant. Utility is to be maximized subject to the budget constraint

$$q(t)y_0 + y(p(t)) = x_1(t) + p(t)x_2(t).\tag{2}$$

However the (identical) young of period t know that, in equilibrium,

$$x_0(t+1) = y_0,\tag{3}$$

and[2]

$$q(t)y_0 = (1-\delta)x_1(t-1).\tag{4}$$

Hence the task of the young is to maximize

$$U(x_1(t), x_2(t)) \equiv u(x_1(t), x_2(t)) + \beta v(y_0)\tag{1'}$$

subject to

$$(1-\delta)x_1(t-1) + y(p(t)) = x_1(t) + p(t)x_2(t).\tag{2'}$$

Let us introduce the expenditure function

$$E(p,U) \equiv \min_{x_1, x_2} x_1 + px_2 \quad \text{s.t.} \quad U \leq U(x_1, x_2).\tag{5}$$

Then the closed economy can be represented by the four equations

$$E(p(t), U(t)) = (1-\delta)x_1(t-1) + y(p(t)),\tag{6}$$

$$E_p(p(t), U(t)) = y_2,\tag{7}$$

$$E(p(t), U(t)) - p(t)E_p(p(t), U(t)) = y_1 + (1-\delta)x_1(t-1),\tag{8}$$

$$x_1(t) = y_1 + (1-\delta)x_1(t-1), \qquad\qquad\qquad (9)$$

where (6) is obtained from (5), (7) and (8) stipulate market clearing for commodities 2 and 1, respectively, (9) describes the accumulation of the durable commodity 1, and $E_p \equiv \partial E/\partial p$. (Note that, by Walras' Law, one of the three equations (6)–(8) is redundant.) A steady state of the closed economy can then be represented by the pair of equations

$$y_1/\delta = E(\overline{p},\overline{U}) - \overline{p}E_p(\overline{p},\overline{U}) \qquad \text{[from (8) and (9)]} \qquad (10)$$

and

$$y_2 = E_p(\overline{p},\overline{U}). \qquad\qquad\qquad (11)$$

We shall need these equations in section 4.

3. An Open Economy

Suppose that at some point in time the hitherto closed and stationary economy acquires the opportunity to freely trade commodities 1 and 2 at the given and constant world price $p, p < \overline{p}$, with commodity 0 traded only on the domestic market. Thereafter the economy can be described by the equations

$$E(p, U(t)) = (1-\delta)x_1(t-1) + y(p), \qquad\qquad (12)$$

$$x_1(t) = E(p, U(t)) - pE_p(p, U(t)), \qquad\qquad (13)$$

which are obtained from (6)–(9) by applying Walras' Law to delete (7) and by combining (8) and (9). Equations (12) and (13) can be solved for $x_1(t)$ and $U(t)$ in terms of $x_1(t-1)$. In particular, $x_1(t) = \Gamma(x_1(t-1))$, where Γ is a continuous function. It will be convenient to denote the nth iterate of $\Gamma(x)$ by $\Gamma^n(x)$.

We now seek restrictions on Γ, and hence on $E(p, U)$, which ensure the existence of a chaotic equilibrium. Since p is given, only the income–consumption relationship can be freely chosen. Thus we seek to construct an income–consumption path which satisfies the well-known sufficient conditions for a chaotic equilibrium provided by Li and Yorke (1975).

THEOREM (LI AND YORKE). *Let Γ: [a, b] → [a, b] be a continuous map of the interval [a, b] into itself, and suppose that there is $x \in$ [a, b] such that $\Gamma(x) > x$, $\Gamma^2(x) > x$ but $\Gamma^3(x) \le x$. Then:*

  (i) *for any integer $k > 1$ there is some $x(0) \in$ [a, b] such that the solution to the system $x(t) = \Gamma(x(t-1))$, $t = 1, 2, \ldots$, with the initial condition $x = x(0)$, is a period-k cycle, and*

  (ii) *there is a set S of uncountably many initial points on [a, b] such that no solutions to the system $x(t) = \Gamma(x(t-1))$, $t = 1, 2, \ldots$, which start in S converge to each other or to any periodic path.*

Part (ii) of the theorem is the mathematical expression of the existence of chaotic solutions. The set S is sometimes referred to as the *scrambled set* of the dynamical system $\Gamma:[a, b] → [a, b]$.

Consider Figure 1, in which OF is the 45°-line and BC is the graph of $(1-\delta)x_1(t) + y(p)$, so that OB represents $y(p)$. Now we add the scaffolding required for the

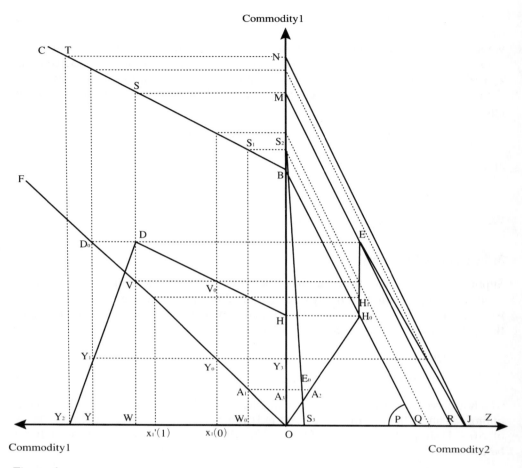

Figure 1.

construction of a suitable income–consumption curve and an associated "distorted tent map," which is the graph of the equation $x_1(t) = \Gamma(x_1(t-1))$.

   (i)   Choose point M above B so that point S on BC is above the 45°-line OF.
   (ii) Choose point D on the vertical line through S so that DV is smaller than MB.
   (iii) Draw the line DH parallel to BC.
   (iv) Draw the horizontal line DD_0 and the vertical line D_0Y.
   (v)   Draw the horizontal line VV_0, the vertical line V_0Y_0, and the horizontal line Y_0Y_1.
   (vi) Extend the straight line through D and Y_1 to meet the horizontal axis at Y_2. Then draw the vertical line Y_2T and the horizontal line TN.
   (vii) Draw the three parallel lines BQ, MR and NJ with the common slope $-p$.
   (viii) Draw the horizontal lines DE and HH_0. Then draw the lines OH_0, H_0E (which is vertical) and EJ.

Thus we arrive at the required income–consumption curve OH_0EJZ and the associated tent map Y_2DH. It is easy to verify that the income–consumption curve is compatible with the strict quasi-concavity of $U(x_1, x_2)$.

To assist in the understanding of Figure 1, suppose that $x_1(t - 1)$ is represented by OW. Then, from BC, we find that WS (= OM) represents $(1 - \delta)x_1(t - 1) + y(p)$. Hence MR is the upper boundary of the budget constraint and E is the optimal consumption point. Reading across to the 45°-line, we then find that $x_1(t)$ is represented by OY.

We can now establish the existence of a chaotic solution to $x_1(t) = \Gamma(x_1(t - 1))$. Suppose that the initial value of x_1 is $x_1(0)$, chosen so that $\Gamma(x_1(0))$ is represented by OW. Then, as we have seen, $\Gamma^2(x_1(0))$ is represented by OY; and, finally, $\Gamma^3(x_1(0)) = x_1(0)$. That is, there exists a period-3 solution such that

$$x_1(0) < \Gamma(x_1(0)), \tag{14a}$$

$$\Gamma(x_1(0)) < \Gamma^2(x_1(0)), \tag{14b}$$

$$x_1(0) \geq \Gamma^3(x_1(0)) \quad [= x_1(0)]. \tag{14c}$$

From the Li–Yorke theorem, therefore, there exist both chaotic and periodic solutions. In particular, there exists a point x_1^* in the open interval $(x_1(0), \text{OY})$ which provides the initial value of a chaotic solution.

4. Gains From Trade

It remains to establish the existence of a chaotic solution with trade gains. This cannot be achieved simply by referring to the general proposition of Kemp and Wolik. They have shown that, in a general OLG context, suitably *compensated* free trade is gainful, whereas we have shown by example that an *uncompensated* free-trade equilibrium may be chaotic. From these two demonstrations we cannot immediately conclude that a compensated free-trade equilibrium may be chaotic. Further analysis of our example is needed. It will be shown that, given an initial (autarkic) steady state and given a suitable value of the parameter y_1/δ (which, from (9), is the steady-state consumption of commodity 1 under autarky), all individuals are better off under free trade *even in the absence of redistributive transfers*. In other words, it will be shown that, under the specified assumptions, the null vector of transfers is an acceptable scheme of lumpsum compensation.

By assumption, before the opening of trade, the economy is in a steady state. Mathematically, the steady state can be represented by (10) and (11). It can also be depicted in Figure 1. Thus suppose that y_1/δ is smaller than $x_1/(0)$ and represented by OW_0. Let us add the vertical line W_0S_1, the horizontal lines S_1S_2 and A_1A_2, and the straight line S_2S_3 with slope $-\bar{p}$. Next we reproduce in Figure 2 the relevant part of Figure 1, in magnified form; and we insert the dashed indifference curve, U^a, tangential to S_2S_3 at E_0. Evidently E_0 represents the stationary equilibrium of the closed economy. In that equilibrium, consumption of the first commodity is equal to y_1/δ and is represented by OA_3, and the demand for the second commodity is equal to y_2 and represented by A_3E_0.

Now let free trade begin in period 1; and let us denote by $x_1'(t), t = 1, 2, \ldots$, the first-commodity consumption sequence under free trade. Since autarkic consumption is equal to $y_1/\delta, x_1'(1)$ must lie in the open interval $(x_1(0), OY)$. Moreover it can be verified that, having entered that interval, $x_1'(t)$ never leaves it for $t > 1$. It follows that, for $t > 1, x_2'(t)$ never falls below OY_3, which exceeds the autarkic consumption OA_3 of the second commodity. For any $t \geq 1$, therefore, $U(t)$ exceeds U^a. And since the consumption of the old is unchanged by the opening of trade, $U(0) = U^a$. Thus the opening of trade enhances the wellbeing of generations $1, 2, \ldots$ and leaves unchanged the

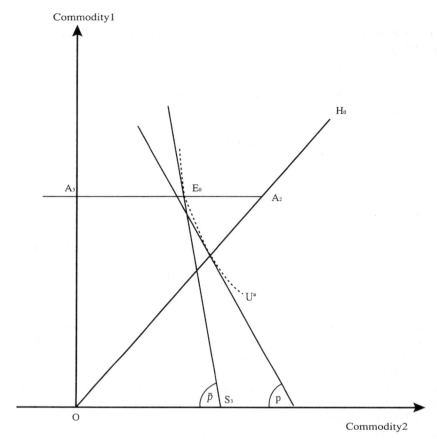

Figure 2.

wellbeing of generation 0; it therefore is beneficial in the sense of Pareto. This is always the case if y_1/δ lies in the open interval $(0, x_1(0))$.

It remains to demonstrate that, for some initial value in $(0, x_1(0))$, the solution is chaotic. Now we know from section 3 that there exists x_1^* in the open interval $(x_1(0), OY)$ such that the solution to the dynamic equation $x_1(t+1) = \Gamma(x_1(t))$, starting from x_1^*, is chaotic. It therefore suffices to show that x_1^* can be reached from some point in $(0, x_1(0))$ by applying the map Γ finitely many times. To this end, consider an arbitrary interval I and define

$$\Lambda(I) \equiv \{x : \exists y \in I \text{ such that } x = \Gamma(y)\}. \tag{15}$$

Clearly $\Lambda(I)$ is also an interval. Now consider the particular interval $(0, x_1(0))$. It can be verified that

$$\Lambda^2(0, x_1(0)) \cup \Lambda^4(0, x_1(0)) = (OW, OY), \tag{16a}$$

$$\Lambda(0, x_1(0)) \cup \Lambda^3(0, x_1(0)) = (x_1(0), OW), \tag{16b}$$

where $\Lambda^2(I) \equiv \Lambda(\Lambda(I))$, etc. It follows from (16) that x_1^* can be reached from some point in the open interval $(0, x_1(0))$ by applying the map Γ at most four times. Since the required point in $(0, x_1(0))$ is the stationary equilibrium point in the closed economy for a suitably chosen y_1/δ, we have established the existence of gainful trade in a chaotic equilibrium.

PROPOSITION 1. *For sufficiently small* y_1/δ, *there is a stationary autarkic equilibrium such that the opening of international trade generates a chaotic equilibrium which is Pareto-preferred to the autarkic equilibrium.*

Remark. We have shown that a compensated and therefore Pareto-improving equilibrium can be chaotic. In our simple example, the compensating transfers form a null vector. However, other examples of compensated but chaotic trade surely can be constructed without that special feature.

Next, we record a further implication of the Li–Yorke Theorem or of the earlier Sarkovskii (1964) Theorem, which can be viewed as a corollary of the Li–Yorke Theorem.

PROPOSITION 2. *For any integer* k *there is a stationary autarkic equilibrium such that the opening of international trade generates a period-*k *cyclical equilibrium which is Pareto-preferred to the autarkic equilibrium.*

References

Kemp, M. C. and H. Y. Wan, Jr, "The Gains from Free Trade," *International Economic Review* 13 (1972):509–22.
———, "An Elementary Proposition Concerning the Formation of Customs Unions," *Journal of International Economics* 6 (1976):95–7.
———, "The Comparison of Second-Best Equilibria: The Case of Customs Unions," in D. Bös and C. Seidl (eds), *The Welfare Economics of the Second Best*, Suppl. 5 to the *Zeitschrift für Nationalökonomie* (1986):161–7, Vienna: Springer-Verlag.
Kemp, M. C. and N. Wolik, "The Gains from International Trade in a Context of Overlapping Generations," in M. C. Kemp (ed.), *The Gains from Trade and the Gains from Aid*, London: Routledge (1995):129–46.
Kemp, M. C. and K.-y. Wong, "Gains from Trade with Overlapping Generations," *Economic Theory* 6 (1995):283–303. Reprinted in M. C. Kemp (ed.), *The Gains from Trade and the Gains from Aid*, London: Routledge (1995):105–28.
Li, T. Y. and J. Yorke, "Period Three Implies Chaos," *American Mathematical Monthly* 82 (1975):985–92.
Sarkovskii, A., "Coexistence of Cycles of a Continuous Map of a Line into Itself, *Ukrainian Mathematical Journal* 16 (1964):61–71.

Notes

1. Roughly speaking, equilibrium trajectories are chaotic if they are not asymptotic to a steady state or to a periodic trajectory and if they do not converge to each other. Typically, chaotic equilibria are highly sensitive to small changes in initial conditions.

2. The identical young of period t also know that, in equilibrium:

$$x_2(t) = y_2, \tag{i}$$

$$x_1(t+1) = (1-\delta)x_1(t) + y_1, \tag{ii}$$

implying that, in autarky, choice is quite mechanical. However, neither (i) nor (ii) necessarily holds under free trade; hence no use will be made of them here.

4
Hong Kong: The Fragile Economy of Middlemen

Henry Y. Wan, Jr and Jason Weisman*

Abstract

The paper shows that standard trade models can be adapted to address crucial policy issues in our dynamic, imperfect-information world. It also shows that intermediated trade is essential to the modernization of the 1.2 billion-person Chinese economy; yet, notwithstanding sincere intentions in Beijing and Hong Kong, subtle changes may deny Hong Kong its irreplaceable catalyst role, leaving China ultimately to technical stagnation.

1. Introduction

With the approach of *la fin de siècle*, it is tempting to speculate about what will be counted as the most important legacies of the latter part of this century. Three candidates seem to be obvious: (1) the microelectronics revolution, (2) the entry of East Asia into the trading world, and (3) the rise and fall of centrally planned economies. The first development spawned the globalized economy and quickened the product cycle. The second led to the rise of Japan and the Asian NIEs as major players in the world economic system. The third allowed China to open up and re-enter the world society after a 30-year hiatus.

Without 1.2 billion-person China, East Asia's impact on the world economy would be only modest in scale. Without modernization, even an "open" China would have only a marginal impact on the rest of the world. Without Hong Kong's involvement, China would face a much more difficult, if not impossible, task of successfully growing and modernizing its economy. Therefore, given the importance of Hong Kong in China's recent success and the ramifications of this relationship for the entire global economy, a deeper understanding of the role played by Hong Kong in mainland China's development is much needed.

Sung (1991) pointed to several important functions of Hong Kong in this relationship: (1) provider of a variety of trade and transport services, (2) source of capital and foreign exchange, (3) market for Chinese primary goods and light manufactures, (4) channel of information between China and foreign businesses, and (5) middleman between China and other countries. The first three factors are associated with tastes, technology, and factor endowments, the importance of which is easily grasped by most policymakers. With the development of Shanghai and many other regional ports along the eastern coast of the mainland, over time these traditional economic contributions are likely to decline in their importance. The last two functions (i.e., conveyor of information and middleman in trade) are more basic and crucial to Hong Kong's role in bringing about long-term sustained development.[1] At the same time these factors are the least understood by both laymen and academics. It will be argued, however, that it is in large part because of Hong Kong's success in these roles that Chinese manu-

* Wan: Cornell University, Ithaca, NY 14853, USA. Tel: (607) 255-6211; Fax: (607) 255-2818; E-mail: hyw1@cornell.edu. Weisman: GE Capital Structured Finance Group, International Country Risk, 180 Glenbrook Rd, Stamford, CT 06902, USA. Tel: (203) 359-9479; E-mail: jlw12@cornell.edu. The second author wishes to state that this work was done privately, and the views expressed do not purport directly or indirectly to represent the official or unofficial views of GE Capital, any unit or officers thereof.

facturing exports have scored unprecedented growth in the past two decades, in quality as well as in value.

With Hong Kong's participation as an intermediary/catalyst, trade in "challenging" goods provides China the incentive to gain information and technology required to successfully participate in the dynamic global economy. This is the same self-sustaining mechanism which benefited Japan and all the NIEs. On the other hand, the absence of strong ties with the more advanced economies made development of Brazil, India, and the former Soviet Union extremely difficult. In this century of fast-moving technological frontiers those who fail to keep up with the latest developments quickly suffer technical obsolescence. In fact, no economy has ever managed to catch up with the industrially advanced world without a close linkage to it.

We believe that the quick modernization of China has and will continue to depend critically on Hong Kong facilitating connections between Chinese enterprises and the more technologically developed world. For historical and cultural reasons Hong Kong is uniquely suited to provide this linkage, and in fact, China needs this linkage more than any other developing economy. This seems to be broadly recognized in Beijing as well as Hong Kong. However, the degree of understanding may not yet be sufficient to preserve the fragile mechanism which maintains this relationship. It is illustrated below that owing to the nature of the "middleman economy" there is a clear risk that Hong Kong's current role may well dissipate unless it is assiduously safeguarded. So, now that the handover is over, a proper study of Hong Kong's important middleman role in mainland China's economic maturation may be essential to all concerned.

This paper examines from the perspective of economic theory the role of middlemen in bringing about economic efficiency. Understanding the middleman's role is also important in other cases, so the Hong Kong–China relationship is far from unique. Currently, Singapore serves a similar role for other ASEAN economies, and in other parts of the developing world new middlemen may conceivably emerge.

Section 2 introduces several stylized assumptions about the important features of an economic system in which middleman trade is carried out within a rapidly evolving world economy. These assumptions are justified by examples from recent experiences of East Asian development. Section 3 is the core of the paper, laying out an explicit model for the middleman economy. In that section it is shown that, owing to an asymmetry in information available to buyers and middlemen, there may be benefits for all involved from the middlemen's participation, bringing about the possibility of moving the economy from stagnation to dynamic growth. On the other hand, using that same model it is shown that the equilibrium with middleman participation may be quite fragile, possibly disintegrating if corruption is allowed to creep into the system. Section 4 discusses the relevance of this model and its results for China and Hong Kong in the wake of reunification. Section 5 concludes.

2. Some Preliminaries

A Stylized World

For simplicity, a stylized world with rapidly changing technology is considered. We focus on manufactured goods, Y, which differ in quality, $q \in \mathcal{R}$, with goods ranked along some quality ladder (Grossman and Helpman, 1991). A good of quality q is denoted by $y(q)$, with the minimum quality which poses challenge denoted as Q. A cardinal fact of life is:

STYLIZED FACT 1. *A developing economy can keep up (let alone catch up) with the current technological advances only through the learning effect of manufactured goods production.*

To capture the principle of "bounded learning" (Young, 1993) it is taken that:

STYLIZED FACT 2. *What is relevant for catching up is to produce manufactured goods of such quality which pose challenge, specifically* $q \geq Q(I, t)$. *Here the "challenge threshold," $Q(I, t)$, is specific to the country (I) and variable over time (t). What is usefully challenging for Korea at time t may not be so for Japan at the same instant, nor for Korea later, by the mechanism of the product cycle.*

Still another fact one must contend with is:

STYLIZED FACT 3. *Only by exporting can developing economies afford to produce manufactured goods posing challenge. In symbols, if $q \geq Q(I, t)$ then $y(q)$ is not affordable to consumers in developing country I at time t.*[2]

Our three stylized facts are neither deduced from more general assumptions nor expected to hold exactly in all possible worlds. By nature, the validity of these is tested empirically. The central role of manufacturing exports in the catching-up process has been observed in the ongoing econometric inquiry by Hong et al. (1998). Independently, Chapter 2 of *Emerging Asia* (Asian Development Bank, 1997) and Coe et al. (1997) provide descriptive corroborative evidence of this phenomenon.

Some discussion of the plausibility of these stylized facts is now in order. To be sure, the learning effect is also present in many primary industries. Yet, in comparison, manufacturing activities are much less dependent on sector-specific natural endowments. Furthermore, unlike activities such as prospecting minerals, tending tropical plants or harvesting marine products, skill and information in manufacturing is much less industry-specific in nature. Hence, in the context of catching up with the developed world, the learning effect arising from manufacturing activities is most conducive to rapid and sustained growth. This characteristic is important, and perhaps increasingly so in our time, when new technologies and products have caused the rapid and widespread obsolescence of older ones. Few people today care much about the elaborate, time-honored art of the *mahout*; i.e., taming the elephant.

In general, there is also less point today in pursuing specialized expertise for extended periods. Indeed, not everything can be learned overnight. Yet in a fast-moving world with intense cross-product competition "the best may well be the enemy of good." This underlies the principle of bounded learning. One does not have to go so far as Nathan and Ross (1997) to derogate the newly developed Chinese fighter planes as "the most perfected obsolete planes in the world." The difficulty of going it alone in technology is well understood to all, the Chinese leadership included.

Most modern technology calls for costly, specialized equipment. For example, clean rooms for fabricating memory chips come at a cost of one billion US dollars each. Facing such a fixed cost, a developing economy—even one as large as India or China—has few domestic consumers who can afford such products with sufficiently challenging qualities to bring about learning. Hence, for producers of such goods, to export is to survive. Conversely, for developing economies, to de-link is to resign from the game.

Moreover, in East Asia, export activities are often collaborative ventures between the developing South and the more developed North. In the intense North–North competition, reliable outsourcing to the low-cost South, when done before one's rivals, offers Northern firms a clear edge. The same holds for the Northern suppliers of key parts to Southern assemblers/exporters. It therefore pays for individual Northern firms to selectively tutor their Southern partners.[3]

Furthermore, to be complete, one may add that Northern firms can hardly use the potential benefit of such tutoring as a bargaining chip to entice Southern firms. Managerial decisions in the South are not generally swayed by the potential efficiency gains of their footloose Southern workers. Poorly developed Southern capital markets would never support Southern workers to work for even lower wages just for the sake of learning. In such deals, therefore, weakness is strength.

Korean Lessons

We now demonstrate the essential validity of the above discussion using an example from economic history: evidence from South Korea over the last four decades. On the whole, postwar Korea stagnated before the early 1960s under President Rhee and Premier Chang, but took off after the export drive of President Park.

First, it can be seen that exporting is important, yet not all exports are equally important. Following up the Filipino-Korean comparison of Lucas (1993), it is noted that the early export of wigs from Korea eventually led to textiles, which after time led to supertankers and computer chips.[4] However, sugar exports from the Philippines now cannot even hold their own against Thai competition in that market. Skills Koreans learned in exporting wigs—quality control and punctual delivery—have allowed them to move on to pursuits with ever-increasing challenge.

Second, industry upgrading is important. The Korean aspiration to catch up could hardly have had much future if they continued to specialize in wigs after 30 years.

Third, for industries with learning potential such as automaking, the home market of a developing economy hardly supplies the clientele necessary to stimulate dynamic learning. This is partly a matter of numbers, partly a matter of income, but also partly a matter of "cosmopolitan" tastes. For example, to earn US dollars in the 1950s automakers had to produce stylish high tailfins. Close attention to Northern consumer tastes help to explain why in world markets Korean cars have far outsold their Brazilian, Russian and Indian rivals, all of which were designed with domestic consumers in mind. The parallel experience of Japan served as a blueprint for the Koreans, which further laid the foundation for the Malaysian movement, "Look East."

The Sino-Hong Kong Context

We have introduced a few symbols to sharpen our discourse, but have made no attempt to fully analyze this problem as a dynamic general equilibrium system. The formulation in Wan (1993) supplies a basis for doing just that, assuming Stylized Facts 1 and 2.[5] For our purpose now, however, such a complex exercise would serve only to distract readers from the main focus. In fact a convenient shortcut is readily available in this analysis. That is, although the crux of our study may be dynamic, *to continue the catching-up process*, one may well focus upon its static dual; i.e., *to escape from the steady state of stagnation*.

To sum up, we take as given that for China to modernize, it must produce goods of ever-more challenging quality, and with export appeal. This is consistent with the observation of Lucas (1988) that for economies with sustained rapid growth (the NIEs) goods produced primarily for export were not produced domestically in the past. Lucas's focus is that these goods are not new globally, only locally; our focus is on the fact that *what is new is exported—to the North.*[6] In our model the main benefit of trade comes from the dynamic effect of learning, not merely from increased employment, higher wages or larger reserves of foreign exchange, as discussed in the Ricardian tradition of static gains.

Furthermore, we note that that even today Russia remains far more technically advanced than China. Yet, in the former Soviet era that nation's economy stagnated owing to isolation. Still today, in areas in which it is isolated, the Chinese economy apparently faces similar difficulties. We believe the mechanism of learning-by-exporting will remain essential to the Chinese effort to modernize for many years to come.

Under "reform and opening" policies of the last twenty years China has supplied labor-intensive goods of foreign design, produced with foreign technology, to foreign markets. Thus, conveniently, the small country assumption in trade theory applies well even for the most populous nation in the world. This is because waiting in the wings are economies like Vietnam, Myanmar, and several African countries, ready to enter these same markets with wages even lower than China's. Thus, we have formally:

STYLIZED FACT 4. *The prices (and designs) of exports from rapidly growing developing countries are set by world markets.*

A stunning implication of our argument is that, notwithstanding its recent raging growth, Chinese development can still be stunted (like the former Soviet Union's) unless its exports are continuously upgraded with an appeal to Northern tastes. In the past such upgrading depended on the intermediation of Hong Kong, a process which as is shown below to be quite fragile. To assess the future of Hong Kong, one must have a firm grasp of (a) *what* function intermediation served in the past, and (b) *whether* the environment will be conducive to such intermediation in the future. A critical question is: precisely which features of the former environment, if any, may defy emulation? The answer to this turns on both the aspects of information and incentives existing in the intermediation process. These issues are examined more closely in the following sections.

3. The Economics of the Middleman

The role of middlemen is critically related to an asymmetry in information available to these market intermediaries and to consumers. Employing a simple bargaining model with search costs, Rubinstein and Wolinsky (1987) were the first to present an explicit model showing how middlemen serve to create more efficient markets by facilitating contacts. Contributions by Yavas (1994, 1996) generalized the basic framework by endogenizing various aspects of the trading process, providing conditions under which the existence of middlemen results in positive welfare effects. Biglaiser (1993) developed a bargaining model to show that middlemen who have large present and future stakes in a market can resolve inefficiencies when adverse selection exists. Biglaiser and Friedman (1994) discussed how the existence of intermediaries can improve quality of products by acting as quality inspectors. They observe that the existence of intermediaries can have several types of effects on markets; including reducing search costs, reducing selling costs, reducing the price premium needed to induce firms to produce better quality goods, and resolving the adverse selection problem. For our part, the model introduced below is most closely linked to this last issue.

Although the works cited above on middlemen have motivated our analysis, in order to more efficiently study the interactions among various economies, we have instead fashioned a much more tractable model out of four building blocks, familiar to researchers in trade and growth.

First, for the international division of labor, we follow the production specification of Dornbusch–Fischer–Samuelson (1977). A representative good can be produced in a continuum of quality grades, $q \in \mathcal{R}$, using Ricardian technology. This model has been extended by Collins (1985) to apply to a three-region trading world, including the North, the South and the newly industrialized economies (NIEs). In contrast, our focus is on the vertical division of labor between a developing economy (China) and a NIE (Hong Kong), which coordinate to export goods to the North. To focus on the price-taking behavior of exporting firms we take as given that all equilibrium prices of goods are determined in the world market.

Second, on the issue of dynamic evolution, we adopt the well-known "principle of bounded learning" of Young (1993); i.e., learning is possible only when producers venture beyond the current-day "mature technology." Thus, we can concentrate on the question of "escaping from stagnation" rather than its less tractable dual of "achieving sustained growth." In doing this we actually demonstrate the versatility of Young's principle in a model where conclusions are in direct variance with Young's.[7]

Third, in dealing with trade under imperfect information, we build upon the models of Chiang and Masson (1988) and Pomery (1984), which show that when consumers cannot easily differentiate products of individual firms, adverse selection (the "lemons" problem analyzed by Akerlof (1970)) may ensue. Consequently, a firm which undertakes the expense of improving the quality of its products will not receive the full benefit. At the same time, those firms which do not attempt to produce better goods gain by free-riding. In this situation a suboptimal equilibrium may result wherein no firms in the economy are willing to undertake costly improvements in the qualities of their products. Chiang and Masson suggest various methods to internalize this negative information externality, including industrial consolidation, limiting export licenses and industrial export quality standards. Our departure from them is to study the effect of a neutral middleman in resolving this adverse selection problem.

Lastly, in discussing the effect of increased corruption, the model developed here treats the gathering of quality information as costly in terms of labor and importable inputs, under a standard production function. Hence, we can measure the effect of corruption on the system, including determining the particular critical point where intermediation becomes economically nonviable.

Formally, we introduce and characterize three different types of equilibria: (1) the perfect-information equilibrium, (2) the (unintermediated) imperfect-information equilibrium, and (3) the intermediated equilibrium. Like Chiang and Masson, we show that quality of exported goods is lower in an unintermediated imperfect-information equilibrium situation than it is when buyers have perfect information about the products they purchase. We also illustrate that, under suitable conditions, the intermediated equilibrium implies the same equilibrium product quality as under perfect information. We then show that if corruption erodes the effectiveness of intermediation, beyond a threshold level of corruption, intermediation stops and equilibrium product quality and net social welfare decline. Under the condition that equilibrium product quality levels under imperfect information correspond to mature technology only, the learning process may then come to an end and the economy cease to grow.

Practically speaking, the information asymmetry we consider is clearly evident in China owing to the character of its social and economic systems. As observed in *Emerging Asia*, the most dynamic and export-oriented components of China's economy today are the rural cooperatives and foreign-related joint venture enterprises. These institutional arrangements vary widely from case to case. However, high transaction costs and low transparency in laws and regulations remain the rule, not the exception. To get the best deal, foreigners need the Hong Kong-based Chinese, who are well-informed about China but not located on the mainland. Their effectiveness in this endeavor rests not only upon their understanding of China, but also on their independence, and here there may be some problem.

To be more precise, in the context of the middleman's role, the perception of independence (in this case by Westerners) is more important in driving this system than the reality. So whether or not Hong Kong continues to have "a high level of autonomy" after the return of sovereignty is less important than whether this perception is maintained, particularly in the minds of Westerners. That is why the role of the popular press is so crucial in this case. As a typical example of popular impressions, seven months before the return of sovereignty of Hong Kong, Gargan (1996) reported in *The New York Times* that "in many respects China—its businesses, its way of operating, its politics—have so permeated this territory that little is left to be done but to lower the Union Jack." Given his description in the same article of key "mainland business practices—bribery, padded commissions, reliance on political contacts to cut deals," it is not surprising that there is some concern in the minds of potential business partners about the stability and independence of Hong Kong's middlemen.

In that same article Gargan described an unusual defense used by the lawyer for the chairman of a Hong Kong company who was accused of dumping his company's shares. The lawyer argued for a light sentence for his client on account that he was "an honorary citizen of China," and because it was necessary for him to have contact with officials in the future. Now, whether or not that defense was successful in winning a more lenient punishment in that particular case is somewhat besides the point.[8] What is quite telling is that, at least as perceived by the lawyer, that line of argument had some chance of being considered positively by a supposedly impartial justice system. Widely held perceptions today about the utility of special connections, if pervasive throughout many levels of the society, may turn out to become self-fulfilling prophecies.

The Model

We adopt the following seven assumptions and definition.

ASSUMPTION 1. *There are three economies in the world, including: A, the $\underline{A}$dvanced economy,[9] B, the $\underline{B}$ackward economy, and C, the $\underline{C}$atalyst economy.*

ASSUMPTION 2. *In each period, all output prices p_t are determined by A, with agents in B and C acting as price-takers in the market for their exported goods.*

ASSUMPTION 3. *Labor is the only primary input, supplied to each economy I in fixed quantity, L_I.*

ASSUMPTION 4. *There are N firms in B, with identical, constant returns to scale, Ricardian technologies. The unit labor requirement for output of a representative good of quality q at time t is $a_t(q)$, which is increasing in q since more labor is needed to produce higher quality goods.*

ASSUMPTION 5. *Individuals in A are risk-neutral with respect to quality, the precise meaning of which will be clarified below.*

ASSUMPTION 6. *The wage rate in B, w_B, is determined by market forces acting to clear the labor market*

$$L_B = \sum_i li,$$ (1)

where l_i is the labor employed by firm i.

ASSUMPTION 7. *In B, given wage w_B, each firm i chooses an ordered pair of labor force employed, l_i, and product quality, q_i, in order to maximize current profit*

$$\pi_i = \rho_i(q_i, .)y_i - w_B l_i = l_i \left\{ \frac{\rho_i(q_i, .)}{a(q_i)} - w_B \right\}.$$ (2)

The (net) unit price received by the firm is $\rho_i(q_i,.)$, which is increasing in q_i but defined differently under different concepts of equilibrium, discussed in more detail below.

(1) Under the *perfect information equilibrium*:

$$\rho_i = p(\mu_i), \text{ and } \mu_i = q_i,$$ (3)

where $p(\mu_i)$ is a continuous, increasing function describing the price buyers in A are willing to pay for goods produced by a firm i which are perceived to have quality μ_i, and with perception in this case mirroring reality.

(2) Under the *imperfect information equilibrium*:

$$\rho_i = p(\mu_i), \text{ and } \mu_i = \frac{q_i \hat{y}_i + \sum_{j \neq i} q_j \hat{y}_j}{\sum_j \hat{y}_j},$$ (4)

where μ_i is the perceived quality of goods produced by firm i, and $\hat{y}_j$ is the expected output of firm j, using information from previous experience. Since buyers cannot identify products of individual firms, they form perceptions on the basis of a weighted average of all firms' production levels.

(3) Under the *intermediated equilibrium*:

$$\rho_i = (1 - f)p(\mu_i), \text{ and } \mu_i = q_i,$$ (5)

where the quality perception (of the buyers in A) mirrors reality and sellers in B pay a fee for the services of middlemen in C, who provide information about the quality of goods of specific exporting firms. The fee structure is such that a fixed fraction f of the sales price is paid for this information, with f dependent on conditions in C, as further explained below.

DEFINITION. *Each equilibrium concept encompasses an ordered triplet:*

$$\left(w_B^*, (l_i^*, q_i^*)_{i=1, 2 ..., N} \right)$$ (6)

which satisfies the twin conditions pertaining to perfect competition:

$$0 = \max_{q_i, l_i} l_i \left\{ \frac{\rho_i(q_i, .)}{a(q_i)} - w_B \right\} \quad \text{(competitive profit condition)},$$ (7)

$$0 = L_B - \sum_{i=1}^{N} l_i \quad \textit{(full employment condition)}. \tag{8}$$

Remark 1. Having assumed that all firms share identical technology and market access, it is reasonable to focus attention on symmetric equilibria, where

$$l_i^* = L_B/N \text{ and } q_i^* = q_1^* \ \forall \ i = 1, 2 \dots, N. \tag{9}$$

Remark 2. Any monotonic transformation of the value of quality leaves all quantities produced and purchased unchanged, hence, without loss of generality units of quality may be redefined such that

$$q = p(q), \tag{10}$$

which reflects the marginal consumer preference in A for a known quality of good.[10] The weighted average of "quality" reflects the weighted average of the marginal utility to consume goods. Under risk neutrality this justifies equation (4).[11] It is now clear that equations (7) and (8) define a Cournot–Nash equilibrium. Players' qualities affect each other through what buyers perceive about a "Made in China" label.

Remark 3. Figure 1 illustrates the implication of equation (7). By definition, from any equilibrium, however reached, a firm can never make more profit by changing its quality decision, given the value of l_i. Nor can one make more profit by changing l_i. Under constant returns, profit must be zero anywhere on the horizontal line illustrated, which maximizes the revenue per worker, given the wage rate and other firms' production decisions. Therefore no individual firm will gain by deviating from the symmetric equilibrium shown in the figure.

Results

From the above analysis we can deduce the following proposition.

PROPOSITION 1. *Under a perfect information equilibrium:*[12]

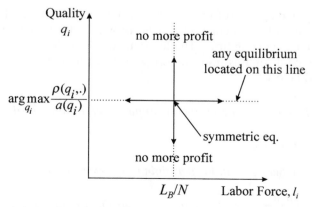

Figure 1. Illustration of a Firm's Optimization Decision

$$q^* = q^*_i = arg\ max_q[p(q)/a(q)] = arg\ max_q[q/a(q)]\ \forall\ i = 1, 2, ..., \text{N}. \tag{11}$$

PROOF. If the claim is false, there exists some q_0 such that

$$[q_0/a(q_0)] > [q^*/a(q^*)]. \tag{12}$$

Since firm i is free to choose independently its product quality and labor force, it can hire the same labor force but produce q_0 instead of q^* and increase its profit by an amount $\{[q_0/a(q_0)] - [q^*/a(q^*)]\}l_i$, contary to equations (3) and (7).   □

COROLLARY 1. *Under a perfect information equilibrium:*

$$w^* = max_q[q/a(q)]. \tag{13}$$

PROOF. This follows directly from equations (6) and (7).[13]   □

Remark 4. In a perfect information equilibrium, l_i is indeterminate. If symmetry is assumed, however, $l_i = L_B/N$.

Remark 5. The above findings hold even if arg $\max_q [p(q)/a(q)]$ is a set with more than one element, in which case there are multiple potential equilibria.

To sharpen the analysis, the quality elasticity of per unit labor input, $\varepsilon(q)$, is defined as

$$\varepsilon(q) \equiv \frac{da(q)/a(q)}{dq/q} = \frac{qa'(q)}{a(q)}, \tag{14}$$

with assumptions[14] that:

ASSUMPTION 8. $\varepsilon(q)$ *exists and is a continuous, strictly increasing function of output quality.*[15]

ASSUMPTION 9. *There exist some* $\underline{q}$ *and* $\bar{q}$ *such that:*

$$\varepsilon(q) < 1/\text{N}\ \forall\ q < \underline{q},$$

$$\varepsilon(q) > 1\ \forall\ q < \bar{q}.$$

COROLLARY 2. *For the perfect information case, a necessary and sufficient condition for equilibrium is*

$$\varepsilon(q^*) = 1. \tag{15}$$

PROOF. Note that profit is

$$\pi_i = l_i\left\{\frac{p_i(q_i, .)}{a(q_i)} - w^*\right\} = l_i\left\{\frac{q_i}{a(q_i)} - w^*\right\}, \tag{16}$$

using equation (3). The first-order condition for profit maximization, choosing quality level results in equation (15) as a necessary condition for profit maximization for each firm. Assumption 9 along with continuity guarantees the existence of some equilibrium quality. Uniqueness is assured since elasticity increases with increasing quality level.   □

COROLLARY 3. *For the symmetric, imperfect information case a necessary and sufficient condition for equilibrium is*

$$\varepsilon(q^0) = 1/N.$$ (17)

PROOF. Profit is

$$\pi_i = l_i \left\{ \frac{\rho_i(q_i, .)}{a(q_i)} - w^0 \right\} = l_i \left\{ \frac{q_i + \sum_{j \neq i} q_j}{Na(q_i)} - w^0 \right\}.$$ (18)

The above expression is obtained using equation (4) along with the assumption that firms are perceived by buyers in A to be equal in size; i.e., $\hat{y}_j$ are identical for all j. The first-order condition, maximizing profit with respect to quality choice for firm i, gives the desired necessary condition. Existence and uniqueness follow as above for the perfect-information case.   □

Hence, the quality/cost tradeoff is affected by the spillover effect of a shared image: a firm receives just $1/N$ of the fruits of its effort to improve the collective image of the quality of goods, but bears the full share of costs. Figure 2 illustrates and provides some intuition about the effect of imperfect information on the quality level of firms' products.

We can now surmise the consequences of imperfect information.

PROPOSITION 2. *Under an unintermediated, imperfect-information equilibrium, both the equilibrium product quality and market-clearing wage rate are lower than in a perfect-information equilibrium.*

PROOF. That the equilibrium quality level is higher under perfect information is obvious from Assumption 8 given the results from equations (15) and (17), since there

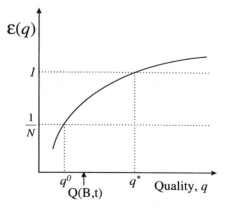

Figure 2. Equilibrium Quality Levels With and Without Intermediation

are assumed to be many producing firms in B ($N > 1$). Next, to show that the wage rate under perfect information is higher than it would be under imperfect information, note that w^* has been found to be the unique solution to the unconstrained maximization of $q/a(q)$. In a symmetric, imperfect-information equilibrium the zero-profit condition using equation (16) gives

$$w^0 = q^0/a(q^0),$$ (19)

which since $q^0 \neq q^*$ implies $w^* > w^0$.

Now we consider the intermediated equilibrium, in which a large number of perfectly competitive firms in economy C charge a proportional fee, f^* per unit of goods, to provide buyers in A perfect information about the quality of products.

Remark 6. Economies B and C are small and therefore have no effect on world prices. The incidence of the middleman's fee must fall on individuals in B.

Remark 7. With intermediation, economy B can export under conditions of perfect information, guaranteeing that the quality level of products would be the same as q^*, above. The wage rate under perfect competition in B is

$$w_B^{**}(1-f^*)q^*/a(q^*).$$ (20)

Alternatively, under imperfect-information equilibrium, the wage rate would be

$$w_B^0 = q^0/a(q^0).$$ (21)

A symmetric, intermediated equilibrium exists only if no firm would find it profitable to sell low-quality goods in order to avoid the middleman's fee. The equilibrium exists, therefore, as long as

$$(1-f^*)q^*/a(q^*) \geq q^0/a(q^0).$$ (22)

Remark 8. Information gathering is costly. The magnitude of f^* depends on the efficiency of economy C in that activity, and that effectiveness may erode because of corruption, which enters as a parameter to the production function for information gathering.

We illustrate this situation with a simple example based upon some special assumptions. To determine the quality of goods produced by each unit of labor in economy B, the required resources for this activity are described by a linear homogeneous production function of the form:

$$F(a_M, a_C; \theta) = 1.$$ (23)

Here a_M and a_C are the unit requirements of imported capital and local labor, respectively. θ is an institutional parameter describing the efficiency of the intermediation activity, equivalent to the degree of corruption in C, with $\theta = 1$ denoting "normal" (or "uncorrupted") institutions and $\theta = 0$ the maximum level of corruption in the society. For concreteness a Cobb–Douglas technology for intermediation is assumed, with capital and labor used as inputs. This production function is represented by

$$F(a_M, a_C; \theta) = \theta a_M^{1-\gamma} a_C^{\gamma} \qquad (24)$$

With all of C's labor force employed in intermediation activities, in equilibrium

$$a_C^* = L_C/Y, \qquad (25)$$

where L_C is the size of the labor force and Y the total quantity of exports from country B. Using the above production function for intermediation, this implies a corresponding value of a_M^*. Given the world market price for imported inputs, m, and the implied marginal rate of factor substitution from the production function for intermediation, the market-clearing wage for country C, w_C^*, can be obtained. Finally, using the fact that the market for intermediation is perfectly competitive, the unit cost (price) of the value of intermediation services (k) is derived:

$$k(w_C, m; \theta) = a_C(\theta)w_C(\theta) + a_M(\theta)m. \qquad (26)$$

With the cost of intermediation set as a fixed fraction of the price of exported goods, independent of quality level, this condition determines the fee schedule:

$$f^* = k(w_C^*, m; \theta)/p(q^*). \qquad (27)$$

Note that since the intermediation process is quality-neutral, a proportional fee schedule will not affect the choice of product quality by firms in B[16] provided that

$$p(q^*) - p(q^0) \geq k(w_C^*, m; \theta). \qquad (28)$$

If this condition is not met then firms in country B would opt to sell their products directly to world markets, forgoing intermediation.

Using the above Cobb–Douglas form to describe the intermediation activities, the quantity of capital imported to C is

$$M^* = \left(Y/L_C^{1-\gamma}\right)^{1/\gamma} \theta^{-1/\gamma}. \qquad (29)$$

The wage rate for labor in C is

$$w_C^* = \frac{(1-\gamma)mM^*}{\gamma L_C}, \qquad (30)$$

with the imputed value of intermediation services therefore

$$kY = \frac{mM^*}{\gamma}. \qquad (31)$$

In fact, the intermediation process described above is no different from any production process in C which incurs some real "cost of doing business" in order to transform a "quality lottery" into its sure-quality component. Analytically, to receive the higher value for quality-certified products, agents in B treat the for-fee service from C just like a transport cost under the "iceberg" hypothesis in the trade literature.

PROPOSITION 3. *With Cobb-Douglas technology for intermediation, a small incremental decrease in efficiency (increase in corruption), $d\theta$, will result in: (1) an increase in the level of imported capital by $[M^*/(\gamma\theta)]\, d\theta$, (2) an increase in wage rate of country C by*

$(w_C^*/(\gamma\theta)d\theta$, and (3) a decrease in income of country B by (m/γ^2) $(Y/L<_C^{1-\gamma})^{1/\gamma}\theta^{-(1+\gamma)/\gamma}d\theta$.

PROOF. The first result above can be obtained by taking the natural logarithm of equation (29), differentiating with respect to θ and rearranging the result. The second expression follows similarly after substituting (29) into (30). The third relation results from the fact that country B's income equals $[1 - f^*(\theta)]q^*Y$, with $f^*(\theta) = (mM^*)/(\gamma q^*Y)$ from equation (27) and $p(q^*) = q^*$. Substituting for M^*, differentiating with respect to θ and rearranging gives the desired expression.   □

Ironically, as efficiency declines in C owing to increased corruption, incomes decline in country B but not C. The quality choice for exports by B is unaffected. If corruption proceeds to the point where

$$q^* - q^0 < k(w_C^*, m; \theta), \tag{32}$$

country B will revert to the unintermediated equilibrium, with product quality declining to q^0 from q^*. This is equivalent to the condition that $\theta < \hat{\theta}$ in Figure 3. Once the intermediary role is lost, individuals in country C would be exactly like those in B, a situation residents of Hong Kong faced under Japanese rule during the Second World War.

This bleak scenario is a cautionary tale, certainly not inevitable. Over time, B may have no need for intermediation. Corruption in C may not go unchecked, or C may find other export of its own, beside serving as a middleman. On the other hand it is a logically consistent scenario, not to be dismissed out of hand. A rather gloomy passage in Lucas (1993) seems to corroborate our view.[17]

We now come to the heart of our inquiry, namely, export is essential to the Chinese ambition to modernize. As we move from a static to a dynamic analysis, quantities are now labeled with time indices. For this analysis we adopt Young's Principle of Bounded Learning and assume that with experience producing "challenging goods" labor productivity increases and costs of production decline.

PROPOSITION 4. *For some "challenge threshold" level, Q(B, t), in country B*

$a_{t+1}(q_i) < a_t(q_i)$, *for all* $q_i \geq Q(B, t)$,

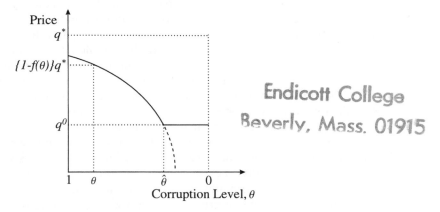

Figure 3. Price Received by B for Exports vs. Corruption Level, θ

$$a_{t+1}(q_i) = a_t(q_i), \text{ for all } q_i < Q(B, t).$$

Some observations are in order. First, it has been assumed that labor turnover in B is so high that firms would not sacrifice current profits just to make their labor force more experienced. Next, under autarky economy B would produce only for domestic demand and output may be positive only for goods with quality lower than some level, $q'(B, t)$, since in general less-developed countries have little demand for goods near the frontiers of current technology.

LEMMA. *If $q'(B, t) < Q(B, t)$ learning is impossible without trade and an import substitution policy would be futile.*

This brings up the rather disturbing possibility that an import substitution policy provides some initial benefit, but proves to be ultimately futile after much of the labor force is trapped in "uneconomic" production activities. This situation may describe what happened to many Eastern European nations after the Second World War. For those countries inward-looking policies sustained some degree of technological progress for a time, but eventually led to stagnation.

PROPOSITION 5. *Intermediation may improve product quality, thus presenting the possibility of firms in B securing dynamic learning.*

As illustrated in Figure 2, if at some point in time the challenge threshold $Q(B, t)$ for country B is in the range between q_t^0 and q_t^*, then the availability of intermediation by C would spell the difference between perpetual stagnation and sustained growth.

4. Discussion

What Hong Kong Provided

At this point, some institutional discussion is in order. We take for granted that the quality decision is made by management but the benefit of learning accrues to workers. The possibility of labor turnover will consequently make learning into an externality from the perspective of individual firms.

In contrast to the buyer, the advantage enjoyed by the middleman is partly cultural but also partly a matter of scale. Individual importers in country A need not purchase repeatedly. They are in no position to keep tabs on individual suppliers in country B and pose the threat of the "grim trigger" strategy; i.e., no future business if the quality standard is not met. On the other hand, the middleman, whether as an independent professional or in the employment of a multinational firm, is distinguished by both capability and intention. Such an actor plays for the long haul, and has his own reputation to care for. As a group, free entry into the ranks of middlemen serves to keep incumbents honest under competitive pressure. In short, the middlemen intermediate best when rent-seeking is conspicuous by its absence.

It is significant that professional middlemen thrive in an environment with an independent judiciary, laws against restrictive business practices, as well as an administration tempered internally by checks and balances and externally by public hearings and an uninhibited press. Formally speaking, the mechanics of governance does not have to be multiparty parliamentary democracy. Certainly, during the former period of the British Crown Colony, residents of Hong Kong had little political role to play compared with citizens of most participatory democracies. Yet, there has been the rule of law, not the rule of men, especially since 1974 with the establishment of the Hong Kong Independent Commission Against Corruption.

What China Needs

The People's Republic of China arose out of a baptism of revolutionary fire. In the first three decades after its founding the PRC confronted both superpowers with arms and fought border wars with India and Vietnam. An argument might be made that in times like those judiciary independence and so forth cannot rank high in the list of public priorities. Understandably, when the survival of the Great Cause is not yet assured, the separation of powers means a divided command, which can only cause mischief and grief. At any rate, the Constitution of the People's Republic of China states that the nation's economic system is based on "socialist public ownership of the means of production, namely, ownership by the whole people." How effectively middlemen can intermediate in this environment seems to be rather a non-sequitur. It is no coincidence then that after 1978, when the "Four Modernizations" became the Chinese national policy and economic growth was promoted to a top priority, the Chinese economy has been intermediated by Hong Kong, and not Shanghai—a metropolis with twice the population and a much larger and centrally placed hinterland. Institutionally, Hong Kong was uniquely qualified to be China's middleman.

The Intermediated Equilibrium with Corruption

In analyzing the future of Hong Kong we are least impressed by some Western media perceptions that Hong Kong capitalist captains are threatened by Beijing ideologues. Even in China, political leaders are trying hard to convince the people that their rule is good for China as a state and for the population in bringing people greater economic benefits. Ideological purity is far from the top item in the current government's agenda. More likely, any threat to the system after the handover will come from Hong Kong rent-seekers perverting a status quo which has been crucial to the long-run benefit of the Chinese economy.

A foretaste of this occurred in 1994 when, two years after it opened its largest restaurant in the world in downtown Beijing, McDonald's was evicted from the site by the Beijing Municipal Government in order to make room for another project. Apparently McDonald's 20-year lease was no match for the behind-the-scenes influence of a consortium controlled by one of Hong Kong's richest men, property developer Li Ka-shing (Roberts, 1997). Whatever the merit of this particular case, Mr Li has apparently gained and Chinese credibility lost in Western eyes. *Ipso facto*, the vigor of Hong Kong capitalism can be easily lost by leaving matters to the most successful Hong Kong capitalists.

To begin with, judging from how much the People's Republic has tried to develop the Shenzhen Special Economic Zone in Hong Kong's image, it should be apparent that the Chinese leadership recognizes: (1) it is to the interest of the mainland for Hong Kong to survive and thrive, (2) Chinese economic institutions are not to be transplanted to Hong Kong, and (3) the administration and economic policy of Hong Kong can be best handled locally. However, we shall argue below that this recognition need not be sufficient at all to preserve the middleman role of Hong Kong.

Certainly, our analysis of these issues in this essay does not imply we are pessimistic about the future of the Hong Kong–China relationship. From an academic perspective these issues should be discussed and possible economic pitfalls addressed. Certainly, nothing is inevitable. Even if Hong Kong can no longer serve as middleman, for some time to come at least, Hong Kong businessmen can still contribute their current skill and information to Chinese development, and receive economic benefit in the bargain. It is a matter of Chinese prestige that Hong Kong should prosper. At the worst, Hong Kong can serve as a second Beidaihe—the Chinese answer to the Soviet government resort towns of Yalta and Sochi. Yet, in the large scheme of things, without Hong Kong as intermediary, the continued upgrading of Chinese manufacturing exports would prove difficult—to the detriment of Chinese development.

Rather than burdening our discussion with analytic formalism, we shall try to make our point with a few purely hypothetical scenarios below. The degrading of Hong Kong's ability as a middleman must take one of two forms: (1) an erosion of efficiency of intermediation, or (2) the development of distortions. It is neither hoped nor predicted that either of these will occur, yet each of these possibilities must be examined dispassionately. The point of departure is to see how the end of the colonial period may trigger such happenings.

Erosion of Efficiency

Hong Kong became effective thanks to the Darwinian process of market competition. First, however imperfect, judiciary independence, a rule of law and certain traditions against conflicts of interest as well as restrictive business practices came with the British system. Second, the top of the colonial administration had insufficient local contact to develop suffocating corruption. Certainly, it is not true that the playing field was ever really level or that British merchants never profited from their privileged positions. Far from it. But the point is that there was still breathing room left for emerging entrepreneurs (mostly, but not all, Chinese) to survive and thrive. From the ranks of the obscure, those both capable and lucky could still emerge (Chau, 1993). Finally, historically opportunities to succeed in Hong Kong were in enterprises related to foreign commerce.

After the return of sovereignty all these things are changed, and not clearly in ways favorable to the trade of middlemen. It is possible that now the cost of doing business may rise so much for intermediaries that Chinese exporters can no longer benefit from Hong Kong middlemen. In this event Hong Kong would be functionally no different from Shanghai—in the period before Chinese reforms.

Development of Distortions

Specific bias may arise to directly compromise the intermediation function. For example, suppose it is well understood by all that a would-be Hong Kong investor in China is personally very close to a high official in Hong Kong. Seeking advantage for her own investment interest, this would-be investor recommends to a Hong Kong middleman a very well-connected (but quite inexperienced) Chinese supplier who "just might prove to be useful" for some ongoing deal. Although it is not the usual practice to select an inexperienced supplier, this middleman has a critical petition (say, the confirmation of the temporary operation license) coming soon under a discretionary government review. A quick cost–benefit calculation causes this Hong Kong-based middleman to feel obliged to select the recommended Chinese supplier for the foreign client.

Now, the intermediated deal eventually goes wrong. Under normal circumstances any deal has some possibility of failing, but given the conditions described here, more deals will go wrong than previously expected. Sooner or later foreign firms would begin to feel less confident about Hong Kong middlemen as well as the Chinese suppliers of goods. This change in attitudes towards the region may result in foreign firms shifting their choice of suppliers from China toward competitors from other countries, to Southeast Asia or elsewhere. By that time the damage would be already done to Chinese national interest. The ultimate effect of this process would be to shift the equilibrium quality in Figure 2 back toward q^0.

Such a development may have happened even if Hong Kong had remained under the Union Jack. Yet, no matter whether the British are or are not more corrupt than the Chinese, for reasons of "cultural distance" the transaction costs of lobbying are certainly much lower now than before. When nonprofessional considerations enter into professional decisions, unjustified risks will be taken more often, and things begin to go sour. In the political economy literature this is the well-known principle of "logrolling" among lobbying parliamentarians. Such practice is present in London and New Delhi, and it is not realistic for anyone to seriously guarantee its absence in Hanoi or Beijing.

Worthwhile to notice is that the change (for the worse) in our hypothetical scenario happens without a single move (good or bad) made by any Mainland Chinese. And yet the perception about the Chinese system as compared with the departed British system has played a role somewhere. Chinese "connections" are believed to be more essential. It does not really matter what is the truth and what is the perception, or where indeed may be some "source most foul" promoting such perception. The critical question is how to head off this type of mischievous development in advance. As has been shown here, it is in the economical interest of both the Chinese mainland and Hong Kong to take preventive countermeasures, soon.

5. Conclusion

It is clear, especially now that Hong Kong is formally a part of the People's Republic of China, that the destinies of these two regions are fundamentally linked. Although Hong Kong has been designated as a Special Administrative Region with a "large degree of autonomy," still the Basic Law of Hong Kong is subordinate to the Constitution of China. Without a doubt the economic future of Hong Kong hinges on the success of Chinese development and the benevolence of the mainland leaders. So, today and in the future what is good for the Chinese mainland will also prove to be good for Hong Kong.

Part of the measures necessary to avoid decay of this mutually beneficial middleman system may rest on what may be called "openness." During the British period, the press was fully free and economic scandals involving Colonial officials presumably could be laid bare by the press. Parliamentary questions could also be raised in London if there were serious economic scandals. Although local residents of Hong Kong never had any formal means to vote out any particular Royal Governor (let alone to affect how Royal Governors were appointed), at least the perception was that officials under suspicion would be readily investigated and probably removed. It is presumably achievable for Beijing to demonstrate the presence of some similar mechanism with respect to Hong Kong corruption now that the territory is under the sovereignty of China.

Part of such measures concern how to deal with potential conflicts of interest between local businesses and the local administration. Again, this presumably can have no ramifications one way or another on the internal security or stability of China. Yet, it should be understood in Beijing that in economically thriving Western societies monopolies and cartels are treated as public enemies. Restrictive business practices are and have been guarded against in Britain under both Labor and the Tories. The anti-trust provisions in America are not just propaganda nor a means to bamboozle the proletariat. These policies serve to preserve free entry against currently entrenched firms, so that the economy can have sustained vitality. Just a few years back Intel and Microsoft were fledgling firms challenging the incumbents.

Capitalism withers if capitalists are not under leash. If Hong Kong is to enjoy fifty years of thriving economic conditions, the current capitalists must be under proper legal constraint, as is standard under capitalism anywhere else. With capitalism everywhere else surviving as before, a prematurely withered capitalist Hong Kong will be to neither the credit nor the interest of Chinese socialism.

References

Akerlof, George A., "The Market for 'Lemons': Quality Uncertainty and the Market Mechanism," *Quarterly Journal of Economics* 84 (1970):488–500.

Asian Development Bank, *Emerging Asia, Changes and Challenges*, Manila: Asian Development Bank (1997).

Biglaiser, Gary, "Middlemen as Experts," *RAND Journal of Economics* 24 (1993):212–23.

Biglaiser, Gary and James W. Friedman, "Middlemen as Guarantors of Quality," *Journal of Industrial Organization* 12 (1994):509–31.

Chau, Leung Chuen, *Hong Kong: A Unique Case of Development*, Washington, DC: World Bank (1993).

Chiang, Shih-Chen and Robert T. Masson, "Domestic Industrial Structure and Export Quality," *International Economic Review* 29 (1988):261–70.

Coe, David T., Elhanan Helpman, and Alexander W. Hoffmaister, "North–South R&D spillovers," *Economic Journal* 107 (1997):134–49.

Collins, Susan M., "Technical Progress in a Three-Country Ricardian Model with a Continuum of Goods," *Journal of International Economics* 19 (1985):171–9.

Dornbusch, Rudiger, Stanley Fischer, and Paul A. Samuelson, "Comparative Advantage, Trade and Payments in a Ricardian Model with a Continuum of Goods," *American Economic Review* 67 (1977):823–39.

Gargan, Edward A., "China Already Entrenched as a Hong Kong Capitalist," *New York Times*, 5 December, 1996.

Grossman, Gene M. and Elhanan Helpman, "Quality Ladders in the Theory of Growth," *Review of Economic Studies* 58 (1991):43–61.

Hong, Yongmiao, Man-Lui Lau, and Henry Y. Wan, Jr, "A Non-parametric, Panel Study of Convergence, and the Trade-Development Nexus," unpublished manuscript, Cornell University, 1998.

Kim, Kihwan and Danny M. Leipziger, *Korea: A Case of Government-Led Development*, Washington, DC: World Bank (1993).

Lau, Man-Lui and Henry Y. Wan, Jr, "The Hong Kong–Guangdong Nexus," in *Proceedings of the International Conference, Financing Development in Guangdong*, Hong Kong: City Polytechnic University of Hong Kong (1994).

Lucas, Robert E., Jr, "On the Mechanics of Economic Development," *Journal of Monetary Economics* 22 (1988):3–42.

———, "Making a Miracle," *Econometrica* 61 (1993):251–72.

Nathan, Andrew J. and Robert S. Ross, *Great Wall and Empty Fortress: China's Search for Security*, New York: Norton (1997).

Pomery, John, "Uncertainty in Trade Models," in Ronald W. Jones and Peter B. Kenen (eds.), *Handbook of International Economics*, Vol. I, New York: North-Holland (1984):419–65.

Roberts, Dexter, "Maybe Guanxi Isn't Everything After All," *Business Week* (International Edition), 24 February 1997.

Rubinstein, Ariel and Asher Wolinsky, "Middlemen," *Quarterly Journal of Economics* 102 (1987):581–93.

Sung, Yun Wing, *The China–Hong Kong Connection: The Key to China's Open–Door Policy*, Hong Kong: Cambridge University Press (1991).

Van, Pham H. and Henry Y. Wan, Jr, "Emulative Development Through Trade Expansions: East Asian Evidence," in John Pigott and Alan D. Woodland (eds.), *International Trade and the Pacific Rim*, London: Macmillan (1998).

Wan, Henry Y., Jr., "Trade, development and inventions," in Horst Herberg and Ngo Van Long (eds.), *Trade, Welfare and Economic Policies: Essays in Honor of Murray C. Kemp*, Ann Arbor: University of Michigan Press (1993).

Yavas, Abdullah, "Middlemen in Bilateral Search Markets," *Journal of Labor Economics* 12 (1994):406–29.

——, "Search and trading in intermediated markets," *Journal of Economics and Management Strategy* 5 (1996):195–216.

Young, Alwyn, "Learning by Doing and the Dynamic Effects of International Trade," *Quarterly Journal of Economics* 106 (1991):369–405.

——, "Invention and Bounded Learning-by-Doing," *Journal of Political Economy* 101 (1993):443–72.

——, "Lessons from the East Asian NICs: A Contrarian View," *European Economic Review* 38 (1994):964–73.

Notes

1. In Lau and Wan (1994), the emphasis was placed on information. What will be argued here is that the best means of acquiring information is through intermediated export trade. The two views are thus intertwined.

2. The special cases cited by Van and Wan (1998) suggest that only by satisfying the quality requirement for developed countries can producers in developing countries learn to improve their technology.

3. For a collection of case histories, see Van and Wan (1998).

4. Kim and Leipziger (1993) documented this type of transformation of the Handok Company over the fifteen years between 1971 and 1985.

5. Stylized Fact 3 may take more doing since it is complicated by heterogeneous preferences.

6. See Young (1993) for an example of a model in which production of challenging goods provides a means of learning-by-doing and brings about the possibility of escape from technical stagnation. In contrast to Coe et al. (1997) which focuses on trade in general, this specification emphasizes export as the trigger for learning.

7. Young (1991) shows theoretically that autarky promotes growth for less-developed regions, while Young (1994) gives empirical evidence that trade is irrelevant for dynamic gain.

8. The insider-trading tribunal fined the businessman one-third the maximum allowable penalty, and banned him from his company for one year, deferring the ban for 12 months.

9. Alternatively, A may be the "rest of the world" relative to B and C, which includes some advanced economies.

10. Quality is an ordinal variable, so any monotonic transformation can be adopted.

11. That is why, should the market care only about the average quality, purchasing a good under information imperfection is equivalent to a quality lottery.

12. This implies that for a given cost of production the producer has achieved the maximum value of output.

13. This means equilibrium profit must be zero under constant returns and free entry; wage is equal to the average product of labor when labor is the only input of production.

14. It is possible to use weaker assumptions to derive the results below. For simplicity and to avoid distracting the reader from the main focus here, these more straightforward and intuitive conditions are utilized.

15. If ε is increasing but not strictly increasing, then there may be alternative equilibrium product mixes of output, some of which imply stagnation and others allow for continued progress. We appreciate the comments of an anonymous referee which alerted us to this possibility.

16. This is because including a multiplicative constant (independent of quality level) in the firm revenue relation will still result in the same quality choice; i.e., $q_i^* = \arg \max[p(q_i)/a(q_i)]$.

17. Lucas (1993) acknowledged the success of the Asian NIEs while expressing his pessimism about the situation after the handover by noting, "never before have the lives of so many people undergone so rapid an improvement over so long a period, nor (with the exception of Hong Kong) is there any sign that this progress is near its end."

5
Catching-up and Regulation in a Two-Sector Small Open Economy

*Theo van de Klundert and Sjak Smulders**

Abstract

Deregulation is often aimed at reducing mark-up pricing in technologically stagnant sheltered sectors. The paper shows that this may decrease the process of catching-up and welfare since it shifts resources away from R&D-intensive tradables sectors. Catching-up and deregulation are analyzed in an R&D-based growth model that allows for international capital mobility, trade, and spillovers. Knowledge spillovers raise the productivity of R&D in the exposed sector which results in catching-up. In the long run, the economy grows at the exogenous world growth rate. Capital mobility speeds up convergence. Temporary shocks have long-lasting effects as the economy exhibits hysteresis.

1. Introduction

In neoclassical growth theory, emerging economies are characterized by a relatively low capital intensity. The scarcity of capital implies a high rate of return on investment and a corresponding high rate of growth. Alternatively, one could assume that emerging economies lack the knowledge to produce at the same level as developed economies. Knowledge can of course be imitated and the relevance of international knowledge spillovers is well documented (e.g., Coe and Helpman, 1995; Coe et al., 1997). However, technological knowledge may be assumed to be firm-specific, at least to an important degree. This implies that knowledge spillovers have to be absorbed by own R&D outlays. Emerging economies may then be characterized by a technical disadvantage, which can be overcome by investing sufficiently in domestic R&D. Therefore, emerging economies may grow fast because there is potential for "catching-up."

In this paper we analyse catching-up in the context of a small open economy with two sectors. The exposed or tradables sector consists of a number of specialized producers which have to compete in the international market by setting prices and investing in R&D. The economy is relatively backward because firms in the exposed sector stay behind in knowledge *vis-à-vis* the rest of the world. This implies two things. First, there is a potential for imitation. Second, investment in R&D in the emerging economy commands a relatively high rate of return. Both factors contribute to a rate of growth in excess of that in the rest of the world, so that the exposed sector catches up. There is no technological change in the sheltered or nontradables sector, but workers in this sector benefit from growth in the exposed sector as the terms of trade move in favor of nontradables (the Balassa effect).

It is assumed that the sheltered sector is subject to a form of regulation that restricts the number of firms by preventing entry. Therefore, regulation gives room to oligopolistic price-setting, allowing firms to set a mark-up over marginal cost. As a result, output in the sheltered sector is restricted. More resources are available for the exposed sector so that investment in R&D becomes more profitable. The implication

---

*Van de Klundert and Smulders: Tilburg University, PO Box 90153, 5000 LE Tilburg, The Netherlands. E-mail: jasmulders@kub.nl. We wish to thank Bjarne S. Jensen and three anonymous referees for useful comments on earlier drafts. Smulders thanks the Dutch Science Foundation NWO for financial support.

is that regulation in the sheltered sector speeds up growth and may for that reason be seen as a kind of development strategy, be it deliberate or not. Whether it is also optimal from the point of consumer welfare remains to be seen.

An important aspect of the present analysis is the prevailing regime with respect to international capital mobility. We distinguish two extreme cases: balanced trade and perfect capital mobility. The results differ substantially among regimes. Under capital mobility, the relatively backward economy is able to smooth consumption by borrowing in the early stages of growth and by servicing the incurred debt later on. Long-run consumption will be lower than under the regime of balanced trade, which means that fewer resources are needed to meet the demand for nontradables. As a consequence, firm size in the tradables sector will be larger, which makes R&D more attractive. The economy catches up to higher levels of productivity, the more debt is accumulated, which in turn depends on the initial knowledge gap. This shows that hysteresis applies, not only with respect to foreign asset positions, but also with respect to the allocation of nonreproducible resources.

It may be useful to relate our analysis to the existing literature. The engine of growth applied in the present paper is borrowed from our earlier work on endogenous growth (Smulders and Van de Klundert, 1995; Van de Klundert and Smulders, 1997). There are a number of theoretical papers on catching-up driven by a knowledge gap but most papers assume that emerging economies learn from doing (e.g., Lucas, 1993; Maggi, 1993; Van de Klundert and Smulders, 1996; Basu and Weil, 1998). In the present model the backward economy has a substantial potential for investing in new knowledge. In Barro and Sala-i-Martin (1997) international diffusion of knowledge requires investment by the recipient country, but there is no international trade in the model. Two-sector open economies are analysed in Turnovsky and Sen (1991, 1995). The authors discuss changes in government expenditure and supply shocks in a neoclassical world with homogenous capital. As the regime of balanced trade is not analysed, it is not possible to isolate the implications of introducing perfect capital mobility in their model.

The paper is organised as follows. In section 2 we present the model for the dependent economy and its behavioral implications. Section 3 is devoted to an analysis of the steady-state characteristics of the system. Equilibrium dynamics are discussed in section 4, applying a linearized version of the model. The dynamics in case of capital mobility turn out to be rather complicated. For this reason catching-up phenomena and regulation in the sheltered sector are discussed in more detail by presenting numerical examples in section 5. The paper closes with some conclusions. Technicalities are relegated to an Appendix.

2. The Dependent Economy

Feasible Growth

Preferences and technology are specified in Table 1. Consumers trade off future consumption for present consumption according to an intertemporal utility function that features a constant elasticity of intertemporal substitution $1/\rho$ (assumed to be smaller than unity) and a pure rate of time preference ϑ, as in equation (1.1). They make a choice at every instant of time between nontradables Y_c and tradables X_c according to the Cobb–Douglas specification in equation (1.2). The X-good in the consumption menu consists of a bundle of N domestic goods and $n\bar{N}$ foreign goods. Here n stands for the number of countries from which goods are imported. Variables with an upper

Table 1. Structure of the Model

Preferences:	$U = \int_0^\infty (1-\rho)^{-1} C(t)^{1-\rho} \exp(-\vartheta t) dt$	(1.1)

$$C = X_c^\sigma Y_c^{1-\sigma}, \quad 0 < \sigma < 1 \tag{1.2}$$

$$X_c = \left(\sum_{i=1}^{N} x_{ci}^{\frac{\varepsilon-1}{\varepsilon}} + \sum_{j=1}^{n\overline{N}} \overline{x}_{cj}^{\frac{\varepsilon-1}{\varepsilon}} \right)^{\frac{\varepsilon}{\varepsilon-1}}, \quad \varepsilon > 1 \tag{1.3}$$

Technology:
$$Y = h_Y L_Y \tag{1.4}$$

$$x_i = h_{xi} L_{xi}^\gamma Y_{xi}^{1-\gamma} \tag{1.5}$$

$$\dot{h}_{xi} = \xi \left(h_{xi}^{1-\alpha_h-\alpha_f} H^{\alpha_h} \overline{H}^{\alpha_f} \right) L_{ri} \tag{1.6}$$

Resource constraints:
$$L_Y + \sum_{i=1}^{N} (L_{xi} + L_{ri}) = L \tag{1.7}$$

$$Y_c + \sum_{i=1}^{N} Y_{xi} = Y \tag{1.8}$$

$$x_{ci} + n x_{\bar{c}i} = x_i \tag{1.9}$$

$$\sum_{i=1}^{N} (x_i - x_{ci}) p_{xi} - \sum_{j=1}^{n\overline{N}} \overline{x}_{cj} \overline{p}_{xj} = \begin{cases} 0 \\ \dot{A} - \bar{r} A \end{cases} \tag{1.10}$$

bars denote a foreign variable.

Y_c	nontradable consumption
x_{ci}	domestic production of tradable good i that is consumed domestically
N	number of firms in a country
Y	total domestic nontradables production
L_{ki}	labor allocated in sector k, firm i
h_{ki}	labor productivity in sector k, firm i
L	labor supply
$x_{\bar{c}i}$	exports of tradable good i

C	aggregate consumption index
X_c	tradables consumption index
$\overline{x}_{cj}$	foreign production of tradable good j that is consumed domestically (imports)
n	number of countries in ROW
x_i	total domestic production of tradable good i
Y_{xi}	(nontradable) intermediates
H	average labor productivity in national high-tech sector
A	Net foreign assets

bar relate to the outside world. The number of domestic and foreign varieties of X-goods is given. These goods are imperfect substitutes as shown in equation (1.3). The elasticity of substitution is constant and equals $\varepsilon > 1$.

Nontradables are produced by applying labor with fixed productivity h_Y as shown in equation (1.4). There is no technical change in the Y-goods sector. Goods in the tradables sector are produced by labour and intermediary inputs from the nontradables sector with a Cobb–Douglas technology, as in equation (1.5). Factor productivity in each branch of the tradables sector can be improved by employing labor in R&D activities, as appears from equation (1.6). Innovation builds upon a knowledge base, which is the result of in-house or firm-specific knowledge accumulated in the past (h_x) and of domestic spillovers as well as of foreign spillovers. These spillover effects are related to average knowledge levels at home (H) and abroad ($\overline{H}$). There are diminishing returns with respect to firm-specific knowledge ($0 < \alpha_h + \alpha_f < 1$) but constant returns with respect to the knowledge base as a whole.

Labor market equilibrium implies that the amount of labour available (L) equals total labour demand, as in equation (1.7). Non-tradables are consumed or used as inputs in the production of tradables, as in equation (1.8). Tradables are consumed at home or exported as appears from equation (1.9). Trade with the outside world is governed by alternative assumptions with respect to international capital mobility. In equations (1.10) we consider two regimes. In case of current account equilibrium, exports equals imports and the LHS of (1.10) equals zero. The other case considered is perfect international capital mobility, which allows the domestic economy to accumulate foreign assets, A, which bear a fixed rate of interest ($r = \bar{r}$). It should be observed that prices of domestic varieties of the X-good are not given. Each producer of X-goods holds a unique position in the world economy because he or she is the sole supplier of a product variety. Therefore prices of export goods or import-competing goods can be set in the domestic economy. Prices of imported goods are of course determined abroad.

Feasible growth paths satisfy equations (1.1)–(1.10). We assume that the domestic economy is small relative to the ROW. Hence, foreign variables are determined by foreign conditions only and can be considered as exogenous variables. Preferences as well as production technology and R&D technology in the ROW are the same as in the domestic economy. In addition, it will be assumed that the ROW exhibits steady-state growth with $\dot{\bar{h}}_{xj}/\bar{h}_{xj} \equiv \bar{g}$ constant, and that all foreign firms are the same so that there is a single price of foreign tradables ($\bar{p}_{xj} = \bar{p}_x$ for all j).

Behavior

Consumers maximize the intemporal utility function in three stages subject to budget constraints. The three-stage budgeting system is formulated in Table 2. In the first stage, each consumer decides on the path of aggregate consumption over time, taking into account the accumulation of financial assets F.[1] The nominal interest rate r is exoge-

Table 2. Consumer Behavior

Maximization of consumer preferences (1.1), (1.2), and (1.3) subject to, respectively:

$$\dot{F}(t) = r(t)F(t) + w(t)L - C(t)P_C(t) \tag{2.1}$$

$$X_c P_X + Y_c p_Y = C P_C \tag{2.2}$$

$$X_c P_X = \sum_{i=1}^{N} x_{ci} p_{xi} + \sum_{j=1}^{n\bar{N}} \bar{x}_{cj} \bar{p}_{xj} \tag{2.3}$$

yields: $\quad \dot{C}/C = (1/\rho)(r - \dot{P}_C/P_C - \vartheta) \tag{2.4}$

$$Y_c p_Y = (1 - \sigma) C P_C \tag{2.5}$$

$$x_{ci} = X_c (p_{xi}/P_X)^{-\varepsilon} \tag{2.6}$$

$$\bar{x}_{cj} = X_c (\bar{p}_{xj}/P_X)^{-\varepsilon} \tag{2.7}$$

where $\quad P_C = (P_X/\sigma)^\sigma (p_Y/(1-\sigma))^{1-\sigma} \tag{2.8}$

$$P_X = \left(\sum_{i=1}^{N} p_{xi}^{1-\varepsilon} + \sum_{j=1}^{n\bar{N}} \bar{p}_{xj}^{1-\varepsilon} \right)^{1/(1-\varepsilon)} \tag{2.9}$$

P_C, P_X price indices of consumption and tradables respectively
$p_Y, p_{xi}, \bar{p}_{xj}$ prices of nontradables, home-produced tradables and imports respectively
w, r wage and interest rate respectively

nous in case of perfect international capital mobility. Otherwise r is determined endogenously by domestic savings and investment. The wage rate is denoted by w. The second stage divides consumption over tradables and nontradables. In the third stage, consumers decide about spending on the different varieties of the tradable good produced at home or produced abroad.

The maximization procedure gives rise to the familiar Ramsey rule, equation (2.4), and demand equations for nontradables, (2.5), domestically produced tradables, (2.6), and imported goods, (2.7). The procedure also generates price indices for consumption, (2.8), and tradables, (2.9), in the domestic economy.

Producer behavior is summarized in Table 3. Demand for each product variety comes from domestic and from foreign consumers as shown in equation (3.2). Producers consider total consumer demand X_C and $\overline{X}_C$ as well as the corresponding price indices P_X and $\overline{P}_X$ as given. Profit maximization therefore results in a mark-up over marginal cost which is equal to the factor $\varepsilon/(\varepsilon-1) \equiv \mu_X$, as in equation (3.3). The cost-minimizing factor input combination follows from equation (3.4).

The optimal R&D strategy implies that the marginal value product of labor employed in research $p_{hi}\xi K_i$ should be equated to the marginal cost of labor (w), as is shown in equation (3.5). The shadow price of the knowledge base p_{hi} is introduced as a Lagrangian multiplier in the maximization procedure. Firms face a tradeoff with respect to investing in knowledge as appears from the no-arbitrage condition in equation (3.6). This condition says that investing a fixed amount of money in the capital market (the RHS of (3.6)) should yield the same revenue as investing that same amount of money in knowledge production. The latter raises factor productivity in commodity production and hence revenue (first term on the LHS of (3.6)), it raises also the knowledge base in R&D (second term) and it yields a capital gain (last term).

Table 3. Producer Behavior

X-sector:
$$V_i = \int_0^\infty [x_i(t)p_{xi}(t) - Y_{xi}(t)p_Y(t) - (L_{xi}(t) + L_{ri}(t))w(t)]\exp\left(-\int_0^t r(s)ds\right)dt \qquad (3.1)$$

$$x_i = X_c(p_{xi}/P_X)^{-\varepsilon} + n\overline{X}_c(p_{xi}/\overline{P}_X)^{-\varepsilon} = \Omega p_{xi}^{-\varepsilon} \qquad (3.2)$$

maximization of (3.1) w.r.t. p_{xi}, Y_{xi} and L_{ri}, s.t. (1.5), (1.6) and (3.2) yields

$$p_{xi} = (\mu_X/h_{xi})(w/\gamma)^\gamma (p_Y/(1-\gamma))^{1-\gamma} \qquad (3.3)$$

$$p_Y Y_{xi}/w L_{xi} = (1-\gamma)/\gamma \qquad (3.4)$$

$$p_{hi} = w/\xi K_i \qquad (3.5)$$

$$(p_{xi}/\mu_X)(x_i/h_{xi}) + p_{hi}\xi(1-\alpha_h-\alpha_f)(K_i/h_{xi})L_{ri} + \dot{p}_{hi} = r p_{hi} \qquad (3.6)$$

where $K_i \equiv h_{xi}^{1-\alpha_h-\alpha_f} H^{\alpha_h}\overline{H}^{\alpha_f}$

$$\mu_X \equiv \varepsilon/(\varepsilon-1)$$

Y-sector: $p_Y = \mu_Y w/h_Y \qquad (3.7)$

where $\mu_Y = m/(m-1)$

K_i firm i's knowledge base in R&D
μ_k mark-up rate in sector k
m number of firms in Y-sector

In the nontradables sector, a regulated number of symmetric firms compete in homogenous markets. Competition *à la* Cournot prevails so that each firm takes as given total spending in his market as well as output of rival firms. Profit maximization results in the market price that is defined in equation (3.7), where m is the number of homogenous and symmetric firms in the Y-sector.[2] Regulation exogenously limits the number of firms m, for instance through a system of licenses or permits. In the sequel we study changes in regulation that directly affect the number of firms in the non-tradables sector. This change affects the economy only through the resulting change in the mark-up rate. Hence, we capture changes in regulation by exogenous changes in the variable μ_Y.

Throughout the paper we assume that also in the tradables sector firms are symmetric. Hence we drop all subscripts i and j (for all i we have $h_{xi} = h_x, p_{xi} = p_x$, etc.).

3. The Steady State

The model can be conveniently reduced to a number of key relationships. In Appendices A and B we derive six semireduced forms which can be interpreted as the savings decision, investment decision, labor market equilibrium, equilibrium in the markets for tradables and for nontradables, balance of payment equilibrium, and the balance of payment regime (see Table 4). As shown in Appendix C, the semireduced model easily reveals the steady-state conditions which are further discussed in this section.

In the steady state, productivity levels in the domestic tradables sector grow at the same rate as abroad; i.e., at given rate $\bar{g}$. The allocation of labor and the knowledge gap $\bar{h}_x/h_x$ are constant. The balanced growth path can be characterized as

Table 4. Key Relationships

Consumption decision (Ramsey):

$$\hat{C} = \frac{1}{\rho}\left[r - (1-\sigma)\hat{h}_x + \left(\frac{1-\sigma}{\varepsilon}\right)\left(\hat{L}_x + \hat{h}_x - \bar{g}\right) - \vartheta\right] \tag{4.1}$$

Investment decision:

$$r = \xi\left(h_x/\bar{h}_x\right)^{-\alpha_f} L_x/\gamma + (1-\alpha_h)\hat{h}_x - \alpha_f \bar{g} + \left(\bar{g} - \hat{h}_x - \hat{L}_x\right)/\varepsilon \tag{4.2}$$

Labor market equilibrium:

$$\hat{h}_x = \xi\left(h_x/\bar{h}_x\right)^{-\alpha_f}\left[\frac{L}{N} - \frac{Y_c}{h_Y N} - \left(\frac{1-\gamma+\gamma\mu_Y}{\mu_Y}\right)\frac{L_x}{\gamma}\right] \tag{4.3}$$

Equilibrium in the (world) market for tradables:

$$p_x = \left(\frac{h_x}{\bar{h}_x}\frac{L_x}{\bar{L}_x}\right)^{-1/\varepsilon}\left(\frac{\mu_Y/h_Y}{\bar{\mu}_Y/\bar{h}_Y}\right)^{(1-\gamma)/\varepsilon} \tag{4.4}$$

Equilibrium in the market for nontradables:

$$Y_c = (1-\sigma)(h_Y/\mu_Y)CP_C/w \tag{4.5}$$

Balance of payments equilibrium:

$$\mu_x wNL_x/\gamma - \sigma CP_C = \dot{A} - \bar{r}A \tag{4.6}$$

Balance of payments regime:

$$\dot{A} = A = 0 \text{ (balanced trade) or } r = \bar{r} \text{ (perfect capital mobility)} \tag{4.7}$$

$$\frac{\dot{h}_x}{h_x}=\frac{\dot{x}}{x}=\frac{\dot{X}_c}{X_c}=\frac{1}{\sigma}\frac{\dot{C}}{C}=\frac{1}{1-\sigma}\frac{\dot{P}_C}{P_C}=\frac{\dot{w}}{w}=\frac{\dot{A}}{A}=\overline{g}.$$

By choice of numéraire, the price of imported goods is set equal to unity ($\overline{p}_x = 1$). The steady-state price of tradables should therefore be constant in the domestic economy ($\dot{p}_x = 0$).

Table 5 displays key relationships that hold in the steady state. Equations (5.1)–(5.5) can be used to find the steady-state solutions in h_x and L_x. Substitution of (5.1) in (5.2) results in a first equation in these variables. Substitution of CP_C/w according to equation (5.5) in (5.4) and substitution of the result in equation (5.3) gives the second equation in h_x and L_x. From these equations we get

$$\frac{h_x}{\overline{h}_x}=\left(\frac{\xi\beta}{\vartheta+[\sigma(\rho-1)+\alpha_h+\alpha_f+\beta]\overline{g}}\left[\frac{L}{N}-\frac{A}{N}\frac{r-g}{w}\frac{1-\sigma}{\sigma\mu_Y}\right]\right)^{1/\alpha_f}, \tag{1}$$

$$L_x=\beta\gamma\left(\frac{\vartheta+[\sigma(\rho-1)+\alpha_h+\alpha_f]g}{\vartheta+[\sigma(\rho-1)+\alpha_h+\alpha_f+\beta]g}\right)\left[\frac{L}{N}-\frac{A}{N}\frac{r-g}{w}\frac{1-\sigma}{\sigma\mu_Y}\right], \tag{2}$$

where

$$\beta\equiv\frac{\sigma\mu_Y}{(1-\sigma)\mu_X+\sigma(1-\gamma+\gamma\mu_Y)}.$$

In case of current account equilibrium or balanced trade, the net foreign asset position equals zero ($A = 0$). In that case the sign of the partial derivations with respect to the parameters can easily be established:

$$\frac{\partial h_x/\overline{h}_x}{\partial N}<0, \quad \frac{\partial h_x/\overline{h}_x}{\partial \xi}>0, \quad \frac{\partial h_x/\overline{h}_x}{\partial \vartheta}<0, \quad \frac{\partial h_x/\overline{h}_x}{\partial \rho}<0, \quad \frac{\partial h_x/\overline{h}_x}{\partial \sigma}>0,$$

$$\frac{\partial h_x/\overline{h}_x}{\partial \alpha_h}<0, \quad \frac{\partial h_x/\overline{h}_x}{\partial \alpha_f}<0, \quad \frac{\partial h_x/\overline{h}_x}{\partial \mu_Y}>0, \quad \frac{\partial h_x/\overline{h}_x}{\partial \mu_X}<0,$$

Table 5. Key Relationships in the Steady State

Consumption decision (Ramsey):

$$r=\vartheta+(\rho\sigma+1-\sigma)\overline{g}=\overline{r} \tag{5.1}$$

Investment decision:

$$\xi\left(h_x/\overline{h}_x\right)^{-\alpha_f}L_x/\gamma=r-(1-\alpha_h-\alpha_f)\overline{g} \tag{5.2}$$

Labor market equilibrium:

$$\overline{g}=\xi\left(h_x/\overline{h}_x\right)^{-\alpha_f}\left[\frac{L}{N}-\frac{Y_c}{h_Y N}-\left(\frac{1-\gamma+\gamma\mu_Y}{\mu_Y}\right)\frac{L_x}{\gamma}\right] \tag{5.3}$$

Equilibrium in the market for nontradables:

$$Y_c=(1-\sigma)(h_Y/\mu_Y)CP_C/w \tag{5.4}$$

Balance of payments equilibrium:

$$\mu_X NL_x/\gamma-\sigma CP_C/w=-(\overline{r}-\overline{g})A/w \tag{5.5}$$

Balance of payments regime:

$A = 0$ (balanced trade) or $A \neq 0$ (perfect capital mobility) $\tag{5.6}$

$$\frac{\partial L_x}{\partial N} < 0, \quad \frac{\partial L_x}{\partial \xi} = 0, \quad \frac{\partial L_x}{\partial \vartheta} > 0, \quad \frac{\partial L_x}{\partial \rho} > 0, \quad \frac{\partial L_x}{\partial \sigma} < 0,$$

$$\frac{\partial L_x}{\partial \alpha_h} > 0, \quad \frac{\partial L_x}{\partial \alpha_f} > 0, \quad \frac{\partial L_x}{\partial \mu_Y} > 0, \quad \frac{\partial L_x}{\partial \mu_X} < 0.$$

An increase in the number of firms (N) or a fall in R&D efficiency (ξ) leads to a lower productivity level in the exposed sector in relation to the productivity level abroad ($\bar{h}_x$). The same result is obtained if the rate of time preference (ϑ), the rate of risk aversion (ρ) or the share of income spend on tradables (σ) is raised. Spillover effects whether of domestic origin (α_h) or of foreign origin (α_h) have a negative impact on the knowledge gap. An increase in μ_Y, which can be associated with more regulation in the sheltered sector, has a positive effect on the productivity level in the exposed sector. It can be concluded that regulation in the sheltered sector helps to modernize the exposed sector. On the other hand, less intensive competition in the exposed sector leading to a higher mark-up factor (μ_X) induces a lower productivity level.

The signs of the partial derivatives with respect to employment in the production of tradables (L_x) help in explaining the results with respect to changes in the level of knowledge in the domestic economy. An increase in N reduces the size of firms in the exposed sector, which makes R&D less attractive. A rise in μ_X leads to a reduction in the production of tradables with a similar effect on R&D. A higher time preference, an increase in risk aversion or a shift in preferences towards tradables induces a higher consumption level. In this case labor is reallocated from R&D activities towards production of tradables as well as nontradables. Higher spillover effects have a negative impact on the incentive to invest in R&D. As a result some labor in R&D laboratories becomes redundant so that a reallocation towards production in both sectors becomes necessary. More regulation in the sheltered sector sets labor free for production and R&D activities in the exposed sector. Finally, it should be noted that an increase in ξ has no effect on the allocation of labor. The rise in productivity comes entirely from the increase in R&D efficiency.

In case of perfect capital mobility, the dependent economy may accumulate foreign assets. Equations (1) and (2) reveal that any level of foreign assets (A/w) can be maintained in a steady state if the long-run productivity gap and labor allocation take the appropriate value. Hence, there is a continuum of steady states. The impact of a change in real foreign assets on $h_x/\bar{h}_x$ and L_x can be found by differentiation of equations (1) and (2) with respect to the level of real foreign assets:

$$\frac{\partial h_x/\bar{h}_x}{\partial A/w} < 0, \quad \frac{\partial L_x}{\partial A/w} < 0.$$

An increase in foreign assets expressed in wage units raises capital income from abroad in real terms. Higher income boosts consumption and production of nontradables, and crowds out domestic high-tech production and R&D. Lower investment in national research results in a larger productivity gap. Alternatively, one could say that there is a tradeoff between the two assets, foreign claims and firm-specific knowledge.

The long-run equilibrium level of foreign assets is determined by history; i.e., the initial knowledge gap and all shocks during transition to the steady state. Perfect capital mobility gives rise to path-dependency, as will be shown in the next section.

4. Equilibrium Dynamics

To study the dynamics it is convenient to linearize the model around the steady state. The key relationships in linearized form are given in Table 6. Variables with a tilde relate to percentage deviations from their steady-state solutions; i.e., $\tilde{x}(t) \equiv dx(t)/x(t)$. Dependence on time index t is omitted where no confusion arises. The variable $\tilde{a}$ is defined as the absolute deviation of $A/\bar{h}_x$ from its steady-state solution; i.e., $\tilde{a} \equiv d(A/\bar{h}_x)$. The linearization procedure is explained in Appendix D.

Balanced Trade

In case of equilibrium on the current account, equation (6.6) can be simplified by setting $\dot{\tilde{a}} = \tilde{a} = 0$. The equations (6.1)–(6.6) can then be applied to derive a set of two linear differential equations in the level of knowledge (h_x) and production labor in the exposed sector (L_x). Equations (4.5)–(4.7) can be used to arrive at

$$\frac{Y_c}{h_Y N} = \frac{1-\sigma}{\sigma} \frac{\mu_X}{\mu_Y} \frac{L_x}{\gamma}. \tag{3}$$

Linearization of equation (3) implies

Table 6. Key Relationships in Linearized Form

Consumption decision (Ramsey):

$$\dot{\tilde{C}} = \frac{1}{\rho}\left[r\tilde{r} - (1-\sigma)\dot{\tilde{h}}_x + \left(\frac{1-\sigma}{\varepsilon}\right)\left(\dot{\tilde{L}}_x + \dot{\tilde{h}}_x\right)\right] \tag{6.1}$$

Investment decision:

$$r\tilde{r} = (\zeta L_x/\gamma)\left[\tilde{L}_x - \alpha_f \tilde{h}_x\right] + (1-\alpha_h)\dot{\tilde{h}}_x - (1/\varepsilon)\left(\dot{\tilde{L}}_x + \dot{\tilde{h}}_x\right) \tag{6.2}$$

Labor market equilibrium:

$$\dot{\tilde{h}}_x = -\left(\frac{\zeta Y_c}{h_Y N}\right)\left(\tilde{Y}_c - \tilde{h}_Y\right) - \left(\frac{\zeta L_x}{\gamma}\right)\left(\frac{1-\gamma+\gamma\mu_Y}{\mu_Y}\right)\tilde{L}_x + \left(\frac{\zeta L_x}{\gamma}\right)\left(\frac{1-\gamma}{\mu_Y}\right)\tilde{\mu}_Y - (\alpha_f g)\tilde{h}_x \tag{6.3}$$

Equilibrium in the (world) market for tradables:

$$\tilde{p}_x = \frac{1-\gamma}{\varepsilon}\left(\tilde{\mu}_Y - \tilde{h}_Y\right) - \frac{1}{\varepsilon}\left(\tilde{h}_x + \tilde{L}_x\right) \tag{6.4}$$

Equilibrium in the market for nontradables:

$$\tilde{Y}_c = \tilde{C} - \sigma\left(\tilde{h}_x - \frac{1}{\varepsilon}\left(h_{\tilde{x}} + \tilde{L}_x\right)\right) - \sigma\left(\gamma + \frac{1-\gamma}{\varepsilon}\right)\left(\tilde{\mu}_Y - \tilde{h}_Y\right) \tag{6.5}$$

Balance of payments equilibrium:

$$\dot{\tilde{a}} = (\tilde{r} - \tilde{g})\tilde{a} + \left(\frac{Nxp_x}{\bar{h}_x}\right)(1-\varepsilon)\tilde{p}_x - \left(\frac{\sigma CP_C}{\bar{h}_x}\right)\left[\tilde{C} + (1-\sigma)\left(\tilde{p}_x + \tilde{h}_x + \gamma\left(\tilde{\mu}_Y - \tilde{h}_Y\right)\right)\right] \tag{6.6}$$

Balance of payments regime:

$$\dot{\tilde{a}} = \tilde{a} = 0 \text{ (balanced trade)} \quad \text{or} \quad \tilde{r} = 0 \text{ (perfect capital mobility)} \tag{6.7}$$

Note: We have assumed $s \to 0$ (small country assumption) and defined $\zeta \equiv \xi\left(h_x/\bar{h}_x\right)^{-\alpha_f}$.

$$\tilde{L}_{YC} - \tilde{h}_Y = \tilde{L}_x - \tilde{\mu}_Y. \tag{4}$$

Substitution of equation (4) in (6.3), taking account of the definition of β, results in the first differential equation:

$$\dot{\tilde{h}}_x = -(\alpha_f g)\tilde{h}_x - \left(\frac{\zeta L_x}{\beta \gamma}\right)\tilde{L}_x + \left(\frac{\zeta L_x(1-\beta\gamma)}{\beta\gamma}\right)\tilde{\mu}_Y. \tag{5}$$

Substitution of equation (4) in (6.5) gives an expression for $\tilde{C}$ which can be differentiated with respect to time. Applying equations (6.1) and (6.5) to eliminate the growth rate of consumption ($\dot{\tilde{C}}$), we arrive after some manipulation at

$$\dot{\tilde{L}}_x\left(\frac{\rho(\varepsilon-\sigma)+\sigma}{\varepsilon}\right) = [\beta+\alpha_h+\sigma(\rho-1)/\mu_X]\left(\frac{\zeta L_x}{\beta\gamma}\right)\tilde{L}_x$$
$$-\alpha_f\left[\vartheta+\left(\frac{\sigma(\rho-1)}{\varepsilon}+\alpha_f\right)g\right]\tilde{h}_x$$
$$-[\alpha_h+\sigma(\rho-1)/\mu_X]\left(\frac{\zeta L_x(1-\beta\gamma)}{\beta\gamma}\right)\tilde{\mu}_Y. \tag{6}$$

From equations (5) and (6) we see that the $\dot{\tilde{h}}_x = 0$ locus slopes downward and that the $\dot{\tilde{L}}_x = 0$ locus slopes upward. Moreover, it can be easily checked that the determinant of the matrix of coefficients with respect to $\tilde{h}_x$ and $\tilde{L}_x$ is negative. Therefore, the model is saddlepoint stable. The phase diagram is shown in the left panel of Figure 1. The broken line represents the stable arm of the saddlepath which is upward-sloping as is illustrated in the figure. For an initial value of the level of knowledge, $h_x(0)$, the amount of labor allocated to the production of tradables, L_x, jumps to the stable arm. Thereafter both variables h_x and L_x adjust towards the steady state as indicated in the figure. The speed of adjustment is determined by the negative eigenvalue of the matrix of coefficients with respect to the state variables in equations (5) and (6).

More regulation in the sheltered sector goes along with an increase in μ_Y. This leads to an upward shift of the stable arm of the saddlepath as shown in the right panel of Figure 1. From equation (6.1) it appears that the rate of interest $\tilde{r}(t)$ does not change in the long run, $\tilde{r}(\infty) = 0$. Substitution of this result in equation (6.2) gives

$$\tilde{L}_x(\infty) = \alpha_f \tilde{h}_x(\infty). \tag{7}$$

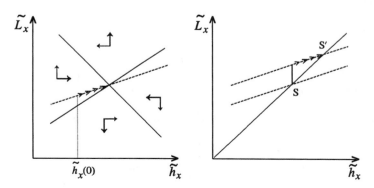

Figure 1. Balanced Trade

If the rate of interest is constant, a rise in L_x, inducing a higher rate of return on investment in R&D, has to be compensated by an increase in h_x, which lowers productivity in the R&D department. Equation (7) leads to a proportional change of both variables along the ray OS in the right panel of Figure 1. The new steady state is found at point S'. On impact of the shock, L_x jumps towards the new stable arm. From there on the economy gradually approaches the new long-run equilibrium. More regulation in the sheltered sector increases prices of nontradables relative to importables. Imports rise and domestic production has to rise in order to pay for these imports. Hence L_x jumps up on impact. Larger sales stimulate incentives for innovation and firms increase R&D efforts. As productivity levels in the exposed sector rise faster, the price of domestic tradables declines and consumers shift their consumption further away from nontradables. Whether it is optimal from a welfare point of view to increase μ_Y will be discussed in section 4.

Perfect Capital Mobility

Under perfect international capital mobility the domestic rate of interest equals the foreign rate of interest which is constant. As a consequence: $\tilde{r} = 0$. Substitution of this result in (6.1) and (6.2) along with substitution of (6.5) in (6.3) results in a system of four differential equations in C, h_x, L_x, and a. In the steady state $\dot{\tilde{C}} = \dot{\tilde{h}}_x = \dot{\tilde{L}}_x = \dot{\tilde{a}} = 0$, but that leaves us with three equations in four unknowns, because equation (6.1) with $\tilde{r} = 0$ is always satisfied. This implies that the model exhibits hysteresis: we need to know the entire transition dynamics to solve for the steady state.[3]

The information contained in equation (6.1) can be preserved by integration of this equation which yields

$$\tilde{C} = \tilde{v} - \left(\frac{1-\sigma}{\rho\varepsilon}\right)[(\varepsilon - 1)\tilde{h}_x - \tilde{L}_x], \tag{8}$$

where $\tilde{v}$ is the constant of integration, which can be interpreted as the permanent change in consumption (due to a shock that hits the economy) for given values of $\tilde{h}_x$ and $\tilde{L}_x$. Access to the international borrowing at a given rate allows for consumption smoothing in response to shocks. A shock that increases the ex-ante domestic rate of return above the international interest rate will induce borrowing in the international market at the cost of incurring a debt and the associated long-run interest burden. In this case, the long-run permanent change in consumption is negative. Indeed, in general, the permanent consumption change, or wealth effect, $\tilde{v}$, crucially depends on the size of the shock and on its impact on the development of the ex-ante domestic rate of return over time.

Equation (8) can be used to eliminate L_x from the equations in Table 6. The variable $\dot{\tilde{L}}_x$ can be eliminated by using equation (6.1). As shown in Appendix E, the model can be reduced to a system of differential equations in three state variables, which can be written in matrix notation as

$$\begin{bmatrix} \dot{\tilde{h}}_x \\ \dot{\tilde{C}} \\ \dot{\tilde{a}} \end{bmatrix} = \begin{bmatrix} a_{11} & a_{12} & 0 \\ a_{21} & a_{22} & 0 \\ a_{31} & a_{32} & r-g \end{bmatrix} \begin{bmatrix} \tilde{h}_x \\ \tilde{C} \\ \tilde{a} \end{bmatrix} + \begin{bmatrix} a_{14} & (\frac{1-\sigma}{\sigma})a_{14} & a_{16} \\ a_{24} & (\frac{1-\sigma}{\sigma})a_{24} & -a_{22} \\ a_{34} & -a_{34} & a_{36} \end{bmatrix} \begin{bmatrix} \tilde{\mu}_Y \\ \tilde{h}_Y \\ \tilde{v} \end{bmatrix}. \tag{9}$$

As explained in Appendix E, the permanent consumption effect $\tilde{v}$ can be found along with the time paths of $\tilde{h}_x$, $\tilde{C}$, and $\tilde{a}$ by imposing solvability with respect to the net foreign position and assuming $\tilde{a}(0) = 0$. Moreover, it is shown there that the dynamics of the

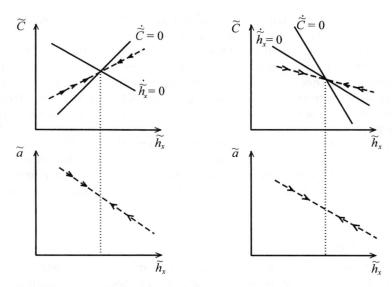

Figure 2. Capital Mobility, large α_f (left panel) and small α_f (right panel)

model can be represented by a phase diagram in $\tilde{h}_x$ and $\tilde{C}$. The slope of the stable manifold depends on the intensity of foreign spillovers and the elasticity of demand ε. For α_f larger (smaller) than $\varepsilon - 1$, consumption and productivity change in the same (opposite) direction along the transition path. The intuition behind this result is given below. The relation between net foreign assets (a) and productivity (h_x) is negative. Intuitively, investment in domestic knowledge and investment in foreign assets are substitutes. The two-panel diagrams in Figure 2 depict the relations among the three state variables $\tilde{h}_x$, $\tilde{C}$, and $\tilde{a}$ for a large and a small value of α_f, respectively. The broken curve in both figures indicates the stable arm of the saddlepath with respect to $\tilde{h}_x$ and $\tilde{C}$.

In order to gain some insight into the time path of consumption, we combine equations (7) and (8), which results in

$$\tilde{C}(0) - \tilde{C}(\infty) = \frac{1-\sigma}{\rho\varepsilon}[(\varepsilon - 1 - \alpha_f)\tilde{h}_x(\infty) + \tilde{L}_x(0)]. \qquad (10)$$

The initial jump in high-tech employment ($\tilde{L}_x$) can be derived from (6.2)[4] and substituted into (10), which yields

$$\tilde{C}(0) - \tilde{C}(\infty) = \frac{1-\sigma}{\rho}\left[\eta\alpha_h + (1-\eta)\left(\frac{\varepsilon - 1 - \alpha_f}{\varepsilon}\right)\right]\tilde{h}_x(\infty), \qquad (11)$$

where $\eta \equiv -\lambda/[\varepsilon(\zeta L_x/\gamma) - \lambda]$ and $\lambda < 0$ is the stable root of the dynamic model.

Equation (11) shows that the timing of consumption depends crucially on the balance between the elasticity of demand for exportables (ε) and spillover parameters. If α_f is small relative to $\varepsilon - 1$, consumption grows less over time; i.e., $\tilde{C}(0) > \tilde{C}(\infty)$. In other words, consumers wait to save and draw a bill on the future. The reason is that consumer prices tend to rise over time. Note that only prices of nontradables matter for the consumer price index, since the share of home-produced tradables in total tradables consumption of the small open economy is negligible. Prices of nontradables depend on wage costs. Higher productivity in the exposed sector drives up wage costs for the sheltered sector. Price increases in this sector fuel consumer price inflation[5]

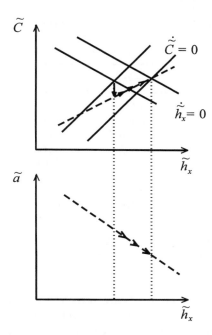

Figure 3. Increase in μ_Y

which makes it attractive to consume now rather than in future. However, if α_f is large, a counterforce becomes important. Employment and production in the tradables sector will increase substantially in response to productivity changes (see (7)), which lowers the price of tradables. Consequently, wage costs fall, and the consumer price index falls. Note that the price fall in response to a productivity improvement is steeper the lower the price elasticity ε is. Hence, if α_f is large relative to ε, consumption levels will rise over time (more than in the initial steady state), and if α_f is small relative to ε, consumption will rise less over time.

The effects of an increase in μ_Y are illustrated in Figure 3 for the case $\alpha_f > \varepsilon - 1$. The $\dot{\tilde{h}}_x = 0$ locus shifts upward and the $\dot{\tilde{C}} = 0$ locus shifts downward. These shifts imply a downward movement of the stable arm of the saddlepath. On impact of the shock consumption declines, but as productivity in the exposed sector improves consumption goes up again. The amount of foreign assets declines, because consumers incur foreign debt to smooth consumption over time.[6]

The picture shown in Figure 3 is merely an illustration, because the shift of the $\dot{\tilde{h}}_x = 0$ locus and the $\dot{\tilde{C}} = 0$ locus cannot be directly determined from (9) as $\tilde{v}$ has to be solved for first. To get a better understanding of the implications of a change in μ_Y, numerical examples may therefore be useful.

5. Numerical Examples

Although in case of balanced trade the model can be solved analytically, it is instructive to compare numerical results under both regimes with respect to the balance of payments. The parameter values for the reference path are equal to:[7]

$$\rho = 2, \vartheta = 0.03, \sigma = 0.8, \varepsilon = 2.5, \alpha_h = 0.5, \alpha_f = 0.4, \xi = 0.01, \gamma = 0.8, \mu_Y = 1.1,$$
$$h_Y = 1, L = 82.4, n = 25, N = \overline{N} = 8, \overline{g} = 1.877\%.$$

Table 7. Catching-up $\tilde{h}_x(0) = -1$

Variable	Balanced trade		Capital mobility	
	$t = 0$	$t \to \infty$	$t = 0$	$t \to \infty$
Price tradables $\tilde{p}_x$	0.440	0.000	0.550	−0.248
Productivity $\tilde{h}_x$	−1.000	0.000	−1.000	0.444
Growth rate $\tilde{g}$	0.850	0.000	1.622	0.000
Consumption $\tilde{C}$	−0.562	0.000	−0.386	−0.438
Tradables cons. $\tilde{X}_c$	−0.677	0.000	−0.480	−0.397
Non-tradables cons. $\tilde{Y}_c$	−0.100	0.000	−0.009	−0.602
Labor tradables $\tilde{L}_x$	−0.100	0.000	−0.374	0.175
Rate of interest $\tilde{r}$	0.416	0.000	0.000	0.000
Foreign assets $\tilde{a}$	—	—	0.000	−5.102
Rate of convergence $|\lambda|$ (%)	1.596		2.109	

In the reference path, net foreign assets are zero. The calculations presented for both regimes are percentage deviations from this reference path. Because the time paths of the variables are monotonic it is sufficient to present results for the periods $t = 0$ and $t = \infty$.

Catching-up

Catching-up occurs when the level of knowledge in relation to the foreign level lies below the steady-state values. In a linearized version of the model this boils down to a negative deviation of $h_x/\bar{h}_x$ from its (future) steady-state level. The outcomes in case the initial level of knowledge in the domestic economy lies 1% below its steady-state value under balanced trade are given in Table 7.

Under balanced trade the system converges to a unique steady state. Catching-up implies a rise in the knowledge level and a temporary higher rate of growth of total factor productivity in the exposed sector. As a result of this process, consumption of tradables and nontradables rises. The initial rate of interest lies above the world level. This makes it attractive for firms to employ a large share of employment in R&D initially. As the level of knowledge approaches its steady-state level the rate of interest converges towards the level prevailing in the rest of the world. In the steady state both rates of interest should be equal because the rates of growth are then equal and consumer preferences are assumed to be the same everywhere—equation (5.1).

In case of perfect international capital mobility there is an inflow of foreign capital to equate interest rates in every period. Consumers as a group are in a position to borrow abroad in order to smooth consumption over time. The preference for current consumption implies that consumption declines over time, in contrast with the case of balanced trade. In the long run, consumers have to service foreign debt, incurred in the course of the transition to a new steady state. Long-run consumption is lower than under balanced trade. Therefore, less labor needs to be allocated to produce nontradable consumption goods. More labor is allocated to tradables production which increases firm size. R&D becomes more attractive, and the level of productivity rises above the steady-state level attained under balanced trade ($\tilde{h}_x(\infty) > 0$).

There is no unique steady-state solution under capital mobility for a given set of structural parameters. If the economy starts at a level of knowledge which is 2% below the value attained in the steady state under balanced trade, all results for $t = \infty$ in case of capital mobility double. Therefore, productivity levels are path-dependent and convergence of countries in terms of productivity levels depends on initial positions. This result flies in the face of the standard views on convergence in neoclassical theory. Moreover, most of this literature is based on the notion of a closed economy (e.g., Barro and Sala-i-Martin, 1995). If capital mobility is assumed in a neoclassical context the economy jumps instantaneously to its unique steady-state levels. Physical capital is imported so as to equate the marginal product of capital with the going rate of interest on world capital markets. Partial international mobility of capital, in the sense that physical capital can be used as collateral for international borrowing but human capital cannot, gives standard neoclassical results with the economy adjusting gradually to its unique long-run equilibrium (cf. Barro et al., 1995).

Path-dependency of consumption levels is a well-known feature of small open economies. In response to adverse temporary domestic shocks, foreign borrowing allows consumers to mitigate the short-run fall in consumption, at the cost of higher debt service and lower long-run consumption. In a one-sector economy, the accumulation of capital is not affected as long as the supply of other factors of production (labor) remains the same so that the physical marginal productivity of capital is not affected (cf. Blanchard and Fisher, 1989, p. 66). However, if the path-dependent change in consumption affects both tradable and nontradable production, as in our model, the allocation of labor over the two sectors is permanently affected. Then also the incentives to accumulate capital in the different sectors of the economy are permanently affected, which results in a long-run change in the domestic capital stock. (See in this connection also Turnovsky and Sen (1991, 1995).)

Increasing Regulation

Table 8 presents the results of a 1% permanent rise in μ_Y. This corresponds to a change in regulation such that a smaller number of firms is allowed to operate in the nontradable sector. An increase of the mark-up factor in the sheltered sector induces a fall in output and employment on impact of the shock. Labor is relocated from the sheltered to the exposed sector so that R&D becomes more attractive.

Under balanced trade the interest rate rises to generate the necessary savings. This implies that the level of consumption declines in the short run. Productivity in the tradables sector rises over time. The additional products can be sold, because the rise in productivity allows for a reduction in prices. The increase in knowledge reduces the rate of return on investment, and in the long run the rate of interest falls back to its original level as does the rate of growth. However, the long-run consumption level increases because of a rise in productivity in the exposed sector.

In case of capital mobility, consumption goes up in the short run and the economy runs a balance-of-trade deficit. The inflow of capital is sufficient to keep the rate of interest at the level in the outside world. Compared with the case of balanced trade, there is now less need to increase the production of tradables at $t = 0$. As a consequence there is more labor available for R&D activities and the level of productivity in the exposed sector rises faster than under balanced trade as appears from the rate of growth. The increase in foreign debt induces a burden in the long run. In the new steady state the economy must run a trade surplus to service debt. Compared with the

Table 8. *Increasing Regulation* ($\tilde{\mu}_Y = 1$)

Variable	Balanced trade		Capital mobility	
	$t = 0$	$t = \infty$	$t = 0$	$t = \infty$
Price tradables $\tilde{p}_x$	−0.021	−0.392	0.071	−0.601
Productivity $\tilde{h}_x$	0.000	0.842	0.000	1.216
Growth rate $\tilde{g}$	0.716	0.000	1.367	0.000
Consumption $\tilde{C}$	−0.124	0.350	0.024	−0.020
Tradables cons. $\tilde{X}_c$	0.032	0.603	0.198	0.268
Non-tradables cons. $\tilde{Y}_c$	−0.748	−0.663	−0.670	−1.170
Labor tradables $\tilde{L}_x$	0.252	0.337	0.022	0.486
Rate of interest $\tilde{r}$	0.350	0.000	0.000	0.000
Foreign assets $\tilde{a}$	—	—	0.000	−4.298
Intertemporal welfare $\tilde{U}$	+0.000	0.350	0.010	−0.020
Rate of convergence $|\lambda|$ (%)	1.596		2.109	

balanced-trade regime, long-run consumption both of tradables and nontradables is lower, while productivity in the exposed sector is higher.

Despite increased regulation, intertemporal welfare calculated at time zero rises under both regimes. Whether this conclusion is robust will be investigated below.

Welfare considerations   Changes in welfare depend on the initial value of μ_Y. This can be shown by a sensitivity analysis with respect to the mark-up factor in the sheltered sector in the initial steady state. Figure 4 presents the results. On the horizontal axis is the initial value of μ_Y. On the vertical axis is the change in intertemporal welfare as a result of a small increase in μ_Y. Welfare is the present discounted value of consumption as of the period of the policy shock. The optimal value μ_Y^* for which the change in welfare equals zero exceeds unity in both balance of payment regimes.

Optimal mark-up rates are lower than in a closed economy without growth where welfare is not distorted if mark-up rates are equal across sectors. This would imply $\mu_Y^* = \mu_X = \varepsilon/(\varepsilon - 1) = 1.67$ in this example. In the open economy, a rise in μ_Y induces an expansion of the tradables sector and a loss in the terms of trade as more goods have to be sold abroad. Therefore the optimal mark-up rate in the nontradables sector has to be lower than the mark-up rate prevailing in the tradables sector. Indeed, it can be proven that a value of μ_Y that equals $\mu_X(\varepsilon - 1)/\varepsilon$ (= 1) maximizes national welfare of the small open economy without growth by optimally trading off terms of trade gains and domestic price distortions.[8]

Next, growth effects should be taken into account in the determination of the welfare-maximizing value of μ_Y. Because of knowledge spillovers, high-tech firms invest too little in R&D. When μ_Y is raised, demand for high-tech products increases which boosts the rate of return to innovation. Hence, higher mark-ups in the sheltered sector provide a second-best instrument to compensate the dynamic distortion in the exposed sector.[9]

Finally, the balance-of-payment regime plays a role. Capital mobility provides an additional reason to regulate the sheltered sector. Under capital mobility, regulating the sheltered sector is a more efficient instrument to compensate the knowledge externality than under balanced trade, so that the optimal μ_Y is larger under the former

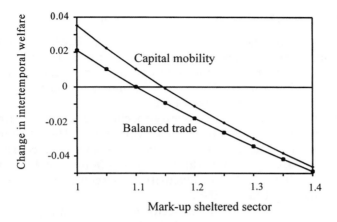

Figure 4. Welfare Effects of Deregulation

regime than under the latter one. Stimulating investment is less costly when the supply of foreign savings is perfectly elastic. In contrast, when trade has to be balanced, increasing μ_Y results in temporarily high rates of interest which impose an intertemporal welfare cost. In the absence of national knowledge spillovers ($\alpha_h = 0$), both regimes call for zero regulation ($\mu_Y = 1$).[10]

Excessive regulation (policies that set μ_Y above μ_Y^*) bring about welfare losses. Figure 4 shows that the welfare losses are smaller in the regime of capital mobility than in the regime of balanced trade if regulation is modest. However, if the sheltered sector is heavily regulated (that is, if $\mu_Y \gg 1.4$, not shown in Figure 4), balanced trade performs better. First note that under capital mobility, the optimal level of regulation is higher, so that starting from modestly high μ_Y society still reaps welfare gains by regulating under capital mobility, while under balanced trade it incurs losses. However, note also that welfare is more sensitive to regulation under capital mobility than under balanced trade (compare the slope of the two curves in Figure 4). Supply of funds is perfectly elastic which allows investment to be more sensitive to changes in innovation incentives. Excess regulation creates overaccumulation of the national knowledge stock and expansion of tradables that is larger than under balanced trade. The associated larger deterioration in the terms of trade makes capital mobility perform worse.

X-inefficiency Returning to regulation, it is often argued that regulation in the sheltered sector induces X-inefficiency. In our model a change in X-inefficiency can be introduced in the form of an autonomous change of labor productivity in the sheltered sector (h_Y). A rise in h_Y leads to an immediate decline in consumption levels, but has no effect on the accumulation of knowledge. This can easily be checked in case of balanced trade. Inspection of the equations (5) and (6) reveals that there is no term in $\tilde{h}_Y$. A similar result holds in case of capital mobility as appears from numerical simulation of the system of equations in (9). Intuitively, a decline in output of nontradables caused by a fall in labor productivity induces a proportional increase in the price of these goods. This induces a proportial decline of the demand for nontradables. This implies that there is no need for a reallocation of labor. Consumption of tradables also declines, because producers apply less nontradables in the production process. The welfare consequences of induced X-inefficiency, if any, have to be taken into account in a final assessment of regulation in the sheltered section.

6. Conclusions

Emerging economies are able to catch up by investing in R&D. The larger the knowledge gap, the higher the rate of return and the faster growth. The international capital market can boost convergence because additional investment can be financed without inducing a rise in the interest rate. This allows consumers to take an advance on future welfare by smoothing consumption over time.

Under capital mobility, temporary country-specific shocks have permanent effects on net foreign asset positions and productivity (hysteresis). Hence, countries that are symmetric in economic structure and in technological and social capability may hold different net foreign asset positions which result in different total factor productivity levels. This may explain the lack of productivity convergence in exposed sectors of the economy (cf. Bernard and Jones, 1996).

In developing countries, the sheltered sector may be operating on the basis of traditional rules and norms. As a result, the absence of perfectly competitive markets may cause mark-up rates to be substantial in this sector. Deregulation would lower mark-up rates. However, national economic policies that deliberately abstain from reducing high mark-up rates in the sheltered sector of the economy may boost national productivity growth. Such a strategy may offset dynamic distortions in the economy because of knowledge spillovers, so that regulation in the sheltered sector may improve welfare.

However, when mark-up rates in the sheltered sector become too large, welfare losses will occur. Productivity growth in the dynamic exposed sector of the economy will be high, but at the cost of severe price distortions. Capital flows will exacerbate the overaccumulation of capital, so that welfare losses are larger under capital mobility than under balanced trade. International capital mobility aggrevates policy mistakes. National policy authorities may therefore adopt capital flow restrictions in small open economies in order to mitigate the adverse welfare effects of mistakes in regulation.

Appendix

A. Solving for Price Variables

With symmetric firms within the country, all domestic firms charge the same price and consumption levels of any good from a certain country are the same. The foreign price of high-tech goods is taken as the *numéraire*. Hence, $p_{xi} = p_x$ for all i, $x_{ci} = x_c$ for all i, $\bar{p}_{xj} = 1$ for all j and all t. The value share of home-produced high-tech goods in total high-tech consumption, s, can be found from (2.6) and (2.7):

$$s \equiv \frac{N x_c p_x}{N x_c p_x + n \bar{N} \bar{x}_c \bar{p}_x} = \frac{1}{1 + (n\bar{N}/N)p_x^{\varepsilon-1}}. \tag{A.1}$$

The small-open-economy assumption implies that N is negligible relative to $n\bar{N}$, so that $s \to 0$. Hence, the consumer price index P_C depends on P_Y and $\bar{p}_x$ only. We find an expression for P_Y by eliminating w between (3.7) and (3.5):

$$P_Y = (p_x h_x/\mu_x)(\mu_Y/h_Y)^{\gamma} \gamma^{-\gamma}(1-\gamma)^{\gamma-1}. \tag{A.2}$$

From (2.8), (A.2), the small-country assumption ($s \to 0$), and the choice of *numéraire* ($\bar{p} = 1$ for all t), we find, using hats to denote growth rates:

$$\hat{P}_C = (1-\sigma)(\hat{h}_x + \hat{p}_x). \tag{A.3}$$

We assume that preferences are homothetic and equal across the world. This means that any pair of goods is consumed everywhere in the same ratio as it is produced:

$$x_c/\overline{x}_c = x_{\overline{c}}/\overline{x}_{\overline{c}} = x/\overline{x} = p_x^{-\varepsilon}. \tag{A.4}$$

where the last equality follows from (2.6) and (2.7).

Combining (1.5), (3.4) and (3.7), we find

$$x = h_x L_x [h_Y(1-\gamma)/\gamma\mu_Y]^{1-\gamma}, \tag{A.5}$$

which holds also for foreign variables. Substitution of (A.5) in (A.4) gives

$$p_x = \left(\frac{h_x}{\overline{h}_x}\frac{L_x}{\overline{L}_x}\right)^{-1/\varepsilon}\left(\frac{\mu_Y/h_Y}{\overline{\mu}_Y/\overline{h}_Y}\right)^{(1-\gamma)/\varepsilon}, \tag{A.6}$$

$$\hat{p}_x = (\overline{g} - \hat{h}_x - \hat{L}_x)/\varepsilon, \tag{A.7}$$

where we have assumed that balanced growth prevails in the rest of the world so that $\overline{L}_x$ is constant.

B. Key Relationships (Table 4)

Table 4 contains seven key relationships of the model in the variables C, r, h_x, L_x, Y_c, p_x, P_C, w, and A. This section explains how to derive these semireduced forms. In the next sections of the appendix, we use the results, first, to characterize the steady state, and, second, to linearize the model and study the dynamics.

We derive the Ramsey equation in (4.1) by combining (2.4), (A.3) and (A.7).

The equation that characterizes the investment decision is found by substitution of the appropriate equations in equation (3.6). First, divide the equation by p_{hi}. Eliminate x, p_x, and p_{hi} in the first term by substituting (3.3), (A.5), and (3.5) respectively. Eliminate L_{ri} in the second term by substituting (1.6). The rate of change of the price of knowledge that appears in the third term can be rewritten as $\hat{p}_h = \hat{p}_x + \alpha_f(\hat{h}_x - \overline{g})$ by differentiating (3.5) with respect to time, taking into account that $h_x = H$, and using (3.3) and (3.7) to eliminate $\hat{w}$. We find (4.2) when we finally substitute (A.7) to eliminate $\hat{p}_x$ and introduce the definition

$$\zeta \equiv \xi K_i/h_{xi} = \xi(h_x/\overline{h}_x)^{-\alpha_f}, \tag{B.1}$$

where the last equality follows from the symmetry assumption.

The labor market equation in (4.3) is derived as follows. From equations (3.4) and (3.7), we find

$$NY_x/h_Y = (1-\gamma)NL_x/\gamma\mu_Y. \tag{B.2}$$

Substituting (1.4), (1.8), (B.1), and (B.2) into (1.7), we find (4.3).

Equation (4.4) replicates (A.6). Equation (4.5) is found by combination of equations (2.5), (3.7) and (1.4).

In order to find the balance of payments equation, we substitute (2.3), (2.2) and (2.5) into (1.10), take into account symmetry, and find

$$Nxp_x - \sigma CP_C = \dot{A} - \overline{r}A. \tag{B.3}$$

Eliminating x and p_x, by substituting (A.5) and (3.3) respectively, we arrive at (4.6).

C. Steady State (Table 5)

The steady state is characterized (defined) by constant growth rates. Equation (4.3) implies that L_x, Y_c and $h_x/\bar{h}_x$ should be constant. It can be checked from (4.5) and (4.6) that A/w should be constant. Hence, in the steady state we may write

$$\dot{L}_x = \dot{Y}_c = 0, \quad \hat{h}_x = \hat{\bar{h}}_x \equiv \bar{g}, \quad \hat{A} = \hat{w}. \tag{C.1}$$

Then it follows from (4.4) and from (A.3), (A.5), (A.2), (3.7), and (4.5) respectively that

$$\hat{p}_x = 0, \tag{C.2}$$

$$\bar{g} = \hat{P}_C/(1-\sigma) = \hat{x} = \hat{P}_Y = \hat{w} = \hat{C}/\sigma. \tag{C.3}$$

Substituting (C.1)–(C.3) into the key relationships in Table 4, we find their steady-state counterparts which are displayed in Table 5.

D. Linearization of the Model (Table 6)

The purpose of this section is to find the linearized version of the model in terms of the four main variables, viz. h_x, L_x, c, and a, and three variables of secondary interest, viz. p, r, Y_c. We introduce the variable $a \equiv A/\bar{h}_{xi}\bar{p}_{xi}$ (which equals $a = A/\bar{h}_x$ by our choice of the *numéraire*) which should be interpreted as the ratio of net foreign assets to domestic assets. We choose this variable because it is a predetermined variable (note that the ratio A/w which is used in section 3 is not), which allows us to exploit the condition $da(0) \equiv \tilde{a}(0) = 0$. Our linearization procedure involves taking total differentiation, where all parameters except μ_Y and h_Y are considered as constants. Tilded variables are expressed as relative deviations from the initial balanced growth path; i.e., for any variable u, $\tilde{u} \equiv du/u$ or $du = u\tilde{u}$, so that $d\hat{u} = \dot{\tilde{u}}$. An exception is $\tilde{a}$ which is defined as the absolute (rather than relative) deviation from the original growth path; i.e., $\tilde{a} \equiv da$ and $d\dot{a} = \dot{\tilde{a}}$, which allows us to consider the situation in which $A = a = 0$ initially (balanced trade).

Equations (6.1)–(6.4) follow directly from linearization of equations (4.1)–(4.4). In order to find equation (6.5), we first linearize (4.5). The resulting equation contains terms with $\tilde{P}_C - \tilde{w}$, which we want to eliminate. In order to find an expression for $\tilde{P}_C - \tilde{w}$, first note from (2.8), (2.9), the symmetry assumption, the small-country assumption ($s \to 0$), and the choice of the *numéraire* ($\bar{p}_x = 1$) that

$$\tilde{P}_C = (1-\sigma)\tilde{P}_Y. \tag{D.1}$$

Linearization of (3.7) and (3.3) gives

$$\tilde{w} = \tilde{h}_x + \tilde{p}_x - (1-\gamma)(\tilde{\mu}_Y - \tilde{h}_Y), \tag{D.2}$$

$$\tilde{P}_Y = \tilde{w} + \tilde{\mu}_Y - \tilde{h}_Y. \tag{D.3}$$

Linearizing (4.5) and substituting (D.1)–(D.3), and (6.4), we find (6.5).

In order to find a convenient balance-of-payments relationship, we divide (4.5) by $\bar{h}_x$ and rewrite the equation in terms of $a \equiv A/\bar{h}_x$ instead of A:

$$Nxp_x/\bar{h}_x - \sigma CP_C/\bar{h}_x = \dot{a} + \bar{g}a - \bar{r}a.$$

Linearizing this expression (recalling our definition $\tilde{a} \equiv da$), substituting (D.1)–(D.3) to eliminate $\tilde{P}_C$ and $\tilde{w}$, and substituting (6.4), we arrive at (6.6).

The six equations (6.1)–(6.6) contain seven variables ($\tilde{w}$, $\tilde{r}$, $\tilde{C}$, $\tilde{L}_x$, $\tilde{h}_x$, $\tilde{Y}_c$, $\tilde{a}$). The equation that completes the system depends on which of the two balance-of-payments regimes applies. Equation (6.7) summarizes the two regimes.

E. Solving the Dynamics under Perfect Capital Mobility

Representation of the model by three differential equations   Substitution of (6.4), (6.5) and (6.7) into (6.1)–(6.3) and (6.6) yields a system of four differential equations in the variables $\tilde{c}$, $\tilde{L}_x$, $\tilde{h}_x$, and $\tilde{a}$. As explained in the main text, the dynamic system exhibits hysteresis and we need to further reduce the system. To this end we take the integral of (6.1) with $\tilde{r} = 0$. It gives the expression that allows us to eliminate L_x:

$$\tilde{L}_x = [\rho\varepsilon/(1-\sigma)](\tilde{C}-\tilde{v})+(\varepsilon-1)\tilde{h}_x, \tag{E.1}$$

where $\tilde{v}$ is the constant of integration. Using this result to eliminate $\tilde{L}_x$ and $\dot{\tilde{L}}_x$ in (6.2), we find (for $\tilde{r} = 0$):

$$\dot{\tilde{C}} = \left(\frac{\zeta L_x}{\gamma}\right)\left[\varepsilon(\tilde{C}-\tilde{v})+\left(\frac{(1-\sigma)(\varepsilon-1-\alpha_f)}{\rho}\right)\tilde{h}_x\right]-\frac{\alpha_h(1-\sigma)}{\rho}\dot{\tilde{h}}_x. \tag{E.2}$$

The elimination of $\tilde{Y}_c$ between (6.3) and (6.5) and substitution of (E.1) in the resulting expression gives the expression for $\dot{\tilde{h}}_x$. Since we want to compare the regime of perfect capital mobility to that of balanced trade, we linearize around an initial steady state without net foreign assets. Hence we may substitute equation (3) from the main text. The resulting expression is displayed in the matrix in (9) in the main text. The coefficients are defined as

$$a_{11} = -\left(\frac{\zeta L_x}{\gamma}\right)\left(\frac{1-\gamma+\gamma\mu_Y}{\mu_Y}\right)(\varepsilon-1)-\alpha_f g \qquad <0$$

$$a_{12} = -\left(\frac{\zeta L_x}{\gamma}\right)\left[\left(\frac{1-\gamma+\gamma\mu_Y}{\mu_Y}\right)\left(\frac{\rho}{1-\sigma}\right)\varepsilon+\left(\frac{1-\sigma}{\sigma}\right)\left(\frac{\mu_X}{\mu_Y}\right)\left(\frac{\sigma\rho+1-\sigma}{1-\sigma}\right)\right] \qquad <0$$

$$a_{16} = \left(\frac{\zeta L_x}{\gamma}\right)\left[\left(\frac{1-\gamma+\gamma\mu_Y}{\mu_Y}\right)\left(\frac{\rho}{1-\sigma}\right)\varepsilon+\left(\frac{1-\sigma}{\sigma}\right)\left(\frac{\mu_X}{\mu_Y}\right)\left(\frac{\sigma\rho}{1-\sigma}\right)\right] \qquad >0$$

$$a_{14} = \left(\frac{\zeta L_x}{\gamma}\right)\left(\frac{(1-\sigma)\mu_X+\sigma(1-\gamma)}{\mu_Y}\right) \qquad >0$$

$$a_{21} = -\alpha_h a_{11}(1-\sigma)/\rho+(\zeta L_x/\gamma)(\varepsilon-1-\alpha_f)(1-\sigma)/\rho \qquad ?$$

$$a_{22} = -\alpha_h a_{12}(1-\sigma)/\rho+(\zeta L_x/\gamma)\varepsilon \qquad >0$$

$$a_{24} = -\alpha_h a_{14}(1-\sigma)/\rho \qquad <0$$

$$a_{31} = (Nxp_x/\bar{h}_x)(\varepsilon-1) \qquad >0$$

$$a_{32} = (Nxp_x/\bar{h}_x)[\rho(\varepsilon-\sigma)/(1-\sigma)-1] \qquad >0$$

$$a_{36} = -(Nxp_x/\bar{h}_x)\rho(\varepsilon-\sigma)/(1-\sigma) \qquad <0$$

$$a_{34} = -(Nxp_x/\bar{h}_x)[(1-\sigma)\mu_X+\sigma(1-\gamma)]/\mu_X \qquad <0$$

Finally we derive a differential equation for net foreign assets a. Use (E.1) to eliminate $\tilde{L}_x$ in (6.6). Under the condition of zero initial net foreign assets, this gives the third differential equation in (9).

Solving the dynamic system   From (9) and the initial conditions for the predetermined variables h_x and a, we have to solve the time paths of $\tilde{h}_x$, $\tilde{c}$, and $\tilde{a}$, and the unknown constant $\tilde{v}$.

To start with, note that the first two differential equations can be solved independently of $\tilde{a}$. In particular, we can draw a phase diagram in an $\tilde{h}, \tilde{C}$ plane. Saddlepoint stability applies under mild conditions (if downward-sloping, the $\dot{C} = 0$ locus should be less steep than the $\dot{h}_x = 0$ locus, which is violated only for very small values of ρ). Two possibilities arise because of the ambiguous sign of a_{21}. If α_f is large, a_{21} is negative, implying that the $\dot{C} = 0$ locus and the stable manifold slope upward (a sufficient condition is $\alpha_f > \varepsilon - 1$). If α_f is small, the $\dot{C} = 0$ locus and the stable manifold slope downward.

Ignoring the third differential equation, we can solve $\tilde{h}_x$ and $\tilde{C}$ as a function of time t, the unknown constant $\tilde{v}$, and the given shocks to the system $\tilde{h}_x^0$, $\tilde{\mu}_Y$, and $\tilde{h}_Y$, where $\tilde{h}_x^0$ is the predetermined value for $\tilde{h}_x$ on time zero. Denoting the vector of these shocks by $\tilde{z}$, and the stable (negative) root by λ, we can express the solutions as

$$\tilde{h}_x = \tilde{h}_x(t, \tilde{v}, \tilde{z}) = e^{\lambda t} \cdot \tilde{h}_x^0 + (1 - e^{\lambda t}) \cdot \tilde{h}_x(\infty, \tilde{v}, \tilde{z}), \tag{E.3}$$

$$\tilde{C} = \tilde{C}(t, \tilde{v}, \tilde{z}) = e^{\lambda t} \cdot \tilde{C}(0, \tilde{v}, \tilde{z}) + (1 - e^{\lambda t}) \cdot \tilde{C}(\infty, \tilde{v}, \tilde{z}). \tag{E.4}$$

We now make explicit the dependence of solutions not only on t but also on the shocks $\tilde{z}$ and on $\tilde{v}$.

Next we have to solve for $\tilde{a}$ and $\tilde{v}$. To this end we use the third differential equation and two natural restrictions on the value of net foreign assets $\tilde{a}$. First, we impose the condition that the long-run value of a is finite. The country has to be solvent: an exploding foreign debt ("Ponzi-game", $a \to -\infty$) should be excluded. The transversality condition rules out an infinitely large net foreign asset position ($a \to \infty$). Second, we impose that net foreign assets are a predetermined variable: $\tilde{a}(0, \tilde{v}, \tilde{z}) = \tilde{a}^0$, where $\tilde{a}^0 = 0$.

The procedure is as follows. We substitute the solutions for $\tilde{h}_x$ and $\tilde{C}$ in the third differential equation. The resulting differential equation in $\tilde{a}$ and the constants $\tilde{\mu}_Y$, $\tilde{h}_Y$, and $\tilde{v}$ can be solved. Imposing the conditions that a is finite for $t \to \infty$ and that $\tilde{a} = 0$ for $t = 0$, we find a relation between $\tilde{h}^0$, $\tilde{\mu}_Y$, $\tilde{h}_Y$, and $\tilde{v}$ which is the solution for $\tilde{v}$. To simplify notation, write the third differential equation in (10) as

$$\dot{\tilde{a}} = (r - g)\tilde{a} + \tilde{x},$$

where

$$\tilde{x} = \tilde{x}(t, \tilde{v}, \tilde{z}) \equiv a_{31}\tilde{h}_x(t, \tilde{v}, \tilde{z}) + a_{32}\tilde{C}(t, \tilde{v}, \tilde{z}) + a_{34}(\tilde{\mu}_Y - \tilde{h}_Y) + a_{36}\tilde{v}. \tag{E.5}$$

Substituting the solutions for $\tilde{h}_x$ and $\tilde{C}$, we can write

$$\dot{\tilde{a}}(t, \tilde{v}, \tilde{z}) = (r - g) \cdot \tilde{a}(t, \tilde{v}, \tilde{z}) + e^{\lambda t} \cdot [\tilde{x}(0, \tilde{v}, \tilde{z}) - \tilde{x}(\infty, \tilde{v}, \tilde{z})] + \tilde{x}(\infty, \tilde{v}, \tilde{z}). \tag{E.6}$$

Integrating and imposing the no-Ponzi game condition, we arrive at

$$\tilde{a}(t, \tilde{v}, \tilde{z}) = \left[\frac{\tilde{x}(\infty, \tilde{v}, \tilde{z}) - \tilde{x}(0, \tilde{v}, \tilde{z})}{r - g - \lambda} - \frac{\tilde{x}(\infty, \tilde{v}, \tilde{z})}{r - g} \right] e^{\lambda t} + \left[\frac{-\tilde{x}(\infty, \tilde{v}, \tilde{z})}{r - g} \right] (1 - e^{\lambda t}). \tag{E.7}$$

The expression in the first brackets equals $\tilde{a}(0, \tilde{v}, \tilde{z})$ which should be equal to zero. From this equality, $\tilde{v}$ is solved in terms of the vector of exogenous shocks $\tilde{z}$.

The lower panel in Figures 2 and 3 in the main text is found in the following way. First, find the relation between $\tilde{C}$ and $\tilde{h}_x$ along the stable manifold by substituting $\dot{\tilde{C}}(t, \tilde{v}, \tilde{z}) = \lambda[\tilde{C}(t, \tilde{v}, \tilde{z}) - \tilde{C}(\infty, \tilde{v}, \tilde{z})]$ into the second differential equation. Next, substitute the resulting expression and the relation $\dot{\tilde{a}} = -\lambda\tilde{a}(\infty, \tilde{v}, \tilde{z})$ in the third differential equation. This gives an expression for $\tilde{a}(t, \tilde{v}, \tilde{z})$ as the sum of a term multiplied by $\tilde{h}_x$ and a term involving constants. With $\tilde{a}(0, \tilde{v}, \tilde{z}) = 0$, this constant should be zero (in fact this is an alternative way to find $\tilde{v}$). The term premultiplying $\tilde{h}_x$ is the slope of the stable manifold depicting the relation between a and h_x. We find this slope to be equal to $(a_{21}a_{32} - a_{22}a_{31} + \lambda a_{31})/(\lambda - a_{22})(\lambda - (r - g))$, which is most likely to be negative.

F. Welfare

Welfare at time $t = 0$ (see equation (1.1)) can be written as

$$W(t) = \left(\frac{1}{1-\rho}\right)C(t)^{1-\rho}\int_t^\infty e^{-R(S)}ds,$$

where R is the cumulative growth-corrected discount rate, defined as

$$R(s) \equiv \int_0^s \left[\vartheta + (\rho-1)\cdot\hat{C}(\tau)\right]d\tau.$$

Hence, welfare depends on the time path of consumption, captured by $C(t)$ and $\hat{C}$. Taking total differentials, solving the resulting integrals by using the fact that all variables develop monotonically with speed of adjustment λ (see (E.4)), and taking into account that consumption grows at rate σg in the steady state, we derive for welfare at $t = 0$:

$$\left(\frac{1}{1-\rho}\right)\frac{dW(t)}{W(t)} \equiv \tilde{W}(t) = \tilde{C}(t) + \left(\frac{\lambda}{\vartheta + (\rho-1)\sigma g - \lambda}\right)[\tilde{C}(t) - \tilde{C}(\infty)].$$

$\tilde{W}$ is defined as $\tilde{W} \equiv dW/[(1 - \rho)W]$, so that $\tilde{W} > 0$ if welfare rises. (Note that $W < (>)0$ if $\rho > (<)1$.)

References

Barro, Robert J. and Xavier Sala-i-Martin, *Economic Growth*, New York: McGraw Hill (1995).

———, "Technological Diffusion, Convergence, and Growth," *Journal of Economic Growth* 2 (1997):1–26.

Barro, Robert J., N. Gregory Mankiw, and Xavier Sala-i-Martin, "Capital Mobility in Neoclassical Models of Growth," *American Economic Review* 85 (1995):103–15.

Basu, Susanto and David N. Weil, "Appropriate Technology and Growth," *Quartarly Journal of Economics* 113 (1998):1025–54.

Bernard, Andrew B. and Charles I. Jones, "Comparing Apples to Oranges: Productivity Convergence and Measurement Across Industries and Countries," *American Economic Review* 86 (1996):1216–38.

Blanchard, Olivier J. and Stanley Fischer, *Lectures on Macroeconomics*, Cambridge, MA: MIT Press (1989).

Coe, David T. and Elhanan Helpman, "International R&D Spillovers," *European Economic Review* 39 (1995):859–87.

Coe, David T., Elhanan Helpman, and Alexander W. Hoffmaister, "North–South R&D Spillovers," *Economic Journal* 107 (1997):134–49.

Klundert, Theo van de and Sjak Smulders, "North–South Knowledge Spillovers and Competition: Convergence versus Divergence," *Journal of Development Economics* 50 (1996):213–32.

———, "Growth, Competition and Welfare," *Scandinavian Journal of Economics* 99 (1997):99–118.

Lucas, Robert E., "Making a Miracle," *Econometrica* 61 (1993):251–72.

Maggi, Giovanni, "Technology Gap and International Trade: An Evolutionary Model," *Journal of Evolutionary Economics* 2 (1993):109–26.

Smulders, Sjak and Theo van de Klundert, "Imperfect Competition, Concentration and Growth with Firm-specific R&D," *European Economic Review* 39 (1995):139–60.

Turnovsky, Stephen J. and Partha Sen, "Fiscal Policy, Capital Accumulation and Debt in an Open Economy," *Oxford Economic Papers* 43 (1991):1–24.

——, "Investment in a Two-Sector Dependent Economy," *Journal of the Japanese and International Economies* 9 (1995):29–55.

Uzawa, Hirofumi, "Time Preference, the Consumption Function and Optimum Asset Holdings," in J. N. Wolfe (ed.), *Value, Capital and Growth: Papers in Honour of Sir John Hicks*, Edinburgh: University of Edinburgh Press (1968).

Notes

1. Financial assets (F) include shares issued by domestic firms, domestic consumer loans and foreign assets (A). Firms' profits accrue to the holders of the first type of assets. Firms in the tradables sector have to issue new shares to finance R&D investments. In the absence of capital mobility, foreign assets are equal to zero $(A = 0)$. Note that we restrict the analysis to a perfect capital market in which the rate of return to any of the assets to which the investor has access bears the same rate of interest.

2. The nontradables sector can be thought of as being subdivided in a large number of symmetric subsectors in each of which a small number (m) of homogenous producers that compete *à la* Cournot.

3. A steady state arises only if foreign and domestic rates of time preference (ϑ) are equal. We have assumed that both are exogenous and we imposed equality. Alternatively, the domestic rate of time preference may be endogenous along the lines of Uzawa (1968). If ϑ changes in response to other variables of the model, these changes will be reflected in equation (6.1) so that this equation can be used to determine the steady state. Accordingly, the multiplicity of steady states vanishes. Two problems, however, arise. First, the well-known objection against the Uzawa formulation applies, viz. for stability reasons, ϑ should be *in*creasing in utility which seems difficult to defend a priori (Blanchard and Fisher, 1989, p. 73). Second, Uzawa analyzed the case that the rate of time preference depends on utility in a model without long-run growth. In our model long-run utility is growing so that no steady state arises if ϑ depends on utility.

4. Note that if the stable root of the dynamic model equals λ, for any variable $\tilde{x}$ we may write $\dot{\tilde{x}}(t) = \lambda[\tilde{x}(t) - \tilde{x}(\infty)]$. Using this result to eliminate $\dot{\tilde{h}}_x$ and $\dot{\tilde{L}}_x$ in (6.4), and subsequently substituting $\tilde{r} = 0$, $\tilde{h}_x(0) = 0$ and equation (7), we find $\tilde{L}_x(0) = \eta[\varepsilon\alpha_h - (\varepsilon - 1 - \alpha_f)]\tilde{h}_x(\infty)$, where η is defined as in the main text.

5. This can be clearly seen by inspecting equations (D.1)–(D.3) in the Appendix.

6. The stable arm of the saddlepath shown in the lower panel of Figure 3 does not shift, because $\tilde{a}(0) = 0$. See Appendix E and also Turnovsky and Sen (1991).

7. In our numerical example, the rest of the world is characterized by exactly the same parameters as the domestic economy. Hence, we linearize around a steady state with $h_x/\bar{h}_x = 1$. Note that by setting $h_x/\bar{h}_x = 1$ and $A = 0$ in equation (1), we find $\bar{g}$. The ROW can be considered as a closed economy with endogenous growth as in Smulders and van de Klundert (1995).

8. This result only holds if the share of domestically produced tradables is negligible in total consumption $(s \rightarrow 0)$, which is the natural assumption if the country is really small and there is no "home-preference." With a larger share, we have $\mu_Y^* > 1$: production of tradables should be stimulated and their price should be lower, since prices of tradables now influence consumer prices. Intuitively, the larger s, the more we move to the closed economy case and the closer μ_Y^* will be to μ_X.

9. Only domestic spillovers matter in this respect. Foreign spillovers provide a flow of knowledge like manna from heaven. From a national perspective, no policy can influence this so it is not an externality that a small open economy can internalize.

10. Provided again that $s \rightarrow 0$.

6
Migration under Asymmetric Information and Human Capital Formation

Nancy H. Chau and Oded Stark*

Abstract

We study the migration of skilled workers, along with the skill acquisition incentives created by the prospect of migration. We trace out the dynamics of migration as foreign employers accumulate experience in deciphering the skill levels of individual migrants. It is found that migration by the relatively highly skilled is followed by return-migration from both tails of the migrant skill distribution; that the possibility of migration induces skill acquisition at home; that until the probability of discovery reaches its steady state equilibrium, migration consists of a sequence of moves characterized by a rising average skill level; and that migration of skilled workers can entail a home-country welfare gain.

1. Introduction

Whatever workers may take with them when they migrate, they cannot possibly transfer their home country's information structure. Consequently, foreign-country employers are not as well informed about home-country workers as are home-country employers. Typically, migration runs across cultures as well as countries. Foreign-country employers who do not share the culture, background, and language of migrants as do home-country employers lack a common framework for assessing the quality and individual merits of migrant workers. For these reasons, the skills of migrant workers cannot be easily discerned, and screening is likely to be imprecise and expensive. In mainstream migration research, incorporation of the natural assumption that migration is inherently associated with a heterogeneous information structure (as opposed to the homogeneous information structure that characterizes nonmigrant employment relationships) has, somewhat surprisingly, been an exception rather than the rule (Kwok and Leland, 1982; Katz and Stark, 1987, 1989; Stark, 1991, 1995). The relative ignorance of foreign employers should not be taken as a constant, however. Exposure breeds familiarity, and increased experience with employing migrants is bound to reduce information asymmetries. Such a change can entail interesting dynamics. For example, the accumulation of information erodes both the pooling of low-skill migrant workers with high-skill migrant workers and the associated wage determination rule (i.e., paying all migrants the same wage, based on the average productivity of the entire cohort of migrants). Absent pooling, however, low-skill migrant workers may find it advantageous to return-migrate (Stark, 1995).

There is little doubt that, in general, migration gives rise to human capital depletion in the home country. The standard argument holds that, absent migration, the home country would have had available to it a more skilled workforce and, concomitantly, would have enjoyed higher per capita output. Indeed, the "drain-of-brains" view has influenced migration research for at least three decades (Grubel and Scott, 1966), with

---

* Stark: University of Oslo, PO Box 1095 Blindern, N-0317 Oslo, Norway; and University of Vienna. Tel: (47)22-855112; Fax: (47)22-857946. Chau: Cornell University, Ithaca, NY 14853, USA. Tel: (607)255-7602; Fax: (607)254-5269. We thank Yoram Weiss, Kar-yiu Wong, and Ilyse Zable for helpful comments. Partial financial support from the Austrian Science Foundation under contract P10967-SOZ is gratefully acknowledged.

the associated literature concentrating largely on how to mitigate this adverse consequence (Bhagwati and Wilson, 1989). However, that migration induces skill *formation* has essentially escaped analysis. Obviously, workers are not endowed with marketable skills at birth. Skills are acquired, and their level determined by optimizing workers who, given their innate learning ability (efficiency in skill formation), weigh the prospective market rewards for enhanced skills, both at home *and* abroad, in addition to the cost of acquiring those skills.

The possibility of migration thus changes the opportunities set, the incentive structure, and the information environment. Herein we study these simultaneous changes and trace their implications. Specifically, we depart from earlier approaches by dropping the strong simplifying assumptions that the distribution of migrants' abilities and the monitoring capabilities of migrants' employers are exogenously given. We endogenize the human capital formation decisions of migrant workers and allow the monitoring capabilities of employers to improve over time as their experience with employing migrants accumulates. This allows us to explore the intertemporal interactions among the decision to migrate, the choice to undertake education, and the monitoring capabilities of migrants' employers.

Our framework explains a number of pertinent characteristics of the migration of skilled workers (the brain drain). For example, as the experience of employing migrants accumulates, the resulting intertemporal adjustments in the probability of deciphering true skill levels leads to a sequence of migratory moves that progressively selects higher skilled workers. We argue that by raising the likelihood of discovering the true qualities of workers, accumulation of experience with migrant employment enhances the incentive for brighter brains to migrate permanently, while it reduces the incentive for low-ability workers to pursue migration. As the probability of discovery of abilities rises, the ability composition of subsequent migrant cohorts shifts rightward. Whenever the average quality of a migrant cohort exceeds that of a previous cohort, wage offers are bidded upward, prompting a subsequent wave of migration involving workers who are even more able. However, this is just a first-round effect. The accumulation of experience in employing migrants also implies that both high- and low-ability workers are more likely to be discovered. Accordingly, the probability of permanent migration by high-ability workers, and the extent of return migration by low-ability workers, rise simultaneously. The result is continuing improvements in the average ability of migrant workers remaining in a country. Until the steady-state equilibrium probability of discovery is reached, a virtual cycle of migration of the more able ensue, as wage offers are adjusted over time in favor of migration of higher ability workers. Meanwhile, the wages of the migrants who stay increase, though not because of an increase in their human capital.

Our model extends earlier work by Katz and Stark (1987). We introduce endogenous human capital formation and examine the dynamics of human capital formation as well as the corresponding intertemporal pattern of migration and return migration. We derive several dynamic predictions that are consistent with a considerable body of empirical literature, as reviewed and synthesized by LaLonde and Topel (1997) and Razin and Sadka (1997). Migration is a process, not an event. It is phased, and it is sequential: not all workers who migrate will move at the same time. Each cohort of migrants includes workers who will stay and workers who, with a well-defined probability, will return-migrate. Ravenstein's century-old "law of migration" (1885, p. 199), which predicts that "each main current of migration produces a compensating countercurrent"—often quoted but not demonstrated analytically—turns out to be an implication of our model. Within cohorts, migration is positively selective (Stark, 1995).[1]

Cohort by cohort, the average quality of migrants rises.[2] The "cost of migration" is a decreasing function of the stock of previous migrants for some workers, but it is an *increasing* function of that stock for others, contrary to the findings of Carrington et al. (1996): migration of low-skill workers pulls down the average of the marginal products of the contemporaneous group of migrant workers, thereby lowering the wage of high-skill workers. Conversely, the presence of high-skill migrant workers in a pool of low-skill and high-skill workers enables low-skill workers to enjoy a wage higher than their marginal product. As migration proceeds and the cumulative stock of migrants rises, the probability of discovery rises. This favors high-skill would-be migrants but dissuades low-skill would-be migrants. Thus an increase in the stock of migrant workers confers a positive externality on subsequent migration of high-skill workers, but a negative externality on the migration of low-skill workers.

We pay particular attention to the change in the welfare of the home-country population in the wake of international migration. In contrast to the received welfare-theoretic analysis of the brain drain,[3] we show that when potential migrant workers incorporate the feasibility of migration in their education decisions, not only does the level of education acquisition in the home country rise, but national welfare may rise as well if the contribution to national income by educated workers increases. We show that a gain in national welfare generated by migration of educated workers is possible given a positive probability of return migration by educated workers once their true productivities are deciphered.

The remainder of this paper is organized as follows. In section 2, we model a home economy not open to migration and determine the extent of education acquisition and the per capita output as benchmarks for subsequent comparisons. In section 3, we present a two-country framework. The information asymmetry between foreign employers and home-country workers is introduced and the effect of migrant employment experience on the probability of deciphering the true ability of individual migrant workers is incorporated. In addition, we study the education and migration decisions of home-country workers in the presence of asymmetric information. We also compare the resulting level of education with that obtained in the absence of the possibility of migration. Section 4 analyzes the relationship between the dynamic process of skilled-worker migration and the probability of discovery, as well as the associated steady-state equilibrium probability of discovery. We trace the circumstances under which migration progressively selects higher ability workers. In section 5, we conduct a welfare analysis and define conditions under which national welfare improves when free migration of skilled workers is permitted. Section 6 summarizes the analysis.

2. An Open Economy Without Migration

Production

During each time period t, the home economy h produces a single composite good in two sectors: an unskilled sector, u, and a skilled sector, s. Output in the unskilled sector during time t is generated through a simple constant-returns-to-scale production function, $X_t^u = a_u^h L_t$, where L_t denotes the number of workers employed in sector u. Similarly, output in the skilled sector is given by a constant-returns-to-scale production function, $X_t^s = a_s^h E_t$, where E_t is the input of skilled labor measured in efficiency units. Thus, a_u^h is the marginal and average product of a worker in sector u, and a_s^h is the marginal and average product of an efficiency unit of labor in the skilled sector. Output prices in the small open home economy are internationally given and, without loss of generality, the price of a unit of output is assumed to be equal to one. There is perfect competition in both output and factor markets. Therefore, the wage paid by profit-maximizing employers to a worker in the unskilled sector is $w_u^h = a_u^h$, and the wage paid for an efficiency unit of work in the skilled sector is $w_s^h = a_s^h$.

Individuals and the Population

In each period N individuals are born. Individuals live for two periods. Thus, the population size during any time period is $2N$. Individuals are characterized by endowments and preferences. Each individual is endowed with one unit of physical labor (a pair of hands) and with innate ability (talent) $\theta \in [0, \infty]$. The distribution of θ over the population is summarized by a cumulative distribution function $F(\theta)$, where $F(\theta)$ is continuously differentiable and is associated with a strictly positive density function $f(\theta)$. Assume, in addition, that the expectation of θ $[\int_0^\infty \theta f(\theta) d\theta]$ is finite. Denote by y_t the income of the individual in period t. The individual's preferences are summarized by a utility function $u(y_t, y_{t+1})$. To simplify, we take $u(y_t, y_{t+1}) = y_t + \beta y_{t+1}$, where $0 < \beta < 1$ is the time discount rate.

An individual born during any time period t faces the following choice: remain uneducated and work in the u sector for the two periods of his life, or spend the first time period acquiring education and work in the s sector in the second period of his life. Acquiring education involves a direct cost c that is incurred at the beginning of period t. Having no funds, the individual borrows c in a perfectly competitive credit market where the interest rate is assumed to be zero. The educated individual, whose innate ability is θ, supplies θ efficiency units of labor to the skilled sector. The supply of efficiency units of labor by an uneducated individual in the s sector is zero, irrespective of his level of innate ability. The labor input supplied by a worker in the unskilled sector is independent of his innate abilities and is equal to his physical labor endowment (one unit).

It follows that the discounted lifetime utility of an educated worker is equal to his discounted second period income, net of education costs:

$$Y_t^s(\theta) \equiv \beta(w_s^h \theta - c).$$

The discounted lifetime utility of an uneducated worker is

$$Y_t^u \equiv (1+\beta)w_u^h.$$

Thus, an individual whose innate ability is θ will decide to acquire education if $Y_t^s(\theta) \geq Y_t^u$, but will choose to remain uneducated otherwise. We thus have

$$Y_t^s(\theta) \geq Y_t^u \Leftrightarrow \beta(w_s^h \theta - c) \geq (1+\beta)w_u^h,$$

or

$$\theta \geq \frac{1}{w_s^h}\left[\frac{(1+\beta)w_u^h}{\beta} + c\right] \equiv \theta^*.$$

That is, individuals whose $\theta \geq \theta^*$ will become skilled workers, and individuals whose $\theta < \theta^*$ will remain unskilled.

Therefore, the $2N$ individuals from the "young" and the "old" generations are distributed across three activities: work in the u sector, work in the s sector, and acquisition of education. Because the fraction of uneducated workers per generation is $F(\theta^*)$, the number of uneducated workers in the population is $2NF(\theta^*)$. The fraction of the old generation employed in the s sector is $[1 - F(\theta^*)]$. The number of individuals employed in the s sector is thus $N[1 - F(\theta^*)]$. Finally, because a fraction $1 - F(\theta^*)$ of the young generation pursues education, the number of individuals being educated during any time period is $N[1 - F(\theta^*)]$. Of course, $2NF(\theta^*) + N[1 - F(\theta^*)] + N[1 - F(\theta^*)] = 2N$. From our previous analysis, it can be confirmed that θ^* is decreasing in w_s^h: the higher the rewards to education, given θ, the larger the fraction of individuals who will invest in education, $[1 - F(\theta^*)]$, and the larger the number of individuals who will do so: $N[1 - F(\theta^*)]$.

Production and Equilibrium

An equilibrium in the economy, at any time, is fully characterized by the parameter θ^*. Once θ^* is known, the allocation of labor across the two employment options and the associated outputs of the two sectors are given.[4] The output of the u sector is $X_t^u = w_u^h 2NF(\theta^*)$. In addition, total labor input (measured in efficiency units) in the skilled sector is $E_t = N\int_{\theta^*}^{\infty}\theta f(\theta)d\theta$.[5] The resulting s sector output is therefore $X_t^s = N\int_{\theta^*}^{\infty}w_s^h\theta f(\theta)d\theta$.

We can now calculate the value of national output, net of education expenditures, and investigate the dependence of national output on θ^*. We denote by $V(\theta^*)$ the time-invariant value of national output net of the cost of education. We have

$$V(\theta^*) = N\Big\{2w_u^h F(\theta^*) + \int_{\theta^*}^{\infty} w_s^h \theta f(\theta)d\theta - c[1 - F(\theta^*)]\Big\}.$$

Output per capita is thus

$$v(\theta^*) = \frac{1}{2}\Big\{2w_u^h F(\theta^*) + \int_{\theta^*}^{\infty} w_s^h \theta f(\theta)d\theta - c[1 - F(\theta^*)]\Big\}. \tag{1}$$

It follows that[6]

$$\frac{\partial v(\theta^*)}{\partial \theta^*} = \frac{1}{2}[-w_s^h\theta^* f(\theta^*) + 2w_u^h f(\theta^*) + cf(\theta^*)]$$

$$= -\frac{1}{2} f(\theta^*)(w_s^h\theta^* - 2w_u^h - c)$$

$$= -\frac{1}{2} f(\theta^*)w_u^h \frac{1-\beta}{\beta}$$

$$< 0. \tag{1'}$$

The value of per capita output is decreasing in θ^*. Recall that an increase in θ^* is equivalent to a reduction in the fraction of the educated workforce. Starting from an equilibrium in which there is no governmental interference in individuals' decisions to acquire education, it follows that per capita output increases as the share of educated workers increases. Note that if $\beta = 1$ in equation (1'), then $\partial v(\theta^*)/\partial \theta^* = 0$. In other words, if individuals do not discount future income, the invisible hand is nicely at work: the level of θ^* chosen by individuals who maximize expected lifetime utility is exactly the same level of θ^* that a social planner will choose to maximize per capita output.

3. A Two-Country World With Migration

The Foreign Economy

The foreign economy, f, also consists of a u sector and an s sector. We denote by $\tilde{L}_t$ and L_t^m the number of foreign workers and migrant workers employed in the u sector, respectively. The output of the u sector is $\tilde{X}_t^u = a_u^f(\tilde{L}_t + L_t^m)$. The output of the s sector, $\tilde{X}_t^s$, is governed by the production function $\tilde{X}_t^s = a_s^f(\tilde{E}_t + E_t^m)$, where $\tilde{E}_t$ denotes the foreign workforce (measured in efficiency units) employed in the s sector and E_t^m is the input of the migrant workforce, also measured in efficiency units. We shall assume that the foreign country uses superior technologies relative to economy h in both its u and s sectors so that $a_i^f > a_i^h$, $i = u, s$. Perfect competition in both output and factor markets guarantees that the wage paid by profit-maximizing employers to a worker in the unskilled sector is $w_u^f = a_u^f > a_u^h = w_u^h$ and the wage paid to an efficiency unit of work in the skilled sector is $w_s^f = a_s^f > a_s^h = w_s^h$.

Foreign employers are assumed to be perfectly aware of the true abilities of indigenous workers. However, the true abilities of individual migrant workers are unknown. Each migrant worker can nevertheless be distinguished as belonging to one of two identifiable groups of workers: educated or uneducated. Following our specification in section 2, wage payments to uneducated migrant workers by profit-maximizing employers depend only on the sector of employment, not on individual abilities. In particular, an uneducated migrant worker receives zero wages in the s sector because the efficiency labor input of such a worker in this sector is zero. Similarly, an uneducated migrant worker in the u sector receives w_u^f as a wage payment because the physical labor input of such a worker in the u sector is one. The same wage-determination procedure no longer applies to educated migrant workers, however, when the educated migrant workforce consists of individuals with heterogeneous abilities.

At any time t, let the wage offer to an educated migrant worker whose true ability is unknown to foreign employers be $w_s^f\theta_t^a$, where θ_t^a denotes the average supply of efficiency labor inputs by the migrant population having unknown individual abilities. In addition, let the total number of migrants at any time τ be $\mathcal{M}_\tau$, and let the cumulative number of migrants until time $t - 1$ be $M_{t-1} = \sum_{\tau=0}^{t-1}\mathcal{M}_\tau$. We assume that with probability $m_t = m(M_{t-1})$ the actual productivity of a worker who supplies $\theta \neq \theta_t^a$ amount of skilled labor will be discovered. The probability of discovery, m_t, is taken to be strictly positive, increasing in migrant hiring experience, $m'(M_{t-1}) > 0$,[7] and bounded from above with $\lim_{M_{t-1}\to\infty} m(M_{t-1}) = \hat{m} < 1$. Once the true ability of a worker is discovered by one foreign employer, the same information becomes instantly available to all foreign employers (this follows from our assumption of perfect competition in factor markets); hence the wage payment for such a worker in the s sector of the foreign country is determined by his true ability, θ.

The Individuals Revisited

Migration entails a per-period cost k that can be perceived as the cost of separation from home. We take this cost to be independent of the level of education acquired and of the stock of migrants. Accordingly, under symmetric information, the per-period income net of the separation cost for an educated worker who migrates to the foreign country is just $w_s^f\theta - k$. Figure 1 illustrates the income schedules for an educated worker in the home country and in the foreign country. The value of θ corresponding to the point of intersection, $\bar{\theta} = k/(w_s^f - w_s^h)$, denotes a critical level of innate ability such that any educated home-country worker with an innate ability $\theta \geq \bar{\theta}$ enjoys a higher income in the foreign country, net of the migration cost, than at home. In the absence of asymmetric information, the most talented will migrate whereas skilled workers endowed with ability less than $\bar{\theta}$ will remain in the home country because the per-period foreign wage net of the cost of migration ($w_s^f\theta - k$) is less than the corresponding home-country wage ($w_s^h\theta$).

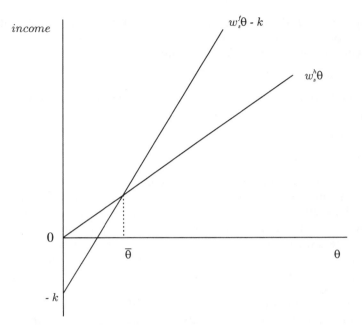

Figure 1. Migration under Symmetric Information

Once the prevalence of asymmetric information and the possibility of migration are incorporated into the decision-making calculus of the home-country workers, the problem of a worker born at any time t spans two consecutive periods. In the first period, an individual may acquire education and incur its cost, c. Otherwise, the individual finds employment in the unskilled sector of the home country or the foreign country. In the second period, the uneducated individual reviews his migration decision and chooses to work either in the home country or in the foreign country. For an educated worker, there are four possible, more elaborate second-period employment options:

(1) An educated worker of ability θ chooses to migrate. With probability m_t, the true ability of the worker is discovered, and the worker return-migrates. With the complementary probability $1 - m_t$, the true ability of the worker is not discovered and he remains in the foreign country. The expected income of such a worker, net of the cost of education, y_t^{rd}, is thus

$$y_t^{rd}(\theta) = m_t w_s^h \theta + (1 - m_t)(w_s^f \theta_t^a - k) - c.$$

(2) An educated worker of ability θ chooses to migrate. With probability m_t, the true ability of the worker is discovered, and the worker remains in the foreign country, receiving $w_s^f \theta$. With the complementary probability $1 - m_t$, the true ability of the worker is not discovered and the worker remains in the foreign country, in which case he receives $w_s^f \theta_t^a$. In this case, the expected income net of the education cost, $y_t^f(\theta)$, is thus

$$y_t^f(\theta) = m_t(w_s^f \theta - k) + (1 - m_t)(w_s^f \theta_t^a - k) - c.$$

(3) An educated worker of ability θ chooses to migrate. With probability m_t, the true ability of the worker is discovered, and the worker remains in the foreign country,

receiving $w_s^f\theta$. With the complementary probability $1 - m_t$, the true ability of the worker is not discovered, and the worker return-migrates. The expected income of such a worker, net of the cost of education, $y_t^{ru}(\theta)$, is thus

$$y_t^{ru}(\theta) = m_t(w_s^f\theta - k) + (1 - m_t)w_s^h\theta - c.$$

(4) An educated worker of ability θ chooses not to migrate and receives a net income, $y_t^h(\theta)$, of

$$y_t^h(\theta) = w_s^h\theta - c$$

with probability one.[8]

Figure 2 depicts these four options and the choices among them. Given θ_t^a and M_{t-1}, the expected income schedules in the four regimes, $y_t^i(\theta) + c$ ($i = rd, f, ru, h$), are illustrated by the lines R^dR^d, FF, R^uR^u, and HH, respectively. R^dR^d is the income schedule of migrant workers who return upon discovery. R^uR^u represents the income schedule of migrant workers who return if their true abilities remain undiscovered. HH and FF denote the income schedules of permanent home-country workers and permanent migrants, respectively. Note in particular that R^dR^d and FF coincides with the horizontal income schedule $w_s^f\theta_t^a - k$, and R^uR^u coincides with the home wage schedule HH whenever $m_t = 0$. In addition, R^dR^d coincides with the home wage schedule and R^uR^u and FF coincide with the foreign wage schedule whenever $m_t = 1$—the case of perfect information elaborated earlier.

Observe from Figure 2 that when $0 < m_t < 1$, the maximum second-period expected income of an educated worker (indicated by the bold segmented line) is demarcated by two critical values of innate abilities: $\bar\theta$ and θ_t^f, where the former (latter) denotes the innate ability of a migrant who is indifferent between regimes 1 and 2 (regimes 2 and 3). A comparison of the migration patterns shown in Figures 1 and 2 reveals that

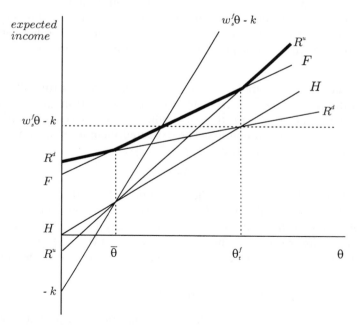

Figure 2. Migration and Return-Migration under Asymmetric Information

under asymmetric information, the most talented workers (with $\theta > \theta_t^f$) will return-migrate with strictly positive probability $1 - m_t$. The inability of foreign employers to decipher the true ability of migrant workers thus acts as a tax on the returns to migration for the most talented workers. In particular, the innate ability of a migrant who is indifferent between regimes 2 and 3, θ_t^f, can be found by noting that

$$(1 - m_t)(w_s^f \theta_t^a - k) + m_t(w_s^f \theta - k) = (1 - m_t)w_s^h \theta + m_t(w_s^f \theta - k)$$

$$\Leftrightarrow \theta = \frac{w_s^f \theta_t^a - k}{w_s^h} \equiv \theta_t^f.$$

Note further that because $R^d R^d$ and FF intersect only once, all educated migrants with ability $\theta \leq \theta_t^f$ can be classified into one of two groups once their true capabilities are detected: return-migrants and permanent migrants. This follows from the definition of $\bar{\theta}$, the critical innate ability level at which the home and the foreign wage schedules intersect. Once his true ability is discovered, an educated worker with low-ability $\theta < \bar{\theta}$ will choose to work in the home country, where the per-period return is the highest. To see this, note that a migrant with innate ability θ is indifferent between regimes 1 and 2 if and only if

$$(1 - m_t)(w_s^f \theta_t^a - k) + m_t w_s^h \theta = (1 - m_t)(w_s^f \theta_t^a - k) + m_t(w_s^f \theta - k)$$

$$\Leftrightarrow w_s^h \theta = w_s^f \theta - k$$

$$\Leftrightarrow \theta = \frac{k}{w_s^f - w_s^h} \equiv \bar{\theta}.$$

Finally, HH lies below the bold segmented line for all values of θ. As long as $\theta_t^a > \bar{\theta}$ and m_t is strictly between zero and unity, the probability that an educated migrant will earn a higher wage in the foreign country is strictly positive. In particular, from the definition of $\bar{\theta}$, if $\theta \leq \bar{\theta}$, $w_s^f \theta_t^a - k > w_s^h \theta$. In addition, $w_s^f \theta - k > w_s^h \theta$ if $\theta > \bar{\theta}$. It follows that if return migration is always an option open to migrant workers, an educated worker will never choose to work only in the home country. We summarize this discussion in the following proposition. (All proofs are relegated to the Appendix.)

PROPOSITION 1. *If $\theta_t^a > \bar{\theta}$*

(1) *Educated workers with innate ability $\theta \leq \bar{\theta}$ migrate. In addition, return-migration yields the maximum second-period income once the true ability of such educated workers is discovered.*
(2) *Educated workers with innate ability $\theta \in (\bar{\theta}, \theta_t^f]$ migrate. In addition, employment in the foreign country yields the maximum second-period income once the true ability of such educated workers is discovered.*
(3) *Educated workers with innate ability $\theta > \theta_t^f$ migrate. In addition, return-migration yields the maximum second-period income if the true ability of such educated workers is not discovered.*

We now proceed to the first-stage education choice by comparing the expected utilities for an educated worker and an uneducated worker over the two periods. To focus on the analysis of migration of skilled workers, we assume that k is sufficiently large with $w_u^f - k < w_u^h$: the per-period foreign income net of the migration cost for an uneducated worker is lower than his unskilled wage in the home country. It follows that

$$w_u^h > w_u^f - k \Rightarrow w_u^h(1+\beta) > (w_u^f - k) + \beta w_u^h,$$
$$\Rightarrow w_u^h(1+\beta) > w_u^h + \beta(w_u^f - k).$$

The inequality on the right-hand side in the first line states that the lifetime utility from working at home is higher than the utility from migrating in the first period of life and the utility from working at home in the second period. The inequality on the right-hand side in the second line states that the lifetime utility from working at home is higher than the utility from working at home in the first period of life and the utility from migrating in the second period. Because $(1 + \beta)w_u^h > (1 + \beta)(w_u^f - k)$ follows from $w_u^h > w_u^f - k$, it follows that migration of the unskilled always yields a lower lifetime utility, irrespective of the timing and duration of migration.

With that in mind, we denote the expected lifetime utility $u_{t-1}(\theta)$ of a worker with innate ability θ born at time $t - 1$ as

$$u_{t-1}(\theta) = E_{t-1}\{\max[\beta y_t(\theta), (1+\beta)w_u^h]\},$$

where $y_t(\theta) = \max[y_t^{rd}(\theta), y_t^f(\theta), y_t^{ru}(\theta), y_t^h(\theta)]$, and $E_{t-1}(\cdot)$ denotes the expectation operator, with the expectation taken over all possible values of m_t at time $t-1$. The expected lifetime utility $u_{t-1}(\theta)$ can be determined by comparing the expectation of the discounted lifetime income of an educated worker, $E_{t-1}[\beta y_t(\theta)]$, and the discounted lifetime income of an uneducated worker, $(1 + \beta)w_u^h$. To do so, additional assumptions regarding the determination of the expected future foreign wage offers, θ_t^a, and the probability of discovery, m_t, are required. In what follows, we endow individuals with the faculty of rational expectations, such that $E_{t-1}(x_t) = x_t$.

Consider, then, the lifetime utility of an individual born at time $t - 1$, with $\theta < \bar{\theta}$. From Proposition 1, such a worker strictly prefers regime 1 if educated, and hence the expectation of his discounted lifetime income is just $\beta y_t^{rd}(\theta)$. Education therefore yields a higher lifetime utility than no education if and only if $\beta y_t^{rd}(\theta) > (1 + \beta)w_u^h$, or if and only if

$$\beta[m_t w_s^h \theta + (1 - m_t)(w_s^f \theta_t^a - k) - c] > (1+\beta)w_u^h$$
$$\Leftrightarrow \theta > \left[\frac{1+\beta}{\beta}w_u^h - (1 - m_t)(w_s^f \theta_t^a - k) + c\right]\frac{1}{m_t w_s^h}$$
$$\equiv \theta_t^{er}.$$

Note that θ_t^{er} is strictly increasing in w_u^h, c, and k. We thus have the following result: all else remaining constant, *the higher is the unskilled wage and the higher is the cost of education, the smaller will be the fraction of the home-country population acquiring education* $[1 - F(\theta_t^{er})]$. Interestingly, *an increase in the cost of migration, k, also deters education by home-country workers.* Education not only varies wage earnings at home and abroad, it also renders migration a feasible option. An increase in the cost of migration weakens the migration incentive for acquiring education. Finally, θ_t^{er} is also increasing in m_t whenever $\partial \theta_t^{er}/\partial m_t = (1/w_s^h m_t)(w_s^f \theta_t^a - k - w_s^h \theta_t^{er}) > 0$, which, in turn, holds since $\theta_t^{er} < \bar{\theta}$. An increase in the probability of discovery, m_t, lowers the education incentives of low-ability workers—the probability that these workers will be pooled with high-ability workers is lower; therefore, the expected returns to their acquisition of skills are lower. It follows that the fraction of the home-country workers who remain uneducated rises as m_t rises, all else remaining constant.

Similarly, the lifetime utility of an educated individual with $\theta \in [\bar{\theta}, \theta_t^f)$ is higher than the utility of an unskilled worker if and only if $\beta y_t^f(\theta) > (1 + \beta)w_u^h$, or if and only if

$$\beta[m_t(w_s^f\theta - k) + (1 - m_t)(w_s^f\theta_t^a - k) - c] > (1 + \beta)w_u^h$$

$$\Leftrightarrow \theta > \left[\frac{1+\beta}{\beta}w_u^h - (1 - m_t)(w_s^f\theta_t^a - k) + c + m_t k\right]\frac{1}{m_t w_s^f}$$

$$\equiv \theta_t^{ef},$$

where θ_t^{ef} is increasing in w_u^h, c, and k as well as in m_t, provided that $\partial\theta_t^{ef}/\partial m_t = (1/w_s^f m_t)(w_s^f\theta_t^a - w_s^f\theta_s^{ef}) > 0$.

With θ_t^{er} and θ_t^{ef} now established, there are two critical levels of innate ability that further divide the home-country population into two groups: uneducated and educated.[9] Simple manipulation of the definitions of θ_t^{er} and θ_t^{ef} yields the following result.

PROPOSITION 2
(1) *If $\theta_t^{er} < \bar\theta$: workers with innate ability $\theta > \theta_t^{er}$ are better off acquiring education. The lifetime utility of workers with $\theta \le \theta_t^{er}$ is maximized by remaining uneducated.*
(2) *If $\theta_t^{er} \ge \bar\theta$: workers with innate ability $\theta > \theta_t^{ef}$ are better off acquiring education. The lifetime utility of workers with $\theta \le \theta_t^{ef}$ is maximized by remaining uneducated.*

If $\theta_t^{er} < \bar\theta$, θ_t^{er} defines a critical ability level that divides the home-country population into educated and uneducated workers. Now the home-country population consists of four groups of individuals: uneducated home-country workers (with $\theta < \theta_t^{er}$), educated workers who migrate and return upon discovery (with $\theta_t^{er} \le \theta < \bar\theta$), educated permanent migrants (with $\bar\theta \le \theta < \theta_t^f$), and educated workers who migrate and return if their true ability is not discovered (with $\theta \ge \theta_t^f$). This partitioning is as shown in Figure 3.

Note again that under asymmetric information, all individuals with $\theta \ge \bar\theta$ do not permanently migrate. As noted earlier, asymmetric information penalizes high-ability migrant workers because, with probability $1 - m_t$, such migrants do not receive the foreign wage that accords with their abilities. More importantly, upon return-migration, the home-country population consists of individuals with the lowest and highest ability levels.

If $\theta_t^{er} \ge \bar\theta$, then workers with $\theta < \bar\theta$, as well as workers with $\bar\theta < \theta < \theta_t^{ef}$, remain uneducated. Therefore, the home-country population consists of only three groups: uneducated home-country workers (with $\theta \le \theta_t^{ef}$), educated permanent migrants (with $\theta_t^{ef} \le \theta < \theta_t^f$), and educated home-country workers who return upon nondiscovery (with $\theta \ge \theta_t^f$). Again, the partitioning is as shown in Figure 4.

As in the previous case, home-country workers consist of individuals with the lowest ability levels and the highest ability levels upon return-migration. The possibility of migration leads to the home country's permanent loss of all migrant workers with skill levels $\theta_t^{ef} < \theta < \theta_t^f$ because, from part 2 of Proposition 1, $y_t^f(\theta) > y_t^{rd}(\theta)$ for every $\theta_t^{ef} \le \theta \le \theta_t^f$. Note also that because, by definition, θ_t^a is the average skill level of all

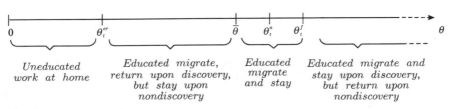

Figure 3. Critical Ability Levels if $\theta_t^{er} < \bar\theta$

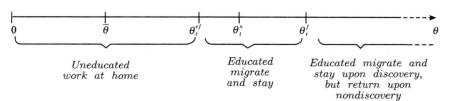

Figure 4. Critical Ability Levels if $\theta_t^{er} > \bar{\theta}$

undiscovered migrant workers at time t, while θ_t^{ef} is the skill level for the lowest ability migrant worker, it must be the case that $\theta_t^a > \theta_t^{ef}$, as shown in Figure 4.

Comparisons of θ^* and θ_t^{er}, and of θ^* and θ_t^{ef} yield the following proposition.

PROPOSITION 3. *The fraction of the home-country population pursuing education in the presence of migration opportunities is always higher than the fraction of the home-country population pursuing education in the absence of migration opportunities.*

Proposition 3 reveals that the increase in the incentive to pursue education when migration offers a more attractive wage to the educated leads the home country to a higher degree of educational attainment. Yet, it should also be noted that the increase in the fraction of educated workers in the home country owing to the prospect of migration does not necessarily imply that the number of educated workers who *stay and work* in the home country increases. To see this, consider the case of $\theta_t^{er} > \bar{\theta}$. From the definitions of θ_t^{ef} and θ^* we have

$$w_s^h \theta^* = m_t \left(w_s^f \theta_t^{ef} - k \right) + (1 - m_t)\left(w_s^f \theta_t^a - k \right)$$
$$\Leftrightarrow w_s^h \theta^* = m_t \left(w_s^f \theta_t^{ef} - w_s^f \theta_t^a \right) + w_s^f \theta_t^a - k$$
$$\Leftrightarrow w_s^h \theta^* < w_s^f \theta_t^a - k,$$

where the last inequality follows because $\theta_t^{ef} < \theta_t^a$. In addition, because, by definition, $w_s^f \theta_t^a - k = w_s^h \theta_t^f$, we have $w_s^h \theta^* < w_s^h \theta_t^f$, or, $\theta^* < \theta_t^f$. Hence, the group of workers who acquire education in response to the prospect of migration (with skill levels $\bar{\theta} < \theta_t^{ef} \leq \theta < \theta^* < \theta_t^f$) belongs to the group of permanent migrants. As a result, the prospect of migration not only leads to a loss for the home country of those educated workers with $\theta > \theta_t^f (> \theta^*)$, who stay in the foreign country upon discovery, it also leads to the preclusion of any increase in the educated workforce in the home country, as a result of the possibility of migration. In what follows, we therefore focus our attention on the case in which $\theta_t^{ef} < \bar{\theta}$, where the four "modes of employment" are present simultaneously.[10] As we elaborate further, the possible return migration of those workers who would not have had the incentive to acquire education in the absence of migration opportunities, allows a possible economy-wide gain in spite of, and along with, a brain drain.

4. The Dynamics of Migration

With θ_t^{er} and θ_t^f defined, we now analyze the process of migration and the evolution of wage offers as experience with employing migrants accumulates over time. Given an initial experience associated with M_0, migration from the home country in subsequent periods can be summarized by the vector $\{\theta_t, \theta_t^{er}, \theta_t^f\}$, the elements of which are in turn solutions to the following system of simultaneous equations:

$$\theta_t^a = \frac{\int_{\theta_t^{er}}^{\theta_t^f} \theta f(\theta) d\theta}{F(\theta_t^f) - F(\theta_t^{er})}, \tag{2}$$

$$\theta_t^f = \frac{w_s^f \theta_t^a - k}{w_s^h}, \tag{3}$$

$$\theta_t^{er} = \frac{1}{m_t w_s^h} \left[\frac{1+\beta}{\beta} w_u^h - (1 - m_t)(w_s^f \theta_t^a - k) + c \right]. \tag{4}$$

On multiplying both sides of equation (2) by w_s^f, the equation can be interpreted as requiring the wage offer to each migrant with unknown ability at time t to be equal to the average ability of the migrant cohort with unknown individual ability at time t, multiplied by the wage rate per efficiency unit of labor. Equations (3) and (4) require, respectively, that the extent of migration and the education decision follow from the expected utility maximization described in section 3.[11] From equation (3), we observe further that

$$\theta_t^a = \frac{w_s^h \theta_t^f + k}{w_s^f} \tag{5}$$

and on rewriting equation (2):

$$\theta_t^a = \frac{\int_{\theta_t^{er}}^{\theta_t^f} \theta f(\theta) d\theta}{F(\theta_t^f) - F(\theta_t^{er})}. \tag{6}$$

Equation (5) captures the supply side of the migrant labor market; that is, the foreign-country wage of an undiscovered migrant worker at time t, $w_s^f \theta_t^a$, is just sufficient to induce the supply of educated workers with ability $\theta \le \theta_t^f$ who are willing to stay and work in the foreign country at the wage $w_s^f \theta_t^a$. Equation (6) holds that if θ_t^f represents the ability of the most able migrant worker who prefers $w_s^f \theta_t^a - k$ to his home wage, and θ_t^{er} represents the ability of the least able migrant worker, $1/w_s^f$ of the wage offer at time t (which reflects the willingness to pay for migrant work) is equal to the average ability of the migrant workforce, with unknown individual abilities, at time t.

Figures 5 and 6 depict the supply (SS) and demand (DD) relationships spelled out in equations (5) and (6) respectively. The intersection points A in Figure 5 and B in Figure 6 depict equilibrium combinations of θ_t^a and θ_t^f that simultaneously satisfy equations (2) through (4), given m_t. It can be confirmed that both DD and SS are upward-sloping.[12] Note also that in general, DD can be flatter or steeper than SS, depending on the exogenous parameters of the model. Consider, for example, the effect of an exogenous increase in the probability of discovery m_t when SS is steeper than DD, as in Figure 5. An increase in m_t shifts the DD curve upward, while the SS curve remains unchanged.[13]

An increase in m_t reduces the number of workers with low ability who acquire education at time $t - 1$, $[1 - F(\theta_t^{er})]$, because workers endowed with rational expectations correctly anticipate the future value of m_t in their human capital calculus. As a result, the average ability (and hence the demand price) of migrants rises for any given θ_t^f because an increase in m_t shifts the skill composition of the migrant population in the foreign country to the right.

Note further that an increase in m_t has no direct effect on the supply side of the migrant labor market. θ_t^f divides the home-country population into two subgroups: a

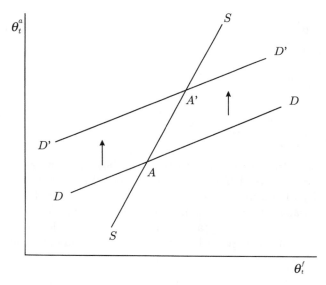

Figure 5. An Increase in m_t when Supply is Steeper than Demand

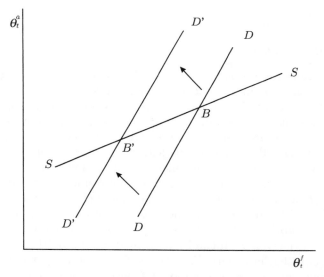

Figure 6. An Increase in m_t when Demand is Steeper than Supply

subgroup that consists of low-ability individuals (with $w_s^h \theta < w_s^f \theta_t^a - k$) who are better off remaining in the foreign country only if their true abilities are *not* discovered, and a subgroup that consists of individuals (with $w_s^h \theta \geq w_s^f \theta_t^a - k$) who receive a higher home wage than $w_s^f \theta_t^a - k$. It follows that θ_t^a alone determines the value of θ_t^f, given the wage schedules in the home country and the foreign country.

The new equilibrium pair θ_t^a and θ_t^f is depicted as point A′ in Figure 5, where both the average ability of migrants and θ_t^f rise as a result of an increase in m_t. In contrast, starting from a point such as B in Figure 6, where *SS* is flatter than *DD*, an increase in

m_t, together with the associated shift of the DD curve, implies a reduction in both θ_t^a and θ_t^f, as depicted by point B′. We denote the solutions to the system of simultaneous equations (2)–(4) as $\theta_t^j(m_t, c, w_u^h), j = a, f, er$. Applying our preceding arguments for the case of an increase in c and for the case of an increase in w_u^h, we obtain the first two parts of the following result; the third part will be reasoned in what follows.

PROPOSITION 4

(1) $\theta_t^a(m_t, c, w_u^h)$ is increasing in m_t, c, and w_u^h if and only if SS is steeper than DD or, equivalently, if and only if

$$1 - \frac{(\theta_t^f - \theta_t^a)f(\theta_t^f)}{F(\theta_t^f) - F(\theta_t^{er})} \frac{w_s^f}{w_s^h} + \frac{(\theta_t^a - \theta_t^{er})f(\theta_t^{er})}{F(\theta_t^f) - F(\theta_t^{er})} \frac{(1 - m_t)w_s^f}{m_t w_s^h} > 0. \tag{7}$$

(2) $\theta_t^f(m_t, c, w_u^h)$ is increasing in m_t, c, and w_u^h if and only if equation (7) is satisfied.

(3) $\theta_t^{er}(m_t, c, w_u^h)$ is increasing in m_t if and only if

$$\frac{w_s^f\theta_t^a - k - w_s^h\theta_t^{er}}{(1 - m_t)w_s^f} > \frac{\partial\theta_t^a}{\partial m_t}. \tag{8}$$

Regarding part 3 of Proposition 4, note that from equations (2)–(4), $\partial\theta_t^{er}/\partial m_t = [(w_s^f\theta_t^a - k - w_s^h\theta_t^{er}) - (1 - m_t)w_s^f\partial\theta_t^a/\partial m_t]/(m_t w_s^h)$. In general, therefore, an increase in m_t has an ambiguous effect on the incentives of workers with low ability levels to acquire education and migrate. The term $(w_s^f\theta_t^a - k - w_s^h\theta_t^{er}) > 0$, which is equal to the reduction in wages when the true ability of the marginal educated worker (the worker whose skill level is θ_t^{er}) is discovered, captures the negative incentive that an increase in m_t has on the education-cum-migration decision of low-ability workers. This negative incentive, however, coincides with the positive incentive that arises owing to the increase in θ_t^a that, contingent on equation (7) holding, occurs as more high-ability workers migrate abroad because of an increased m_t. It follows that the negative incentive effect of an increase in m_t dominates the positive incentive effect whenever the increase in θ_t^a with respect to m_t is sufficiently low, as in equation (8), in which case, $\partial\theta_t^{er}/\partial m_t > 0$.

Proposition 4 completely summarizes the intertemporal variations of θ_t^a, θ_t^f, and θ_t^{er} for any given probability of discovery, m_t. Because migrant employment experience is cumulative, and the probability of discovery at any time $t + 1$ depends on the accumulation of migrant employment experience until time $t - 1$, $[m^{-1}(m_t)]$, plus the increment in the total volume of migration at time t ($\mathcal{M}_t = N[(1 - m_t)\{F(\bar\theta) - F[\theta_t^{er}(m_t, c, w_u^h)]\} + F[\theta_t^f(m_t, c, w_u^h)] - F(\bar\theta) + m_t\{1 - F[\theta_t^a(m_t, c, w_u^h)]\}]$), the law of motion governing the process of migration therefore depends only on the evolution of m_t, with

$$m_{t+1} = \begin{cases} m[m^{-1}(m_t) + \mathcal{M}_t] & \text{if } m_t < \hat{m} \\ \hat{m} & \text{otherwise} \end{cases} \tag{9}$$

where $m^{-1}(m_1) = M_0$ is given.

A steady state of equation (9) is denoted m^* such that $m_t = m_{t+1} = m^*$. The steady-state values of θ_t^j will be denoted as $\hat\theta^j, j = a, f, er$. The values of $\hat\theta^j$ are determined using equations (2)–(4) once m^* is determined.

PROPOSITION 5. If equation (7) is satisfied and the initial probability of discovery m_1 is such that $\theta_1^a(m_1, c, w_u^h) > \bar\theta$, then the only steady state equilibrium probability of discovery, m^*, is equal to $\hat{m}$.

This result is straightforward from Proposition 4.[14] In essence, the requirement that equation (7) be satisfied guarantees that accumulation of migrant employment experience and hence the probability of discovery will lead to a sequence of migratory moves from the home country over time. In the process, the average productivity of the migrants improves, not only because of an increase in the incentive for brighter individuals to migrate as the probability of discovery rises, but also because of the simultaneous decline in the willingness of the lowest-ability individuals to acquire education and migrate. Such a cumulative process implies that the only long-run equilibrium consistent with an initial condition that yields a positive rate of migration is such that the probability of discovery no longer improves even when $\mathcal{M}_t$ increases.[15]

5. The Possibility of a Welfare Gain

Denote by $\hat{\theta}^{er}$ and $\hat{\theta}^{f}$ the solutions derived from the system of simultaneous equations (equations (2)–(4)) given $\hat{m}$.

During any time period, the total home-country population $(2N)$ is distributed as follows: the N young individuals are divided into two groups: $NF(\hat{\theta}^{er})$, those who are uneducated and work, and $N[1 - F(\hat{\theta}^{er})]$, those who acquire education and do not work. The N old individuals are divided into two groups: $NF(\hat{\theta}^{er})$, those who are uneducated and work in the home country, and the rest, who engage in migration. These workers, in turn, are divided into three groups of migrants who, with probability $\hat{m}$, will return-migrate and, with probability $1 - \hat{m}$, will remain in the foreign country (consisting of $N[F(\bar{\theta}) - F(\bar{\theta}^{er})]$ individuals); permanent migrants (consisting of $N[F(\hat{\theta}^{f}) - F(\bar{\theta})]$ individuals); migrants who, with probability $1 - \hat{m}$, will return-migrate and, with probability $\hat{m}$, will remain in the foreign country (consisting of $N[1 - F(\hat{\theta}^{f})]$ individuals). There are thus $N\{\hat{m}[F(\bar{\theta}) - F(\hat{\theta}^{er})] + (1 - \hat{m})[1 - F(\hat{\theta}^{f})]\}$ workers at home who are return migrants, and there are $N\{(1 - \hat{m})[F(\bar{\theta}) - F(\hat{\theta}^{er})] + [F(\hat{\theta}^{f}) + F(\bar{\theta})] + \hat{m}[1 - F(\hat{\theta}^{f})]\} \equiv \hat{\mathcal{M}}^{p}$ workers who remain abroad.

Therefore, national output accrues from $2NF(\hat{\theta}^{er})$ workers who each produce w_{u}^{h}, from $\hat{m}N[F(\bar{\theta}) - F(\hat{\theta}^{er})]$ workers who each produce w_{s}^{h} times their individual θ, and from $(1 - \hat{m})N[1 - F(\hat{\theta}^{f})]$ workers who each produce w_{s}^{h} times their individual θ.

Denote by $V^{m}(\hat{\theta}^{er}, \hat{\theta}^{f})$ the long-run equilibrium value of the per-period national output in the home country, net of the cost of education. It follows that

$$V^{m}(\hat{\theta}^{er}, \hat{\theta}^{f}) = 2NF(\hat{\theta}^{er})w_{u}^{h} + N\hat{m}\int_{\hat{\theta}^{er}}^{\bar{\theta}}(w_{s}^{h}\theta - c)f(\theta)d\theta$$

$$+ N(1 - \hat{m})\int_{\hat{\theta}^{f}}^{\infty}(w_{s}^{h}\theta - c)f(\theta)d\theta$$

$$= N\Big[2F(\hat{\theta}^{er})w_{u}^{h} + \hat{m}\int_{\hat{\theta}^{er}}^{\bar{\theta}}(w_{s}^{h}\theta - c)f(\theta)d\theta$$

$$+ (1 - \hat{m})\int_{\hat{\theta}^{f}}^{\infty}(w_{s}^{h}\theta - c)f(\theta)d\theta\Big]$$

$$= N\Big[2F(\hat{\theta}^{er})w_{u}^{h} + \int_{\hat{\theta}^{er}}^{\infty}(w_{s}^{h}\theta - c)f(\theta)d\theta$$

$$- (1 - \hat{m})\int_{\hat{\theta}^{er}}^{\bar{\theta}}(w_{s}^{h}\theta - c)f(\theta)d\theta - \int_{\bar{\theta}}^{\hat{\theta}^{f}}(w_{s}^{h}\theta - c)f(\theta)d\theta$$

$$- \hat{m}\int_{\hat{\theta}^{f}}^{\infty}(w_{s}^{h}\theta - c)f(\theta)d\theta\Big]$$

$$= N\Big[2F(\hat{\theta}^{er})w_{u}^{h} + \int_{\hat{\theta}^{er}}^{\infty}(w_{s}^{h}\theta - c)f(\theta)d\theta - (w_{s}^{h}\hat{\theta}^{p} - c)\frac{\hat{\mathcal{M}}^{p}}{N}\Big],$$

where

$$\hat{\theta}^p = \frac{N}{\hat{\mathcal{M}}^p}\left[(1-\hat{m})\int_{\hat{\theta}^{er}}^{\bar{\theta}}\theta f(\theta)d\theta + \int_{\bar{\theta}}^{\hat{\theta}^f}\theta f(\theta)d\theta + \hat{m}\int_{\hat{\theta}^f}^{\infty}\theta f(\theta)d\theta\right]$$

is the average ability of all migrant workers who stay abroad. The term $(w_s^h\hat{\theta}^p - c)\hat{\mathcal{M}}^p$ thus refers to the home-country output, net of the cost of education, that the home country forgoes when $\hat{\mathcal{M}}^p$ of its workers migrate and stay in the foreign country. To recall, $\hat{\mathcal{M}}^p$ is the per-period number of home-country workers employed abroad in a steady-state. Therefore, per capita output at home is

$$v^m(\hat{\theta}^{er}, \hat{\theta}^f) = \frac{V^m(\hat{\theta}^{er}, \hat{\theta}^f)}{2N - \hat{\mathcal{M}}^p}.$$

Thus, $v^m(\hat{\theta}^{er},\hat{\theta}^f) > v(\theta^*)$ if and only if

$$\frac{1}{2 - \hat{\mathcal{M}}^p/N}\left[2F(\hat{\theta}^{er})w_u^h + \int_{\hat{\theta}^{er}}^{\infty}(w_s^h\theta - c)f(\theta)d\theta - (w_s^h\hat{\theta}^p - c)\frac{\hat{\mathcal{M}}^p}{N}\right]$$

$$> \frac{1}{2}\left[2w_u^hF(\hat{\theta}^*) + \int_{\theta^*}^{\infty}(w_s^h\theta - c)f(\theta)d\theta\right] \equiv v(\theta^*)$$

or if and only if

$$\frac{1}{2 - \hat{\mathcal{M}}^p/N}\left[2F(\hat{\theta}^{er})w_u^h + \int_{\hat{\theta}^{er}}^{\theta^*}(w_s^h\theta - c)f(\theta)d\theta + \int_{\theta^*}^{\infty}(w_s^h\theta - c)f(\theta)d\theta\right.$$

$$\left. - (w_s^h\hat{\theta}^p - c)\frac{\hat{\mathcal{M}}^p}{N}\right] > \frac{1}{2}\left[2w_u^hF(\hat{\theta}^*) + \int_{\theta^*}^{\infty}(w_s^h\theta - c)f(\theta)d\theta\right].$$

On manipulating the preceding equation, we obtain the following necessary and sufficient condition for $v^m(\hat{\theta}^{er}, \hat{\theta}^f) > v(\theta^*)$:

$$\left\{\int_{\hat{\theta}^{er}}^{\theta^*}(w_s^h\theta - c - 2w_u^h)f(\theta)d\theta + \frac{\hat{\mathcal{M}}^p}{N}[v(\theta^*) - (w_s^h\hat{\theta}^p - c)]\right\}\frac{1}{2 - \hat{\mathcal{M}}^p/N} > 0. \qquad (10)$$

The first term in the curly brackets on the left-hand side of equation (10) reflects the gain in per capita output when the number of educated workers in the home country increases from $N[1 - F(\theta^*)]$ to $N[1 - F(\hat{\theta}^{er})]$ as a result of the prospect of migration. In particular:

$$\int_{\hat{\theta}^{er}}^{\theta^*}(w_s^h\theta - c - 2w_u^h)f(\theta)d\theta \equiv (w_s^h\hat{\theta}^d - c - 2w_u^h)[F(\theta^*) - F(\hat{\theta}^{er})] > 0$$

if and only if $w_s^h\hat{\theta}^d - c > 2w_u^h$, where $\hat{\theta}^d$ denotes the average skill level of workers in the range $[\hat{\theta}^{er}, \theta^*]$. Hence, the first term of equation (10) is positive if and only if the average product of the increase in the educated workforce in the s sector, net of the cost of education, is higher than the forgone output in the u sector. In particular, a sufficient condition for the foregoing is that $w_s^h\hat{\theta}^{er} - c - 2w_u^h > 0$. From the definition of $\hat{\theta}^{er}$, this requires that

$$\left(2\hat{m} - \frac{1+\beta}{\beta}\right)w_u^h < (1-\hat{m})(c + k - w_s^f\hat{\theta}^a),$$

which, for example, is satisfied for sufficiently small $\hat{m}$ and/or sufficiently large c and k. From Proposition 3, it follows that $w_s^h\hat{\theta}^{er} - c < w_u^h\theta^* - c$, and from the definition of

θ^*, it follows that when $\beta = 1$, $w_s^h \theta^* = 2w_u^h + c$. Therefore, when $\beta = 1$, $w_s^h \hat{\theta}^{er} - c < 2w_u^h$. But if $w_s^h \hat{\theta}^{er} - c - 2w_u^h < 0$, the sufficient condition just referred to may not hold. That is, a gain in per capita income is less likely to occur. Recall our discussion in section 2 (*Production and Equilibrium*), in which we pointed out that when $\beta = 1$, individual utility maximization corresponds to the social optimum. Here again we find that when $\beta = 1$, it is less likely that the migration prospect will lead to an improvement. However, if $\beta < 1$, the smaller the β, the larger the gain that will result from the increase in education prompted by the prospect of migration. This is nicely reflected by the increased likelihood that equation (10) will hold.

The second term in the curly brackets on the left-hand side of equation (10) reflects the change in per capita income resulting from a reduction in total population due to the loss of educated workers. In particular, this term is positive whenever the per capita home-country income of steady-state migrant workers, $w_s^h \hat{\theta} p - c$, is less than the per capita home-country income in the absence of migration, $v(\theta^*)$. Note that the larger the total number of workers abroad in a steady state ($\mathcal{M}^p$), the more significant will be the effect of this source of change in per capita output.

PROPOSITION 6. *The per capita output in a country vulnerable to migration of skilled workers is higher than the per capita output in a country that is immune to migration if and only if equation (10) is satisfied.*

It is quite straightforward to write an equation analogous to (10) for the purpose of examining per capita output along the transition path, in the presence of migration or in its absence. In particular, from the discussion of equation (10), it can be verified that if the following inequality holds at each time period, t:

$$\left\{ \int_{\theta_t^{er}}^{\theta^*} (w_s^h \theta - c - 2w_u^h) f(\theta) d\theta + \frac{\mathcal{M}_t^p}{N} \left[v(\theta^*) - w_s^h \theta_t^p - c \right] \right\} \frac{1}{2 - \mathcal{M}_t^p / N} > 0 \qquad (10')$$

per capita home-country output during the transition toward the steady state is higher in every time period t than it would have been had the country been immune to migration. Furthermore, if equation (10) holds in a steady state for an $\hat{m}$ which is sufficiently small (indicating a welfare improvement owing to the possibility of migration), equation (10') will hold if $m_t \le \hat{m}$. To see this, recall from Proposition 5 that $\mathcal{M}_t$ is increasing in t along the transition path toward the steady state. It follows, therefore, that $m_t \le \hat{m}$ and hence the home country is better off in the wake of migration.

6. Conclusions

When an economy opens up to migration, workers in the economy are presented with a new set of opportunities and a new structure of incentives. Although the expansion of opportunities results in human capital depletion, the revised incentives induce human capital formation: higher returns to skills in the foreign country prompt more skill formation in the home country. We have shown that the fraction of the home-country workforce acquiring education in the presence of migration opportunities is higher than the fraction of the home-country workforce undertaking education in the absence of migration opportunities.

Migration is also associated with a changing information environment, implying, in particular, that foreign-country employers are imperfectly informed about the skill levels of individual migrant workers. Consequently, migrants with different skill levels are pooled together and all are paid the same wage, which is based on the average product of the entire cohort of migrants. The imperfect but nonzero capability of employers to decipher true skill levels of individual migrants—captured in the probability of discovery—results in return-migration of both the highest and lowest skilled migrant workers, whereas permanent migrants are not drawn from the extremes of the skill distribution. Employers nevertheless become less ignorant over time. As their experience with employing migrants builds up, the probability of discovery rises. This progressive rise prompts a sequence of migratory moves characterized by a rising average level of skills, until the probability of discovery reaches its steady-state equilibrium.

Accounting for the steady-state goings, comings, and skill formation, we have shown that under well-specified conditions, per capita output in the home country is higher than what would have obtained had the country altogether been immune to migration. An intriguing implication of this is that if migration of skilled workers is allowed (rather than hindered), the home-country population can enjoy higher welfare.[16] A drain of brains and a welfare gain need not be mutually exclusive and, as we have demonstrated, the former can be the very cause of the latter.

Appendix

Proof of Proposition 1

We proceed by stating the conditions under which $y_t^f(\theta) > y_t^{rd}(\theta)$ and $y_t^f(\theta) > y_t^{ru}(\theta)$. Now,

$$y_t^f(\theta) - y_t^{rd}(\theta) = (1 - m_t)(w_s^f \theta_t^a - k) + m_t(w_s^f \theta - k) - (1 - m_t)(w_s^f \theta_t^a - k) - m_t(w_s^h \theta)$$
$$= m_t(w_s^f \theta - k - w_s^h \theta) > 0$$

if and only if $\theta > \bar{\theta}$. Similarly

$$y_t^f(\theta) - y_t^{ru}(\theta) = (1 - m_t)(w_s^f \theta_t^a - k) + m_t(w_s^f \theta - k) - (1 - m_t)(w_s^h \theta) - m_t(w_s^f \theta - k) > 0$$

if and only if $\theta < \theta_t^f$ with

$$\theta_t^f = \frac{w_s^f \theta_t^a - k}{w_s^h}.$$

It remains to be shown that $\theta_t^f > \bar{\theta}$ and that $y_t^h(\theta) < \max[y_t^{rd}(\theta), y_t^f(\theta), y_t^{ru}(\theta)]$ for all θ. Now:

$$\theta_t^f - \bar{\theta} = \frac{w_s^f \theta_t^a - k}{w_s^h} - \frac{k}{w_s^f - w_s^h}$$
$$= \frac{w_s^f \theta_t^a}{w_s^h} - \frac{kw_s^h + k(w_s^f - w_s^h)}{w_s^h(w_s^f - w_s^h)}$$
$$= \frac{w_s^f \theta_t^a}{w_s^h} - \frac{w_s^f}{w_s^h} \frac{k}{w_s^f - w_s^h}$$
$$= \frac{w_s^f \theta_t^a}{w_s^h} - \frac{w_s^f \bar{\theta}}{w_s^h}$$
$$> 0$$

if and only if $\theta_t^a > \bar{\theta}$ (where the first and the fourth equalities follow from the definition of $\bar{\theta} = k/(w_s^f - w_s^h)$). In addition, for $\theta < \theta_t^f$:

$$y_t^{rd}(\theta) - y_t^h(\theta) = (1 - m_t)(w_s^f \theta_t^a - k) + m_t w_s^h \theta - w_s^h \theta$$
$$= (1 - m_t)(w_s^f \theta_t^a - k) - (1 - m_t)w_s^h \theta$$
$$= (1 - m_t)(w_s^f \theta_t^a - k - w_s^h \theta) > 0.$$

Hence, $y_t^{rd}(\theta) > y_t^h(\theta)$ for $\theta < \theta_t^f$. Also, because $y_t^f(\theta) > y_t^{rd}(\theta)$, it must also be the case that $y_t^f(\theta) > y_t^h(\theta)$ for $\theta \in [\bar{\theta}, \theta_t^f)$. Finally, for $\theta \geq \theta_t^f$:

$$y_t^{ru}(\theta) - y_t^h(\theta) = (1 - m_t)(w_s^h \theta) + m_t(w_s^h \theta - k) - w_s^h \theta$$
$$= m_t(w_s^f \theta - k) - m_t w_s^h \theta$$
$$= m_t(w_s^f \theta - k - w_s^h \theta) > 0.$$

It follows, therefore, that for all $\theta < \bar{\theta}$, $y_t(\theta) = y_t^{rd}(\theta)$; $\theta \in [\bar{\theta}, \theta_t^f)$, $y_t(\theta) = y_t^f(\theta)$; otherwise, $y_t(\theta) = y_t^{ru}(\theta)$, where $y_t(\theta)$, recall, is equal to $\max[y_t^{rd}(\theta), y_t^f(\theta), y_t^{ru}(\theta), y_t^h(\theta)]$. $\square$

Proof of Proposition 2

(1) The case of $\theta_t^{er} < \bar{\theta}$: we need to show that $\beta y_t(\theta) > (1 + \beta)w_u^h$ for every $\theta > \theta_t^{er}$. From the proof of Proposition 1, we have, for all $\theta < \bar{\theta}$, $y_t(\theta) = y_t^{rd}(\theta)$; $\theta \in [\bar{\theta}, \theta_t^f)$, $y_t(\theta) = y_t^f(\theta)$; and otherwise, $y_t(\theta) = y_t^{ru}(\theta)$. Hence, it is sufficient to show the following: (A) for $\theta \in [\theta_t^{er}, \bar{\theta})$, $\beta y_t^{rd}(\theta) > (1 + \beta)w_u^h$; (B) for $\theta \in [\bar{\theta}, \theta_t^f)$, $\beta y_t^f(\theta) > (1 + \beta)w_u^h$; and (C) $\beta y_t^{ru}(\theta) > (1 + \beta)w_u^h$ for $\theta \geq \theta_t^f$.

(A) By the definition of θ_t^{er}:

$$\frac{1+\beta}{\beta} w_u^h = m_t w_s^h \theta_t^{er} + (1 - m_t)(w_s^f \theta_t^a - k) - c$$
$$\Leftrightarrow \frac{1+\beta}{\beta} w_u^h < m_t w_s^h \theta + (1 - m_t)(w_s^f \theta_t^a - k) - c$$
$$\Leftrightarrow (1 + \beta)w_u^h < \beta y_t^{rd}(\theta)$$

for any $\theta \geq \theta_t^{er}$. Clearly, it must also be the case that $(1 + \beta)w_u^h < \beta y_t^{rd}(\theta)$ for any $\theta \in [\theta_t^{er}, \bar{\theta})$.

(B) Making use of the definition of θ_t^{er}, suppose that $\theta_t^{er} < \bar{\theta}$. We have

$$\left[\frac{1+\beta}{\beta} w_u^h - (1 - m_t)(w_s^f \theta_t^a - k) + c\right]\frac{1}{m_t w_s^h} < \bar{\theta}$$
$$\Leftrightarrow \frac{1+\beta}{\beta} w_u^h - (1 - m_t)(w_s^f \theta_t^a - k) + c < m_t w_s^h \bar{\theta}$$
$$\Leftrightarrow \frac{1+\beta}{\beta} w_u^h < m_t w_s^h \bar{\theta} + (1 - m_t)(w_s^f \theta_t^a - k) - c$$
$$\Leftrightarrow \frac{1+\beta}{\beta} w_u^h < m_t(w_s^h \bar{\theta} - k) + (1 - m_t)(w_s^f \theta_t^a - k) - c$$
$$\Leftrightarrow \frac{1+\beta}{\beta} w_u^h < m_t(w_s^h \theta - k) + (1 - m_t)(w_s^f \theta_t^a - k) - c = y_t^f(\theta)$$

for every $\theta > \bar{\theta}$. Note that the next-to-last inequality follows from the definition of $\bar{\theta}(w_s^f \bar{\theta} - k = w_s^h \bar{\theta})$. It follows, therefore, that for every $\theta > \bar{\theta}$, $(1 + \beta)w_u^h < \beta y_t^f(\theta)$ whenever $\theta_t^{er} < \bar{\theta}$.

(C) Because $y_t^f(\theta) < y_t^{ru}(\theta)$ for $\theta > \theta_t^f$ it follows from (B) that $(1 + \beta)w_u^h < \beta y_t^f(\theta) < \beta y_t^{ru}(\theta)$ for every $\theta > \bar{\theta}$. In the proof of Proposition 1, we have that $\theta_t^f > \bar{\theta}$. Hence, for every $\theta > \theta_t^f (> \bar{\theta})$, $(1 + \beta)w_u^h < \beta y_t^f(\theta) < \beta y_t^{ru}(\theta)$.

(2) The case of $\theta_t^{er} \geq \bar{\theta}$: we need to show that $\beta y_t(\theta) > (1 + \beta)w_u^h$ for every $\theta > \theta_t^{ef}$. In particular, we need to show the following: (D) for all $\theta < \bar{\theta}$, $(1 + \beta)w_u^h > y_t^{rd}(\theta)$; (E) for $\theta \in [\bar{\theta}, \theta_t^{ef})$, $(1 + \beta)w_u^h > \beta y_t^f(\theta)$; (F) for $\theta \in [\theta_t^{ef}, \theta_t^f]$, $(1 + \beta)w_u^h < \beta y_t^f(\theta)$; and (G) for $\theta > \theta_t^f$, $(1 + \beta)w_u^h < \beta y_t^{ru}(\theta)$.

(D) Suppose that $\theta_t^{er} \geq \bar{\theta}$. By the definition of θ_t^{er} we have

$$\left[\frac{1+\beta}{\beta}w_u^h - (1 - m_t)(w_s^f\theta_t^a - k) + c \right]\frac{1}{m_t w_s^h} \geq \bar{\theta}$$

$$\Leftrightarrow \frac{1+\beta}{\beta}w_u^h - (1 - m_t)(w_s^f\theta_t^a - k) + c \geq m_t w_s^h\bar{\theta}$$

$$\Leftrightarrow \frac{1+\beta}{\beta}w_u^h \geq m_t w_s^h\bar{\theta} + (1 - m_t)(w_s^f\theta_t^a - k) - c$$

$$\Leftrightarrow \frac{1+\beta}{\beta}w_u^h > m_t w_s^h\theta + (1 - m_t)(w_s^f\theta_t^a - k) - c = y_t^{rd}(\theta)$$

for $\theta < \bar{\theta}$. It follows, therefore, that for $\theta < \bar{\theta}$, $(1 + \beta)w_u^h > \beta y_t^{rd}(\theta)$.

(E) We shall first establish that $\theta_t^{ef} \geq \bar{\theta}$. If $\theta_t^{er} \geq \bar{\theta}$, we have

$$\left[\frac{1+\beta}{\beta}w_u^h - (1 - m_t)(w_s^f\theta_t^a - k) + c \right]\frac{1}{m_t w_s^h} \geq \bar{\theta}$$

$$\Leftrightarrow \frac{1+\beta}{\beta}w_u^h - (1 - m_t)(w_s^f\theta_t^a - k) + c \geq m_t w_s^h\bar{\theta}$$

$$\Leftrightarrow \frac{1+\beta}{\beta}w_u^h \geq m_t w_s^h\bar{\theta} + (1 - m_t)(w_s^f\theta_t^a - k) - c$$

$$\Leftrightarrow \frac{1+\beta}{\beta}w_u^h \geq m_t(w_s^f\bar{\theta} - k) + (1 - m_t)(w_s^f\theta_t^a - k) - c = y_t^f(\bar{\theta})$$

$$\Leftrightarrow y_t^f(\theta_t^{ef}) = \frac{1+\beta}{\beta}w_u^h \geq y_t^f(\bar{\theta})$$

$$\Leftrightarrow \theta_t^{ef} \geq \bar{\theta}$$

where the next-to-last line follows from the definition of θ_t^{ef}. Now, we can make use of the definition of θ_t^{ef} once more to establish that for $\theta \in [\bar{\theta}, \theta_t^{ef})$, $(1 + \beta)w_u^h > \beta y_t^f(\theta)$. From the definition of θ_t^{ef} we have

$$\frac{1+\beta}{\beta}w_u^h = m_t(w_s^f\theta_t^{ef} - k) + (1 - m_t)(w_s^f\theta_t^a - k) - c$$

$$\Leftrightarrow \frac{1+\beta}{\beta}w_u^h > m_t(w_s^f\theta - k) + (1 - m_t)(w_s^f\theta_t^a - k) - c$$

for every $\theta < \theta_t^{ef}$. It follows, therefore, that for every $\theta < \theta_t^{ef}$, $(1 + \beta)w_u^h > \beta y_t^f(\theta)$. This includes, of course, all $\theta \in (\bar{\theta}, \theta_t^{ef})$.

(F) Making use of the definition of θ_t^{ef}:

$$\frac{1+\beta}{\beta} w_u^h = m_t(w_s^f \theta_t^{ef} - k) + (1 - m_t)(w_s^f \theta_t^a - k) - c$$

$$\Leftrightarrow \frac{1+\beta}{\beta} w_u^h < m_t(w_s^f \theta - k) + (1 - m_t)(w_s^f \theta_t^a - k) - c$$

for every $\theta > \theta_t^{ef}$. It follows, therefore, that for every $\theta > \theta_t^{ef}$, $(1 + \beta)w_u^h < \beta y_t^f(\theta)$. This includes, of course, all $\theta \in [\theta_t^{ef}, \theta_t^f]$.

(G) Recall that (F) states that $\beta y_t^f(\theta) > (1 + \beta)w_u^h$ for every $\theta > \theta_t^{ef}$. This includes, as a subset, $\theta > \theta_t^f$ so that for $\theta > \theta_t^f$, $\beta y_t(\theta) > (1 + \beta)w_u^h$. But for $\theta > \theta_t^f$, $y_t^{ru}(\theta) > y_t^f(\theta)$ or $\beta y_t^{ru}(\theta) > \beta y_t^f(\theta)$. Therefore, for $\theta > \theta_t^f$, $\beta y_t^{ru}(\theta) > \beta y_t^f(\theta) > (1 + \beta)w_u^h$. □

Proof of Proposition 3

We need to show that $\theta_t^{er} < \theta^*$. From Figure 2, observe that to the left of $\bar{\theta}$, $y_t^{rd}(\theta) > y_t^h(\theta)$. Take $\theta = \theta_t^{er}$. Because

$$y_t^{rd}(\theta_t^{er}) = m_t w_s^h \theta_t^{er} + (1 - m_t)(w_s^f \theta_t^a - k) - c,$$

$$y_t^h(\theta_t^{er}) = w_s^h \theta_t^{er} - c.$$

$$w_s^h \theta_t^{er} - w_s^h \theta^* < m_t w_s^h \theta_t^{er} + (1 - m_t)(w_s^f \theta_t^a - k) - w_s^h \theta^*$$

$$= \frac{w_u^h(1 + \beta)}{\beta} + c - w_s^h \theta^*$$

$$= 0,$$

where the next-to-last equality follows from the definition of θ_t^{er}, and the last equality follows from the definition of θ^*. Thus, $w_s^h \theta_t^{er} < w_s^h \theta^*$ or $\theta_t^{er} < \theta^*$.

To show that $\theta_t^{ef} < \theta^*$, observe from Figure 2 that to the left of θ_t^f, $y_t^f(\theta) > y_t^h(\theta)$. Taking $\theta = \theta_t^{ef}$, we have

$$y_t^f(\theta_t^{ef}) = m_t(w_s^f \theta_t^{ef} - k) + (1 - m_t)(w_s^f \theta_t^a - k) - c,$$

$$y_t^h(\theta_t^{ef}) = w_s^h \theta_t^{ef} - c.$$

Hence

$$w_s^h \theta_t^{ef} - w_s^h \theta^* < m_t(w_s^f \theta_t^{ef} - k) + (1 - m_t)(w_s^f \theta_t^a - k) - w_s^h \theta^*$$

$$= \frac{w_u^h(1 + \beta)}{\beta} + c - w_s^h \theta^*$$

$$= 0,$$

where the next-to-last equality follows from the definition of θ_t^{ef}, and the last equality follows from the definition of θ^*. Thus, $w_s^h \theta_t^{ef} < w_s^h \theta^*$ or $\theta_t^{ef} < \theta^*$. □

The Slope of the Curve DD

Because the DD curve depends on both θ_t^f and θ_t^{er}, we first make use of equation (4) to determine that

$$\frac{\partial \theta_t^{er}}{\partial \theta_t^a} = -\frac{(1 - m_t)w_s^f}{m_t w_s^h}.$$

Differentiation of equation (6) yields

$$\frac{\partial \theta_t^a}{\partial \theta_t^f}|DD = \frac{\theta_t^f f(\theta_t^f)}{F(\theta_t^f) - F(\theta_t^{er})} - \frac{\theta_t^{er} f(\theta_t^{er})}{F(\theta_t^f) - F(\theta_t^{er})} \frac{\partial \theta_t^{er}}{\partial \theta_t^a} \left(\frac{\partial \theta_t^a}{\partial \theta_t^f}|DD \right)$$

$$- \frac{\int_{\theta_t^{er}}^{\theta_t^f} \theta f(\theta) d\theta}{(F(\theta_t^f) - F(\theta_t^{er}))^2} \left[f(\theta_t^f) - f(\theta_t^{er}) \frac{\partial \theta_t^{er}}{\partial \theta_t^a} \left(\frac{\partial \theta_t^a}{\partial \theta_t^f}|DD \right) \right]$$

$$= \frac{\theta_t^f f(\theta_t^f)}{F(\theta_t^f) - F(\theta_t^{er})} - \frac{\theta_t^{er} f(\theta_t^{er})}{F(\theta_t^f) - F(\theta_t^{er})} \frac{\partial \theta_t^{er}}{\partial \theta_t^a} \left(\frac{\partial \theta_t^a}{\partial \theta_t^f}|DD \right)$$

$$- \frac{\theta_t^a}{F(\theta_t^f) - F(\theta_t^{er})} \left[f(\theta_t^f) - f(\theta_t^{er}) \frac{\partial \theta_t^{er}}{\partial \theta_t^a} \left(\frac{\partial \theta_t^a}{\partial \theta_t^f}|DD \right) \right]$$

$$= \frac{(\theta_t^f - \theta_t^a) f(\theta_t^f)}{F(\theta_t^f) - F(\theta_t^{er})} - \frac{(\theta_t^{er} - \theta_t^a) f(\theta_t^{er})}{F(\theta_t^f) - F(\theta_t^{er})} \frac{\partial \theta_t^{er}}{\partial \theta_t^a} \left(\frac{\partial \theta_t^a}{\partial \theta_t^f}|DD \right)$$

$$= \frac{1}{\Delta} \frac{(\theta_t^f - \theta_t^a) f(\theta_t^f)}{F(\theta_t^f) - F(\theta_t^{er})},$$

where the second-to-last equality follows from the definition of θ_t^a in equation (2). Hence, because $\theta_t^f > \theta_t^a$, a necessary and sufficient condition for DD to be upward-sloping is that $\Delta > 0$. To see that this is indeed the case, note that

$$\Delta = 1 + \frac{(\theta_t^{er} - \theta_t^a) f(\theta_t^{er})}{F(\theta_t^f) - F(\theta_t^{er})} \frac{\partial \theta_t^{er}}{\partial \theta_t^a}$$

$$= 1 + \frac{(\theta_t^a - \theta_t^{er}) f(\theta_t^{er})}{F(\theta_t^f) - F(\theta_t^{er})} \frac{(1 - m_t) w_s^f}{m_t w_s^h} > 0.$$

Proof of Proposition 4

(1) We need to determine the relationships between $\theta_t^j, j = a, f, er$ and the exogenous variables $m_t, c,$ and w_u^h, which are implicit in equations (2)–(4). By totally differentiating equation (2), we get

$$d\theta_t^a = \frac{\theta_t^f f(\theta_t^f)}{F(\theta_t^f) - F(\theta_t^{er})} d\theta_t^f - \frac{\theta_t^{er} f(\theta_t^{er})}{F(\theta_t^f) - F(\theta_t^{er})} d\theta_t^{er}$$

$$- \frac{\int_{\theta_t^{er}}^{\theta_t^f} \theta f(\theta) d\theta}{[F(\theta_t^f) - F(\theta_t^{er})]^2} [f(\theta_t^f) d\theta_t^f - f(\theta_t^{er}) d\theta_t^{er}]$$

$$= \frac{\theta_t^f f(\theta_t^f)}{F(\theta_t^f) - F(\theta_t^{er})} d\theta_t^f - \frac{\theta_t^{er} f(\theta_t^{er})}{F(\theta_t^f) - F(\theta_t^{er})} d\theta_t^{er}$$

$$- \frac{\theta_t^a}{F(\theta_t^f) - F(\theta_t^{er})} [f(\theta_t^f) d\theta_t^f - f(\theta_t^{er}) d\theta_t^{er}]$$

$$= \frac{(\theta_t^f - \theta_t^a) f(\theta_t^f)}{F(\theta_t^f) - F(\theta_t^{er})} d\theta_t^f + \frac{(\theta_t^a - \theta_t^{er}) f(\theta_t^{er})}{F(\theta_t^f) - F(\theta_t^{er})} d\theta_t^{er} \qquad (A1)$$

where the next-to-last line follows from the definition of θ_t^a in equation (2). Because $(\theta_t^f - \theta_t^a) > 0$ and $(\theta_t^{er} - \theta_t^a) < 0$, θ_t^a is increasing in θ_t^f and θ_t^{er}. The foregoing derivation, of course, also confirms our claim in section 4 that θ_t^a is strictly increasing in θ_t^f.

By totally differentiating equation (3), we obtain

$$d\theta_t^f = \frac{w_s^f}{w_s^h} d\theta_t^a. \tag{A2}$$

Hence θ_t^f is increasing in θ_t^a.

Turning now to the determination of θ_t^{er}, we get, by totally differentiating equation (4):

$$
\begin{aligned}
d\theta_t^{er} &= \frac{1+\beta}{\beta m_t w_s^h} dw_u^h + \frac{1}{m_t w_s^h} dc - \frac{(1-m_t)w_s^f}{m_t w_s^h} d\theta_t^a + \frac{w_s^f \theta_t^a - k}{m_t w_s^h} dm_t \\
&\quad - \frac{1}{(m_t w_s^h)^2}\left[\frac{1+\beta}{\beta} w_u^h - (1-m_t)(w_s^f \theta_t^a - k) + c\right] w_s^h dm_t \\
&= \frac{1+\beta}{\beta m_t w_s^h} dw_u^h + \frac{1}{m_t w_s^h} dc - \frac{(1-m_t)w_s^f}{m_t w_s^h} d\theta_t^a + \frac{w_s^f \theta_t^a - k}{m_t w_s^h} dm_t - \frac{w_s^h \theta_t^{er}}{m_t w_s^h} dm_t \\
&= \frac{1+\beta}{\beta m_t w_s^h} dw_u^h + \frac{1}{m_t w_s^h} dc - \frac{(1-m_t)w_s^f}{m_t w_s^h} d\theta_t^a + \frac{w_s^f \theta_t^a - k - w_s^h \theta_t^{er}}{m_t w_s^h} dm_t.
\end{aligned}
$$

$$\tag{A3}$$

It follows that θ_t^{er} is increasing in w_u^h and c but decreasing in θ_t^a. Also, because $\theta_t^a > \bar{\theta}$ by the assumption in section 3 (*The Individuals Revisited*), $w_s^f \theta_t^a - k > w_s^f \bar{\theta} - k = w_s^h \bar{\theta} > w_s^h \theta_t^{er}$, where the last inequality follows from our assumption that $\theta_t^{er} < \bar{\theta}$ in section 3. Hence, θ_t^{er} is increasing in m_t, all else remaining constant.

We next examine the relationship between θ_t^a and m_t, holding all else constant. By substituting equations (A2) and (A3) into (A1), we obtain

$$
\begin{aligned}
d\theta_t^a &= \frac{(\theta_t^f - \theta_t^a)f(\theta_t^f)}{\mathcal{M}_t / N}\left(\frac{w_s^f}{w_s^h} d\theta_t^a\right) \\
&\quad - \frac{(\theta_t^a - \theta_t^{er})f(\theta_t^{er})}{F(\theta_t^f) - F(\theta_t^{er})}\left(\frac{(1-m_t)w_s^f}{m_t w_s^h} d\theta_t^a - \frac{w_s^f \theta_t^a - k - w_s^h \theta_t^{er}}{m_t w_s^h} dm_t\right) \\
&= \frac{1}{\Omega}\left[\frac{(\theta_t^a - \theta_t^{er})f(\theta_t^{er})}{F(\theta_t^f) - F(\theta_t^{er})}\frac{w_s^f \theta_t^a - k - w_s^h \theta_t^{er}}{m_t w_s^h}\right] dm_t
\end{aligned}
\tag{A4}
$$

where

$$\Omega = 1 - \frac{(\theta_t^f - \theta_t^a)f(\theta_t^f)}{F(\theta_t^f) - F(\theta_t^{er})}\frac{w_s^f}{w_s^h} + \frac{(\theta_t^a - \theta_t^{er})f(\theta_t^{er})}{F(\theta_t^f) - F(\theta_t^{er})}\frac{(1-m_t)w_s^f}{m_t w_s^h}.$$

The numerator in the last line of equation (A4) is positive because $w_s^f \theta_t^a - k - w_s^h \theta_t^{er} > 0$. Therefore, θ_t^a is increasing in m_t if and only if $\Omega > 0$, as stated in Proposition 4.

Substituting equation (A3) into equation (A1), keeping m_t and w_u^h constant, we obtain

$$d\theta_t^a = \frac{1}{\Omega}\frac{(\theta_t^a - \theta_t^{er})f(\theta_t^{er})}{F(\theta_t^f) - F(\theta_t^{er})}\frac{1}{m_t w_s^h} dc. \tag{A5}$$

It follows that θ_t^a is increasing in c if and only if $\Omega > 0$. Finally, holding m_t and c constant, we obtain, on substituting equation (A3) into (A1):

$$d\theta_t^a = \frac{1}{\Omega} \frac{(\theta_t^a - \theta_t^{er})f(\theta_t^{er})}{F(\theta_t^f) - F(\theta_t^{er})} \frac{1+\beta}{\beta m_t w_s^h} dw_u^h. \tag{A6}$$

Hence θ_t^a is also increasing in w_u^h if and only if $\Omega > 0$.

(2) Turning now to θ_t^f, from equation (A2) we obtain

$$d\theta_t^f = \frac{w_s^f}{w_s^h} \frac{\partial \theta_t^a}{\partial m_t} dm_t.$$

Hence, a necessary and sufficient condition for θ_t^f to be increasing in m_t is that $\partial \theta_t^a / \partial m_t > 0$. From equation (A4), we have already determined that θ_t^a is increasing in m_t if and only if $\Omega > 0$. It follows that $\Omega > 0$ is necessary and sufficient for θ_t^f to be increasing in m_t.

In a similar fashion, we can determine, using equations (A2) and (A5), that

$$d\theta_t^f = \frac{w_s^f}{w_s^h} \frac{\partial \theta_t^a}{\partial c} dc.$$

It follows that θ_t^f is also increasing in c under the condition $\Omega > 0$, because $(\partial \theta_t^a / \partial c) > 0$, from equation (A5). Finally:

$$d\theta_t^f = \frac{w_s^f}{w_s^h} \frac{\partial \theta_t^a}{\partial w_u^h} dw_u^h.$$

From equation (A6), $(\partial \theta_t^a / \partial w_u^h) > 0$ if $\Omega > 0$; hence, θ_t^f is increasing in w_u^h under the condition $\Omega > 0$.

(3) To determine the relationship between θ_t^{er} and m_t, note, from equation (A3), that all else remaining constant:

$$d\theta_t^{er} = -\frac{(1-m_t)w_s^f}{m_t w_s^h} \left(\frac{\partial \theta_t^a}{\partial m_t} \right) dm_t + \frac{w_s^f \theta_t^a - k - w_s^h \theta_t^{er}}{m_t w_s^h} dm_t.$$

From equation (A4), we obtain the result that $(\partial \theta_t^a / \partial m_t) > 0$, if and only if $\Omega > 0$. Because $(w_s^f \theta_t^a - k - w_s^h \theta_t^{er}) > 0$, as already pointed out in our discussion following equation (A3), we have that θ_t^{er} is increasing in m_t if and only if

$$\frac{w_s^f \theta_t^a - k - w_s^h \theta_t^{er}}{m_t w_s^h} > \frac{(1-m_t)w_s^f}{m_t w_s^h} \left(\frac{\partial \theta_t^a}{\partial m_t} \right)$$

or if and only if

$$\frac{w_s^f \theta_t^a - k - w_s^h \theta_t^{er}}{(1-m_t)w_s^f} > \frac{\partial \theta_t^a}{\partial m_t}$$

as stated in equation (8).   □

Proof of Proposition 5

Because $\theta_1^a > \bar{\theta}$:

$$\theta_1^f - \theta_1^a = \frac{w_s^f \theta_1^a - k}{w_s^h} - \theta_1^a$$

$$= \frac{w_s^f \theta_1^a - k}{w_s^h} - \frac{w_s^h \theta_1^a}{w_s^h}$$

$$= \frac{w_s^f \theta_1^a - k - w_s^h \theta_1^a}{w_s^h} > 0$$

and hence, there is positive migration at $t = 1$ with $M_1 = M_0 + \mathcal{M}_1 > M_0$ or, equivalently, $m_2 = m(M_1) > m(M_0) = m_1$. Also, because M_t can be no less than M_0, satisfaction of equation (6) implies that $\theta_t^a(m_t, c, w_u^h) > \theta_1^a(m_1, c, w_u^h)$ and hence $\theta_t^a(m_t, c, w_u^h) > \bar{\theta}$ for all $t = 2, 3, 4. \ldots$. In addition, equation (6) also guarantees that $\theta_t^f(m_t, c, w_u^h) > \theta_1^f(m_1, c, w_u^h)$, because θ_t^f is increasing in m_t for any t.

Finally, because $\theta_t^{er} < \bar{\theta}$, we have $\theta_t^f > \theta_t^a > \bar{\theta} > \theta_t^{er}$ and $M_t = M_{t-1} + \mathcal{M}_t > M_{t-1}$ for all t. It follows immediately that $M_{t+i} \geq M_t, i = 1, 2, \ldots$. Hence, the only long-run equilibrium probability of discovery must correspond to the upper bound $\hat{m}$.   □

Existence

To determine whether or not there exists at least one set of solutions $\theta_t^j, (j = a, f, er)$, to equations (2)–(4) for every m_t that satisfies the requirement in Proposition 1 that $\theta_t^a > \bar{\theta}$, we need only show that there exists at least one θ_t^f for every m_t at which the *SS* and *DD* curves intersect. Once θ_t^f is determined, equation (5) can be used to determine θ_t^a. Finally, the value of θ_t^{er} can also be calculated from equation (4) once θ_t^a is determined.

Consider the right-hand side of equation (5). Note that as $\theta_t^f \to \infty, \theta_t^a \to \infty$. In addition, as $\theta_t^f \to \infty$, the right-hand side of equation (6) is finite because, by assumption, θ has a finite expectation. It follows that for sufficiently large θ_t^f, *SS* lies above *DD*. By the intermediate-value theorem, existence is guaranteed if and only if *DD* lies above *SS* for some $\theta_t^f > \bar{\theta}$ or if and only if

$$\frac{\int_{\theta_t^{er}}^{\theta_t^f} \theta f(\theta) d\theta}{F(\theta_t^f) - F(\theta_t^{er})} > \frac{w_s^h \theta_t^f}{w_s^f}.$$

The requirement that there exists a $\theta_t^f > \bar{\theta}$ such that *DD* lies above *SS* guarantees that the *equilibrium* value of θ_t^a is strictly greater that $\bar{\theta}$. From the definition of θ_t^f in section 3, $\theta_t^f > \bar{\theta}$ implies that

$$\frac{w_s^f \theta_t^a - k}{w_s^h} > \bar{\theta}$$

$$\Leftrightarrow w_s^f \theta_t^a > w_s^h \bar{\theta} + k$$

$$\Leftrightarrow w_s^f \theta_t^a > w_s^h \bar{\theta} + (w_s^f - w_s^h)\bar{\theta}$$

$$\Leftrightarrow w_s^f \theta_t^a > w_s^h \bar{\theta}$$

$$\Leftrightarrow \theta_t^a > \bar{\theta}.$$

References

Berry, Albert R. and Ronald Soligo, "Some Welfare Aspects of International Migration," *Journal of Political Economy* 77 (1969):778–94.

Bhagwati, Jagdish and John D. Wilson, *Income Taxation and International Mobility*. Cambridge, MA: MIT Press (1989).

Borjas, George J., "Self-selection and the Earnings of Immigrants," *American Economic Review* 77 (1987):531–53.

Carrington, William J., Enrica Detragiache, and Tara Vishwanath, "Migration with Endogenous Moving Costs," *American Economic Review* 86 (1996):909–30.

DaVanzo, Julie, "Repeat Migration in the United States: Who Moves Back and Who Moves On?" *Review of Economics and Statistics* 65 (1983):552–9.

Grubel, Herbert G. and Anthony Scott, "The International Flow of Human Capital," *American Economic Review* 56 (1966):268–74.

Katz, Eliakim and Oded Stark, "International Migration under Asymmetric Information," *Economic Journal* 97 (1987):718–26.

———, "International Migration under Alternative Informational Regimes: A Diagrammatic Analysis," *European Economic Review* 33 (1989):127–42.

Kwok, Peter V. and Hayne Leland, "An Economic Model of the Brain Drain," *American Economic Review* 72 (1982):91–100.

LaLonde, Robert J. and Robert H. Topel, "Economic Impact of International Migration and the Economic Performance of Migrants," in Mark R. Rosenzweig and Oded Stark (eds.), *Handbook of Population and Family Economics*. Amsterdam: North-Holland (1997):799–850.

Ravenstein, Ernest George, "The Laws of Migration," *Journal of the Royal Statistical Society* 48 (1885):167–227.

Razin, Assaf and Efriam Sadka, "International Migration and International Trade," in M. R. Rosenzweig and Oded Stark (eds.), *Handbook of Population and Family Economics*. Amsterdam: North-Holland (1997):851–87.

Reilly, Barry, "What Determines Migration and Return? An Individual Level Analysis using Data for Ireland," unpublished manuscript, University of Sussex (1994).

Stark, Oded, *The Migration of Labor*. Oxford: Blackwell (1991).

———, "Frontier Issues in International Migration," in *Proceedings of the World Bank Annual Conference on Development Economics, 1994*. Washington, DC: International Bank for Reconstruction and Development (1995):361–86.

Notes

1. Returnees tend to be less well educated than the migrants who stay (DaVanzo, 1983; Reilly, 1994).

2. Borjas (1987) provided evidence that the quality of migrant workers from Western Europe to the United States was increasing over the period 1955–79. However, his measures of quality are different from those we use.

3. The primary conclusion of Grubel and Scott (1966) and Berry and Soligo (1969) was that, whereas very low levels of migration have no impact on the welfare of those who stay behind, finite levels of migration unambiguously reduce welfare.

4. With linear production technologies in the skilled and unskilled sectors, production in our model is akin to production in the standard Ricardian model of international trade. However, the home country remains incompletely specialized in the production of the two outputs under free trade. This outcome follows from the heterogeneity of the home-country workers in terms of their endowed abilities and their irreversible decisions to undertake education. Consequently, workers in the two sectors do not instantaneously switch between sectors even if the returns to a unit of unskilled labor differ from the returns to a unit of skilled labor (which, to recall, is measured in efficiency units).

5. The average number of efficiency units of labor supplied by a skilled worker is $\int_{\theta^*}^{\infty} \theta f(\theta) d\theta / \int_{\theta^*}^{\infty} f(\theta) d\theta$. Since there are $N(1 - F(\theta^*))$ skilled workers, their total supply of skilled work is $[\int_{\theta^*}^{\infty} \theta f(\theta) d\theta / \int_{\theta^*}^{\infty} f(\theta) d\theta] N[1 - F(\theta^*)] = N \int_{\theta^*}^{\infty} \theta f(\theta) d\theta$.

6. To derive the last equality, note that from the definition of θ^*, $w_s^h \theta^* - c = (1 + \beta) w_u^h / \beta$. Hence, $w_s^h \theta^* - 2 w_u^h - c = (1 - \beta) w_u^h / \beta$.

7. A prime denotes the first derivative with respect to M_{t-1}.

8. In general, there can be two additional migration regimes for educated home-country workers: (5) An educated worker migrates. With probability m_t, the true ability of the worker is discovered, and the worker remains in the foreign country to engage in u-sector employment. With probability $1 - m_t$, the worker receives $w_s^f \theta_t^a$ in the foreign country. (6) An educated worker migrates. With probability m_t, the true ability of the worker is discovered, and the worker return-migrates to engage in u-sector employment in the home country. With probability $1 - m_t$, he receives $w_s^f \theta_t^a$ in the foreign country. Later, we show that neither of these options will be pursued by educated migrant workers as long as w_u^h is sufficiently small and k is sufficiently large.

9. Given θ_t^{er} and θ_t^{ef}, we are now in a position to demonstrate the conditions under which no educated return-migrant will be employed in the u sector of the home country. To this end, note that in equilibrium, $\beta y_t^{rd}(\theta_t^{er}) = (1 + \beta)w_u^h$. An educated worker is strictly better off working in the skilled sector if and only if $w_s^h \theta_t^{er} > w_u^h$ as the skill level of all educated workers is no less than θ_t^{er}. From the definition of θ_t^{er}, we have

$$w_s^h \theta_t^{er} = \frac{1}{m_t}\left[\frac{(1+\beta)w_u^h}{\beta} - (1-m_t)(w_s^f \theta_t^a - k) + c\right]$$

$$= w_u^h + \frac{1}{m_t}\left[\frac{[1+\beta(1-m_t)]w_u^h}{\beta} - (1-m_t)(w_s^f \theta_t^a - k) + c\right]$$

$$> w_u^h$$

if w_u^h is sufficiently small. In addition, because $w_u^f - k < w_u^h$, by transitivity, $w_s^h \hat{\theta}_t^{er} > w_u^h > w_u^f - k$. Hence, migration regimes 5 and 6, as discussed in note 8, will not be pursued by any educated migrant worker.

10. For $\theta_t^{er} \bar{\theta}$, we require that

$$m_t w_s^h \bar{\theta} + (1-m_t)(w_s^f \theta_t^a - k) - c \geq \frac{(1+\beta)w_u^h}{\beta}.$$

Because $\theta_t^a > \bar{\theta}$, the left-hand side of the preceding inequality is greater than $m_t w_s^h \bar{\theta} + (1 - m_t)$ $(w_s^f \bar{\theta} - k) - c = w_s^h \bar{\theta} - c = w_s^h k/(w_s^f - w_s^h) - c$. It follows that

$$m_t w_s^h \bar{\theta} + (1-m_t)(w_s^f \theta_t^a - k) - c > w_s^h \frac{k}{w_s^f - w_s^h} - c \geq \frac{(1+\beta)w_u^h}{\beta},$$

whenever w_u^h is sufficiently small and k is sufficiently large.

11. A natural question is whether or not a solution to the preceding system exists. In the Appendix we provide an existence proof and spell out the required assumptions.

12. From equation (5), the slope of the supply relationship $(\partial\theta_t^a/\partial\theta_t^f)|_{SS}$ can be written as

$$\frac{\partial\theta_t^a}{\partial\theta_t^f}|_{SS} = \frac{w_s^h}{w_s^f} > 0.$$

From the demand relationship in equation (6), we confirm in the Appendix that the slope $(\partial\theta_t^a/\partial\theta_t^f)|_{DD}$ is

$$\frac{\partial\theta_t^a}{\partial\theta_t^f}\bigg|_{DD} = \frac{(\theta_t^f - \theta_t^a)f(\theta_t^f)/[F(\theta_t^f) - F(\theta_t^{er})]}{1+\{(\theta_t^a - \theta_t^{er})f(\theta_t^{er})/[F(\theta_t^f) - F(\theta_t^{er})]\}[(1-m_t)w_s^f/m_t w_s^h]} > 0.$$

13. To see this, note from equation (6) that for any given value of θ_t^f, an increase in m_t leads to an upward shift of the DD curve, because

$$\frac{\partial\theta_t^a}{\partial m_t}\bigg|_{\theta_t^f const.} = \frac{(\theta_t^a - \theta_t^{er})f(\theta_t^{er})}{F(\theta_t^f) - F(\theta_t^{er})}\frac{\partial\theta_t^{er}}{\partial m_t}$$

$$= \frac{(\theta_t^a - \theta_t^{er})f(\theta_t^{er})}{F(\theta_t^f) - F(\theta_t^{er})}\frac{w_s^f \theta_t^a - k - w_s^h \theta_t^{er}}{m_t w_s^h} > 0,$$

where the first equality follows from equation (A1) in the Appendix, and the second equality follows from equation (A3). It follows, therefore, that DD shifts upward when m_t increases, or

$$\frac{\partial \theta_t^a}{\partial m_t}\bigg|_{\theta_t^f \text{ const.}} > 0.$$

In addition, from equation (5):

$$\frac{\partial \theta_t^a}{\partial m_t}\bigg|_{\theta_t^f \text{ const.}} = 0.$$

Hence, SS is independent of m_t.

14. We are grateful to Yoram Weiss for pointing out that the steady-state assumption can also be supported by an alternative experience accumulation formulation, in which a per-period depreciation rate can be used to capture the fact that recent migrants provide more information on the quality of the current wave of migrants.

15. It bears emphasizing that Proposition 5 also relies on an assumption made in Proposition 1, that is, that $\theta_t^a > \bar{\theta}$. Otherwise, from equation (3):

$$\theta_t^f - \theta_t^a = \frac{w_s^f \theta_t^a - k}{w_s^h} - \theta_t^a$$

$$= \frac{w_s^f \theta_t^a - k - w_s^h \theta_t^a}{w_s^h} < 0$$

as $\theta_t^a < \bar{\theta}$. It follows that equation (2), which requires that θ_t^f be no smaller than θ_t^a, can never be satisfied and accordingly migration never takes off.

16. Note that this outcome holds independently of migrants remitting either some or none of their higher foreign earnings.

7
Chaotic Equilibria in a Small, Open, Overlapping-Generations Economy with Child–Parent Externality

Kazuo Nishimura and Koji Shimomura*

Abstract

This paper presents a simple overlapping-generations model of a small open economy with child–parent externality that exhibits chaotic equilibrium dynamics.

1. Introduction

One of the most important issues in dynamic economics is the choice of framework—linear, stochastic and inherently stable models, or nonlinear, deterministic and inherently unstable models—that can best explain economic movements. The issue is important for each analyst because it is closely related to his/her fundamental view on market mechanisms; that is, whether he/she sees market mechanisms as dynamically stable or not. The recent revival of interest in the endogenous cycle hypothesis suggests the importance of constructing dynamic general equilibrium models with perfect foresight that exhibit persistent (either cyclical or chaotic) fluctuations without exogenous shocks (Boldrin and Woodford, 1990).

This line of research has generated a vast literature on nonlinear dynamics in the framework of a representative agent (see Nishimura and Sorger (1996) for a recent survey), and in the framework of overlapping generations (OLG) with no bequest motive (Grandmont, 1985; Reiclin, 1986; Farmer, 1986).

In a recent paper, de la Croix (1996) presented a simple OLG model to show that cyclical oscillations can be generated by child–parent externality. We believe that child–parent externality is ubiquitous; children are most strongly influenced by their parents, under whatever cultural backgrounds they are brought up.

This paper presents another simple example of an OLG dynamic equilibrium model with child–parent externality that exhibits complicated dynamics. A main feature that differentiates our model from de la Croix's is that the former can generate chaotic dynamics as well as cyclical ones, while the latter focuses on cycles. The other main feature of our model is that, under the assumption that agents are intra-generationally identical, international trade and child–parent externality *together* contribute to generating chaos.

2. The Model

Our model is an overlapping-generations one in which each individual lives two periods, as child and parent. There are two types of good, good 1 and good 2, both of

---

* Nishimura: KIER, Kyoto University, Yoshida-Honmachi, Sakyo, Kyoto, Japan 606-01. Tel: +81-75-753-7124; Fax: +81-75-753-7198; E-mail: nishimura@kier.kyoto-u.ac.jp. Shimomura: RIEB, Kobe University, 2-1 Rokkodai, Nada, Kobe, Japan 657-0013. Tel: +81-78-881-1212; Fax: +81-78-861-6434; E-mail: simomura@rieb.kobe-u.ac.jp. We are grateful to Rodney Chun and Kar-yiu Wong for constructive comments. The comments and suggestions from two anonymous referees have much improved the paper. All remaining errors are ours.

which are tradable consumption goods. Each parent generation is endowed with the same amounts of primary factors of production and earns income by supplying their endowments to factor markets, while each child generation has no initial endowment and is completely fed by their parent generation.

Let us define *generation t* as the one that is born at period t. The utility function of each household in generation t is denoted as

$$u = u(c_1(t+1), c_2(t+1); c_1(t), c_2(t)), \tag{1}$$

where $(c_1(t + 1), c_2(t + 1))$ is the household consumption bundle that was purchased by generation t, which uses a part of the bundle for their own consumption and the rest for feeding their child generation; and $(c_1(t), c_2(t))$ is the household consumption purchased by generation; $t - 1$. Concerning the relationship between u and $(c_1(t + 1), c_2(t + 1))$, we make a standard assumption:

ASSUMPTION 1. $u(c_1(t + 1), c_2(t + 1); c_1(t), c_2(t))$ *is twice-differentiable, increasing and strictly quasiconcave in* $c_1(t + 1)$ *and* $c_2(t + 1)$.

The main feature of equation (1) is that the purchasing pattern of each parent generation has an externality effect on the preferences of the next child generation. Let us specify in what way the decision $(c_1(t), c_2(t))$ by generation $t - 1$ affects the preferences of generation t.

ASSUMPTION 2. *The marginal rate of substitution (MRS) between good 1 and good 2*

$$MRS[c_1(t+1), c_2(t+1); c_1(t), c_2(t)] \equiv [\partial u/\partial c_2(t+1)]/[\partial u/\partial c_1(t+1)]$$

has the following properties:

(i) *It is increasing in both* $c_1(t)$ *and* $c_2(t)$: $\partial MRS/\partial c_i(t) > 0$, $i = 1, 2$.
(ii) *For any nonnegative* $c_1(t + 1)$, $c_2(t + 1)$, *and* c:

$$MRS[c_1(t+1), c_2(t+1); c, 0] = MRS[c_1(t+1), c_2(t+1); 0, c] = 0.$$

Remark 1. Consider the following form of utility function:

$$u(\cdot) = \Lambda(c_1(t), c_2(t))U[g_1(c_1(t), c_2(t))h_1((c_1(t+1)) + g_2(c_1(t), c_2(t))h_2(c_2(t+1))], \tag{1a}$$

where

$$\Gamma(c_1(t), c_2(t)) \equiv g_2(c_1(t), c_2(t))/g_1(c_1(t), c_2(t))$$

$$\Gamma(0, c_2(t)) = \Gamma(c_1(t), 0) = 0.$$

If $\Gamma(c_1(t), c_2(t))$ is increasing in both $c_1(t)$ and $c_2(t)$, then (1a) satisfies Assumption 2. The following two examples are special cases of (1a).

Example 1

$$u = \left[\alpha(c_1(t))^a (c_2(t))^b (c_1(t+1))^{-1/\rho} + (1-\alpha)(c_1(t))^\alpha (c_2(t))^\beta (c_2(t+1))^{-1/\rho}\right]^{-\rho},$$

where $a < \alpha$, $b < \beta$, and $\rho > 0$.

Example 2

$$u = (1/A)c_1(t+1)/c_1(t) + \frac{c_2(t)}{\rho}(c_2(t+1))^\rho,$$

where $0 < \rho < 1$ and $A > 0$.

Remark 2. Note that what matters in Assumption 2 is the *relative* degree of externalities g_2/g_1, and not whether externalities are positive or negative in the sense that $\partial U/\partial c_i(t)$, $i = 1, 2$, is positive or negative.

For simplicity, it is also assumed that each adult has just one child, which implies that the population of each generation is constant over time. We normalize the population to be one.

We assume that the production side of the economy is the standard two-good, two-(primary) factor Heckscher–Ohlin model. The two factors of production are assumed to be internationally immobile, which implies that the production possibility curve is concave to the origin (Figure 1(a)).

Now let us formulate the optimization problem that generation t solves:

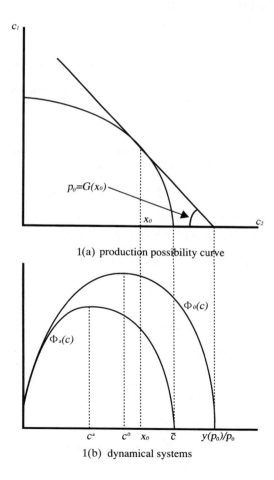

1(a) production possibility curve

1(b) dynamical systems

Figure 1.

$$\max_{c_i(t+1),\, i=1,2} u(c_1(t+1), c_2(t+1); c_1(t), c_2(t))$$

$$\text{s.t. } c_1(t+1) + p_{t+1}c_2(t+1) \leqq y(p_{t+1}),$$

where p_{t+1} is the price of good 2 in terms of good 1 at period $t+1$, and $y(p_{t+1})$ is the GNP function of the economy. For the time being, let us assume that the above optimization problem has an interior solution $(c_1(t+1), c_2(t+1))$ for given $c_1(t), c_2(t), p_{t+1}$ and $y(p_{t+1})$. Then the solution satisfies the well-known condition

$$
\begin{aligned}
p_{t+1} &= MRS[c_1(t+1), c_2(t+1); c_1(t), c_2(t)] \\
&= MRS[y(p_{t+1}) - p_{t+1}c_{t+1}, c_{t+1}; y(p_t) - p_t c_t, c_t],
\end{aligned}
\tag{2}
$$

where $c_{t+1} \equiv c_2(t+1)$ and $c_t \equiv c_2(t)$.

First, let us consider the case in which the economy is autarkic. We then have as the market-clearing condition:

$$y'(p_{t+1}) = c_{t+1} \quad \text{and} \quad y'(p_t) = c_t. \tag{3}$$

Inverting the function $y'(.)$, we can rewrite (3) as

$$p_{t+1} = G(c_{t+1}) \quad \text{and} \quad p_t = G(c_t). \tag{3a}$$

Substituting (3a) into (2), we obtain the dynamical system for the autarkic economy:

$$G(c_{t+1}) = MRS(y(G(c_{t+1})) - G(c_{t+1})c_{t+1}, c_{t+1}; y(G(c_t)) - G(c_t)c_t, c_t). \tag{4}$$

Next, let us consider the case in which the economy is a small open one that is facing a given international price p_0. Substituting p_0 into (2), we obtain the dynamical system for the small open economy:

$$p_0 = MRS(y(p_0) - p_0 c_{t+1}, c_{t+1}; y(p_0) - p_0 c_t, c_t). \tag{5}$$

The difference equations (4) and (5) are our models to be examined.

3. Dynamical Equations

To derive clear results for the dynamic behavior of (4) and (5), we have to specify the utility function (1). Let us specify it as (1a). Then, one may verify that (4) and (5) can be respectively rewritten as

$$G(c_{t+1}) = H(c_{t+1})\Gamma(y(G(c_t)) - G(c_t)c_t, c_t) \tag{4a}$$

$$p_0 = \tilde{H}(c_{t+1})\Gamma(y(p_0) - p_0 c_t, c_t), \tag{5a}$$

where

$$H(c_{t+1}) \equiv \frac{h_2'(c_{t+1})}{h_1'(y(G(c_{t+1})) - G(c_{t+1})c_{t+1})} \quad \text{and} \quad \tilde{H}(c_{t+1}) \equiv \frac{h_2'(c_{t+1})}{h_1'(y(p_0) - p_0 c_{t+1})}.$$

Considering the standard properties of the utility function and the GNP function, one can verify that both $G(c_{t+1})/H(c_{t+1})$ and $1/\tilde{H}(c_{t+1})$ are increasing in c_{t+1}. Inverting these functions, we obtain

$$c_{t+1} = F[\Gamma(y(G(c_t)) - G(c_t)c_t, c_t)] \equiv \Phi_a(c_t) \qquad (3b)$$

$$c_{t+1} = Z[\Gamma(y(p_0) - p_0 c_t, c_t)/p_0] \equiv \Phi_0(c_t) \qquad (4b)$$

where $F[.]$ and $Z[.]$ are the inverse functions of $G(.)/H(.)$ and $1/\tilde{H}(.)$.

LEMMA.

(i) $\Phi_a(0) = \Phi_a(\bar{c}) = 0$ and $\Phi_0(0) = \Phi_0(y(p_0)/p_0) = 0$, where $\bar{c}$ is the solution to $y(G(c))$ $- G(c)c = 0$ and is smaller than $y(p_0)/p_0$. See Figure 1(b).

(ii) Each of $\Phi_a(c)$ and $\Phi_0(c)$ has a unique maximum point, say c^a and c^0, in the intervals $(0, \bar{c})$ and $(0, y(p_0)/p_0)$, respectively, if $\Gamma(c_1, c_2)$ is strictly concave in c_i, $i = 1, 2$.

PROOF. (i) Trivial. (ii) Each function has a global maximum point within the respective interval, because of (i). Uniqueness is clear from

$$\text{sign}[\Phi_a''(c^a)] = \text{sign}[G^2\Gamma_{11} - 2G\Gamma_{12} + \Gamma_{22} - G'\Gamma_1] < 0,$$

$$\text{sign}[\Phi_0''(c^0)] = \text{sign}[p_0^2\Gamma_{11} - 2p_0\Gamma_{12} + \Gamma_{22}] < 0,$$

where $\Gamma_{ij}(c_1, c_2) \equiv \partial^2\Gamma/\partial c_i\partial c_j$ and $\Gamma_i(c_1, c_2) \equiv \partial\Gamma/\partial c_i$, $i, j = 1, 2$. $\qquad\square$

Note that c^a and c^0 are independent of the functions $F[.]$ and $Z[.]$, respectively.

4. Chaotic Equilibria

Set X be a closed and convex interval of real numbers. Let $f: X \to X$ be a continuous function. A pair of X and f, denoted by (X, f), may be called a *dynamical system*. Let us denote the nth iterate of f by f^n. If $x \in X$ satisfies $f^k(x) = x$ for some integer $k > 1$, but $f^n(x) \neq x$ for $n = 1, \ldots, k - 1$, then x is called a *periodic point* of (X, f) with period k. The orbit from a periodic point with period k is said to exhibit *period-k cycles*. In this case, we say that a dynamical system (X, f) has *period-k* cycles.

A subset S of X is called a *scrambled set* of a dynamical system (X, f) if it has the following properties:

(i)   The cardinality of S is uncountable.
(ii) S does not contain any periodic point of (X, f).
(iii) For any $x, y \in S$ such that $x \neq y$:

$$\limsup_{n\to\infty}|f^n(x) - f^n(y)| > 0 \quad \text{and} \quad \liminf_{n\to\infty}|f^n(x) - f^n(y)| = 0.$$

(iv) For any periodic point $z \in X$ and any $x \in S$:

$$\limsup_{n\to\infty}|f^n(z) - f^n(x)| > 0.$$

If a dynamical system has a scrambled set, we say that the dynamical system is *chaotic*.

The following result, which is due to Li and York (1975), relates the existence of a scrambled set to that of period-three cycles.

PROPOSITION 1. *If there is a point $x \in X$ that satisfies*

$$f^3(x) \le x < f(x) < f^2(x) \text{ or } f^3(x) \ge x > f(x) > f^2(x),$$

then (i) there is a scrambled set S in X, and (ii) there is a periodic point of period m for every positive integer m.

Now let us focus on the system

$$c_{t+1} = bF[\Gamma(y(G(c_t)) - G(c_t)c_t, c_t)] \equiv b\Phi_a(c_t), \tag{3c}$$

where b is a parameter. Note that c^a is independent of b. Hence, we can choose a value of b, say b^*, such that

$$\bar{c} = b^* F[\Gamma(y(G(c^a)) - G(c^a)c^a, c^a)].$$

Then the graph of $b^*\Phi_a(c)$ can be drawn as in Figure 2. It is clear that under Assumptions 1–3, there exists a unique stationary state c^{ae}. Let us now prove the main result.

PROPOSITION 2. *Both the dynamical system (3c) with $b = b^*$, and*

$$c_{t+1} = s^* Z[\Gamma(y(p_0) - p_0 c_t, c_t)/p_0] \equiv s^* \Phi_0(c_t), \tag{4c}$$

where s^* is defined as $y(p_0)/[p_0\Phi_0(c^0)]$, are chaotic.

PROOF. See Figure 2. First, draw a vertical line from B and denote by H the intersection of the vertical line and the 45°-line. Draw a horizontal line from H and denote by L the intersection of the horizontal line and the left-hand part of the graph of $b^*\Phi_a(c)$. Draw a vertical line from L and denote by A the intersection of the vertical line and the horizontal axis of coordinates. Then it is clear that if the initial condition $c(0)$ is chosen to be the length of OA, we have

$$b^*\Phi_a(c(0)) > c(0) \qquad (OD > OA \text{ in Figure 2})$$
$$b^*\Phi_a(b^*\Phi_a(c(0))) > c(0) \quad (OE > OA \text{ in Figure 2})$$
$$b^*\Phi_a(b^*\Phi_a(b^*\Phi_a(c(0)))) = 0 < c(0).$$

Therefore, owing to the Li–Yorke Theorem, there is a scrambled S in $(0, \bar{c})$. A parallel argument can be used for (4c). □

5. Can International Trade Induce Chaos?

The foregoing argument suggests that both closed and open economies with child–parent externality can have chaotic dynamics. In this section, we shall show a theoretical possibility that while an economy never has complicated dynamics in an autarkic situation, it starts to exhibit chaotic behavior once it opens its border.

In this section we shall further specify the utility function as

$$u = (1/A)c_1(t+1)/c_1(t) + \frac{c_2(t)}{\rho}[c_2(t+1)]^\rho, \quad 0 < \rho < 1, A > 0$$

which is a special case of (1a). Under this specification, (4) and (5) become

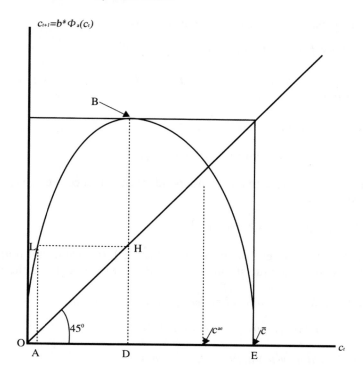

Figure 2.

$$G(c_{t+1})[c_{t+1}]^{1-\rho} = Ac_t[y(G(c_t)) - G(c_t)c_t], \qquad (4d)$$

$$G(x_0)[c_{t+1}]^{1-\rho} = Ac_t[y(G(x_0)) - G(x_0)c_t], \qquad (5d)$$

where x_0 is the output of good 2 when the international price is p_0; i.e., $p_0 = G(x_0)$.

So far we have assumed that the household's optimization problem has an interior solution c_{t+1} for given c_t. Since both

$$\gamma_a(c_{t+1}) \equiv G(c_{t+1})[c_{t+1}]^{1-\rho} \quad \text{and} \quad \gamma_0(c_{t+1}) \equiv G(x_0)[c_{t+1}]^{1-\rho}$$

are monotonically increasing with $\gamma_a(0) \equiv \gamma_0(0) = 0$ and $\gamma_a(\infty) \equiv \gamma_0(\infty) = \infty$, it is clear that for any c_t in the open interval $(0, \bar{c})$, c_{t+1} is uniquely determined from each of (4d) and (5d). Moreover, if

$$A < \frac{G(\bar{c})\bar{c}^{1-\rho}}{c_a[y(G(c_a)) - G(c_a)c_a]},$$

c_{t+1} is in the interval $(0, \bar{c})$. So is c_t, which means that the household's optimization problem has a unique interior solution in the closed economy for any $t > 0$ as far as c_0 is in $(0, \bar{c})$. The parallel argument holds in the open economy if

$$A < \frac{G(x_0)[y(G(x_0))/G(x_0)]^{1-\rho}}{c_0[y(G(x_0)) - G(x_0)c_0]}.$$

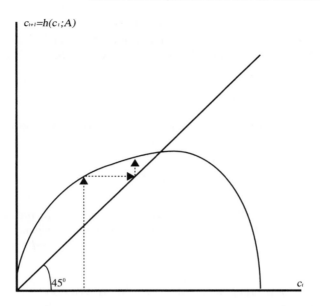

Figure 3.

Note that the household's optimization problem always has an interior solution along any chaotic path, as was discussed in the previous section, even if these expressions are equalities.

From (4d), we see that c^a satisfies $y(G(c)) - 2G(c)c = 0$. Therefore, if

$$A \leqq (c^a)^{-(1+\rho)} = \left[\frac{2G(c^a)}{y(G(c^a))} \right]^{1+\rho},$$

the graph of (4d) can be depicted as in Figure 3. Then it is clear that the dynamical system has either:

  (i) a unique and globally stable positive stationary state and the zero stationary state
 (ii) stable and unstable stationary positive states and the zero stationary state, or
(iii) the zero stationary state only.

In any case, there is neither chaos nor repeated cycles.

Now let us turn to (5d). First, note that it can be rewritten as

$$c_{t+1} = A^{\frac{1}{1-\rho}} [c_t \{(y(G(x_0))/G(x_0) - c_t)\}]^{\frac{1}{1-\rho}} \equiv h(c_t; A). \tag{6}$$

Clearly, c^0 is $y(G(x_0))/2G(x_0)$. Let $\bar{A}$ be $4[G/y]^{1+\rho}$, where $G \equiv G(x_0)$ and $y \equiv y(G(x_0))$. Then one can verify that $h(y/2G; \bar{A}) = y/G$. It follows from Proposition 2 that the dynamical system $c_{t+1} = h(c_t; \bar{A})$ is chaotic.

Next let $c^*(A)$ be the smaller root of the equation

$$c^0 = h(c; A).$$

Since $c^*(\bar{A}) > 0$ and $h(h(h(c^*(\bar{A}); \bar{A}); \bar{A}); \bar{A}) = 0$, the solution to $c_{t+1} = h(c_t; \bar{A})$ that starts from $c^*(\bar{A})$ satisfies the Li–Yorke condition for chaos. Hence, even if A is slightly less than $\bar{A}$, the solution to $c_{t+1} = h(c_t; A)$ that starts from $c^*(A)$ still satisfies the Li–Yorke condition. Since there is no possibility of chaos for sufficiently small and positive A, there should exist the lower bound of A, say $A_{\min}$, that satisfies the Li–Yorke condition. Thus if

$$A_{\min} < A < \bar{A} \equiv 4[G/y]^{1+\rho},$$

then (6) satisfies the Li–Yorke condition. Now we arrive at the following result.

PROPOSITION 3. *If*

$$G(c^a)/y(G(c^a)) > 2^{1-\rho}\, G(x_0)/y(G(x_0)), \tag{7}$$

then for any A in $(A_{min}, 4[G(x_0)/y(G(x_0))]^{1+\rho})$ the economy in the autarkic situation converges to either positive or zero stationary state without repeated cycles or chaos, while it can have chaotic dynamics once it starts international trade under a given international price.

Remark 2. By definition, $G(x_0)$ is the international price of good 2. Since $G(x)/y(G(x))$ is increasing in x, condition (7) in the above proposition tends to hold if the international price of good 2 is sufficiently smaller than $G(c^a)$.

6. Concluding Remarks

First, we have just focused on chaos. It follows from the Li–Yorke Theorem cited above that a dynamic system satisfying the Li–Yorke condition has a periodic orbit of arbitrary number.

Second, we have considered closed and small open economies. We plan to investigate whether chaotic dynamics are still possible in a large country model.

Third, we have used an overlapping-generations model with child–parent externality. However, such a framework is not crucial for our argument. It may be as realistic as child–parent externality to suppose that what a person consumed yesterday affects his preferences today. We could make a parallel argument under such past–present externality without using the overlapping-generations framework.

References

Boldrin, M. and M. Woodford, "Equilibrium Models Displaying Endogenous Growth and Chaos," *Journal of Monetary Economics* 25 (1990):189–222.

de la Croix, D.,"The Dynamics of Bequeathed Tastes," *Economics Letters* 53 (1996):89–96.

Farmer, R., "Deficits and Cycles," *Journal of Economic Theory* 40 (1986):77–88.

Grandmont, J. M., "On Endogenous Competitive Business Cycles," *Econometrica* 22 (1985):995–1037.

Li, T. and J. Yorke, "Period Three Implies Chaos," *American Mathematical Monthly* 82 (1975):985–92.

Nishimura, K. and G. Sorger, "Optimal Cycles and Chaos: A Survey," *Studies in Nonlinear Dynamics and Econometrics* 1 (1996):11–28.

Reiclin, P., "Equilibrium Cycles in an Overlapping Generations Economy with Production," *Journal of Economic Theory* 40 (1986):89–102.

8
Learning-by-Doing and Strategic Trade Policy

Hassan Benchekroun, Ngo Van Long, and Huilan Tian*

Abstract

The paper models international rivalry between a domestic firm that is going through a learning-by-doing phase, and a mature foreign rival. It is shown that the optimal production subsidy for the domestic firm depends on the degree of strategic sophistication of the foreign firm. Optimal production subsidy rules are derived under various scenarios. They are shown to be very sensitive to the specification of the game between the domestic and the foreign firms. Whether the optimal subsidy should decrease over time depends on the strategic sophistication of the foreign firm.

1. Introduction

Learning-by-doing has often been identified as one of the important sources of economic growth. (See Long and Wong (1997) for a survey of theories of growth and trade, and for important references to the learning-by-doing literature.) There is a growing volume of publications on the theory of learning as well as on the phenomenon of learning in manufacturing and other industries.[1] Many Japanese and East Asian firms are believed to have achieved their dominant market positions through learning processes, possibly with the help of their government in ensuring significant local market shares, which is favorable to learning via increased accumulated output. A number of economists believe that appropriate strategic trade policies should be designed to protect domestic firms when they are experiencing learning-by-doing, both to correct for externalities (if learning by one domestic firm confers benefits on other domestic firms) and to shift rents from foreign firms. There are two distinct issues here: knowledge spillovers within the domestic industry, and international market-share rivalry, which affects output and hence learning rate.

   In this paper we focus on the second issue, with particular emphasis on the possibility of sophisticated strategic behavior by a mature foreign firm. We abstract from knowledge spillovers by assuming that there is only one domestic firm. We show that there are basically two different types of policies. The first one would give a great deal of help to the domestic firm during its early infancy, and would decrease this help as the firm becomes more mature—we call this the "weaning policy." The second type of policy would propose a reward that gradually increases in line with the growth of the firm's knowledge capital; we will refer to this as the "coaxing policy." Which of these policies the home government should choose depends on the kind of strategy that the mature foreign firm adopts. To further our understanding of this point, we develop two models of market rivalry between a foreign firm and a domestic firm. The models differ from each other only in one respect: the degree of strategic sophistication of the foreign firm.

---

*Benchekroun: Concordia University, 1455 DeMaisonneuve Blvd W., Montreal, Quebec H3G 1M8, Canada. Tel: 514-848-3909; Fax: 514-848-4536; E-mail: hben@vax2.concordia.ca. Long, Tian: McGill University, 855 Sherbrooke St W., Montreal, Quebec H3A 2T7, Canada. Tel: 514-398-4844; Fax: 514-398-4938; E-mail: innv@musicb.mcgill.ca, and b4nt@musicb.mcgill.ca. We should like to thank Professors Kotaro Suzumura and Koji Shimomura for helpful comments. We thank SSHRC and FCAR for financial support.

In *model 1*, we assume that the foreign firm does not try to interfere with the learning process of the domestic firm: in each period, it behaves as if it were a conventional static Cournot oligopolist. It knows that the domestic firm is learning (i.e., accumulating, via production of the final good, a stock of "knowledge capital" that reduces costs), but it does not take into account the fact that its output strategy may influence the domestic firm's output and hence learning rate. We derive the optimal production subsidy rule and show that it implies a subsidy rate that *increases over time* toward a steady-state subsidy rate. The optimal policy is thus of the "coaxing" variety.

In *model 2*, we consider the case in which the foreign firm is more sophisticated in strategic behavior. It knows it can influence the domestic firm's rate of learning. We find the subgame-perfect Nash equilibrium of this dynamic game between the two firms, and show how the home government can displace this equilibrium by a production subsidy rule in order to achieve a welfare improvement for the home country. We compare the optimal subsidy formula for model 2 with that for model 1. They stand in sharp contrast to each other. In model 2, the subsidy *declines over time*, while the opposite holds in model 1. The intuition behind this result lies in the fact that when the foreign firm is sophisticated, it tends to be relatively more aggressive when the domestic firm is in its early infancy. As a response, the domestic firm tends to under-produce at low knowledge levels. The optimal subsidy policy must provide incentives to counter this intertemporal bias. This policy adopted is thus of the "weaning" variety.

Even though the foreign firm, in model 2, seeks to influence the domestic firm's learning rate, it would not be appropriate to classify that behavior as Stackelberg. In fact, in model 2 both firms move simultaneously. A truly Stackelberg behavior on the part of the foreign firm would require that the foreign firm be the first mover. This distinction is made precise in the Appendix, where we sketch *model 3*, in which the foreign firm is a Stackelberg leader.

An important implication of our analysis is that in order to conduct effective strategic trade policy, the home government must know how sophisticated firms are in their dynamic games. This points to the complexity of intervention in a world of imperfect information. In the concluding section, we offer some pertinent remarks on informational issues relating to strategic trade policy, and on the coordinating role of governments.

2. The Basic Setting

A Simple Model of Learning-by-Doing

Consider a duopoly consisting of a domestic firm and a foreign firm competing as Cournot rivals in the home market, where the inverse demand function is $P = P(Z)$ with $P'(Z) \leq 0$, and Z is the quantity sold in the home market. For simplicity, we assume that $P(Z) = a - bZ$. The foreign firm is technologically more advanced; its cost of production is lower than that of the domestic firm. For simplicity, the foreign firm's unit cost is taken to be a constant which is set at zero by normalization. The domestic firm, on the other hand, is going through a learning-by-doing process. Its unit cost is positive, but the more it produces, the more it accumulates knowledge, which reduces its unit cost.

Let $q(t)$ denote the home firm's output at time t, and $k(t)$ denote its stock of knowledge. We assume that

$$\dot{k}(t) = q(t) - \delta k(t), \quad k(0) = k_0 \tag{1}$$

where $\delta > 0$ is the rate of depreciation of knowledge. The firm's unit cost of production is $c(k) \geq 0$, where $c'(k) \leq 0$, indicating that unit cost falls as the stock of knowlege capital is accumulated. We assume that $c(k)$ is given by

$$c(k) = \begin{cases} \bar{c} - \gamma k & \text{if } \gamma k \leq \bar{c}, \\ 0 & \text{if } \gamma k \geq \bar{c}, \end{cases} \tag{2}$$

where $\gamma \geq 0$ is the parameter describing the productivity of knowledge capital. In the polar case where $\gamma = 0$, all the results reduce to those of the standard static model without learning.

Assume that the domestic firm sells only in the home market. The foreign firm's supply to the home market is $Q(t)$. Thus $Z(t) = q(t) + Q(t)$. The foreign firm also sells in its own country, and its supply in that country, denoted by $Q_F(t)$, is sufficiently great to ensure that its knowledge capital exceeds $\bar{c}/\gamma$, so that its unit cost is always zero regardless of the quantity $Q(t)$ that it supplies to the home market.

Strategic Trade Policy

We now consider the role of a home government that has an objective function to be maximized. Following the political economy approach,[2] we assume that this objective function is a weighted sum of (i) the profit of the domestic firm, (ii) the tax revenue, and (iii) the domestic consumers' surplus. We specify that the weights given to the first two components are unity, and that given to consumers' surplus is $0 \leq \mu \leq 1$. The extreme case where $\mu = 0$ is of some interest, because, first, at the formal level, with $\mu = 0$, the resulting objective function is identical to that of the Brander–Spencer "third market model" of strategic trade policy; and, second, it depicts a polar case where consumers' interests have a negligible weight in the government's political support function.

Consumers' surplus is denoted by $S(Z)$:

$$S(Z) = \int_0^Z P(\tilde{Z})d\tilde{Z} - ZP(Z) = \frac{bZ^2}{2}. \tag{3}$$

In principle, the home government may have many policy instruments at its disposal, such as production subsidy, tariff, quota, and "voluntary export restraints" (VERs). In what follows, for simplicity, we restrict attention to a production subsidy. Note that in the special case where domestic production is only for exports, then a production subsidy is the same as an export subsidy.

Consider the simplest form of subsidy policy: If the home firm produces q, then it receives a subsidy payment $\theta(k)q$ where $\theta(k)$ is the rate of subsidy per unit of output. We suppose that θ is specified as a function of k alone.[3] This kind of subsidy formula is called a "Linear Markov" subsidy rule (LMSR): the payment is linear in q and the rule is Markovian in the sense that the per-unit subsidy depends only on the current value of the state variable (the stock of knowledge capital).

Owing to the linear–quadratic formulation, we can restrict attention to LMSR that are linear k:

$$\theta(k) = \alpha + \eta k,$$

where α and η are to be determined. Under this specification, social welfare, as seen by the government of the home country, may be written as

$$W \equiv v(k_0, \eta, \alpha) - \int_0^\infty (\alpha + \eta k)qe^{-rt}dt + \int_0^\infty \frac{\mu b Z^2}{2}e^{-rt}dt, \tag{4}$$

where $v(k_0, \eta, \alpha)$ is the integral of the discounted stream of profit flow of the domestic firm. The home government seeks to maximize W by choosing α and η. In the following sections, we show that the optimal pair (α^*, η^*) depends on the nature of rivalry between the domestic and the foreign firm, and in particular, on the degree of strategic sophistication of the foreign firm.

3. Model 1: A Foreign Firm with Unsophisticated Behavior

In this section we model the determination of equilibrium in the home market as follows.[4] At each time t, there is an instantaneous Cournot equilibrium, where the quantities supplied by the two firms are determined by their "effective unit costs." The foreign firm's effective unit cost is zero. The domestic firm's effective unit cost at time t is defined to be $c(k(t)) - \lambda(t)$, where $\lambda(t)$ is the marginal contribution of a unit of current output to the future cost reduction. More precisely, $\lambda(t)$ is the shadow price (or costate variable) associated with the knowledge stock $k(t)$.

The domestic firm's payoff is

$$v = \int_0^\infty \{P[Q(t) + q(t)]q(t) - c(k(t))q(t)\}e^{-rt}dt,$$

where $r > 0$ is the rate of discount. The domestic firm takes the output path of the foreign firm as given and seeks to maximize its payoff v subject to the conditions:

$$\dot{k}(t) = q(t) - \delta k(t), \quad k(0) = k_0.$$

The Hamiltonian function for this optimization problem is

$$H = \{a - b[q(t) + Q(t)] - c(k(t))\}q(t) + \lambda(t)[q(t) - \delta k(t)].$$

Maximization with respect to $q(t)$ (taking $Q(t)$ as given) yields

$$a - bQ(t) - 2bq(t) = c(k(t)) - \lambda(t). \tag{5}$$

The shadow price $\lambda(t)$ evolves according to the rule

$$\dot{\lambda}(t) = r\lambda(t) - \frac{\partial H}{\partial k} = (r + \delta)\lambda(t) + q(t)c'(k(t)). \tag{6}$$

The foreign firm takes the time path of $c(k(t)) - \lambda(t)$ (or, equivalently, the time path of $q(t)$) as given. Since the foreign firm's cost is always zero regardless of its supply $Q(t)$, its first-order condition is

$$a - 2bQ(t) - bq(t) = 0. \tag{7}$$

(This formulation assumes that the foreign firm is somewhat myopic: it does not seek to influence the time path of learning of the domestic firm; the case in which the behavior of the foreign firm is more sophisticated will be considered in the next section). Equations (5) and (7) determine the *instantaneous* Cournot *equilibrium* outputs at t:

$$q(t) = \frac{1}{3b}[a - 2c + 2\lambda(t)], \tag{8}$$

$$Q(t) = \frac{1}{3b}[a + c - \lambda(t)]. \tag{9}$$

We substitute (8) into (1) and (6) to obtain a pair of differential equations in k and λ (in what follows, we omit t when there is no risk of confusion):

$$\dot{\lambda} = (r+\delta)\lambda + \left[\frac{a-2c+2\lambda}{3b}\right]c'(k), \tag{10}$$

$$\dot{k} = \frac{a-2c+2\lambda}{3b} - \delta k. \tag{11}$$

To restrict the number of cases to be considered, we introduce the following assumption:

ASSUMPTION 1. γ is sufficiently small and a and b sufficiently great to ensure that

$$a > 2\bar{c}, \quad 3\delta b > \gamma\left[\frac{a}{\bar{c}} + \frac{2\delta}{r+\delta}\right]. \tag{12}$$

From Assumption 1, the system (10) and (11) has the following *positive* steady-state pair $(k_\infty, \lambda_\infty)$:

$$k_\infty = \frac{(r+\delta)(a-2\bar{c})}{3b\delta(r+\delta)-2\gamma(r+2\delta)}, \quad \lambda_\infty = \frac{\delta_\gamma k_\infty}{r+\delta},$$

and, in particular, $\gamma k_\infty < \bar{c}$, and $c(k_\infty) - \lambda_\infty > 0$.

We now investigate the stability property of the steady state. From (1) and (8):

$$\ddot{k} = \dot{q} - \delta\dot{k} = \left[\frac{2}{3b}\right](\dot{\lambda} - \dot{c}) - \delta\dot{k}. \tag{13}$$

From (6) and (8):

$$\dot{\lambda} = -\gamma q + (r+\delta)\left[\frac{3bq + 2c - a}{2}\right]. \tag{14}$$

Substituting (14) into (13), and making use of (1), we obtain

$$\ddot{k} - r\dot{k} + \left[\frac{2\gamma(r+2\delta)}{3b} - \delta(\delta+r)\right]k = \left[\frac{r+\delta}{3b}\right](2\bar{c} - a).$$

The associated characteristic equation has two real roots of opposite signs. We take the negative root as this is associated with the stable branch of the saddlepoint. This negative root is

$$\beta = \frac{1}{2}[r - \sqrt{r^2 + 4\delta(r+\delta) - 8\gamma(r+2\delta)/3b}] < 0. \tag{15}$$

It is convenient to define $\rho \equiv -\beta > 0$. Then the converging time path of the stock of knowledge is

$$k(t) = k_\infty + (k_0 - k_\infty)\exp(-\rho t). \tag{16}$$

It follows that along the converging path

$$\dot{k} = -\rho[k - k_\infty];$$

that is, $\dot{k}$ is positive if $k < k_\infty$. From this we obtain the *feedback representation* of the equilibrium path of domestic output:

$$q = \dot{k} + \delta k = (\delta - \rho)k + \rho k_\infty \equiv q(k). \tag{17}$$

Notice that $q'(k) = \delta - \rho \geq 0$ ($= 0$ if $\gamma = 0$). This result makes sense: as the capital stock accumulates, the domestic firm's Cournot equilibrium output increases over time if $\gamma > 0$.

The equilibrium time path of k is given by (16). Knowing k, the equilibrium domestic output is determined by (17). From this, we can determine the equilibrium path of the shadow price, represented in the feedback form, from the equilibrium time path of k:

$$\lambda(k) = \frac{1}{2}[3bq(k) + 2c(k) - a]. \tag{18}$$

The equilibrium path of foreign output is

$$Q(k) = \frac{1}{3b}[a + c(k) - \lambda(k)] = \frac{1}{2b}[a - bq(k)], \tag{19}$$

and the equilibrium price path is

$$P(k) = \frac{1}{3}[a + c(k) - \lambda(k)] = \frac{1}{2}[a - bq(k)]. \tag{20}$$

The domestic firm's profit in a Cournot equilibrium at time t is a function of $k(t)$:

$$\pi = (P - c)q = -\frac{1}{2}bq(k)^2 + \frac{1}{2}aq(k) - c(k)q(k). \tag{21}$$

Substitute (17) and (20) into (21) to get

$$2\pi(t) = -Ak(t)^2 + Bk(t) + D, \tag{22}$$

where

$$A = [b(\delta - \rho) - 2\gamma](\delta - \rho),$$
$$B = (\delta - \rho)(a - 2\bar{c}) - \rho[b(\delta - \rho) - 2\gamma +]k_\infty,$$
$$D = (a - 2\bar{c} - \rho bk_\infty)\rho k_\infty.$$

Notice that (i) $A < 0$ if $0 < \gamma < b(r + 2\delta)/3$, and $A > 0$ if $\gamma > b(r + 2\delta)/3$; and (ii) if $\gamma = 0$ then $A = B = 0$, and $C = \frac{2}{9b}(a - 2\bar{c})^2$.

The Nash equilibrium payoff to the domestic firm is

$$v(k_0) \equiv \int_0^\infty \pi(t)e^{-rt}dt.$$

From the above analysis we obtain the following result.

PROPOSITION 1. *The integral of the stream of discounted profit of the domestic firm is an increasing function of γ (the productivity of knowledge capital) and a decreasing function of the maximum unit cost $\bar{c}$.*

PROOF. Substitute (16) into (22), and differentiate with respect to γ (or $\bar{c}$), then evaluate the resulting integral (details are omitted). □

We now turn to the question of *optimal intervention*. As mentioned in the preceding section, for simplicity we will restrict attention to only one policy instrument, namely a production subsidy. Other instruments such as a constant tariff rate, or a nonlinear tariff schedule, etc., can be considered by a similar method. As explained in the preceding section, it is appropriate to consider a linear Markov subsidy rule (LMSR) of the form $\theta(k) = \alpha + \eta k$.

For the moment, let us take α and η as given. What are the effects of the LMSR on the equilibrium path and on welfare? To answer these questions, it is convenient to define $C(k) \equiv c(k) - \alpha - \eta k$. Then the analysis of the preceding section follows with a minor modification: c should be replaced by C, $\bar{c}$ by $\bar{c} - \alpha$, and c' by $-\gamma - \eta$. We obtain the following propositions.

PROPOSITION 2. *Starting from a laissez-faire situation, a small increase in α or in η will increase welfare.* (The proof is omitted.)

PROPOSITION 3. *For the case $\mu = 0$, the optimal pair (α^*, η^*) ensures that the domestic firm's output q(t) is equal to that of a Stackelberg leader that maximizes intertemporal profit, in a game where the foreign firm (the follower) takes the leader's output at each t as given. In particular:*

$$\eta^* = \frac{\gamma}{2} > 0, \quad \alpha^* = \frac{a - 2\bar{c}}{4} > 0.$$

PROOF. See the Appendix.

Remark. Proposition 3 implies that if $\mu = 0$, then the optimal subsidy rate consists of a fixed component (α^*) that is *negatively related* to the firm's maximum initial cost $\bar{c}$, and a variable component, $\eta^* k$, which *increases* over time until the stationary state is reached.

PROPOSITION 4. *If $1 \geq \mu > 0$, the optimal subsidy rate per unit of output exceeds the one described in Proposition 3. The optimal pair (α^{**}, η^{**}) is an increasing function of μ:*

$$\eta^{**} = \left[\frac{3}{2 - (\mu/2)} - 1 \right] \gamma > \eta^*, \quad \alpha^{**} = \frac{a[1 + 2\mu] - \bar{c}[2 + \mu]}{4 - \mu} > \alpha^*.$$

Furthermore, $k_\infty^{**} > k_\infty^*$, where k_∞^{**} and k_∞^* denote respectively the steady-state stock of knowledge capital for the case $1 \geq \mu > 0$ and the case $\mu = 0$.

PROOF. Similar to that of Proposition 3.

Remark. Proposition 4 indicates that when consumers' surplus has a positive weight in the government's objective function, then the subsidy rate is greater at each instant of time, *and* it grows at a faster rate. (As will be seen in the following section, these two features need not hold when the foreign firm is strategically more sophisticated.) Concerning the steady state, note that the steady-state knowledge capital is greater, the greater is the weight attached to consumers' surplus. This result is plausible, because a greater k_∞ will decrease price, which implies a higher level of consumers' surplus.

4. Model 2: Rivalry Between a Sophisticated Foreign Firm and a Domestic Firm

In the preceding section we assumed that the behavior of the foreign firm was rather myopic: it takes the time path of accumulation of knowledge of the domestic firm as given. At each point in time it chooses the output level that corresponds to that of a static Cournot equilibrium. Clearly, a more alert foreign firm would recognize that it could influence the domestic firm's time path of accumulation of knowledge by declaring that its output at any t will be conditional on, say, the observed level of knowledge at t. In this section we consider the implication of such a strategy.

Let us assume that the foreign firm chooses a Markovian strategy, that is, a rule that determines its output at t as a function of the observed value of the state variable (the stock of knowledge of the domestic firm) at t. As we are dealing with a linear quadratic model, we restrict attention to linear Markovian strategies; that is, the foreign firm's output follows a rule of the form $Q = e + fk$, where e and f are constants. The domestic firm, on the other hand, chooses a rule of the form $q = X + Yk$. (These assumptions are not too restrictive, because it can be easily shown that a linear rule is in fact a *best response* to one's rival linear rule.)

A Nash equilibrium in linear Markovian strategies is a vector (e^*, f^*, X^*, Y^*) such that if the foreign firm takes (X^*, Y^*) as given, then (e^*, f^*) is its best reply, and, conversely, if the domestic firm takes (e^*, f^*) as given, then (X^*, Y^*) is its best reply.

PROPOSITION 5. *If γ is sufficiently small, then there exists a unique Nash equilibrium in linear Markovian strategies, with*

$$f^* = \frac{-(r+2\delta) + \Delta_I}{4} < 0, \quad e^* = \frac{4af^* + (r+\delta)(a+\bar{c})}{8bf^* + 3b(r+\delta)},$$

$$Y^* = \frac{r+2\delta - \Delta_I}{2} > 0, \quad X^* = \frac{4a - \bar{c}}{b[3 + 8f^*/(r+\delta)]},$$

where

$$\Delta_I \equiv \sqrt{(r+2\delta)^2 - (r+2\delta)(8\gamma/b)} > 0.$$

PROOF. See the Appendix.

Before deriving the optimal subsidy rule, let us note that the equilibrium strategy of the domestic firm has the property that its output is an increasing function of the stock of knowledge. For the foreign firm, the strategic manipulation of its rival's production consists of deterring the domestic firm from learning, by aggressively expanding its output while the learner is at its early infancy. Furthermore, the more sensitive the domestic firm's output is to a change in its stock of knowledge capital, the more aggressive will be the foreign firm's production expansion. As an equilibrium response to this, the domestic firm tilts its production path toward the future; i.e., it tends to "underproduce" in its early infancy.

Now consider the implication of a production subsidy rule that pays the domestic firm for each unit of output an amount $\theta(k) = \alpha + \eta k$. This induces a new Markovian equilibrium which can be readily obtained from Proposition 5: we simply replace γ by $\gamma + \eta$ and $\bar{c}$ by $\bar{c} - \alpha$.

The following proposition can be established concerning strategic trade policy when the foreign firm is sophisticated.

PROPOSITION 6. *If* $\mu = 0$, *then, under the assumption that both firms use linear Markovian strategies, the optimal pair* (α^0, η^0) *ensures that the domestic firm achieves the output path that is equal to that of a Stackelberg leader, with the foreign firm being the follower having as reaction function* $Q(t) = (a - bX - bYk(t))/(2b)$. *More generally, for any* $\mu \in [0, 1]$, *the optimal pair* (α^0, η^0) *is given by:*

$$\eta^0 = \frac{\gamma}{2}\left[\frac{1}{1-(\mu/4)} - 2\right] < 0, \tag{23}$$

$$\alpha^0 = \left[\frac{a - 2\bar{c}}{2}\right]\left[\frac{\rho^0\{3 + 8f^0/(r+\delta)\}}{2\delta\{1-(\mu/4)\}} - 1\right] > 0, \tag{24}$$

where ρ^0 *and* f^0 *are given by*

$$\rho^0 \equiv \frac{-r}{2} + \frac{\Delta_2}{2}\frac{\sqrt{(r+2\delta)^2 - 4\gamma(r+2\delta)/[b-b\mu/4]}}{2} > 0,$$

$$f^0 \equiv \frac{-(r+2\delta) + \Delta_2}{4},$$

$$\Delta_2 \equiv \sqrt{(r+2\delta)^2 - 4\gamma(r+2\delta)/[b-b\mu/4]}.$$

PROOF. See the Appendix.

Remark. Comparing Proposition 6 with Propositions 3 and 4, we find that when the foreign firm is sophisticated, the optimal rate of subsidy per unit, $\theta(k)$, falls over time, as k rises over time, in sharp contrast to the situation where the foreign firm is strategically unsophisticated. The optimal subsidy rule is thus a "weaning policy." The use of a subsidy rule that offers a subsidy rate that is a decreasing function of knowledge capital serves to reduce the sensitivity of the domestic firm's output to a change in its stock of knowledge capital, and thus reduces the power of the foreign firm to manipulate the domestic firm's production. The subsidy rule $\theta^0(k)$ decreases the foreign firm's incentive for aggressive expansion and thus gives a higher market share to the domestic firm.

5. Concluding Remarks

We have shown that optimal strategic trade policies depend on the degree of strategic sophistication of the foreign firm. The optimal policy would become more complicated when the domestic industry consists of several firms and there are knowledge spillovers generated by learning-by-doing. For a first step in this direction, see Benchekroun and Long (1997).

In model 2 and model 3 (see the Appendix), we have assumed that the foreign firm uses linear strategies. This raises an important question: would the foreign firm have an interest in mis-informing the domestic firm? For example, it may play a nonlinear strategy but pretend that it is using a linear one. Such mis-information will of course be detected eventually. A related informational problem is the observability (or non-observability) of knowlege capital. A firm's true cost of production may be unknown to its rivals, or to the government. Modeling mis-information and detection of mis-information constitutes a challenging topic for further research.

This paper has focused on strategic trade policy, and abstracted from other important issues such as the establishment of a collaborative mechanism, such as the one observed in postwar Japan, in which "government bureaucrats, industry representatives, and private and government banks all participated, exchanged information, and negotiated with each other" (Suzumura, 1997, p. 7). In fact, several experts have argued that this type of intervention, rather than rent shifting through tariffs and production subsidies, has been the principal driving force behind the spectacular performance of countries such as Japan and South Korea.[5] While acknowledging the importance of this argument, we believe that learning-by-doing would be quite ineffective if the domestic output were small; and therefore production subsidies (or similar types of subsidies), in ensuring that domestic firms operate at a scale favorable to rapid growth of knowledge capital, have a significant role to play.

Appendix

The Integral of Discounted Profit in Model 1

The Nash equilibrium payoff to the domestic firm is

$$v(k_0) \equiv \int_0^\infty \pi(t) e^{-rt} dt.$$

We now calculate this integral in terms of k_0 and other parameters. We obtain

$$2v(k_0) = -A\left[\frac{k_\infty^2}{r} + \frac{2k_\infty(k_0 - k_\infty)}{r+\rho} + \frac{(k_0 - k_\infty)^2}{r+2\rho}\right] + B\left[\frac{k_\infty}{r} + \frac{k_0 - k_\infty}{r+\rho}\right] + \frac{D}{r}, \quad (25)$$

or, after rearrangement:

$$2v(k_0) = \frac{-Ak_0^2}{(r+2\rho)} + \frac{k_0}{(r+\rho)}\left[B - \frac{2\rho Ak_\infty}{(r+2\rho)}\right] + \frac{D}{r} + \frac{\rho k_\infty}{r(r+\rho)}\left[B - \frac{2\rho Ak_\infty}{(r+2\rho)}\right] \quad (26)$$

Proof of Proposition 3

If the foreign firm takes $q(t)$ as given, then its output is $Q(t) = [a - bq(t)]/2b$. Let us determine what would be the time path of output of the domestic firm if it could be a Stackelberg leader (i.e., if it could precommit itself to a time path of output, before the foreign firm makes its output decision). The Hamiltonian for the domestic firm would then be

$$H = \frac{1}{2}aq - c(k)q - \frac{1}{2}bq^2 + \lambda[q - \delta k].$$

This yields the following differential equation:

$$\ddot{k} - r\dot{k} + \left[\frac{\gamma(r+2\delta)}{b} - \delta(\delta+r)\right]k = (r+\delta)\left[\frac{\bar{c} - (a/2)}{b}\right] \quad (27)$$

with a steady-state capital stock $k_\infty^L = [(r + \delta)(a - 2\bar{c})]/[2\gamma(r + \delta) - 2b\delta(\delta + r)]$. This steady state has the saddlepoint stability.

Next consider the Nash equilibrium of section 3, with $c(k)$ replaced by $C(k)$. The equilibrium time path must satisfy the following equation:

$$\ddot{k} - r\dot{k} + \left[\frac{2\gamma(r+2\delta)}{3b} - \delta(\delta+r)\right] = (r+\delta)\left[\frac{2(\bar{c}-\alpha)-a}{3b}\right]. \tag{28}$$

The two differential equations yield the same solution if and only if $\eta = \gamma/2$ and $\alpha = a - (\bar{c}/2)$. To show that this is the optimal solution for the government when $\mu = 0$, it suffices to note that the home government, by choosing α and η, can choose the time path of q, and that with $\mu = 0$, the interest of the government coincides with that of the domestic firm. Alternatively, after some tedious manipulation, it can be verified directly that $\eta = \gamma/2$ and $\alpha = a - (\bar{c}/2)$ maximize $v(k_0, \alpha, \eta)$ minus the integral of discounted flow of subsidies.

Proof of Proposition 5

Given the foreign firm's rule $Q = e + fk$, the domestic firm, taking e and f as given, solves its optimal control problem:

$$\max \int_0^\infty \{aq - b[e + fk + q]q - c(k)q\}\exp(-rt)dt$$

subject to $\dot{k} = q - \delta k$, $k(0) = k_0$. We now solve this problem by using the Hamilton–Jacobi–Bellman equation.

We must find a function $v(k)$ such that

$$rv(k) = \max_q[aq - b[e + fk + q]q - c(k)q + v'(k)(q - \delta k)]. \tag{29}$$

Let us try the quadratic function $v(k) = G + Ek + (1/2)Fk^2$. Then maximizing the right-hand side of (29) with respect to q yields

$$q = \frac{1}{2b}(a - be - \bar{c} + E) + \frac{k}{2b}(\gamma + F - bf). \tag{30}$$

Substituting (30) into the right-hand side of (29) yields

$$rv(k) = \frac{1}{2b}(a - be - \bar{c} + E)^2 + \left[\frac{1}{4b}(\gamma + F - bf)^2 - \delta F\right]k^2$$

$$+ \left[\frac{1}{2b}(a - be - \bar{c} + E)(\gamma + F - bf) - \delta E\right]k. \tag{31}$$

Since $rv(k) = r[G + Ek + (F/2)k^2]$, for (31) to hold as an identity, we must have

$$rF/2 = \frac{1}{4b}(\gamma + F - bf)^2 - \delta F, \tag{32}$$

$$rE = \left[\frac{1}{2b}(a - be - \bar{c} + E)(\gamma + F - bf) - \delta E\right], \tag{33}$$

and

$$rG = \frac{1}{2b}(a - be - \bar{c} + E)^2. \tag{34}$$

For given e and f, equation (32) is quadratic in F:

$$F^2 + [2(\gamma - bf) - 2b(r + 2\delta)]F + (\gamma - bf)^2 = 0. \tag{35}$$

Its two roots are

$$F_1 = -(\gamma - bf) + b(r + 2\delta) - \Delta, \tag{36}$$

$$F_2 = -(\gamma - bf) + b(r + 2\delta) + \Delta,$$

with

$$\Delta \equiv \sqrt{[b(r + 2\delta)]^2 - 2b(r + 2\delta)(\gamma - bf)}, \tag{37}$$

where $F_1 < F_2$ in the case of real roots. (We assume $2(\gamma - bf) < b(r + 2\delta)$ to ensure that the roots are real.) We would expect that if $\gamma = 0$ (no learning) then k would be irrelevant, and therefore the foreign firm would naturally set $f = 0$. In that case, we would expect k to be irrelevant for the home firm as well, and hence the appropriate root would be $F_1 = 0$. If $\gamma > 0$, then we would expect f to be negative. Then the smaller root F_1 would be positive.

Turning to (33), we obtain

$$E = \frac{(a - be - \bar{c})(\gamma + F_1 - bf)}{2b(r + \delta) - (\gamma + F_1 - bf)}. \tag{38}$$

We expect E to be nonnegative, because it measures the marginal contribution of knowledge capital when $k = 0$. Note that $(\gamma + F_1 - bf) \geq 0$ if $\gamma - bf \geq 0$. Finally:

$$G = \frac{1}{2r}(a - be - \bar{c} + E)^2. \tag{39}$$

It follows that given $Q = e + fk$, the domestic firm's *best reply* is $q = X + Yk$, where

$$Y = Y(f, \gamma) \equiv \frac{1}{2b}[b(r + 2\delta) - \Delta], \tag{40}$$

with $Y(0, 0) = 0$, and

$$X = X(e, f, \gamma) \equiv \frac{1}{2b}\left[\frac{(a - be - \bar{c})(r + \delta)}{r + \delta - Y(f, \gamma)}\right]. \tag{41}$$

Now let us turn to the optimization problem of the foreign firm. This firm takes the domestic firm's Markovian strategy as given: $q = X + Yk$ (X and Y are also taken as given). Let the value function of the foreign firm be $V(k) = G^* + E^*k + (F^*/2)k^2$. The Hamilton–Jacobi–Bellman equation is

$$rV(k) = \max_Q [aQ - b(X + Yk)Q - bQ^2 + V'(k)(X + Yk - \delta k)]. \tag{42}$$

This yields the foreign firm's best reply

$$Q = \frac{1}{2b}(a - bX - bYk). \tag{43}$$

Thus, the foreign firm chooses $Q = e + fk$, where

$$e = e(X) = \frac{1}{2b}(a - bX) \tag{44}$$

$$f = f(Y) = -\frac{Y}{2}. \tag{45}$$

Substitute (43) into (42) to solve for G^*, E^*, and F^*:

$$F^* = \frac{bY^2}{r+2\delta-2Y},$$

(46)

$$E^* = \frac{2F^*X-(a-bX)Y}{(2r+\delta-Y)},$$

(47)

$$rG^* = \frac{a^2}{4b} - \frac{aX}{2} - \frac{bX^2}{2} + E^*X.$$

(48)

We are now ready to determine the equilibrium values of e, f, X, and Y. From the four equations (40), (41), (44) and (45), we obtain

$$-4bf = \gamma + F_1 - bf,$$

(49)

and using (36) we can solve for f. There are two roots:

$$f_1 = \frac{-(r+2\delta)+\Delta_1}{4} \leq 0,$$

(50)

$$f_2 = \frac{-(r+2\delta)-\Delta_1}{4} < 0,$$

with $\Delta_1 = \sqrt{(r+2\delta)^2 - (8\gamma/b)(r+2\delta)}$.

We assume that γ is sufficiently small to ensure that Δ_1 is real. We choose the root f_1 because when $\gamma = 0$ then $f_1 = 0$, which makes sense. The solutions for e, X, and Y can then be obtained.

Proof of Proposition 6

The home government wants to choose a pair (α^0, η^0) that maximizes the objective function

$$\int_0^\infty \left\{ \pi - (\alpha + \eta k)q + \mu \frac{bZ^2}{2} \right\} e^{-rt} dt,$$

where π is the domestic firm's profit (including the subsidy). Given that γ is sufficiently small and that both firms use linear Markovian strategies, any pair (α, η) sufficiently near the optimal pair (α^0, η^0) will yield a pair of converging time paths $(q(t), k(t))$ that can be represented in the feedback form $q(k) = [\delta - \rho(\eta)]k + \rho(\eta)k_\infty(\alpha, \eta)$. The objective function can then be calculated as a function of (α, η), and a maximum is found using ordinary calculus.

Alternatively, one may note that with two parameters to choose, the government is in effect directly controlling the "policy function" $q(k)$ by choosing its slope and its intercept. This function can be determined by finding the time paths for $q(t)$ and $k(t)$. The foreign firm's output, along the equilibrium, is related to the domestic firm's equilibrium output by $Q = (a - bq)/(2b)$. Thus, instead of finding (α, η), we can solve an ordinary optimal control problem for the government. We then obtain the differential equation

$$\ddot{k} - r\dot{k} + k\left[\frac{\gamma(r+2\delta)}{b-(b\mu/4)} - \delta(r+2\delta) \right] = \frac{(r+\delta)}{2b[1-\mu/4]}[2\bar{c} - a(1+\mu/2)].$$

This yields the steady state

$$k_\infty^0 = \frac{(r+\delta)[a(1+\mu/2)-2\bar{c}]}{2\delta(r+\delta)b[1-(\mu/4)]-2\gamma(r+2\delta)},$$ (51)

and along the converging path

$$\dot{k} = -\rho^0[k-k_\infty^0],$$ (52)

where

$$\rho^0 \equiv \frac{-r}{2} + \frac{\Delta_2}{2},$$

$$\Delta_2 \equiv \sqrt{(r+2\delta)^2 - 4\gamma(r+2\delta)/[b-(b\mu/4)]},$$

which is positive for γ sufficiently small.

On the other hand, given a pair (α, η), the Markovian Nash equilibrium in linear strategies yields the following equation:

$$\dot{k} = X + Yk - \delta k,$$ (53)

where X and Y are given by Proposition 5, with γ replaced by $\gamma + \eta$ and $\bar{c}$ replaced by $\bar{c} - \alpha$. For the two equations (52) and (53) to have the same steady state and the same stable branch, it is necessary and sufficient that (α, η) take the value (α^0, η^0) as given in Proposition 6.

Model 3: The Foreign Firm is the Stackelberg Leader

In model 2, the foreign firm is sophisticated enough to realize that it can influence the learning rate of the domestic firm. Therefore it takes the stock of knowledge capital of the domestic firm as a state variable in its own optimization problem. This leads to a linear Markovian strategy $Q = e + fk$ which is the best reply for the domestic firm's strategy $q = X + Yk$. We found a Nash equilibrium pair of strategies that are best replies to each other.

We now consider, for completeness, the case in which the foreign firm is a Stackelberg leader (in linear strategies). This is modeled as follows. We assume that the foreign firm is able to precommit to a linear strategy before the domestic firm chooses its strategy. Suppose the foreign firm announces that its strategy is $Q = e + fk$. (It announces the pair of numbers (e, f), as well as the linear rule $Q = e + fk$.) The domestic firm, having been informed of the values of (e, f), chooses the best reply $q = X(e, f, \gamma) + Y(f, \gamma)k$, where $X(e, f, \gamma)$ and $Y(f, \gamma)$ are described by (41) and (40) respectively. Knowing this, the foreign firm chooses the optimal pair (e, f) so as to maximize its payoff:

$$\max_{e,f} \int_0^\infty e^{-rt}\{a - b[(e + fk(t) + X(e, f, \gamma) + Y(f, \gamma)k(t)]\}(e + fk(t))dt$$ (54)

subject to

$$\dot{k} = X(e, f, \gamma) + Y(f, \gamma)k - \delta k, \quad k(0) = k_0.$$ (55)

The differential equation (55) has the solution

$$k(t) = \frac{X(e, f, \gamma)}{\delta - Y(f, \gamma)} + \left[k_0 - \frac{X(e, f, \gamma)}{\delta - Y(f, \gamma)}\right]\exp[Y(f, \gamma) - \delta]t.$$ (56)

Substituting this into (54), evaluating the integral, then maximizing it with respect to (e, f), we obtain the Stackelberg solution in linear strategies. (It is conceivable that there exist nonlinear strategies which are preferable to the leader.)

References

Benchekroun, Hassan and Ngo Van Long, "Knowledge Spillovers and Market Rivalry," manuscript, McGill University (1997).

———, "Efficiency-Inducing Taxation for Polluting Oligopolists," *Journal of Public Economics* 55 (1998):325–42.

Bhattacharya, Gautam, "Learning and the Behavior of Potential Entrants," *Rand Journal of Economics* 1 (1984):281–9.

Brueckner, Jan and Neil Raymon, "Optimal Production with Learning-by-doing," *Journal of Economic Dynamics and Control* 6 (1983):127–86.

Docker, Engelberg, Steffan Jorgensen, Ngo Van Long, and Gerhard Sorger, *Differential Games in Economics and Management Science*, Cambridge: Cambridge University Press (1998): 1–350.

Fudenberg, Drew and Jean Tirole, "Learning-by-Doing and Market Performance," *Bell Journal of Economics* 14 (1983):522–30.

Grossman, Gene and Elhanan Helpman, "Protection for Sale," *American Economic Review* 84 (1994):833–50.

Hillman, Arye L., "Declining Industries and Political Support Protectionist Motives," *American Economic Review* 72 (1982):1180–7.

Karp, Larry and John Livernois, "On Efficiency-Inducing Taxation for a Non-renewable Resource Monopolist," *Journal of Public Economics* 49 (1992):219–39.

Komiya, Ryutaro, "Planning in Japan," in Morris Bornstein (ed.), *Economic Planning: East and West*, Cambridge, MA: Ballinger (1975):220–54.

Krouse, Clement, "Market Rivalry and Learning-by-Doing," *International Journal of Industrial Organization* 12 (1994):437–56.

Liberman, Marvin, "Patents, Learning-by-Doing, and Market Structure in Chemical Processing," *International Journal of Industrial Organization* 5 (1987):257–76.

———, "The Learning Curve, Technology Barriers to Entry, and Competitive Survival in the Chemical Processing Industries," *Strategic Management Journal* 10 (1989):431–47.

Long, Ngo Van and Neil Vousden, " Protectionist Responses and Declining industries," *Journal of International Economics* 30 (1991):87–103.

Long, Ngo Van and Kar-yiu Wong, "Endogenous Growth and International Trade: A Survey," in Bjarne Jensen an Kar-yiu Wong (eds.), *Dynamics, Economic Growth, and International Trade*, Ann Arbor: University of Michigan Press (1997):11–74.

Rosendorff, B. Peter, "Voluntary Export Restraints, Antidumping Procedure, and Domestic Politics," *American Economic Review* 86 (1996):544–61.

Suzumura, Kotaro, "Japan's Industrial Policy and Accession to the GATT: A Teacher by Positive or Negative Examples?" manuscript, Institute of Economic Research, Hitotsubashi University (1997).

Wan, Henry, Jr, "Trade, Development, and Inventions," in Horst Herberg and Ngo Van Long (eds.), *Trade, Welfare and Economic Policies: Essays in Honor of Murray C. Kemp*, Ann Arbor: University of Michigan Press (1993): 120–30. (An earlier version of this paper appeared as Cornell Working Paper 86, 1975.)

Notes

1. See, for example, Wan (1975, 1993), Brueckner and Raymon (1983), Fudenberg and Tirole (1983), Bhattacharya (1984), Liberman (1987, 1989), Krouse (1994).
2. See, for example, Hillman (1982), Long and Vousden (1991), Grossman and Helpman (1994), Rosendorff (1996).

3. We require that the subsidy rule be time-independent so as to avoid the time-inconsistency problem. See Karp and Livernois (1992) for an example of a time-inconsistent tax rule, and Benchekroun and Long (1998) for time-consistent tax rules when there are polluting oligopolists.

4. Formally, our solution concept here is equivalent to that of an open-loop Nash equilibrium. For a discussion of this concept, and related concepts, see Docker et al. (1998).

5. We should like to thank Professor Suzumura for communicating to us this important point. He has also supplied us with the following quote from the work of Ryutaro Komiya: "Whatever the demerits of the system of industrial policies in postwar Japan, it has been a very efficient means of collecting, exchanging and propagating industrial information. . . . Probably information related to various industries is more abundant and easily obtainable in Japan than in most other countries. Viewed as system of information collection and dissemination, Japan's system of industrial policies may have been among the most important factors in Japan's high rate of industrial growth, apart from the direct or indirect economic effects of industrial policy measures" (Komyia, 1975, p. 221.)

9
Real Exchange Rate Trends and Growth: A Model of East Asia

*Michael B. Devereux**

Abstract

In contrast to the Balassa–Samuelson hypothesis, many fast-growing Asian countries have experienced little trend real exchange rate appreciation, or even depreciation. Moreover, their long-run real exchange rate trend seems to be dominated by movements in traded goods prices. A model is developed which is consistent with these observations. As in the Balassa–Samuelson model, productivity growth is concentrated in the traded goods sector. Nevertheless the real exchange rate may exhibit trend depreciation, driven by persistent deviations in the price of traded goods from those in the reference country. The key feature of the model is the presence of endogenous productivity growth in the distribution services sector.

1. Introduction

What determines a country's long-run real exchange rate? The leading theory is still the celebrated Balassa–Samuelson hypothesis, which ascribes long-run deviations from purchasing power parity to differences in rates of growth of productivity in traded goods industries (Balassa, 1964; Samuelson, 1963; Asea and Mendoza, 1994). According to this hypothesis, faster-growing countries will have relatively higher growth rates of productivity in traded goods. This will generate persistent real exchange rate appreciation through a rate of growth of nontraded goods prices that is higher than that of slower-growing countries.

The most cited example in support of the Balassa–Samuelson hypothesis is the case of Japan. Between 1973 and 1997, the Japanese yen appreciated by 82% in real terms against the US dollar. Many studies have tied this to the differential rate of productivity growth between Japan and the US (e.g., Marston, 1990). But outside Japan, it is rather hard to find strong evidence that fast-growing countries have experienced significant real exchange rate appreciation.[1] Many studies over the last five years, however, have shown that real exchange rates are driven more by differences in price levels across countries, particularly in traded goods, than by differences in movements in the relative price of nontraded goods (e.g., Engel, 1996; Canzoneri et al., 1996; Isard and Symansky, 1995; Chinn, 1997). In particular, Isard and Symansky show that for fast-growing East Asian countries, there is little evidence for real appreciation relative to Japan or the US (even before the current exchange rate crisis in East Asia). Moreover, they show that, even at low frequencies, almost all the trends in real exchange rates are driven by movements across countries in the relative prices of traded goods, rather than by different trends in the relative price of nontraded goods within countries.

Taken at face value, these findings present a puzzle, since they indicate not just a departure from the Balassa–Samuelson hypothesis, but also substantial and persistent deviations from the law of one price in traded goods across countries. It seems hard

* Devereux: University of British Columbia, 997-1873 East Mall, Vancouver, BC, Canada V6T 1Z1. Tel: 604-822-2876; Fax: 604-822-5915. E-mail: devm@unixg.ubc.ca. I thank SSHRC of Canada for financial support. I also thank Partha Sen and Philip Lane for comments on an earlier draft.

to maintain the argument that these can be explained by nominal rigidities, or at least by nominal rigidities alone. But neither, on the other hand, do trade barriers and costs of transportation seem sufficient to explain the magnitude of real exchange rate movements.

In this paper I explore a mechanism for long-run real exchange rate determination that is an alternative to the Balassa–Samuelson model, but which includes that model as a special case. In particular, the model is designed to address two main issues: (a) the tendency for long-run exchange rates to be dominated by differentials in traded goods prices, and (b) the tendency for many faster-growing Asian economies to experience real exchange rate *depreciation* against Japan and the US.

The model is based on the importance of national distribution services sectors for traded goods. The central idea is that even for internationally traded commodities, there is a substantial nontraded element in the final goods price paid by consumers. I think of this as a distribution service. When looking at the fast-growing countries of Asia, it is likely that growth in manufacturing productivity has been mirrored by growth in the national distribution system. If distribution networks exhibit productivity deepening driven by growth in the national economy, then growth that is due to productivity increases in traded goods may in fact lead to continual reductions in traded goods prices.[2] Thus, contrary to the Balassa–Samuelson hypothesis, productivity increases in traded goods may lead to a real exchange rate depreciation. An important point to emphasize is that this result obtains without introducing any additional shocks than exist in the basic Balassa–Samuelson model. That is, it is found that a small, fast-growing economy may exhibit trend depreciation even if the preconditions exist for the Balassa–Samuelson model (high rates of productivity growth in traded goods).

The present model also contains a number of other implications for the determination of the real exchange rate. I show that deregulation in the distributional services sector which allows an increased entry of firms will lead to a depreciation in the real exchange rate.

I also investigate the effects of fiscal policy on the real exchange rate. In the basic Balassa–Samuelson model, the real exchange rate is determined by productivity growth alone, and is independent of the pattern of fiscal policy (e.g., Obstfeld and Rogoff, 1996). However, cross-country empirical evidence shows that government spending is associated with real exchange rate appreciation (De Gregorio et al., 1994). In the present model, it is shown that by reducing the size of the distribution sector and driving up the price of traded goods, higher rates of government spending tend to generate real exchange rate appreciation.

Section 2 introduces the model. Section 3 then shows how the equilibrium real exchange rate is determined, and explores the effect of various shocks on the real exchange rate. Section 4 provides some conclusions.

2. A Model of the Real Exchange Rate

In this section I develop a model of the real exchange rate where distribution costs drive a wedge between the world price of traded goods and the price facing domestic consumers and producers. Consider a small open economy, for which both the world price of traded goods and the world interest rate are taken as given. In the economy there are three types of goods and services produced. Traded goods are produced for consumption or export. Nontraded goods are produced for domestic consumption alone. Finally there are (nontraded) distributional services. These services are required for the distribution and consumption of traded goods.[3]

There is free mobility of financial and physical capital for both firms and consumers in the small economy. I first set out the problem facing consumers.

Consumers

We wish to examine the interaction between consumption, productivity growth, and the real exchange rate. A convenient device for exploring this nexus is to assume that agents in this economy face a finite lifetime in the sense of Blanchard (1985). That is, we assume that there are overlapping generations of agents, all of whom face a constant probability of death at any given time. Time is continuous, and an agent's death is determined by a Poisson process with arrival rate p. That is, p is the "instantaneous" probability of death.

Since lifetime uncertainty is independent across individuals in the economy, at the aggregate level exactly p of the population will die at any instant. Actuarially fair insurance companies will then insure individuals against the risk of death, so that borrowing and lending interest rates will be $r + p$, where r is the world interest rate (Blanchard and Fischer, 1989). In addition, if there is a measure p of people born at any instant, the population will remain constant at 1.

If we assume logarithmic preferences, then Blanchard (1985) shows that utility may be defined as

$$U = \int_t^\infty \log c(s, z) e^{-(\rho+\delta)(z-t)} dz, \tag{1}$$

where $c(s, z)$ is the consumption of an agent born at time s, taking place at time z, and δ is the rate of time preference. Consumption is disaggregated into both traded and nontraded goods, and traded goods consumption in turn is comprised of direct consumption of foreign goods, and consumption of distributional services. That is

$$c(s, t) = c_T(s, t)^\beta c_N(s, t)^{1-\beta},$$

$$c_T(s, t) = v_T(s, t)^\gamma d_T(s, t)^{1-\gamma}.$$

Here c_T and c_N represent the consumption of traded and nontraded goods, respectively. Then v_T represents units of traded goods purchased at the wholesale level, and d_T represents a distribution service. This captures the idea that there is a domestic service component to traded goods consumption. To produce one unit of consumption of the "traded good," the domestic agent must put together the produced good and a distribution service.

Given preferences as in (1), we may define the price index for the composite consumption good as

$$P(P_T, P_N) = \phi_\beta P_T^\beta P_N^{1-\beta},$$

and the sub-price index for traded goods consumption as

$$P_T(P_w, Q) = \phi_\gamma P_w^\gamma P_d^{1-\gamma},$$

where P_N is the price of nontraded goods, P_T is the price index for traded goods consumption, and P_w is the world price of traded goods at the wholesale level, which is taken as given to the small economy.[4] P_d represents the domestic price of distribution services. This will be determined within the domestic economy.

The consumer faces the budget constraint given by

$$P(t)c(s, t) + \dot{B}(s, t) + \dot{K}(s, t) = W(t) + (r + p)(B(s, t) + K(s, t)), \tag{2}$$

where $B(s, t)$ and $K(s, t)$ represent the stock of foreign bonds held by the consumer, and the stock of domestic physical capital held by the consumer, respectively, and $W(t)$ represents the wage rate. Both bonds and capital earn a competitive return at the world interest rate. In addition, the interest rate facing the consumer is augmented by the risk of death, p, as noted above.

The consumer maximizes (1) subject to (2) and the transversality constraint given by

$$\lim_{t \to \infty} e^{-(r+p)t}(B(s, t) + K(s, t)) = 0.$$

The resulting optimal consumption path will be characterized by the condition

$$\dot{c}(s, t) = \left(r - \frac{\dot{P}(t)}{P(t)} - \delta\right)c(s, t).$$

Now, aggregating across all individuals in the economy (Blanchard and Fischer, 1989), we arrive at the two conditions which govern the behavior of aggregate consumption $C(t)$:

$$\dot{C}(t) = \left(r - \frac{\dot{P}(t)}{P(t)} - \delta\right)C(t) - p(p+\delta)\frac{Q(t)}{P(t)}, \tag{3}$$

$$P(t)C(t) + \dot{Q}(t) = W(t) + rQ(t). \tag{4}$$

Because new individuals are continually being born with no assets, the behavior of aggregate consumption in this economy will be determined by the stock of (nonhuman) assets defined by $Q = B + K$, as in (3). The evolution of Q will be determined by the economy-wide resource constraint (4). Since the risk-premium component of interest rates p is just a transfer between individuals, it falls out of the aggregate budget constraint.

We may rewrite (3) by defining total current expenditure $E = PC$, so that

$$\dot{E} = (r - \delta)E - p(p+\delta)Q. \tag{5}$$

Equations (4) and (5) jointly determine the evolution of E and Q, given the wage W and the foreign interest rate r. In general, however, the wage rate in the small economy will be growing, owing to growth in the productivity of the traded goods sector (see below). Let the rate of growth of the wage be g_w. Thus, the wage rate may be written as $W(t) = W_0\exp(g_w t)$. Then in a balanced growth path both Q and E will be rising at rate g_w. We may transform (4) and (5) by defining $e = E/\exp(g_w t)$ and $q = Q/\exp(g_w t)$ to obtain the following conditions:

$$\dot{q} = (r - g_w)q + W_0 - e, \tag{6}$$

$$\dot{e} = (r - g_w - \delta)e - p(p+\delta)q. \tag{7}$$

To avoid a large taxonomy of cases, we assume that $r > g_w + \delta$. Then Figure 1 illustrates the dynamics of e and q outside of the balanced growth path. In order that there exist nonnegative steady-state levels of E and Q, we must make the regularity assumption

$$\frac{p(p+\delta)}{r - g_w - \delta} > r.$$

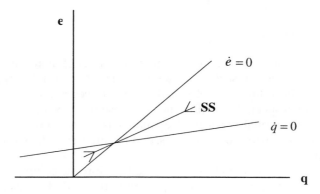

Figure 1.

The locus $\dot{q} = 0$ describes equation (6), while the locus $\dot{e} = 0$ describes equation (7). A unique saddlepath, represented by the locus *SS*, exists, and is upward-sloping. e and q will adjust monotonically to their steady-state $\bar{e}$ and $\bar{q}$.

Finally, the breakdown of consumer expenditure into its constituent parts is governed by the two conditions (at the economy-wide aggregate level)

$$P_T C_T = \frac{\beta}{1-\beta} P_N C_N, \tag{8}$$

$$P_w V_T = \frac{\gamma}{1-\gamma} P_d D_T. \tag{9}$$

Given prices and these conditions, it is straightforward to use (7) to determine the evolution of the consumption of individual goods.

Firms

There are three sectors in the economy: the traded goods sector, the nontraded goods sector, and the distribution sector. In each sector, firms hire capital and labor to maximize profits. It is assumed that the distribution services sector is comprised of a continuum of monopolistic competitive firms of total measure A. The other two sectors are competitive.

The technologies for producing goods are as follows:

$$Y_T = \theta_T(t) K_T^\alpha L_T^{1-\alpha}, \tag{10}$$

$$Y_N = \theta_N(t) K_N^\kappa L_N^{1-\kappa}, \tag{11}$$

$$x(i) + \psi = \theta_x(t) K_x(i)^\alpha L_x(i)^{1-\alpha}. \tag{12}$$

Here y_T and y_N denote output of traded and nontraded goods respectively. The θ terms denote productivity in each sector. Let $\theta_T(t) = \theta_0 \exp(g_T t)$, $\theta_N(t) = \theta_{n0} \exp(g_N t)$, and $\theta_x(t) = \theta_{x0} \exp(g_x t)$.

Output of a distributional services firm, $x(i)$, is subject to a fixed cost ψ. The consumption of distributional services by consumers is then determined by the function

$$D_T = \left(\int_0^A x(j)^\rho \, dj \right)^{\frac{1}{\rho}}, \tag{13}$$

where $0 \le \rho \le 1$. Equation (11) implies that there an effect of increasing returns to specialization in the distribution sector. For a given quantity of total output in the distribution sector, Ax, the total stock of distribution services is greater, the higher is A relative to x. In this respect, fluctuations in A represent a type of *endogenous productivity* effect in distributional services. The smaller is ρ, the lower is the elasticity of substitution between distributional services, and the greater is the strength of this specialization effect.

Given wholesale prices of traded goods fixed by foreign competition, and a fixed foreign rate of return to capital, unit-cost pricing in the traded goods (wholesale) and nontraded goods sectors implies that

$$P_w = \phi_\alpha \frac{W(t)^{1-\alpha} r^\alpha}{\theta_{Tt}}, \tag{14}$$

$$P_{nt} = \phi_\kappa \frac{W(t)^{1-\kappa} r^\kappa}{\theta_{Nt}}. \tag{15}$$

The individual firms that produce specialized distribution services are monopolists, and set price at a mark-up over marginal cost. In a symmetric equilibrium, this gives

$$p_x = \frac{\mu \phi_\alpha W(t)^{1-\alpha} r^\alpha}{\theta_{xt}}, \tag{16}$$

where, $\mu = 1/\rho$.

Then free entry into the distribution services sector implies the zero-profit condition

$$p_x x (1 - \mu) = p_x \psi. \tag{17}$$

Thus, sales per firm, x, is a constant, equal to $\psi/(1 - \mu)$.

Finally, efficient pricing of the distribution composite must imply that (in a symmetric equilibrium)

$$P_d = A^{1-\frac{1}{\rho}} p_x. \tag{18}$$

From (12), given a fixed value of P_w, it follows that the wage rate will be growing at rate $g_T/(1 - \alpha)$; i.e.,

$$W(t) = \left(\frac{P_w \theta_{T0} \exp(g_T t)}{r^\alpha} \right)^{\frac{1}{1-\alpha}}. \tag{19}$$

Note that, from (19), $g_w = g_T/(1 - \alpha)$.

The Real Exchange Rate

The most common definition of the real exchange rate is the ratio of price levels between one country and another, expressed in a common currency. In this model, there is no nominal currency, so the real exchange rate is just the ratio of the home country price to that of the foreign country. Since prices in the rest of the world are taken as given to the small open economy, we can then identify the real exchange rate with the home country CPI, P. A rise in P represents a real exchange rate appreciation.

It is easy to see from above that, at the wholesale level, the Balassa–Samuelson prediction holds true. From the unit price equations for P_N, we have

$$P_N(t) = \frac{\theta_T(t)^{\frac{1-\kappa}{1-\alpha}}}{\theta_{Nt}(t)} r^{\left[\kappa\left(\frac{1-\kappa}{1-\alpha}\right)-\alpha\right]} P_w^{\frac{(1-\kappa)}{(1-\alpha)}}. \tag{20}$$

If productivity growth in the traded goods sector exceeds that in the nontraded goods sector (i.e., $g_T > g_N$), and labor share in nontradeables is not too small, then the price of nontraded goods must be rising over time. The rate of growth of the nontraded is

$$\frac{\dot{P}_N}{P_N} = g_T \left[\frac{(1-\kappa)}{(1-\alpha)}\right] - g_N.$$

Since wholesale traded goods prices are given, a persistent increase in P_N in itself would imply that the country was experiencing a real exchange rate appreciation. This captures the basic Balassa–Samuelson mechanism, as illustrated in Rogoff (1996), for instance.

At the final goods level, however, the same conclusion does not necessarily hold. To see this, use (8), (9), and (18) to solve for the aggregate price index for the economy as

$$P = P_w^{\beta}\left(A^{1-\frac{1}{\rho}}\frac{\theta_T}{\theta_x}\mu\right)^{(1-\gamma)\beta} P_N^{1-\beta}, \tag{21}$$

where P_N is given by (20).

Productivity growth in the traded goods sector will imply increasing P_N, as before. For $\gamma = 1$, this implies that P is rising, and so this would imply persistent real exchange rate appreciation (holding the rest of the world price level fixed). But in general, productivity growth will now have two other effects. First, it may directly lead to a rising P_x, depending on the behavior of exogenous productivity in the distributional sector. If the change in growth θ_T is mirrored by a growing θ_x, then this effect is absent, and P_x is stationary. Otherwise the rise in traded goods productivity will raise P_x, thus causing further real exchange rate appreciation. The second effect goes the other way, however. Rising θ_T will tend to raise consumption, and in doing so, will lead to growth in the size of the distributional sector. This causes an *endogenous* productivity expansion, which leads to a falling value of P_d. Thus, traded goods prices facing the consumer will tend to *fall* owing to this effect alone.

Equation (21) implies, therefore, that the endogenous response of the distributional sector to productivity changes in traded goods will introduce a force for falling prices, conflicting with the basic Balassa–Samuelson mechanism.

In order to see the the strength of each of these individual forces on the real exchange rate, we need to solve for the optimal path of consumption from equations (6) and (7).

3. Determination of the Real Exchange Rate

To fully determine the real exchange rate in this model, we must determine the path of A. To do this, we use (6) and (7), (19), (21), and the condition

$$e = \frac{E}{\exp(g_w t)} = \frac{1}{\beta(1-\gamma)} A x \mu \frac{\theta_{T0}}{\theta_{x0}} \frac{\exp\left(\frac{\alpha}{1-\alpha} g_T t\right)}{\exp(g_x t)}. \tag{22}$$

Equation (22) is obtained from the definition of the consumption composite, and (8), (9), and (18). It implies that expenditure, in "efficiency units" depends on A, and the productivity of traded goods and distributional services.

Assume that the growth in productivity in the distribution sector is a fraction m of that in the traded goods sector; i.e., $g_x = m g_T$, where $0 \le m \le 1$. Then since in a balanced growth path, $\dot{E}/E = g_w$, we must have the balanced growth path of A determined by

$$\frac{\dot{A}}{A} = \left[\frac{1}{1-\alpha} - (1-m) \right] g_T. \tag{23}$$

Equation (23) confirms that growth in productivity in the traded goods sector will generate persistent growth in the size of the distribution sector. The magnitude of this growth depends upon the trend in P_x. Total expenditure E must grow at rate $g_T/(1-\alpha)$. But total expenditure is proportional to $P_x A$. If $m = 1$, then P_x is stationary, and the distribution sector grows at the same rate as the economy's wage rate. Otherwise A will grow at a slower rate.

Since the economy's prices are determined solely by world prices and the level of expenditure, the level of output in each sector is determined residually by labor market clearing. Given a fixed labor force of size L, we must have

$$L = L_T + L_N + A L_x.$$

Using the properties of expenditure functions above, we have

$$L = (1-\alpha)\left(\frac{r}{w}\right)^\alpha \frac{Y_T}{\theta_T} + (1-\kappa)\left(\frac{r}{w}\right)^\kappa \frac{Y_N}{\theta_N} + A(1-\alpha)\left(\frac{r}{w}\right)^\alpha \frac{x+\psi}{\theta_x}. \tag{24}$$

Then, given A determined as above, and Y_N determined recursively from A and (8)–(9), equation (24) determines the output of traded goods Y_T.[5] From (24), it is then easy to establish that, in a balanced growth path, output in the traded and nontraded sector will grow in the following manner:

$$\frac{\dot{Y}_T}{Y_T} = \frac{1}{1-\alpha} g_T,$$

$$\frac{\dot{Y}_N}{Y_N} = g_N + \frac{\kappa}{1-\alpha} g_T.$$

Output of traded goods (at the wholesale level) grows at the same rate as the wage. Output of nontraded goods will grow at a slower rate, since the assumption that the price of nontraded goods is rising over time (i.e., $g_T(1-\kappa)/(1-\alpha) > g_N$) implies that

$$g_T \frac{1}{1-\alpha} > g_T \frac{\kappa}{1-\alpha} + g_N.$$

We now return to the examination of the trend in the real exchange rate.

Productivity Growth and the Real Exchange Rate

From (20), (21), and (24), the rate of growth of the domestic price level is

$$\frac{\dot{P}}{P} = g_T\left[\left(\frac{1}{1-\alpha} - (1-m)\right)\left(1 - \frac{1}{\rho}\right)\beta(1-\gamma) + \beta(1-\gamma)(1-m) + (1-\beta)\frac{1-\kappa}{1-\alpha}\right]$$
$$- g_N(1-\beta) \tag{25}$$

In a balanced growth equilibrium, the real exchange rate may be appreciating or depreciating. If $\gamma = 1$, then, as before, the Balassa–Samuelson hypothesis applies, and there is a trend real appreciation. But when $\gamma < 1$, the first term in equation (25) is negative, and if this is large enough the overall price level may be falling. Take the case where $m = 1$, so that the distributional sector productivity has the same trend as the traded goods sector; then the real exchange rate will exhibit persistent depreciation when

$$\left[\left(1 - \frac{1}{\rho}\right)(1-\gamma)\beta + (1-\kappa)(1-\beta)\right]g_T - (1-\alpha)(1-\beta)g_N < 0. \tag{26}$$

This is more likely, the greater is the degree of increasing returns to specialization in the distributional sector, the higher the share of the distributional sector in final consumption of traded goods, and the lower is the share of labor in nontraded goods.

The explanation for the possibility of trend real exchange rate depreciation is the endogenous productivity "deepening" in the distribution sector. As wage growth drives consumption growth, this will entice more firms to enter the distributional services sector. As seen by (18), this endogenous productivity effect will continually drive down the price of distributional services. If this effect is strong enough, the real exchange rate may be falling over time. Moreover, the fall in the real exchange rate is due to a persistent fall in the price of traded goods relative to those in the rest of the world.

Thus, this model can rationalize the observations noted in the introduction; that (a) many Asian countries have experienced persistent real exchange rate depreciation, despite having higher growth rates, and (b) real exchange rate changes have been associated with changes in the relative prices of traded goods across countries, rather than with changes in the relative price of nontraded to traded goods within countries. Moreover, the model seems to capture well the conjecture of Isard et al. (1997) that the explanation for the lack of strong real appreciation in Hong Kong and Singapore is due to fast productivity growth in the service sector. In our setup, the rate of overall productivity growth in the service sector is in fact endogenously determined.

Figure 2 illustrates the dynamic impact of a rise in productivity growth in the traded goods sector. The $\dot{q} = 0$ locus shifts down and the $\dot{e} = 0$ locus shifts left. The result will be to reduce steady-state e and q. The immediate impact may be either to increase or reduce expenditure e. Figure 2 shows the first case. Beginning from point A, expenditure jumps to point B on impact, and thereafter falls gradually to its new steady state C. The initial impact will lead to an increase in normalized expenditure e, which leads to an immediate real exchange rate depreciation. But e then falls as the economy experiences persistent current account deficits. This must mean that A is rising at a slower rate than its long-run trend. From (19'), the implication then is that along the adjustment path to the new steady state, the real exchange rate is depreciating (appreciating) at a rate lower (higher) than its long-run trend. Figure 3 illustrates two possible adjustment scenarios, depending upon whether the trend in the real exchange rate is positive or negative to begin with. Considering the solid line in Figure 3, the higher growth of θ_T will raise the trend growth in the real exchange rate, but during the adjustment phase, the real exchange rate is appreciating at a faster rate than in the new trend path. Considering the broken line in Figure 3, the higher growth of θ_T leads to a faster

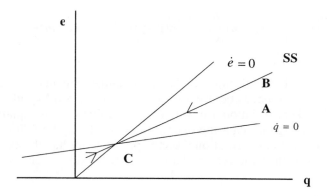

Figure 2.

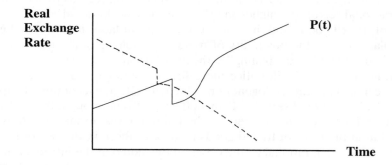

Figure 3.

rate of decline in the real exchange rate. During the adjustment phase here, the real exchange rate will be depreciating at a rate less than the new long run rate.

Deregulation

Many countries have followed policies of deregulation in the services sector in the past decade. One way to motivate this within the present model is through a change in fixed costs ψ. What is the effect of a change in ψ? From (18) we see this has no effect on the equilibrium wage, so it leaves steady-state e and q unchanged. Nor does it change the price of nontraded goods (15), or the price of distributional services (16). But from the definition of e, we see that a fall in the fixed cost will have the effect of reducing x and increasing A, relative to its long-run growth path. Intuitively, a fall in entry costs into the distributional sector will increase production along the *extensive* margin (i.e., the number of firms), while reducing production along the *intensive* margin (output per firm).

But from (21), it follows that a fall in fixed costs of entry to the distribution sector must lead to a fall in P and a real depreciation. Thus, deregulation will tend to reduce the real exchange rate. In the current model, this happens instantaneously, as illustrated in Figure 4. The trend path of the real exchange rate will be permanently lower. There are no dynamic implications for expenditure or the current account.

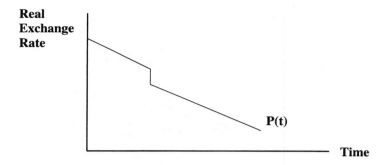

Figure 4.

Fiscal Policy

What is the impact of a rise in government spending and/or government debt in this model? The basic Balassa–Samuelson model as set out above implies that the real exchange rate is unaffected by the size of government spending—it is determined by technology factors solely. However, empirical evidence (e.g., De Gregorio et al., 1994) seems to indicate that a higher share of government leads to a higher (more appreciated) real exchange rate.

Let us alter the model to allow for government spending and government debt in the following way. Assume that government spending is based on a goods composite equivalent to that of private sector consumption. The government budget constraint is then

$$\dot{B}^g = PG - PT + rB^g,$$

while the private budget constraint is now

$$E + \dot{Q} + \dot{B}^g = r(Q + B^g) + W - PT,$$

where G is government real spending, B^g is government debt, and T is real tax revenue.

Let the government maintain a constant real government spending in efficiency units, $\tilde{g} = G/\exp(g_w t)$. The determination of e and q is now written as

$$\dot{q} = W_0 + (r - g_w)q - e - P\tilde{g}, \tag{4''}$$

$$\dot{e} = (r - g_w - \delta)e - p(p + \delta)(q + b^g), \tag{5''}$$

where $b^g = B^g/\exp(g_w t)$. W_0 is again determined by (18).

In Figure 5, a balanced budget tax-financed increase in government spending will lead to a shift downwards in the $\dot{q} = 0$ locus, but leave unchanged the $\dot{e} = 0$ locus. Steady-state e and q fall. The immediate impact is to lead to a shift downwards in e, causing a fall in the growth rate of A, and a real exchange rate appreciation. This is followed by further appreciation as P rises towards its new steady-state growth path associated with a smaller size of the distributional sector. Figure 6 illustrates this. While government spending has no impact on the long-run rate of change in the real exchange rate, it will lead to a shift up in the trend path. Thus, this model implies clearly that a higher share of government in GDP will lead to a higher real exchange rate. Note also that this is not dependent on the government having a bias in spending on nontraded goods.

A higher stock of government debt will also imply a higher trend path of P. A higher b^g leads to shift upwards in the $\dot{e} = 0$ locus. This necessitates a lower value of e and q.

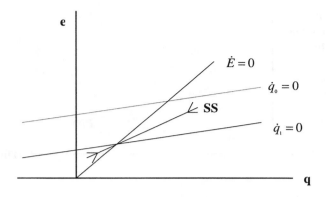

Figure 5.

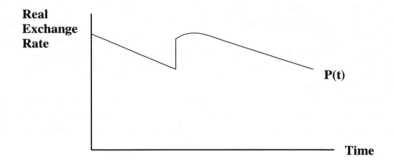

Figure 6.

Government debt crowds out private net wealth, and lowers steady-state expenditure. But in this model, this must imply a lower trend path of A, and a higher real exchange rate.

4. Conclusions

This paper has outlined one mechanism that may be important for movements in the real exchange rate for small economies. The mechanism is one of endogenous productivity-deepening in the services sector that occurs as a country's total income grows. This releases forces that drive down traded goods prices, offsetting the basic Balassa–Samuelson forces for productivity growth to raise domestic prices. The model accords with the evidence for Asian countries that (a) many of the fast-growing countries experienced real exchange rate depreciation, and (b) much of the movement in real exchange rate was accounted for by deviations from the law of one price in traded goods prices across countries.

References

Asea, P. and E. Mendoza, "The Balassa–Samuelson Model: A General Equilibrium Appraisal," *Review of International Economics* 2 (1994):244–67.

Balassa, B. A. "The Purchasing Power Parity Doctrine: A Reappraisal," *Journal of Political Economy* 72 (1964):584–96.

Blanchard, O. J. "Debt, Deficits, and Finite Horizons," *Journal of Political Economy* 93 (1985):223–47.

Blanchard, O. J. and S. Fischer, *Lectures on Macroeconomics*, Cambridge, MA: MIT Press (1989).

Canzoneri, M., R. Cumby, and B. Diba, "Relative Labour Productivity and the Real Exchange Rate in the Long-Run: Evidence for a Panel of OECD Countries," NBER discussion paper 5676 (1996).

Chinn, M. D., "The Usual Suspects? Productivity and Demand Shocks and Asia Pacific Real Exchange Rates," NBER discussion paper 6108 (1997).

De Gregorio, J., A. Giovannini, and H. C. Wolf, "International Evidence in Tradeables and Non-tradeables Inflation," *European Economic Rieview* 38 (1994): 1225–44.

Engel, C., "Accounting for Real Exchange Rate Changes," NBER discussion paper 5394 (1995).

Giovannini, A., "Exchange Rates and Traded Goods Prices," *Journal of International Economics* 24 (1988):45–68.

Isard, P. and S. Symansky, "Real Exchange Rate Experience in APEC Countries," mimeo, International Monetary Fund (1995).

———, "Economic Growth and the Real Exchange Rate: An Overview of the Balassa–Samuelson Hypothesis in Asia," mimeo, International Monetary Fund (1997).

Marston, R. C., "Price Behavior in Japanese and U.S. Manufacturing," in P. Krugman (ed.), *Trade with Japan: Has the Door Opened Wider?*, Chicago: University of Chicago Press (1991): 121–41.

Obstfeld, M. and K. Rogoff, *Foundations of International Macroeconomics*, Cambridge, MA: MIT Press (1996).

Rogoff, K., "The Purchasing Power Parity Puzzle," *Journal of Economic Literature* 34 (1996):647–68.

Samuelson, P. A., "Theoretical Notes on Trade Problems," *Review of Economics and Statistics* 46 (1963):145–54.

Notes

1. Isard et al. (1997) find some evidence of the Balassa–Samuelson hypothesis in the real exchange rate behavior of Japan, Korea, and Taiwan, but none for other Asian countries such as Indonesia, Thailand, and Malaysia.

2. The model might be seen as a formalism of a suggestion of Isard et al. (1997), who conjecture that the reason why countries like Singapore and Hong Kong showed show little real appreciation is due to fast growth in productivity in the services sector.

3. Assuming that distributional services were necessary for the distribution and consumption of nontraded goods would not change the results.

4. We define $\phi_x = [(x)^x(1-x)^{1-x}]^{-1}$.

5. Implicitly, we are assuming that the economy remains within the diversified production equilibrium.

10
Industrialization, Economic Growth, and International Trade

Kar-yiu Wong and Chong K. Yip*

Abstract

This paper analyzes the relationship between economic growth, industrialization, and international trade in a two-sector endogenous growth model. With learning-by-doing, the economy grows perpetually along a balanced growth path, with manufacturing's relative price declining continuously. Under trade, its pattern of trade and growth will be affected by external growth. If it remains diversified under trade, its growth can keep in pace with the rest of the world. If the growth rate of the rest of the world is higher than a certain limit, the economy cannot catch up and will eventually produce agriculture only.

1. Introduction

Industrialization and international trade have long been regarded as two of the most important engines of growth for many countries. Ever since the industrial revolution that brought rapid growth to various countries, industrialization has been regarded by many governments as the key to fast growth. Many government policies have been geared to promote the development of the manufacturing sector, very often at the expense of other sectors such as agriculture. International trade is commonly treated as an important factor of growth (e.g., Boldrin and Scheinkman, 1988; Young, 1991; Wong, 1995). All Asian countries that experienced rapid growth in the previous decades are open economies, and this fact has had great influence on the trade policies of many developing countries.

The objective of this paper is to examine the relationship between industrialization, economic growth, and international trade. In particular, it analyzes how industrialization and international trade may affect the growth performance of a country.

To analyze this relationship, we construct a simple two-sector endogenous growth model. The two sectors are conveniently called the manufacturing sector and the agricultural sector. The manufacturing sector grows over time owing to both the accumulation of physical capital as a result of investment, and the accumulation of human capital through learning-by-doing. The growth of the manufacturing sector pulls the economy with it. The agricultural sector of the economy, however, does not have any learning-by-doing effect, implying no growth in technology. Along a balanced growth path (BGP), the two sectors are growing at different rates, implying a continuous decline in the relative price of manufactures.[1]

It is interesting to compare the present result of falling relative price of manufacturing with the well-known Prebisch–Singer hypothesis that developing countries are facing declining relative prices of primary products. While the hypothesis has been supported in some empirical studies (e.g., Sarkar, 1986, 1994, 1997), it remains a contro-

Wong: University of Washington, Seattle, WA 98195-3330, USA. Tel: 206-685-1859; Fax: 685-7477; E-mail: karyiu@u.washington.edu. Yip: Chinese University of Hong Kong, Shatin, NT, Hong Kong. Tel: (852) 26097057; Fax: 26035805; E-mail: b660732@mailserv.cuhk.edu.hk. Thanks are due to Koon-Lam Shea, Eric Bond, participants at the Hong Kong conference in July 1997 and the ASSA session in January 1998, and an anonymous reviewer, for helpful comments.

versial issue in the literature. Two remarks can be offered here. First, while the two goods in the present model are conveniently labeled manufacturing and agriculture, they can be relabeled for any pair of goods under consideration. Our results suggest only that whether the relative price of one good in a closed economy increases or decreases over time depends on the learning-by-doing effects in the sectors. Second, our model does not predict that a small economy will be facing deteriorating terms of trade because the pattern of trade of the economy has to be determined endogenously. If, for example, the economy exports the agriculture, its terms of trade are actually improved.[2]

In the present model, since manufacturing is getting cheaper relative to agriculture, many new questions arise. For example, how may the growth rate of the rest of the world affect this economy's pattern of trade, pattern of production, and growth? Can the economy ever catch up with the rest of the world? What are the conditions under which an economy can remain diversified, and can that be substainable? What are the features of an economy if it is completely specialized in one good? What can we say about the growth rate of the economy if it is completely specialized under trade? Answers to these questions will be provided later in this paper.

In the next section, the features of the model are presented and its properties, such as the balanced growth path of a closed economy, are derived. Section 3 analyzes the economy under free trade in the case in which both goods are produced (diversification) along a balanced growth path. Whether diversification can be substained is investigated. Section 4 turns to the case in which the economy is completely specialized in the production of the agricultural good. The alternative case in which it is completely specialized in producing the manufacturing good is studied in section 5. These three sections show that the patterns of production of the economy depend crucially on the growth rate of the world. The last section summarizes the main results and offers some concluding remarks.[3]

2. A Closed Economy

Consider an economy of constant size of population, L. Two types of homogeneous products, agricultural good (good A) and manufacturing good (good M), are produced by competitive firms using constant-returns technologies. Both goods are consumed, but the manufacturing good can also be invested to increase the physical capital stock.[4]

Production

The production of the agricultural good is done by competitive firms using only labor input. The sectoral production function at any point of time t can be written as

$$X_t^A = AL_t^A, \tag{1}$$

where X_t^A is the output, L_t^A is the homogeneous labor (number of workers) input, and $A > 0$ denotes the constant labor productivity. Since A is constant, it is equal to the marginal as well as average product of labor of the sector.

Production of the manufacturing good requires two inputs: capital (K_t) and labor ($M_t L_t^M$):

$$X_t^M = F(K_t, M_t L_t^M), \tag{2}$$

where X_t^M is the output and L_t is the number of workers employed. The variable M_t is a labor productivity index, meaning that $M_t L_t^M$ is regarded as the effective labor input. The production function in (2) satisfies the following assumption:

ASSUMPTION 1. *The production function of the manufacturing sector is twice-differentiable and linearly homogeneous in factor inputs, and satisfies $F_i > 0$ and $F_{ii} < 0$, where F_i denotes the partial derivative of F with respect to the ith argument ($i = 1, 2$).*

There are two cases. As L_t^M approaches zero, either (case I) F_2 approaches infinity (the Inada condition); or (case II) F_2 is bounded from above.

All markets are competitive. Define the capital–labor ratio in the manufacturing sector as $k_t \equiv K_t/(M_t L_t^M)$. The manufacturing production function can be rewritten as

$$X_t^M = M_t L_t^M f(k_t),\tag{3}$$

where $f(k_t) \equiv F(k_t, 1)$. With cost minimization, the wage rate, w_t, and rental rate of capital, r_t, in terms of the manufacturing good are equal to

$$w_t = w(k_t) = f(k_t) - k_t f'(k_t),$$

$$r_t = r(k_t) = f'(k_t).$$

Firms are competitive, taking prices and the labor productivity as given.

The growth of the sector, and thus that of the economy, comes from an increase in the manufacturing labor productivity M_t over time. In the present paper, we follow the tradition of Romer (1986) and model the endogenous growth as the result of an external learning-by-doing process.[5] In particular, the increase in labor productivity is assumed to be given by the following condition:

$$\dot{M}_t = \mu X_t^M = \mu F(K_t, M_t L_t^M),\tag{4}$$

where $\mu > 0$ is a measure of the effectiveness of learning by doing. At any point of time, M_t is taken as given and no firm or individual will take condition (4) into consideration.

CONDITION 1. *The learning-by-doing (LBD) effects in the manufacturing sector are weak in the sense that μ is sufficiently small.*

Condition 1 is required for some of the results derived below. Choosing the agricultural good as the *numéraire*, we denote the relative price of the manufacturing good by p_t. In addition, we consider a production subsidy of constant *ad valorem* rate of $s \geq 0$ on the manufacturing sector so that the domestic producers' price of manufacturing becomes $(1 + s)p_t$. Perfect mobility of labor between the two sectors with positive outputs implies equalization of wage rates:

$$A = (1 + s)p_t M_t w(k_t).\tag{5}$$

Consumption and Investment

Consumption of the two goods (C_t^A and C_t^M) and investment ($\dot{K}_t$) are decided by a representative agent.[6] For simplicity, no depreciation of physical capital is considered. Assume that the instantaneous utility function of the representative agent at time t is given by $\beta \ln C_t^A + \ln C_t^M$, where $\beta > 0$. The optimization problem of the representative agent is to choose the consumption and investment streams to

$$\max \int_0^\infty (\beta \ln C_t^A + \ln C_t^M) e^{-pt} dt$$

subject to the standard budget constraint

$$C_t^A + p_t(C_t^M + \dot{K}_t) = AL_t^A + (1+s)p_t F(K_t, M_t L_t^M) - T_t, \tag{6}$$

as well as (4), where ρ is the rate of time preference and T_t denotes the lump-sum tax used to finance the production subsidy. Let λ_t^M and λ_t^C be the costate variables associated with (4) and (6) respectively. Then the first-order conditions for the optimization problem are

$$\beta/C_t^A = \lambda_t^C/p_t, \tag{7}$$

$$1/C_t^M = \lambda_t^C, \tag{8}$$

$$\dot{\lambda}_t^C = \rho\lambda_t^C - [(1+s)\lambda_t^C + \mu\lambda_t^M]F_1, \tag{9}$$

$$\dot{\lambda}_t^M = \rho\lambda_t^M - [(1+s)\lambda_t^C + \mu\lambda_t^M]F_2 L_t^M, \tag{10}$$

as well as (4), (6), and the transversality conditions.

For a closed economy, equilibrium of the goods market requires that

$$C_t^M + \dot{K}_t = F(K_t, M_t K_t^M), \tag{11}$$

$$C_t^A = AL_t^A. \tag{12}$$

Equilibrium of the labor market is described by

$$L_t^A + L_t^M = L. \tag{13}$$

The optimality and equilibrium conditions can be rewritten as follows:

$$C_t^A = \beta p_t C_t^M, \tag{14}$$

$$\frac{\dot{\lambda}_t^C}{\lambda_t^C} = \rho - \left(1 + s + \frac{\mu}{q_t}\right) r(k_t), \tag{15}$$

$$\frac{\dot{\lambda}_t^M}{\lambda_t^M} = \rho - [\mu + (1+s)q_t] L_t^M w(k_t), \tag{16}$$

$$\dot{K}_t = M_t L_t^M f(k_t) - C_t^M, \tag{17}$$

$$\dot{M}_t = \mu M_t L_t^M f(k_t), \tag{18}$$

as well as (5) and (12), where $q_t \equiv \lambda_t^C/\lambda_t^M$. The utility function implies that both goods are consumed at all positive prices, and thus the present economy when closed is diversified.

Balanced Growth Path

The balanced growth path (BGP) equilibrium of the economy is defined as a situation in which all endogenous variables are changing at constant rates (not necessarily the same) while the capital–labor ratio of the manufacturing sector remains constant over time. Based on this definition, the autarkic BGP equilibrium of the economy is described by the following proposition.

PROPOSITION 1. *The autarkic BGP equilibrium of the economy with a given* s ≥ 0 *is a situation where* C_t^M, X_t^M, M_t, *and* K_t *(*λ_t^C, λ_t^M, *and* p_t*) are growing (declining) at a common constant rate of* g^a *while* C_t^A, X_t^A, L_t^A, L_t^M, *and* k_t *are stationary over time.*

The proofs of this and some other propositions are given in the Appendix. Using Proposition 1, we can derive the BGP growth rate. Imposing the BGP equilibrium restrictions on (14)–(18), we get[7]

$$C^A = \beta p_t C_t^M, \tag{19}$$

$$-g^a = \rho - \left(1 + s + \frac{\mu}{q}\right) r(k), \tag{20}$$

$$-g^a = \rho - [\mu + (1+s)q] L^M w(k), \tag{21}$$

$$g^a = f(k)/k - c, \tag{22}$$

$$g^a = \mu L^M f(k), \tag{23}$$

$$A = (1+s) p_t M_t w(k), \tag{24}$$

where $c \equiv C_t^M / K_t$ and condition (24) comes from equalization of the wage rates in the two sectors. From (20)–(21), we have

$$r(k) = q L^M w(k). \tag{25}$$

Combining (20), (23), and (25), we get

$$(1 + s - \mu L^M k) r(k) = \rho. \tag{26}$$

Next, using (12), (19), and (24), we have

$$\beta c = \left(\frac{L - L^M}{L^M}\right) \frac{(1+s) w(k)}{k}. \tag{27}$$

Finally, manipulating (22), (23), and (27), we obtain

$$(1 - \mu L^M k) f(k) = \left(\frac{L - L^M}{L^M}\right) \frac{(1+s) w(k)}{\beta}. \tag{28}$$

Conditions (26) and (28), which describe the autarkic equilibrium, form a system of two equations with two unknowns, L^M and k.

PROPOSITION 2. *Given the Inada conditions, an autarkic equilibrium that satisfies conditions (26) and (28) exists. If the learning-by-doing effect is not significant (Condition 1), and if at the autarkic equilibrium the schedule that represents condition (28) is positively sloped, the autarkic equilibrium is unique.*

For meaningful comparative static experiments, the autarkic equilibrium is assumed to be unique. Note that the Inada conditions assumed in the above proposition are stronger than what are needed for the existence of a BGP.

Once L^M and k are determined, the autarkic BGP growth rate (g^a), agriculture employment, output, and consumption, and the values of $p_t K_t$ and $p_t M_t$ can be obtained from (23), (13), (1), (19), and (24). Note that C_t^M, M_t, and K_t increase at a rate of g^a over time. By (3), the output of manufacturing along a BGP rises at the same rate, implying that $p_t X_t^M$ is a constant. The national income of this economy in terms of agriculture is equal to $Y^a = X^A + p_t X_t^M$, which, by the above analysis, is constant over time.

The BGP equilibrium is illustrated in Figure 1. The value of national income which is the maximum possible output of agriculture, AL, is marked on the vertical axis. The

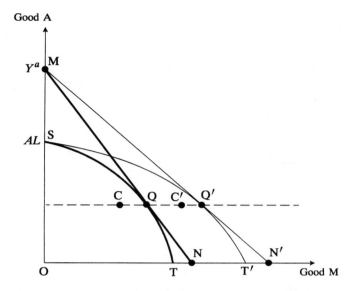

Figure 1.

budget line of the economy, MN, which has a slope of $-p_t$, can be drawn, where p_t is the prevailing price ratio. The corresponding values of K_t and M_t are used to construct the production possibility frontier (PPF), shown as ST in the diagram. This frontier touches line MN at point Q, the autarkic production point. The consumption point is at C, where QC represents the level of investment. Suppose at a later time t' the relative price p'_t is known (noting that its rate of decline is equal to g^a). The above argument can be used again to construct the new budget line (MN') and the new PPF (ST') in Figure 1. The new production point (Q') is shown, where points Q and Q' are on the same horizontal line because the output of agriculture is constant. The new consumption point is at C', where Q'C' of manufacturing has been invested.

Comparative Statics

To determine the effects of a change in some exogenous variables (μ, L, ρ, s), totally differentiate (26) and (28) and rearrange terms to give

$$\begin{bmatrix} a_{11} & a_{12} \\ a_{21} & a_{22} \end{bmatrix} \begin{bmatrix} dL^M \\ dk \end{bmatrix} = \begin{bmatrix} rkL^M & 0 & 1 & -r \\ fkL^M & (1+s)w/\beta L^M & 0 & b \end{bmatrix} \begin{bmatrix} d\mu \\ dL \\ d\rho \\ ds \end{bmatrix},$$

where $a_{11} \equiv -\mu kr < 0$, $a_{12} \equiv (1 + s - \mu L^M k)r' - \mu L^M r < 0$, $a_{21} \equiv (1 + s)wL/[\beta(L^M)^2] - \mu kf$, $a_{22} \equiv (1 - \mu L^M k)r - \mu L^M f - [(L - L^M)(1 + s)w'/(\beta L^M)]$, $b \equiv (1 - \mu L^M k)f/(1 + s) > 0$. Solving the above matrix equation, we obtain

$$\frac{dL^M}{d\rho} = \frac{a_{22}}{D}, \tag{29}$$

$$\frac{dL^M}{d\mu} = \frac{kL^M(ra_{22} - fa_{12})}{D}, \tag{30}$$

$$\frac{dL^M}{dL} = -\frac{a_{12}w(1+s)}{\beta L^M D}, \tag{31}$$

$$\frac{dL^M}{ds} = -\frac{ra_{22} + ba_{12}}{D}, \tag{32}$$

$$\frac{dk}{d\rho} = -\frac{a_{21}}{D}, \tag{33}$$

$$\frac{dk}{d\mu} = \frac{kL^M(fa_{11} - ra_{21})}{D}, \tag{34}$$

$$\frac{dk}{dL} = \frac{a_{11}w(1+s)}{\beta L^M D}, \tag{35}$$

$$\frac{dk}{ds} = \frac{ra_{21} + ba_{11}}{D}, \tag{36}$$

where $D \equiv a_{11}a_{22} - a_{12}a_{21}$ is the determinant of the matrix on the left-hand side. In general, the sign of D is ambiguous. For the time being let us focus mainly on the case in which the learning-by-doing effect is not significant; that is, μ is sufficiently small (Condition 1). In this case, we have $a_{21} > 0$ and $D \approx -wLr'/[\beta(L^M)^2] > 0$.

Invoking Condition 1, we have the following unambiguous comparative statics results:

$$\frac{dL^M}{dL} > 0, \quad \frac{dk}{d\rho} < 0, \quad \frac{dk}{d\mu} < 0, \quad \frac{dk}{dL} < 0. \tag{37}$$

The effects of labor accumulation on economic growth can be derived from (23):

$$\frac{dg^a}{dL} = \frac{\mu w}{\beta L^M D}(-fa_{12} + rL^M a_{11}) > 0, \tag{38}$$

where $-fa_{12} + rL^M a_{11} = \mu L^M rw - (1 - \mu L^M k)fr' > 0$. Also:

$$\frac{dg^a}{d\mu} = \frac{\mu k L^M}{D}[f(-fa_{12} + rL^M a_{11}) + r(-rL^M a_{21} + fa_{22})] + L^M f, \tag{39}$$

$$\frac{dg^a}{d\rho} = \frac{\mu}{D}(-rL^M a_{21} + fa_{22}) < 0, \tag{40}$$

$$\frac{dg^a}{ds} = \frac{\mu}{D}[b(rL^M a_{11} - fa_{12}) + r(rL^M a_{21} - fa_{22})] > 0. \tag{41}$$

Finally, note that the two equilibrium conditions, (26) and (28), do not contain the technology index A. We thus have the interesting result that both L^M and k, and thus the growth rate (g^a), are independent of the value of A. This result, which is not that straightforward, is due to the fact that M_t is a stock variable and cannot adjust instantaneously, implying that a change in A affects the relative price p_t proportionately. Thus all quantity variables such as production, consumption, and growth remain unchanged.

3. A Diversified, Small Open Economy

Suppose now that the economy introduced above, which from now on is called the home economy, is allowed to trade freely with the rest of the world (ROW). To simplify our analysis, we make the following assumptions:

(a) The home economy is small compared with the ROW in the sense that the economic conditions in the ROW are not affected by its trade with the economy.
(b) The structure of the ROW is the same as the home economy.
(c) At the time when trade is allowed, both the economy and the ROW are at their own BGP equilibrium.
(d) There is no production subsidy in the home economy.
(e) There is no international spillover, meaning that the home economy learns from its own manufacturing production only.

Denote the exogenously given BGP growth rate of the ROW by $g^w > 0$. Furthermore, let us denote the relative price of manufacturing in the ROW at time t by $p_t^w > 0$, which is decreasing at a rate of g^w.

Pattern of Production

To determine the home country's pattern of production, let us substitute (1) into (2) and use the labor market equilibrium condition $L_t^M + L_t^A = L$ to get an implicit expression for the equation of the home economy's production possibility frontier:

$$X_t^M = F\left(K_t, M_t\left(L - \frac{X_t^A}{A} \right) \right). \tag{42}$$

Differentiating both sides of condition (42) and rearranging terms, we get the marginal rate of transformation, MRT (the time subscripts being suppressed for simplicity):

$$MRT \equiv -\frac{dX^A}{dX^M} = \frac{A}{MF_2}. \tag{43}$$

Define the extreme values of MRT at time t as (see Figure 2)

$$\underline{\chi}_t \equiv -\frac{dX^A}{dX^M}\bigg|_{L^M \to 0} = -\frac{A}{MF_2(K,0)}, \tag{44}$$

$$\bar{\chi}_t \equiv -\frac{dX^A}{dX^M}\bigg|_{L^M \to L} = -\frac{A}{MF_2(K,ML)}. \tag{45}$$

If $F(\ldots)$ satisfies the Inada condition (i.e., $\lim_{L^M \to 0} F_2 = \infty$), then $\underline{\chi}_t = 0$ at all times. If the Inada condition is not satisfied, $\underline{\chi}_t$ and $\bar{\chi}_t$ generally change over time.

Depending on the technologies of the home economy and the value of p_t^w at any time t, three patterns of production in the economy under the following conditions can be identified:

(a) complete specialization in agriculture: $p_t^w \le \underline{\chi}_t$;
(b) diversification with positive production of both goods: $\bar{\chi}_t > p_t^w > \underline{\chi}_t$;
(c) complete specialization in manufacturing: $p_t^w \ge \bar{\chi}_t$.[8]

In the present section, we focus on the case in which the economy diversifies under free trade along a BGP.

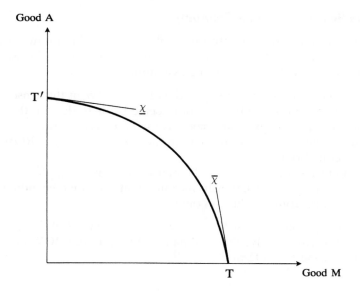

Figure 2.

Free-Trade Balanced Growth Path

Since the derivation of the optimal investment and equilibrium conditions are similar to the one described in the previous section for a closed economy, the details are skipped. The equilibrium conditions along a BGP are

$$C_t^A = \beta p_t^w C_t^M, \tag{46}$$

$$\frac{\dot{\lambda}_t^C}{\lambda_t^C} = \rho - \left(1 + \frac{\mu}{q_t}\right) r(k_t), \tag{47}$$

$$\frac{\dot{\lambda}_t^M}{\lambda_t^M} = \rho - (\mu + q_t) L_t^M w(k_t), \tag{48}$$

$$A = p_t^w M_t w(k_t), \tag{49}$$

$$p_t^w \dot{K}_t = A L_t^A + p_t^w M_t L_t^M f(k_t) - p_t^w C_t^M - C_t^A, \tag{50}$$

$$\dot{M}_t = \mu M_t L_t^M f(k_t), \tag{51}$$

where $q_t \equiv \lambda_t^C / \lambda_t^M$.

PROPOSITION 3. *Under free trade with the ROW in which the relative price of manufacturing,* p_t^w, *is declining at the constant rate of* g^w, *the BGP under diversification of the home economy is a situation in which* C_t^M, X_t^M, M_t, *and* K_t (λ_t^C, λ_t^M) *are growing (declining) at a common constant rate of* g^w *while* C_t^A, k_t, X_t^A, L_t^A, *and* L_t^M *are all positive and stationary over time.*

The BGP under diversification of the home economy can be derived as follows. From (47) and (48) and the fact that both λ_t^C and λ_t^M are decreasing at the same rate of g^w, we get

$$\mu L^M r w = (\rho + g^w - \mu L^M w)(\rho + g^w - r). \tag{52}$$

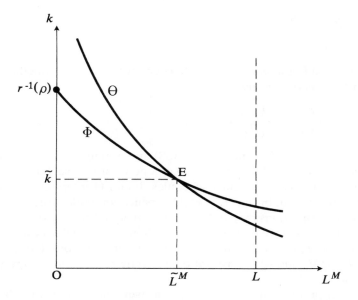

Figure 3.

Condition (51) and the fact that M is growing at the rate g^w are combined together to give

$$g^w = \mu L^M f(k).$$
(53)

Substituting (53) into (52) and rearranging the terms, we get

$$\rho = (1 - \mu L^M k)r.$$
(54)

Based on conditions (54) and (53), let us define the following two functions:

$$\Phi(L^M, k; g^w) \equiv \rho - (1 - \mu L^M k)r(k),$$
(55)

$$\Theta(L^M, k; g^w) \equiv g^w - \mu L^M f(k).$$
(56)

The above analysis suggests that the BGP of the economy is described by $\Phi(L^M, k; g^w) = 0$ and $\Theta(L^M, k; g^w) = 0$.

The derivatives of $\Phi(L^M, k; g^w)$ are (denoted by subindices):

$$\Phi_L = \mu r k > 0,$$

$$\Phi_k = \mu L^M r - (1 - \mu L^M k)r' = \mu L^M r - \rho r'/r > 0,$$

$$\Phi_g = 0.$$

When given g^w, condition $\Phi(L^M, k; g^w) = 0$ is depicted by schedule Φ in Figure 3. The slope of the schedule is equal to

$$\left.\frac{dk}{dL^M}\right|_\Phi = -\frac{\Phi_L}{\Phi_k} = -\frac{rk}{L^M r - \rho r'/(r\mu)} < 0.$$
(57)

The partial derivatives of function $\Theta(k, L^M; g^w)$ can be obtained in a similar way:

$$\Theta_L = -\mu f < 0,$$

$$\Theta_k = -\mu L^M r < 0,$$

$$\Theta_g = 1 > 0.$$

In Figure 3, the condition $\Theta(k, L^M; g^w) = 0$ when given g^w is illustrated by schedule Θ. The slope of the schedule is given by

$$\left.\frac{dk}{dL^M}\right|_\Theta = -\frac{\Theta_L}{\Theta_k} = -\frac{rk + w}{L^M r} < 0. \tag{58}$$

By comparing the expressions in (57) and (58) and noting that $r' < 0$, it is easy to see that schedule Θ is steeper than schedule Φ at a point of intersection (if one exists).

Figure 3 shows the case in which schedules Φ and Θ intersect at point E, which represents the BGP equilibrium $(\tilde{L}^M, \tilde{k})$. Diversification under free trade means that $\tilde{L}^M \in (0, L)$. Using conditions (57) and (58), such an equilibrium, if one exists, is unique.

Once $\tilde{L}^M$ and $\tilde{k}$ are known, the rest of the endogenous variables can be determined easily by making use of the optimality and equilibrium conditions derived earlier. Note that both $p_t^w K_t$, $p_t^w M_t$, and $p_t^w C_t^M$ are stationary, while K_t, M_t, and C_t^M are increasing at a rate of g^w along a BGP.

The change in production and consumption over time can also be illustrated in a diagram similar to Figure 1, with a horizontal line representing the locus of production point (because the production of good A is constant) and another horizontal line representing the locus of consumption point (because the consumption of good A is constant). In the presence of trade, these two horizontal lines may not coincide. The economy exports (imports) good A if and only if the production locus is higher than the consumption locus.

We now determine whether diversification under free trade is sustainable, i.e., whether the condition $\bar{\chi}_t > p_t^w > \underline{\chi}_t$ can hold over time. To answer this question we need to determine how $\bar{\chi}_t$, p_t^w, and $\underline{\chi}_t$ change over time. First note that p_t^w decreases at a rate of g^w. Next, if $F_2(K, L^M)$ approaches infinity as L^M approaches zero, we have $\underline{\chi}_t = 0$ always. If, when $L^M \to 0$, $F_2(K, L^M)$ is bounded from above and is independent of K,[9] $\underline{\chi}_t$ decreases at a rate of g^w along a BGP. Finally, we turn to the change of $\bar{\chi}_t$. Differentiate both sides of (45) to give

$$\hat{\bar{\chi}}_t = -(1 + \sigma_{ML})\hat{M} - \sigma_K \hat{K}, \tag{59}$$

where circumflexes denote growth rates of variables and σ_i is the elasticity of function $F_2(K, ML)$ with respect to variable i, $i = K, ML$. Along a BGP, because both M and K grow at a rate of g^w, (59) reduces to

$$\hat{\bar{\chi}}_t = -(1 + \sigma_{ML} + \sigma_K)g^w = -g^w, \tag{60}$$

where because $F_2(K, ML)$ is homogeneous of degree zero in K and ML, $\sigma_{ML} + \sigma_K = 0$. Condition (60) implies that $\bar{\chi}_t$ decreases at a rate of g^w along the BGP. In other words, $\bar{\chi}_t > p_t^w > \underline{\chi}_t$ can hold over time.

PROPOSITION 4. *Given Assumption 1, the free-trade BGP equilibrium under diversification of the home economy is unique and sustainable.*

Trading Regimes Indexed by g^w

The role of the ROW's growth on the home economy's BGP with diversification can be analyzed further. Let us imagine that there is a continuum of hypothetical trading regimes, in each of which there is one different growth rate of the ROW.[10] We want to examine the balanced growth path of the home economy if it is in different trading regimes.

Let us begin with the regime in which g^w is the same as the home economy's autarkic growth rate, $\bar{g}^a$. In this case, the values of L^M and k that satisfy (54) and (53) are the same as those that satisfy (26) and (28). If at the time of allowing free trade the autarkic relative price is the same as that of the ROW, then no trade exists and the no-trade situation continues indefinitely.

Suppose now that there is a small change in g^w so that the home economy remains diversified under trade. Differentiating both $\Phi(L^M, k; g^w) = 0$ and $\Theta(L^M, k; g^w) = 0$ as defined in (55) and (56), treating g^w as a parameter and rearranging terms, we get

$$\begin{bmatrix} \Phi_L & \Phi_k \\ \Theta_L & \Theta_k \end{bmatrix} \begin{bmatrix} d\tilde{L}^M \\ d\tilde{k} \end{bmatrix} = \begin{bmatrix} 0 \\ -1 \end{bmatrix} dg^w.$$

Solving the two equations to give the effects of a change in g^w:

$$\frac{d\tilde{L}^M}{dg^w} = \frac{\Phi_k}{\tilde{D}} > 0, \tag{61}$$

$$\frac{d\tilde{k}}{dg^w} = \frac{-\Phi_L}{\tilde{D}} < 0, \tag{62}$$

where $\tilde{D} = \mu^2 L^M rw - (1 - \mu L^M k)\mu fr' > 0$. Condition (61) implies that $d\tilde{L}^A/dg^w < 0$ and $dX^A/dg^w < 0$.

The effects of a change in g^w are illustrated in Figure 4. When there is an increase in g^w, schedule Θ shifts up to, say, Θ' while schedule Φ does not move, with the new equilibrium point depicted by point E', showing an increase in $\tilde{L}^M$ but a drop in $\tilde{k}$. These results are summarized in the following proposition.

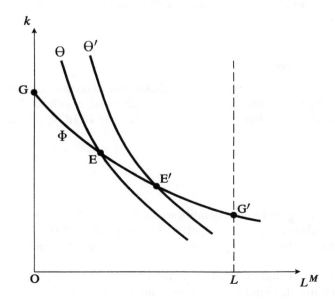

Figure 4.

PROPOSITION 5. *If initially* $g^w = \bar{g}^a$, *and if* g^w *increases slightly, then there is an increase in the BGP values of* L^M, M, *and* X^M, *but a drop in the BPG values of* k *and* X^A.

The pattern of trade of the home economy along a BGP in different regimes can be derived as follows. Define $Z^M \equiv X^M - C^M - \dot{K}$ (time subscript dropped for simplicity) as the export supply of good M, $Z^A \equiv X^A - C^A$ as the export supply of good A, and $E = C^A + pC^M$ as the national expenditure. Whether trade exists, the budget constraint (or the Walras Law, i.e., $Z^A + pZ^M = 0$) of the economy implies that

$$E = X^A + p(X^M - I), \tag{63}$$

where we let $I \equiv \dot{K}$. We are now ready to state and prove the following proposition.

PROPOSITION 6. *Suppose that the home country trades freely with the ROW and remains diversifed. (a) If the ROW grows slightly faster than the home economy and if the home country's investment does not rise as a result of trade, then the home country exports manufacturing and imports agriculture. (b) If the ROW grows slightly slower than the home economy and if the home country's investment does not fall, then the home economy imports manufacturing and exports agriculture.*

The pattern of trade of the home economy suggested in Proposition 6 is not intuitive. One may think that because the manufacturing sector is the engine of growth, if the ROW grows faster then the small economy would have a comparative disadvantage in the good. Proposition 6 shows that this intuition is not correct. The rationale behind the proposition is that if the ROW grows faster, then along a BGP with diversification, the small economy has to catch up by producing more of the manufacturing good. This promotes the export of the good so long as the investment does not increase significantly. The case in which the ROW grows slower can be interpreted in the same way. This analysis shows that, in the present model, the more appropriate way to predict the pattern of trade along a BGP is not to compare the autarkic relative prices of the economies at any point of time, since they keep falling, but to compare the BGP growth rates of the economies.[11]

More Conditions for Diversification

In this subsection, we try to derive more conditions for diversification in the economy along a BGP under free trade. Recall that diversification requires $\tilde{L}^M \in (0, L)$. Now treating L^M as a parameter but k and g as variables, the BGP equilibrium conditions can be written as

$$\Phi(k, g; L^M) = 0, \tag{64}$$

$$\Theta(k, g; L^M) = 0. \tag{65}$$

When $L^M \to 0$, let $(\underline{k}, \underline{g})$ solve the conditions, and when $L^M \to L$, let $(\bar{k}, \bar{g})$ solve the conditions. By condition (55), $\underline{k} = r^{-1}(\rho)$, and by condition (56), $g = 0$. The solution $(\bar{k}, \bar{g})$ can be obtained by replacing L^M with L in conditions (55) and (56). Both $\bar{k}$ and $\bar{g}$ are finite.

It was derived earlier that as g^w rises, the locus of the equilibrium point shifts along schedule Φ in Figure 4. Denote the vertical intercept of the schedule by point G, and the point on the schedule that corresponds to $\tilde{L}^M = \bar{L}$ by point G'. As schedule

Φ is negatively sloped, $\bar{k} < r^{-1}(\rho)$. Therefore condition $\tilde{L}^M \in (0, L)$ is equivalent to $g^w \in (0, \bar{g})$, or $k \in (\bar{k}, r^{-1}(\rho))$.[12] We now have the following proposition.

PROPOSITION 7. *The necessary condition for diversification in a BGP equilibrium under free trade is that* $g^w \in (0, \bar{g})$.

4. Complete Specialization in Agriculture

We now turn to another type of pattern of production under free trade: complete specialization in the agricultural good. This happens when $0 < p_t^w \leq \chi_t$. However, recall that because $p_t^w > 0$, if the Inada conditions are satisfied, then $\chi_t = 0$,[13] meaning that the economy will never specialize in the production of agriculture. So the analysis in this section is applicable in the cases in which the Inada conditions are not satisfied so that $\chi_t > 0$.

When the economy produces only agriculture, we have $\tilde{L}^A = L$ and $\tilde{L}^M = 0$. This means that the wage-equalization condition (49) is no longer valid, since manufactures are not produced.[14] For the same reason, the LBD equation (51) is not applicable.

The absence of LBD effects under free trade has several implications. First, the stocks of physical capital and human capital become idle.[15] Second, the production of agriculture, which depends on L only, has a constant output over time. Third, the lack of learning-by-doing means that the transition of the economy to a new BGP under free trade could be simple. In particular, if labor can move between sectors instantaneously and costlessly, then shifting from diversification under autarky to specialization in agriculture under free trade would require only a quick jump to the new BGP. Fourth, since both K and M are constant over time, χ_t remains stationary over time. On the other hand, the world price p_t^w decreases at a rate of g^w. This means that specialization in agriculture is sustained over time.

The last two remarks have a further implication. Suppose that the economy diversifies right after having free trade with the ROW. The home economy then adjusts along a new path. Suppose at any time during the transition of the economy to a new BGP the world price p_t^w drops below χ_t, which in general is not a constant when the economy is adjusting. If labor movement between the sectors is instantaneous and costless, then the output of good M drops immediately to zero. This eliminates all LBD effects in the future, and the economy will remain specialized in agriculture over time.

PROPOSITION 8. *If at any time in the presence of free trade* $p_t^w < \chi_t$, *the economy is completely specialized in agriculture. No learning-by-doing exists, and the pattern of production remains unchanged over time.*

When the home economy produces only agriculture, it trades with the rest of the world and chooses consumption so that the marginal rate of substitution is equal to the world relative price, as given by (46). However, the external terms of trade of the economy improve over time since the world relative price decreases continuously. The terms-of-trade improvement thus improves the welfare of the economy over time, allowing the economy to benefit from the LBD effect in the rest of the world.

5. Complete Specialization in Manufacturing

If $p_t^w \geq \chi_t$, the home economy will specialize in the production of manufacturing. With learning-by-doing, labor productivity in the sector grows according to equation (4).

Since the economy consumes both goods, it exports manufactures and imports agriculture at the prevailing world prices. Trade is still balanced owing to the budget constraint:

$$p_t^w \dot{K}_t = p_t^w M_t L_t^M f(k_t) - p_t^w C_t^M - C_t^A. \tag{66}$$

As before, the representative agent consumes and accumulates physical capital to maximize her intertemporal welfare. Her maximization problem is similar to that analyzed before, except that production of agriculture is zero, implying that $L^M = L$. The first-order conditions are then given by (46)–(48), (66), and (51).

Can a BGP with complete specialization in manufacturing be sustained? Suppose that it can be. Recall the equilibrium conditions (64) and (65). We showed that with $L^M = L$, the solution to these two conditions is $(\bar{k}, \bar{g})$. This equilibrium is depicted by point G′ in Figure 4. If $g^w = \bar{g}$, the BGP with manufacturing of the home economy with the same growth rate can be sustained. If the $g^w > \bar{g}$, then the home economy will not be able to catch up with the ROW. To see this point more clearly, note that with $g^w > \bar{g}$, the economy has to accumulate physical capital at a rate as required by condition (53). However, by doing so, condition (54) will be violated, meaning that the intertemporal welfare of the representative agent is not being maximized.

We now derive more explicitly the equilibrium when $g^w \geq \bar{g}$. If the economy is growing at its maximum rate, $\bar{g}$, with complete specialization in manufacturing, $\bar{\chi}_t$ is decreasing at the same rate. The minimum value of MRT, χ_t, will either decrease at a rate of $\bar{g}$ (if the Inada conditions are not satisfied) or will remain at a fixed level of zero (if the Inada conditions are satisfied). As a result, in the singular case in which $g^w = \bar{g}$, both p_t^w and $\bar{\chi}_t$ are decreasing at a rate of $\bar{g}$, and the BGP under specialization in manufacturing can be sustained. If, however, the growth rate of the ROW is $g^w > \bar{g}$, then p_t^w decreases faster than $\bar{\chi}_t$. This means that sooner or later p_t^w is less than $\bar{\chi}_t$, and the economy starts producing both goods. However, because $g^w > \bar{g}$, a BGP with diversification does not exist. In this case, the BGP equilibrium of the economy is one with complete specialization in agriculture, which has been described in the previous section. However, if $\chi_t = 0$, then the economy can be completely specialized in agriculture only asymptotically.

PROPOSITION 9. *(a) If* $g^w = \bar{g}$ *then a BGP equilibrium under free trade with complete specialization in manufacturing is sustainable. (b) If* $g^w > \bar{g}$, *then a BGP equilibrium with complete specialization in manufacturing under free trade is not sustainable. The BGP of the economy is one in which the economy is completely specialized in agriculture [asymptotically if the Inada conditions are satisfied].*

6. Concluding Remarks

We have constructed a model to analyze the relationship between industrialization, economic growth, and international trade. This model has some interesting features that distinguish it well from many of the existing growth models in the literature. Probably the most notable one is the fact that the learning-by-doing effect exists in one of the sectors only, making labor in that sector more and more productive. In a closed economy, the widening gap in labor productivity in the two sectors does not imply the decline or disappearance of the stagnant (agriculture) sector, but it does lead to a constant drop in the relative price of the growing (manufacturing) sector. The feature of a declining relative price is consistent with what we usually observe for many manufacturing goods.

The determinants of the growth of the economy is the focus of this paper. When an economy is closed, its growth rate depends on the learning-by-doing effect, which is directly related to the relative output level of the manufacturing sector. This suggests the possible use of production subsidies to promote growth.

Under free trade, the effectiveness of production subsidies in promoting growth is generally limited. The growth of the economy depends on, among other things, its pattern of trade and the growth of the rest of the world. For example, if the economy is diversified along a balanced growth path, then its growth rate is pegged to that of the rest of the world. If the economy is completely specialized in agriculture, then no learning-by-doing effects exist, and the home economy will have no incentive to invest in physical capital because physical capital is not used in the agricultural sector. The growth rate of the economy drops down to zero, showing the importance of the manufacturing sector in its growth performance. For the case of complete specialization in manufacturing, except in the singular case in which $g^w = \bar{g}$, a BGP with complete specialization in manufacturing does not exist. A BGP of the economy, if it exists, is complete specialization in agriculture (asympotically if the Inada conditions are satisfied).

The last remark that may be pointed out is that this paper considers only domestic learning-by-doing as an engine of growth. There could be many other factors that improve the growth performance of an economy resulting from trading with other countries: for example, technology spillover effects, technology transfers through foreign direct investment and international labor migration, and imitation.[16] All these effects, which have been ignored here, could be the topics for future research.[17]

Appendix

Proof of Proposition 1

Along a BGP equilibrium, by definition, k_t is constant. Condition (18) implies that L_t^M is constant over time. Let the BGP equilibrium growth rate of M_t be g^a. Then (5) yields $\dot{p}_t/p_t = -g^a$. Next, (12) and (1) give constancy of L_t^A, X_t^A and C_t^A, while (14) and (17) in turn imply that both C_t^M and K_t (hence X_t^M) are growing at the same rate g^a. Finally, condition (15) implies that q_t is a constant along a BGP, meaning that both λ_t^C and λ_t^M are declining at the same rate g^a.   □

Proof of Proposition 2

Let us first examine the properties of condition (26), and use superscript "I" to denote the corresponding variables. As $L^M \to 0$, $k \to \underline{k}^I \equiv r^{-1}(\rho/(1 + s)) > 0$, where $r^{-1}(.)$ is the inverse function of the rental rate function. As $L^M \to L$, $k \to \bar{k}^I$, where $\bar{k}^I$ solves the following equation:[18]

$$\mu L \bar{k}^I = 1 + s - \frac{\rho}{r(\bar{k}^I)}. \tag{67}$$

Furthermore, the rate of change of k with respect to L^M subject to condition I is equal to

$$\left. \frac{dk}{dL^M} \right|_I = \frac{\mu k r}{\rho r'/r - r\mu L^M} < 0, \tag{68}$$

where $r' \equiv dr/dk < 0$.

We now turn to condition (28) and use superscript "II" to denote the correspond-ing variables. As $L^M \to 0$, $k \to \underline{k}^{II} \equiv 0$, when given the Inada condition.[19] As $L^M \to L$, $k \to \bar{k}^{II} \equiv 1/(\mu L)$. Note that when s is sufficiently small, equation (67) implies that $\bar{k}^{II} > \bar{k}^I$.[20] Furthermore, the rate of change of k with respect to L^M subject to (28) and Condition 1 is equal to

$$\left.\frac{dk}{dL^M}\right|_{II} = \frac{L(1+s)w}{L^M\left[(L-L^M)(1+s)w' - \beta rL^M\right]}. \tag{69}$$

From condition (69), the rate of change of k with respect to L^M approaches positive infinity as $L^M \to 0$. This rate of change is not continuous at $(L - L^M)(1 + s)w' = \beta rL^M$, approaching positive infinity as $[(L - L^M)(1 + s)w' - \beta rL^M]$ approaches 0^+, or negative infinity as $[(L - L^M)(1 + s)w' - \beta rL^M]$ approaches 0^-. Because $\underline{k}^I > \underline{k}^{II}$ and $\bar{k}^I < \bar{k}^{II}$, and owing to continuity of the functions, there exists at least one autarkic equilibrium. Since the rate of change of k with respect to L^M for condition (26) is always negative, if the corresponding rate of change of k with respect to L^M for condition (28) at the autar-kic equilibrium is always positive, the autarkic equilibrium is unique.   □

Proof of Proposition 3

By the definition of a BGP, k_t is constant and M_t is growing at a constant rate of g^w. Condition (51) implies that L_t^M, and hence L_t^A, are stationary. This in turn yields a con-stant K_t/M_t ratio. Since $\dot{p}_t^w/p_t^w = -g^w$, (49) gives the BGP equilibrium growth rate of M_t (and hence K_t) as g^w. Next, (46) and (50) give constancy of $p_t^w C_t^M$ and C_t^A so that C_t^M is growing at the same rate g^w. Finally, from (8) and (47), both λ_t^C and λ_t^M are declining at the same rate g^w.   □

Proof of Proposition 6

(a) Condition (46) implies that $E = (1 + 1/\beta)C^A$, or that

$$\Delta E = (1+1/\beta)\Delta C^A. \tag{70}$$

If investment does not fall, then Proposition 5 implies that $\Delta(X^M - I) > 0$, so that by condition (63), $\Delta E > \Delta X^A$. This result and condition (70) imply that

$$(1+1/\beta)\Delta C^A > \Delta X^A. \tag{71}$$

By Proposition 5, $\Delta X^A < 0$. If $\Delta C^A > 0$, $\Delta Z^A < 0$ and, by Walras' Law, $\Delta Z^M > 0$. If $\Delta C^A < 0$, then (71) implies that $\Delta X^A < \Delta C^A < 0$. So again, $\Delta Z^A < 0$ and $\Delta Z^M > 0$. Part (b) can be proved in a similar way.   □

References

Boldrin, M. and J. A. Scheinkman, "Learning-By-Doing, International Trade, and Growth: A Note," in *The Economy as an Evolving Complex System* (SFI Studies in the Science of Com-plexity), Reading, MA: Addison-Wesley (1988).

Bond, Eric W. and Kathleen Trask, "Trade and Growth with Endogenous Human and Physical Capital Accumulation," in Bjarne S. Jensen and Kar-yiu Wong (eds.), *Dynamics, Economic Growth, and International Trade*, Ann Arbor: University of Michigan Press (1997):211–40.

Bond, Eric W., Ping Wang, and Chong K. Yip, "A General Two-Sector Model of Endogenous Growth Model with Human and Physical Capital: Balanced Growth and Transitional Dynam-ics," *Journal of Economic Theory* 68 (1997):149–73

Conway, Patrick and William A. Darity, Jr, "Growth and Trade with Asymmetric Returns to Scale: A Model for Nicholas Kaldor," *Southern Economic Journal* 57 (1991):745–59.

Dutt, Amitaya K., "Monopoly Power and Uneven Development: Baran Revisited," *Journal of Development Studies* 24 (1988):161–76.

Long, Ngo Van and Kar-yiu Wong, "Endogenous Growth and International Trade: A Survey," in Bjarne S. Jensen and Kar-yiu Wong (eds.), *Dynamics, Economic Growth, and International Trade*, Ann Arbor: University of Michigan Press (1997):11–74.

Matsuyama, Kiminori, "Agricultural Productivity, Comparative Advantage and Economic Growth," *Journal of Economic Theory* 58 (1992):317–34.

Romer, Paul M., "Increasing Returns and Long Run Growth," *Journal of Political Economy* 94 (1986):1002–37.

———, "Growth Based on Increasing Returns Due to Specialization," *American Economic Review, Papers and Proceedings*, 77(2) (1987):56–72.

———, "Endogenous Technological Change," *Journal of Political Economy* 98(5) (1990):71–102.

Sarkar, Prabirjit, "The Singer–Prebisch Hypothesis: A Statistical Evaluation," *Cambridge Journal of Economics* 10 (1986):355–71.

———, "Long-Term Behaviour of Terms of Trade of Primary Products *vis-à-vis* Manufactures: A Critical Review of Recent Debate," *Economic and Political Weekly* 29 (1994):1612–14.

———, "Growth and Terms of Trade: A North–South Macroeconomic Framework," *Journal of Macroeconomics* 19 (1997):117–33.

Wong, Kar-yiu, *International Trade in Goods and Factor Mobility*, Cambridge, MA: MIT Press (1995).

———, "Endogenous Growth and International Labor Migration: The Case of A Small Open Economy," in Bjarne S. Jensen and Kar-yiu Wong (eds.), *Dynamics, Economic Growth, and International Trade*, Ann Arbor: University of Michigan Press (1997):289–336.

Wong, Kar-yiu and Chong K. Yip, "Dynamic Gains from Trade and Industrialization," mimeo University of Washington (1998).

Young, Alwyn, "Learning-By-Doing and the Dynamic Effects of International Trade," *Quarterly Journal of Economics* 106 (1991):369–405.

Notes

1. The feature of the present model that the relative price of manufacturing is declining along a BGP is quite different from many of the existing models; for example, Bond et al. (1997) and Bond and Trask (1997).

2. See Conway and Darity (1991), Darity (1990), and Dutt (1988) for related work.

3. While our paper is limited to a positive theory of trade and industrialization, the analysis provided here certainly has strong welfare and policy implications. In another paper (Wong and Yip, 1998), we examine how the welfare of an economy may be affected by trade and industrialization in a dynamic model, and argue that an economy can still gain from trade even if its terms of trade deteriorate over time. We also identify some cases in which policies such as production subsidies can be used to promote the welfare of an open economy.

4. Our model differs from the Ricardo–Viner–Jones model of Matsuyama (1992).

5. Our assumption of the existence of externality in the accumulation of human capital, which allows us to keep the assumption of perfect competition, is common in the endogenous growth literature. One limitation of this assumption is that firms and individuals do not take into account the learning-by-doing in their choice of optimal actions. An alternative and interesting way to endogenize growth is to internalize the learning-by-doing process so that firms may be facing decreasing costs. The resulting internal economies of scale usually lead to imperfect competition in a dynamic model. See Romer (1987, 1990) for work along this line.

6. An alternative model, suggested by Eric Bond, is one in which investment is determined not by a representative agent but by competitive investors who take prevailing prices as given. This implies that intertemporal disortions in investment may be created. We avoid this approach in order not to model the behavior of the investors separately.

7. Note that endogenous variables that stay stationary along a BGP have no time subindex.

8. The three conditions can be written in an equivalent way: (a) $A \geq p_t^w M_t w(K, 0)$; (b) $A = p_t^w M_t w(K_t, M_t L_t^M)$ for $0 \leq L^M \leq L$; and (c) $A \leq p_t^w w(K_t, M_t L)$.

9. $F_2(K, L^M)$ is homogeneous of degree zero, implying that $KF_{21} + ML^M F_{22} = 0$. Given part (b) of Assumption 1 and when $L^M \to 0$, $F_{21} \to 0$ for any positive amount of K.

10. Note that we are comparing the balanced growth paths of the home economy in different regimes with different growth rates of the ROW. For simplicity, we just say an increase or decrease in g^w as we shift from one regime to another.

11. In the static, neoclassical framework the comparative advantages of economies are defined in terms of the autarkic relative prices. This is the law of comparative advantage (Wong, 1995). This law has been extended to growing economies in their steady states in which autarkic relative prices are stationary. See, for example, Bond and Trask (1997). This law is not applicable in the present model, however.

12. Notice that $d\tilde{L}^M/dg^w > 0$ as derived earlier implies the monotonic relation between the two variables.

13. To get $\chi_t = 0$, all we need is that $F_2(K, 0) \to 0$ as $L^M \to 0$.

14. In fact, (49) is replaced by $A > p_t^w M_t w(k_t)$.

15. Of course, the economy can sell physical and/or human capital, if tradable, to the ROW. The economy will receive a one-time payment.

16. Wong (1997) shows one that international labor migration from a more advanced country to a less advanced country can improve the human capital level in the latter country.

17. For a recent survey of the effects of trade on growth, see Long and Wong (1997).

18. To see whether equation (67) has a solution, note that when $k \to 0$, $r(k) \to \infty$ by the Inada conditions, so that the LHS is less than the RHS; when $k \to \infty$, $r(k) \to 0$, implying that the LHS is greater than the RHS. Continuity of the functions imply that at least one solution with $k^I > 0$ exists. Note further that the LHS is increasing in k while the RHS is decreasing in k. Thus the solution is unique.

19. Rewrite equation (28) as $\beta L^M (1 - \mu L^M k) f(k) = (L - L^M)(1 + s)w(k)$. When $L^M \to 0$, the LHS of the equation approaches zero, requiring that the corresponding $w(k) \to 0$, or $k \to 0$ by the Inada conditions.

20. Actually what we need for this result is that $s < \rho/r(k^I)$.

11
Income Tax, Property Tax, and Tariff in a Small Open Economy

*Charles Ka Yui Leung**

Abstract

Why do some countries enjoy high economic growth rates while some suffer in "low-growth traps"? Why are tax policies in different countries so different? Some suggest that it is exactly these differences in government policies which contribute to the difference in economic growth rates. This paper considers a small open economy which sustains its economic growth by adopting new technologies. When the value of initial wealth is "relatively small," policies which promote growth most result in the highest welfare. In other cases, policies that discourage growth most may be welfare-maximizing.

1. Introduction

Why do some countries enjoy high economic growth rates and some suffer in "low-growth traps"? Why are the tax policies in different countries so different? In particular, why did not the governments in those "low-growth countries" change their policies to improve the welfare of their citizens? To answer these and related questions, economists have proposed many theories, trying to provide scientific explanations of the cross-country difference in economic growth (positive side), and practical policy recommendations for governments (normative side). One of them is particularly interesting: it is exactly the difference in government policies which contributes to the difference in long-term growth rates. Some authors further argue that the existing policies are suboptimal and suggest some alternatives.[1]

This paper attempts to contribute to the literature by focusing on tax policy analysis in a very stylized model. This model considers a small open economy which does not invent new technology. The economic agents purchase intermediate goods from the world market which embodies new technologies, and they sell part of their final outputs. Technological adoption can be achieved only by expanding the scope of intermediate goods imports from aboard.[2] Despite its simplicity, this setting captures many realistic aspects, and models with similar features have been studied widely.[3] Easterly et al. (1993) (hereafter EKLR) modify those models and eliminate the scale effect, which is not supported by empirical research.[4] This paper extends EKLR by incorporating residential capital (or household capital, terms which will be used interchangeably), which is an investment good and also a durable consumption good. The importance of residential capital has been recognized in the real business cycle literature.[5] This paper, however, assumes away business cycle fluctuations and focuses on the comparison of growth and welfare effects of different tax policies: namely, income tax, property tax, and tariffs. The concept of residential capital is particularly important for the "Four Little Dragons", since household capital constitutes an increasing share of their total capital.[6]

* Leung: Chinese University of Hong Kong, Shatin, Hong Kong. Tel: (852) 2609-7158; Fax: (852) 2603-5805; E-mail: charlesl@cuhk.edu.hk. The author thanks Bjarne Jensen, Sailesh Jha, Ronald Jones, Kar-Yiu Wong, Chong Yip, seminar participants, three anonymous referees, and especially Rodney Chun, Totaro Miyashita, Priscilla Ng and Hiroshi Ohta for helpful comments, and Yim Chun Wong for capable research assistance. The usual disclaimer applies.

The results found in this paper are intuitive. The "engine" of growth here is the adoption of new technology, achieved by increasing the range of intermediate goods used in final goods production. Therefore taxes that affect the incentive to adopt "new" intermediate goods most will hurt economic growth most. A property tax has the least effect on that and hence has the least negative impact on growth. And since the returns of using any particular type of intermediate good are diminishing, a tariff has a bigger impact than an income tax. However, "growth-maximizing" is not necessarily "welfare-maximizing." In fact, depending on the initial conditions, the level of social welfare attained can be the lowest. In other words, the governments of slow-growing countries could have chosen the "right policies," which deliver the slowest economic growth yet the highest social welfare.

The organization of this paper is simple. The next section displays the basic model. The growth effects and the welfare effects of different regimes are discussed in turn. Concluding remarks are followed by the Appendix, which contains all the proofs and an extension of the basic model.

2. Basic Model

Owing to the similarity of the present model with that of Easterly et al. (1993), the description of the economic environment will be brief. Time is discrete and the horizon is infinite. The total population of the economy is constant over time and normalized to unity. At period $t, t = 0, 1, 2, \ldots$, the representative agent maximizes the "lifetime utility"

$$\sum_{s=t}^{\infty} \beta^s u(C_s, h_s),$$

which is the discounted sum of "periodic utility" $u(C_s, h_s)$ for period $s = t, (t + 1)$, $(t + 2), \ldots$. The periodic utility function assumed here is adopted from Greenwood and Hercowitz (1991):

$$u(C_s, h_s) = \ln C_s + \omega \ln h_s,$$

where C_s is the nondurable consumption at period s, h_s is the stock of household capital at period s, and $\omega > 0$ is a preference parameter.[7] At period t, the representative agent is able to combine all different intermediate goods $i, i \in [0, A_t]$ and nontradeable inputs N_t, to produce final output, via an aggregate production function. Final output can be consumed (C_t), or used to build household capital, or used to pay for the intermediate goods imported from foreign countries, with the rest used for adopting new technology. Adopting new technology is necessary for sustaining economic growth; and since the new technology is embodied in the "new" intermediate goods, the agent needs to expand the scope of intermediate goods imported from aboard. There is a once-and-for-all "setup" cost or "fixed cost" for learning how to operate with the new intermediate goods, which is equal to $1/B_A$ units of final output. On the other hand, there is no technological change in the onstruction sector. It takes q units of (locally produced) consumption goods to produce one unit of household capital, $q > 0$. For simplicity, the depreciation rate of household capital is assumed to be zero. Since it is a linear production technology, q is also the *relative price* of household capital in terms of consumption goods.

To guarantee time-consistency, the maximization problem is formulated as a dynamic programming problem:

$$V(A_t, h_t) = \max_{C_t, h_{t+1}, A_{t+1}, \{x_t(i)\}} u(C_t, h_t) + \beta V(A_{t+1}, h_{t+1}),$$

s.t.

$$C_t + q(h_{t+1} - h_t) + \frac{(A_{t+1} - A_t)}{B_A} + \int_0^{A_t} p_t(i) x_t(i) di$$

$$\leq B_1(N)^{\alpha_1} \left[\int_0^{A_t} (x_t(i))^{\gamma_1} di \right]^{(1-\alpha_1)/\gamma_1}, \tag{1}$$

where $0 < \alpha_1, \beta, \gamma_1 < 1$. Notice that the household capital h_t is simply a durable consumption but does not contribute to goods production. As will be clear, the only "dynamic" choice variable in the goods production process is the range (or the "scope") of intermediate goods imported, or the "technology level" A_t. The budget constraint restricts the sum of nondurable consumption C_t, consumption goods forgone to purchase additional household capital $q(h_{t+1} - h_t)$, consumption goods forgone to adopt new technology $(A_{t+1} - A_t)/B_A$, and consumption goods forgone to import all different types of intermediate inputs $\int_0^{A_t} p_t(i) x_t(i) di$, not to exceed the total amount of the final goods produced:

$$B_1(N)^{\alpha_1} \left[\int_0^{A_t} (x_t(i))^{\gamma_1} di \right]^{(1-\alpha_1)/\gamma_1}, \quad B_1, B_A > 0.$$

Implicitly, it is assumed that there is an aggregate production technology which combines the intermediate goods $x_t(i), i \in [0, A_t]$, and nontradeable (and nonaccumulative) factor N to produce the final goods. Notice that the intermediate goods are imported and then "used up" in the production process *within the same period*.

Following EKLR, the symmetry assumption is imposed:

$$p_t(i) = p, \quad \forall t, \quad \forall i. \tag{2}$$

In the Appendix, it is shown that the original problem can be simplified as

$$V(A_t, h_t) = \max_{C_t, h_{t+1}, A_{t+1}} u(C_t, h_t) + \beta V(A_{t+1}, h_{t+1}), \tag{3}$$

s.t.

$$C_t + q(h_{t+1} - h_t) + \frac{(A_{t+1} - A_t)}{B_A} \leq A_t R, \tag{4}$$

for some "constant" R. It can be shown that a higher value of p is associated with a lower value of R. The first-order conditions[8] are similar to those in EKLR:

$$h_t = \frac{\beta \omega}{q \left((C_t)^{-1} - \beta(C_{t+1})^{-1} \right)}, \tag{5}$$

$$\frac{C_{t+1}}{C_t} = \beta(1 + B_A R). \tag{6}$$

Notice that t is arbitrary and the right-hand side of (6) is invariant in time. It follows that the growth rate of consumption is constant over time, and so a shorthand $g_{C,t}$ is defined: $g_{C,t} \equiv C_{t+1}/C_t$. Also, $g_{y,t}$, $g_{A,t}$, and $g_{h,t}$ are defined analogously. This paper will restrict itself to the case where $g_{C,t} > 1$, $\forall t$.

Before more explorations on the growth rates of other aggregate variables, observe that the consumption growth rate is positively correlated to B_A and R. The intuition is clear. A higher value of B_A means a lower "learning cost" $1/B_A$, and since the economic growth is sustained by expanding the scope of imported intermediate goods, slower learning cost will speed up learning and growth. A higher value of R is associated with a lower value of p. A lower value of p means that the imported goods can be purchased at a lower price and hence more resources can be invested in learning and more goods can be consumed.

Equation (6) implies that the growth rate of consumption is constant over time: $g_{C,t} = g_C$, $\forall t$. A natural question is, whether $g_{y,t}$, $g_{A,t}$, and $g_{h,t}$ are also constant over time. Put another way, are there any transitional dynamics in this model? In the Appendix it is shown that

$$\left(\frac{h_t}{C_t}\right) = \Psi, \quad \Psi = \frac{\beta\omega}{q}\frac{g_C}{(g_C - \beta)}, \tag{7}$$

for all period t. It implies that the growth rate household capital is also a constant: $g_{h,t} = g_h$, $\forall t$. And for plausible values of β, it is shown in the Appendix that $g_C = g_{A,t}$, $\forall t$. Therefore, this paper will restrict its attention to the balanced growth path where

$$g_C = g_h = g_A. \tag{8}$$

For any given initial household capital stock h_0, the whole path of consumption C_t and household capital h_t can be traced out by (6), (8), and (7). It is interesting to note that the level of the constant cost of producing household capital, q, does not affect the growth rate (see (6)), but only the equilibrium ratio of household capital to non-durable consumption.

In this simple economy, the public finance exercise is straightforward. Assume that the government needs to finance an exogenous path of wasteful expenditure, that will have an effect neither on consumption nor production. Three different ways of financing will be considered. They are tariffs, income tax, and property tax.

3. Growth Effects

This section provides a comparison of the implications of a universal tariff,[9] an income tax and a property tax on the economic growth rate. To keep the discussion tractable, and to provide a benchmark, attention is focused on time-invariant tax rates. As differential factor taxation is not considered, the equilibrium solution will coincide with the planner's problem with aggregate taxation constraints. This observation simplifies the algebra.

A Tariff

It is shown in the Appendix that (4) should be modified as

$$C_t + q(h_{t+1} - h_t) + \frac{(A_{t+1} - A_t)}{B_A} \leq A_t R_x, \tag{9}$$

where $R_x = (1 + \tau_x)^{-(1-\alpha_1)/\alpha_1} * R$, where τ_x is the tariff rate levied on the intermediate inputs. And the common growth rate in this economy is simply

$$g_C^x = \beta(1 + B_A R_x). \tag{10}$$

If all the government expenditure G_t^x is financed by the tariff, the balanced government budget will be

$$\tau_x \int_0^{A_t} x_t(i)p_t(i)di = G_t^x.$$ (11)

Since

$$\int_0^{A_t} x_t(i)p_t(i)di = \frac{A_t R_x}{(1+\tau_x)}\left(\frac{1-\alpha_1}{\alpha_1}\right),$$

equation (11) implies

$$\tau_x = \frac{\alpha_1 G_t^x}{(1-\alpha_1)A_t R_x - \alpha_1 G_t^x}.$$ (12)

It is assumed that $0 < \tau_x < 1$. This expression will be very useful when the analogous formula for the income tax case is computed.

An Income Tax

In this case, (4) should be modified as

$$C_t + q(h_{t+1} - h_t) + \frac{(A_{t+1} - A_t)}{B_A} \le A_t R_y,$$ (13)

where $R_y = [1 - \tau_y]^{1/\alpha_1} * R$. The common growth rate in this economy will be simplified to

$$g_C^y = \beta(1 + B_A R_y).$$ (14)

If all the government expenditure G_t^y is financed by the income tax, the balanced government budget will be

$$\tau_y B_1(N)^{\alpha_1}\left[\int_0^{A_t}(x_t(i))^{\gamma_1}di\right]^{(1-\alpha_1)/\gamma_1} = G_t^y.$$ (15)

Since

$$B_1(N)^{\alpha_1}\left[\int_0^{A_t}(x_t(i))^{\gamma_1}di\right]^{(1-\alpha_1)/\gamma_1} = A_t R_y \alpha_1^{-1}[1-\tau_y]^{-1},$$

then

$$\tau_y = \frac{\alpha_1 G_t^y}{A_t R_y + \alpha_1 G_t^y}.$$ (16)

In order to compare different tax schemes in an endogenous growth model, certain assumptions need to be made. We follow Palivos and Yip (1995) in assuming that government expenditure is a constant share of the total net output: $G_t^i = \xi A_t R_i$, $0 < \xi < 1$, $i = x, y$. This assumption guarantees feasibility and simplifies the exposition. Nevertheless, in reality government expenditure does vary across tax schemes, and so the reader should interpret the results with caution. Hence, for $0 < \tau_x < 1$, it is necessary that $\xi < \alpha_1^{-1} - 1$. By the definitions of R_x, R_y, (10), and (14), it is clear that $g_C^x > g_C^y \Leftrightarrow R_x > R_y \Leftrightarrow (1 + \tau_x)^{-(1-\alpha_1)/\alpha_1} > (1 - \tau_y)^{1/\alpha_1}$. The relative magnitude of the consumption growth rate depends on the relative magnitude of the marginal product of an additional intermediate good under the corresponding tax schemes. With all these results, it is straightforward to derive the following result (all proofs are in the Appendix).

LEMMA 1. *For any given level of government expenditure share* ξ *and* α_1 *not too large,* $0 < \alpha_1 < (1 + \xi)^{-1}$, *and technological level* A_t, *the economy under the income tax regime exhibits a higher economic growth rate than its tariff counterpart:*

$$g_C^x < g_C^y. \tag{17}$$

Notice that for any particular intermediate good, the rate of return is diminishing if the amount of imports of all other intermediate goods is constant. Hence, imposing a tariff could lead to a distortion of the composition of intermediate goods, at least when the economy is off the symmetric equilibrium. An income tax does not have such an effect and hence it delivers a higher economic growth rate.[10]

A Property Tax

It is assumed that the property tax is proportional to the value of the total amount of household capital (stock) possessed by the representative agent. Hence, (4) will be modified as

$$C_t + q(h_{t+1} - h_t) + \frac{(A_{t+1} - A_t)}{B_A} + \tau_h(qh_t) \leq A_t R, \tag{18}$$

and it is easy to see that the economic growth rate will be unchanged:

$$g_C^h = \beta(1 + B_A R). \tag{19}$$

But equation (7) needs to be modified as

$$\frac{h_t}{C_t} = \frac{\beta\omega}{q} \frac{g_C}{[g_C - \beta(1 - \tau_h)]}. \tag{20}$$

This observation is formulated as the following lemma.

LEMMA 2. *The property tax rate in this economy does not affect the economic growth rate.*

For later reference, I also want to derive the level of tax rate needed to finance the public expenditure G_t. To balance the budget:

$$\tau_h(qh_t) = G_t.$$

By the balanced growth condition and $G_t = \xi A_t R$:

$$\tau_h = \frac{\xi R}{q} \frac{A_0}{h_0}. \tag{21}$$

The following proposition summarizes the results.

PROPOSITION 3. *Since* $R > R_y > R_x$, *we have* $g_C^h > g_C^y > g_C^x$.

The intuition is clear. What sustains growth is the learning. The property tax does not affect learning and hence should have no effect on growth. As the other two regimes considered here do affect growth adversely, economic growth under the property tax regime should be the highest. Notice that although the growth effect of a property tax is zero, the wealth effect will not be.

4. Welfare Effects

The previous section examined the implications of different taxation schemes for the economic growth rate. While that gave testable predictions, it was unable to provide answers to normative questions. In this section, the welfare implications of taxation schemes will be examined. The results that can be obtained from a two-sector endogenous growth model are, of course, very limited. The observation that the model economy is always on a balanced growth path greatly simplifies the algebra. Along the balanced growth path, and given the specific functional form I have assumed, the lifetime utility for the case of no tax has a simple representation:

$$V(A_0, h_0) = \sum_{t=0}^{\infty} \beta^t u(C_t, h_t)$$
$$= u(C_0, h_0) + \beta u(g_C C_0, g_C h_0) + \dots$$
$$= \left(\frac{1}{1-\beta}\right)(\ln C_0 + \omega \ln h_0) + (\ln g_C)(\mathcal{B}(1+\omega)), \qquad (22)$$

where h_0 is the initial stock of household capital. C_0, the initial-period consumption, is

$$C_0 = A_0 R - (g_C - 1)\left(qh_0 + \frac{A_0}{B_A}\right), \qquad (23)$$

and

$$\mathcal{B} = \sum_{n=1}^{\infty} n\beta^n = \frac{\beta}{(1-\beta)^2}, \qquad (24)$$

which is a constant.[11] Extending the formula for the nontrivial tax case is straightforward. For the case a of tariff and an income tax, simply replace R by R_i, and g_C by g_C^i, $i = x, y$. For the case of a property tax:

$$C_0^h = A_0 R_h - (g_C^h - 1)\left(qh_0 + \frac{A_0}{B_A}\right), \qquad (25)$$

where $R_h = (1 - \xi)R$. The initial-period consumption is negatively correlated to the growth rate of consumption goods. Notice that the property tax reduces R to R_0^h, and the latter ratio of nondurable consumption and household capital, but does not have any direct impact on the *growth* rate of nondurable consumption. The following lemma dictates the sufficient condition for the lifetime utility to move in the same direction as the economic growth rate increases, which applies to all three cases.

PROPOSITION 4.

$$\frac{dV(A_0, h_0)}{dg_C} > 0$$

$$\Leftrightarrow \quad \frac{g_C^i}{C_0^i} - \mathbb{M} < 0 \qquad (26)$$

$$\Leftrightarrow \quad \beta(1 + B_A R_i) < \left(1 + \frac{A_0 R_i}{\rho_I}\right)\left(\frac{1}{1+s\beta}\right)$$

where $\mathbb{M} = (\beta(1 + \omega)/(1 - \beta))/\rho_I$, $\rho_I = (qh_0 + A_0/B_A)$, *and* $s_\beta = (1 - \beta)/\beta(1 + \omega)$, $i = x$, y, *are constants.*

The proof can be found in the Appendix. Notice that the second term $\mathbb{M}$ is constant across regimes while the first term is strictly increasing in the consumption growth rate g_C^i,[12] as long as a feasibility constraint is satisfied; namely, the initial-period consumption C_0^i does not exceed the total net output A_0R_i.

Here is the plan. First, two corollaries will be presented. Then, interpretation of the proposition will be offered. Assume that the share of government expenditure ξ is held fixed across different regimes.[13] It follows immediately that if the growth rates under all the different regimes deliver a positive sign (negative sign) for $g_C/C_0 - \mathbb{M}$, the regime which has the highest consumption growth rate, namely the property tax, will attain the lowest (highest) welfare level.

COROLLARY 1. *If ξ, g_C^i, are such that $g_C^i/C_0^i - \mathbb{M} < 0$, j = x, y, then, with the same initial conditions (A_0, h_0), $V(.; \tau_h) > V(.; \tau_y) > V(.; \tau_x)$.*

COROLLARY 2. *If ξ, g_C^i, are such that $g_C^i/C_0^i - \mathbb{M} > 0$, j = x, y, h, then, with the same initial conditions (A_0, h_0), $V(.; \tau_h) < V(.; \tau_y) < V(.; \tau_x)$.*

The intuition is simple. To enjoy a higher economic growth rate, agents would need to sacrifice the initial-period consumption. Since the marginal utility of consumption is diminishing and the agents discount future utility, the initial-period consumption "cannot be too low" to have an overall increase in welfare. When the economic growth rate is "not too high" relative to the initial-period consumption, which is the case of $g_C^i/C_0^i - \mathbb{M} < 0, \Leftrightarrow g_C^i < \mathbb{M}C_0^i$, then the future increase in consumption will be high enough to compensate the initial suffering. In this case, the welfare under the property tax regime will be highest since it delivers the highest economic growth rate, $V(.; \tau_h) > V(.; \tau_y) > V(.; \tau_x)$. The same idea applies to the case of $g_C^i/C_0^i - \mathbb{M} > 0$.

There is a shortcoming of this explanation: both the initial consumption level and the economic growth rate are endogenous. To provide for a more satisfactory explanation, the necessary and sufficient condition should be written in terms of fundamentals; i.e., the initial conditions, and the preference and production parameters. This brings in the second part of the proposition: $g_C^i/C_0^i - \mathbb{M} < 0 \Leftrightarrow \beta(1 + B_AR_i) < (1 + A_0R_i/\rho_1)$ $[1/(1 + S_\beta)]$. Notice that the left-hand side is in fact the economic growth rate, $\beta(1 + B_AR_i) = g_C^i$. The right-hand side is more complicated. The second bracket is simply a scaling factor and can be ignored for the moment. Notice that $\rho_1 = qh_0 + A_0/B_A$, which can be interpreted as the total value of "wealth" at the initial period, which is equal to the sum of the value of existing houses, and the amount of learning cost if the initial level of technology is zero instead of A_0. The amount A_0R_i is the total amount produced in the initial period. Thus, the right-hand side can be interpreted as some weighted ratio of the initial period production relative to the initial level of wealth. When the initial period production is "large" relative to the initial amount of wealth, it means that the "long-run utility" or "lifetime utility" will very much depend on the economic growth rate. Thus, the regime which delivers the highest economic growth rate (i.e., the property tax regime) will deliver the highest welfare level. And this is the message of the first corollary. The interpretation of the second corollary is symmetric and is skipped.

However, the amount of information that can be extracted from these two corollaries is limited. For instance, if it happens that in one regime the ratio of economic growth rate relative to the initial consumption is less than the constant $\mathbb{M}$, but the reverse is true in another regime for the same economy (say, $g_C^h/C_0^h - \mathbb{M} < 0$ and

$g_C^y/C_0^y - \mathbb{M} > 0$), it is not possible to compare the welfare levels under different regimes without resort to numerical computations.

5. Concluding Remarks

In fast-growing small open economies such as Hong Kong and Singapore, tariffs are rarely used and government expenditure is financed mainly by income tax. This is not the case for Taiwan and South Korea. Why? Should economists recommend something different? According to the arguments in this paper, the choice of optimal policy depends on *the amount of initial wealth*. If the amount of initial wealth is "small" relative to the initial-period production, then economic growth is very important and the regime which delivers the highest economic growth rate should be chosen. However, when the initial wealth is relatively "large", then the regime which delivers the slowest economic growth rate is optimal. In other words, the difference in initial conditions can lead to a significant difference in economic policies and economic growth rates as well.

This analysis has some shortcomings. Why is income tax still used in all these countries? According to the theory developed here, income tax never delivers the highest welfare level. Second, the model here is very special and the results might not be very robust. The theory should also incorporate more realistic market structures, such as those in Greenhut and Ohta (1976, 1979). Nevertheless, this paper is a preliminary step in understanding the cross-country differences in economic growth and government policies, and poses a challenge to future research.

Appendix

Simplification of the Representative Agent Problem

Following EKLR (1993), the original maximization problem is broken into two stages. Given the prices of the intermediate goods, the first step is to compute the optimal amount of import. This will determine the amount of "net output", the total production net of the payment of imports. The second step is to choose the amounts of consumption goods, household capital goods and the optimal level of technological adoption for the given amount of net output. As in EKLR:

$$(1-\alpha_1)B_1(N)^{\alpha_1}\left[\int_0^{A_t}(x_t(i))^{\gamma_1}\,di\right]^{[(1-\alpha_1)/\gamma_1]-1}(x_t(i))^{\gamma_1-1} = p_t(i). \qquad (A1)$$

Equation (A1) says that the demand for (imported) intermediate goods $i, x_t(i)$, is determined by the equalization of its marginal product and price, $p_t(i)$. The net output is

$$y_t \equiv B_1(N)^{\alpha_1}\left[\int_0^{A_t}(x_t(i))^{\gamma_1}\,di\right]^{(1-\alpha_1)/\gamma_1} - \int_0^{A_t}p_t(i)x_t(i)\,di.$$

By the symmetry assumption (2), it follows that $x_t(i) = x, \forall t, i$. Full employment implies $N = 1$. Following EKLR, it is assumed that $1 - \alpha_1 = \gamma_1$, so that the economy will exhibit balanced growth. Thus:

$$y_t = A_t R, \qquad (A2)$$

where R is by definition both the marginal and the average product of an additional intermediate good:

$$R = \alpha_1 (B_1)^{1/\alpha_1} (1-\alpha_1)^{(1-\alpha_1)/\alpha_1} (p)^{-(1-\alpha_1)/\alpha_1},$$ (A3)

and equation (1) can be rewritten as (4).

Proof of the Constancy of the Growth Rates

Combining (6) with (5) will deliver (7). By (7), the ratio of household capital to non-durable consumption is constant. In other words, the growth rates of the two quantities must be the same: $g_{C,t} = g_{h,t}$, $\forall t$; and since $g_{C,t}$ is a constant, $g_{h,t}$ is also a constant: $g_{h,t} = g_h$, $\forall t$.

Note that (4) holds as an equality and can now be written as

$$C_t + q(g_h - 1)h_t = A_t \left(R + \frac{1}{B_A} - \frac{g_{A,t}}{B_A} \right).$$ (A4)

By (7), the left-hand side of (A4) can be simplified to

$$C_t + q(g_h - 1)h_t = [1 + q(g_h - 1)\Psi]C_t.$$

Updating (A4) by one period and then taking the ratio with the original equation, gives

$$\frac{C_{t+1}}{C_t} = g_C = g_{A,t^*} \frac{\left(R + \dfrac{1}{B_A} - \dfrac{g_{A,t+1}}{B_A} \right)}{\left(R + \dfrac{1}{B_A} - \dfrac{g_{A,t}}{B_A} \right)}.$$ (A5)

An obvious solution of this equation is that the growth rate of the "technology" is constant over time:

$$g_{A,t} = g_{A,t+1} = g_C.$$ (A6)

Suppose now that the growth rate of "technology" is not constant, $g_{A,t} \neq g_{A,t+1}$. Then (A5) can be further simplified as a difference equation:

$$\chi_{t+1} = \chi_a - \frac{\chi_b}{\chi_t},$$ (A7)

where χ_t represents the growth rate of technology; $\chi_t = g_{A,t}$, $\chi_a = B_R/B_G - g_C$, $\chi_b = g_C B_R/B_G$, $B_R = R + 1/B_A$, and $B_G = 1/B_A$. Notice that $B_R/B_G = 1 + B_A R$. By (6), $B_R/B_G = g_C/\beta$. Hence, $\chi_a = g_C(\beta^{-1} - 1) > 0$. Since $g_C > 1$, $\chi_b > 1$. An obvious question is to check whether there is a steady state for χ_t and whether χ_t will converge to its steady state under some conditions. From (A7), it is clear that such a steady state would be a solution of the following quadratic equation:

$$\chi^2 - \chi_a \chi + \chi_b = 0.$$ (A8)

Notice that the discriminant of this equation is

$$(\chi_a)^2 - 4\chi_b = (g_C)^2 \left((\beta^{-1})^2 - 6\beta^{-1} + 1 \right).$$

For $\beta > (3 + \sqrt{8})^{-1} = 0.17$, $((\beta^{-1})^2 - 6\beta^{-1} + 1) = ((\beta^{-1} - 3)^2 - 8) < 0$. From empirical macroeconomics and the asset pricing literature, we know that the annual discount factor is about 0.96.[14] Notice that $\ln(0.17)/\ln(0.96) = 43.407$. This means that if the discount factor is taken to be smaller than 0.17, either the duration of a period is longer than 43 years, or estimates in the whole body of literature fall considerably short of reality.

In sum, for practical purposes, there is no real root of equation (A8). There will be no steady state. Hence, this paper focuses on the case where (A6) holds.

Proof of Equation (9)

In this case, (1) is modified as

$$
C_t + q(h_{t+1} - h_t) + \frac{(A_{t+1} - A_t)}{B_A} + (1 + \tau_x)\int_0^{A_t} p_t(i)x_t(i)di
$$
$$
\leq B_1(N)^{\alpha_1}\left[\int_0^{A_t} (x_t(i))^{\gamma_1} di\right]^{(1-\alpha_1)/\gamma_1},
\tag{A9}
$$

and (A1) as

$$
(1-\alpha_1)B_1(N)^{\alpha_1}\left[\int_0^{A_t} (x_t(i))^{\gamma_1} di\right]^{[(1-\alpha_1)/\gamma_1]-1} (x_t(i))^{\gamma_1-1} = (1+\tau_x)p_t(i),
\tag{A10}
$$

where τ_x is the tariff rate levied on the intermediate inputs. The verification of (9) is simple. It is instructive to start with (A10). Imposing the condition that $1 - \alpha_1 = \gamma_1$:

$$
x_t(i) = \left[\frac{(1-\alpha_1)B_1(N)^{\alpha_1}}{(1+\tau_x)p_t(i)}\right]^{1/\alpha_1} = \left[\frac{(1-\alpha_1)B_1}{(1+\tau_x)p_t(i)}\right]^{1/\alpha_1} N.
\tag{A11}
$$

This implies that $p_t(i)x_t(i) = [((1 - \alpha_1)B_1)/(1 + \tau_x)]^{1/\alpha_1} N(p_t(i))^{-(1-\alpha_1)/\alpha_1}$. Now, as $p_t(i) = p$:

$$
(1+\tau_x)\int_0^{A_t} p_t(i)x_t(i)di = A_t[(1-\alpha_1)B_1]^{1/\alpha_1} N((1+\tau_x)p)^{-(1-\alpha_1)/\alpha_1}.
\tag{A12}
$$

From (A10), it is also simple to derive that

$$
B_1(N)^{\alpha_1}\left[\int_0^{A_t} (x_t(i))^{\gamma_1} di\right]^{[(1-\alpha_1)/\gamma_1]} = (B_1)^{1/\alpha_1} (1-\alpha_1)^{(1-\alpha_1)/\alpha_1} NA_t((1+\tau_x)p)^{-(1-\alpha_1)/\alpha_1}.
$$

$$\tag{A13}$$

By definition, after-tax net output can be obtained by subtracting (A12) from (A13):

$$
B_1(N)^{\alpha_1}\left[\int_0^{A_t} (x_t(i))^{\gamma_1} di\right]^{[(1-\alpha_1)/\gamma_1]} - (1+\tau_x)\int_0^{A_t} p_t(i)x_t(i)di
$$
$$
= \alpha_1(B_1)^{1/\alpha_1} (1-\alpha_1)^{(1-\alpha_1)/\alpha_1} NA_t((1+\tau_x)p)^{-(1-\alpha_1)/\alpha_1}
$$
$$
= R(1+\tau_x)^{-(1-\alpha_1)/\alpha_1} A_t.
$$

The proof of (13) is similar and can be found in Leung (1998).

Proof of Expression (17)

From the definitions of R_x, R_y, (10), and (14), we know that $g_C^x < g_C^y \Leftrightarrow R_x < R_y \Leftrightarrow (1 + \tau_x)^{-(1-\alpha_1)/\alpha_1} < (1 - \tau_y)^{1/\alpha_1}$. By (12) and (16), we have

$$
(1+\tau_x)^{-(1-\alpha_1)/\alpha_1} < (1-\tau_y)^{1/\alpha_1} \Leftrightarrow \phi_1(\alpha_1) < \phi_2(\alpha_1),
$$

where $\phi_1(\alpha_1) = [(1 - \alpha_1 - \alpha_1\xi)/(1 - \alpha_1)]^{1-\alpha_1}$ and $\phi_2(\alpha_1) = 1/(1 + \alpha_1\xi)$ for $0 < \alpha_1 < (1 + \xi)^{-1}$.

Notice that $\phi_1, \phi_2 > 0$ and

$$\phi_1(0) = \phi_2(0) = 1. \tag{A14}$$

In addition, $\phi_2' = -\xi(1 + \alpha_1\xi)^{-2} < 0$, $\phi_2'' > 0$. However, $\phi_1' = -\phi_1 * \phi_3$, where $\phi_3(\alpha_1) = \{\ln[(1 - \alpha_1 - \alpha_1\xi)/(1 - \alpha_1)] + [\xi/(1 - \alpha_1 - \alpha_1\xi)]\} > 0$ for $0 < \alpha_1 < (1 + \xi)^{-1}$. Thus, $\phi_1' < 0$. Notice further that $\phi_2'(0) = -\xi(1 + (0)\xi)^{-2} = -\xi$. And $\phi_1'(0) = -\phi_1(0) * \phi_3(0)$, where $\phi_3(0) = \ln[(1 - 0 - 0 * \xi)/(1 - 0)] + [\xi/(1 - 0 - 0 * \xi)] = \xi$. Thus, $\phi_1'(0) = -\phi_1(0) * \phi_3(0) = -1 * \xi = -\xi$. In other words:

$$\phi_1'(0) = \phi_2'(0) = -\xi. \tag{A15}$$

With (A14) and (A15), if we can also show that $\phi_1'' < 0$, it implies that $\phi_1(\alpha_1) < \phi_2(\alpha_1)$. Since $\phi_1' = -\phi_1 * \phi_3$, $\phi_1'' = -\phi_1 * \phi_3' + \phi_3(-\phi_1') = -\phi_1 * (\phi_3' - (\phi_3)^2)$. Hence:

$$\phi_1'' = -\phi_1 * \left[\frac{\xi}{(1-\alpha_1)^{1/2}(1-\alpha_1-\alpha_1\xi)} + \phi_3 \right] * \left[\frac{\xi}{(1-\alpha_1)^{1/2}(1-\alpha_1-\alpha_1\xi)} - \phi_3 \right].$$

The first bracket is obviously positive. The second one is equal to

$$\frac{\xi}{(1-\alpha_1)^{1/2}(1-\alpha_1-\alpha_1\xi)} - \frac{\xi}{(1-\alpha_1-\alpha_1\xi)} - \ln\left(\frac{1-\alpha_1-\alpha_1\xi}{1-\alpha_1} \right)$$

$$= \frac{\xi}{(1-\alpha_1-\alpha_1\xi)} \left[\frac{1}{(1-\alpha_1)^{1/2}} - 1 \right] - \ln\left(\frac{1-\alpha_1-\alpha_1\xi}{1-\alpha_1} \right)$$

$$> 0 \text{ as } 0 < \left(\frac{1-\alpha_1-\alpha_1\xi}{1-\alpha_1} \right) < 1.$$

Thus, $\phi_1'' < 0$.

Proof of Proposition 4

The first part can be obtained by simple differentiation. For the case of tariff and income tax, recall that

$$C_0^i = A_0 R_i - (g_C^i - 1)\left(qh_0 + \frac{A_0}{B_A} \right) = \left[A_0\left(R_i + \frac{1}{B_A} \right) + qh_0 \right] - \left(qh_0 + \frac{A_0}{B_A} \right)g_C^i$$

$$= \rho_0^i - \rho_1 g_C^i, \quad i = x, y, h.$$

Notice that $\rho_0^i = \rho_1 + A_0 R_i$. Observe that $(g_C^i/C_0^i) - M < 0 \Leftrightarrow g_C^i < C_0^i M \Leftrightarrow (1 + \rho_1 M)g_C^i < \rho_0^i M$. Combine this with (10) and (14) to yield

$$(1 + \rho_1 M)g_C^i < \rho_0^i M \Leftrightarrow \beta(1 + B_A R_i) < M\rho_0^i/(1 + M\rho_1).$$

The final term is

$$\left(\frac{\rho_0^i}{\rho_1} \right)\left[\frac{\beta(1+\omega)}{\beta(1+\omega) + (1-\beta)} \right] = \left(1 + \frac{A_0 R_i}{\rho_1} \right)\left(\frac{1}{1 + s_\beta} \right),$$

where $s_\beta = (1 - \beta)/[\beta(1 + \omega)]$.

References

Backus, David, Patrick Kehoe, and Timothy Kehoe, "In Search of Scale Effects in Trade and Growth," *Journal of Economic Theory* 58 (1992):377–409.

Cooley, Thomas and Gary Hansen, "Money and the Business Cycle," in Thomas Cooley (ed.), *Frontiers of Business Cycle Research*, Princeton: Princeton University Press (1995).

Easterly, William and Sergio Rebelo, "Marginal Income Tax Rates and Economic Growth in Developing Countries," *European Economic Review* 37 (1993a):409–17.

———, "Fiscal Policy and Economic Growth: an Empirical Investigation," *Journal of Monetary Economics* 32 (1993b):417–58.

Easterly, William, Robert King, Ross Levine, and Sergio Rebelo, "Policy, Technology Adoption and Growth," in Robert Solow and Luigi Pasinetti (eds.), *Economic Growth and the Structure of Long Term Development*, New York: International Economic Association (1993).

Greenhut, Melvin and Hiroshi Ohta, "Related Market Conditions and Interindustrial Mergers," *American Economic Review* 66 (1976):267–77.

———, "Vertical Integration of Successive Obligopolists," *American Economic Review* 69 (1979):137–41.

Greenwood, Jeremy and Zvi Hercowitz, "The Allocation of Capital and Time over the Business Cycle," *Journal of Political Economy* 99 (1991):1188–214.

Grossman, Gene and Elhanan Helpman, *Innovation and Growth in the Global Economy*, Cambridge, MA: MIT Press (1991).

Hercowitz, Zvi, "The 'Embodiment' Controversy: A Review Essay," *Journal of Monetary Economics* 41 (1998):217–24.

Jha, Sailesh and Charles Ka Yui Leung, "Price and Sectorial Dynamics in a Growth Model," unpublished, Chinese University of Hong Kong (1998).

Leung, Charles Ka Yui, "Income Tax, Property Tax and Tariff in a Small Open Economy," Chinese University of Hong Kong working paper 104 (1998).

Levine, Ross and David Renelt, "A Sensitivity Analysis of Cross-Country Growth Regressions," *American Economic Review* 82 (1992):942–63.

Palivos, Theodore and Chong Yip, "Government Expenditure Financing in an Endogenous Growth Model: a Comparison," *Journal of Money, Credit and Banking* 27 (1995):1159–78.

Rebelo, Sergio, "Long-Run Policy Analysis and Long-Run Growth," *Journal of Political Economy* 99 (1991):500–21.

Rouwenhorst, Geert, "Asset Pricing Implications of Equilibrium Business Cycle Models," in Thomas Cooley (ed.), *Frontiers of Business Cycle Research*, Princeton: Princeton University Press (1995).

Stokey, Nancy and Sergio Rebelo, "Growth Effects of Flat-Rate Taxes," *Journal of Political Economy* 103 (1995):519–50.

Notes

1. For instance, see Easterly and Rebelo (1993a,b), Rebelo (1991), Stokey and Rebelo (1995).
2. See Hercowitz (1998) for a recent review of the evidence.
3. See Grossman and Helpman (1991) for a survey.
4. For instance, see Backus et al. (1992). Another virtue of the EKLR model is that it is able to mimic the stylized facts found in Levine and Renelt (1992).
5. For instance, Greenwood and Hercowitz (1991) document that the value of residential capital stock in the United States is significantly higher than that of business capital, and the value of the investment flow of residential capital is also higher than that of business capital.
6. For instance, see Jha and Leung (1998) for evidence.
7. Alternatively, it can be interpreted that it is the reduced form of a more complicated structure. Economic agents derive utility from the flows of service generated by the household capital $u(C_t, d_t)$, and that flow is proportional to the amount of stock of household capital, $d_t = d * h_t$, $d > 0$.
8. The derivations can be found in Leung (1998).
9. EKLR, among others, show that a universal tariff is less distorting than a differential tariff. Thus, we are indeed focusing on the less distorting version of tariff. More on this follows.
10. See EKLR (1993) for more discussion.

11. The proof is suggested by Toharo Miyashita. Observe that $\mathcal{B} - \beta\mathcal{B} = \beta + \beta^2 + \ldots = \beta/(1 - \beta)$ and the result is immediate.

12. Notice that $C_0^i = \rho_0^i - \rho_0^i g_C^i$, where $\rho_0^i = A_0(R^i + 1/B_A) + qh_0$, and $\rho_1^i = qh_0 + A_0/B_A$. Hence, $d(g_C^i/C_0^i)/dg_C = \rho_0^i/(C_0^i)^2 > 0$.

13. Similar experiments have been conducted by other researchers. See Cooley and Hansen (1995) for a survey.

14. See Rouwenhorst (1995) for an overview.

Index